The Big Book of
Quilting

The Big Book of
Quilting

*Everything you need
to create beautiful quilts,
decorative accessories,
apparel and more*

CONTRIBUTORS

Cheryl Fall • Bettina Havig • Mary Jo Hiney • Karol Kavaya
Maggie Malone • Fran Roen • Linda Seward • Vicki Skemp

Edited by Cassia B. Farkas

A Main Street Book

A Division of Sterling Publishing Co., Inc.
New York

Material in this book was collected from:
Quilting Shortcuts, © 1986 by Sterling Publishing Co., Inc.; *Small Quilting Projects*, © 1988 by Linda Seward; *Country Quilts in a Day*, © 1991 by Fran Roen; *Amish Quiltmaker*, © 1992 by Bettina Havig; *Classic Quilts in a Day*, © 1994 by Fran Roen; *Treasury of Quilting Patterns*, © 1994 by Cheryl Fall; *Treasury of Appliqué Quilt Patterns*, © 1996 by Maggie Malone; *Speed Quilting*, © 1996 by Cheryl Fall; *Beautiful Foundation-Pieced Quilt Blocks*, © 1999 by Chapelle Limited; published by Sterling Publishing Co., Inc.; *Quilt National 1999*, © 1999 by Lark Books, a division of Sterling Publishing Co., Inc.; *Community Quilts*, © 2001 by Karol Kavaya and Vicki Skemp; and *The Weekend Crafter: Quilting*, © 2002 by Karol Kavaya and Vicki Skemp; published by Lark Books, a division of Sterling Publishing Co., Inc.

Library of Congress Cataloging-in-Publication Data is available upon request.

10 9 8 7 6 5 4 3 2 1

Published by Sterling Publishing Co., Inc.
387 Park Avenue South, New York, NY 10016
© 2003 by Sterling Publishing Co., Inc.
Distributed in Canada by Sterling Publishing
c/o Canadian Manda Group, One Atlantic Avenue, Suite 105
Toronto, Ontario, Canada M6K 3E7
Distributed in Great Britain by Chrysalis Books
64 Brewery Road, London N7 9NT, England
Distributed in Australia by Capricorn Link (Australia) Pty. Ltd.
P.O. Box 704, Windsor, NSW 2756, Australia

Designed by Alan Barnett, Inc. and Tony Meisel

Printed in China

Sterling ISBN 1-4027-0661-8

Contents

Log Cabin blocks arranged in a dramatic chevron. Pieced, embroidered, and quilted by the Community Quilters of Madison County, NC.

Introduction

Why quilt? In today's world, where myriad catalogs glut our mailboxes, at least half of them offering "handcrafted" quilts, what is it about the planning and making of a quilt of our own that calls out to us?

There is something ineffably satisfying about working with cloth, and quilting is a form of needlecraft that can be done either as a highly satisfying journey of self-expression, or by joining with others in a deeply rewarding community endeavor. More important, it is a way of giving a demonstration of love in which the recipient can actually wrap up! Every time we look at a quilt that has been made just for us, we see loving care in all those stitches, and know how much we mean to the person or group who made them. The list of reasons could go on, but it is perhaps this last that is at the heart of it.

Quilting as a medium has the widest scope of all the fiber arts—from fashioning a hat or an evening bag, to crafting an award-winning gallery wall hanging or a treasured family heirloom. The quilter may use the most humble of materials or the most sumptuous. Designs run from homey to sophisticated, austerely symmetrical to wildly freeform. Quilting has even become a manifestation of social expression with such witnesses as the National AIDS Memorial Quilt.

This book encompasses the know-how and expertise of many quilters, all respected in their field. They offer us a cumulative tally of years of quilting experience that, if we could string them together, year-for-year would take us back to the very beginnings of quilting in this country. The aim in bringing together the work of so many writers, quilters, and fiber artists is to explore some of the many ways this craft is carried out. But most of all, it is to distill the best advice about how to plan and create—from the first snip to the last stitch—some of the most marvelous quilting projects available. Many of these projects are rooted in the oldest and best traditions, while others are innovative and contemporary.

Here, then, is a reference that provides easy-to-follow practical steps, encouragement, and an inspirational gallery of examples—a resource that will be useful for years to come. The challenge has been to find a thread or pattern to unify all the varied parts into something beautiful, pleasing, edifying, and entertaining. As an editor, my experience of putting together this book has been like fashioning a crazy quilt of information—rich in texture and color, varied in technique, and dense with delightfully surprising treasures.

Each section retains its own unique character and expression. As they jostled each other for position, there emerged a kind of historical progression. Part I—Quilts from American History and Culture, looks at the roots of the quilting tradition in this country, whereas Part II—Quilting in Today's World, is about new directions this folk art has taken as it approached the turn of the 21st century. The thread is the passing on of patterns, legends, and stories; voicing fancies, foibles and peeves; sharing tips and techniques. History informs us, and we inform the future with what we pass on. We look to how things were done for our instruction, but it is your own personal inspiration, and that of each and every quilter, that carries it all forward.

Although most projects in this book have specific directions included, the information in Part III—The Essentials of Quilting, will provide you with an invaluable background and step-by-step instruction for every phase of the quilting process. It is suggested that you read through this material before beginning a project. Even the experienced quilter might pick up a new trick or two.

PART I

Quilts from American History and Culture

CHAPTER 1

Best-loved Classics

by Fran Roen

A Double Irish Chain quilt. Irish chain quilts have been popular since the mid-1700s.
For other variations and instructions, see pages 73, 111, 156, and 187.

The Queen's Petticoat

This pattern dates from about 1760, a tumultuous time for the British colonies in North America. Look carefully to see how one might achieve a circular "ruffled petticoat" effect if all the small square pieces were set in either light or dark coordinating colors, with the triangle pieces as a contrasting background.

Although it looks complicated, this quilt is fairly easy. The quilt pieces are cut by speed-cutting methods and assembled into seventy-two rows of three kinds, which are then sewn together (see construction diagram, figure 1–1, and figure 1–9). Colors given below in parentheses are the colors used in the model. Use whatever colors are pleasing to you. Yardage for borders is given separately so you may vary their color. Finished quilt size: 59" x 84".

YARDAGE

Fabric A (blue): 1¼ yards
Fabric B (white):
   1½ yards for quilt blocks
   ¾ yard for inner border
Fabric C (red):
   ¾ yard for quilt blocks
   1 yard for outer border
Fabric D (yellow print): ½ yard
Fabric E (dark green print): 1½ yards
Fabric F (light green): 1 yard
4 yards of 45"-wide batting
4 yards of fabric for backing
1 yard of fabric for single-thickness bias binding
1½ yards for double-thickness bias binding

CUTTING

Three 2½" x 45" strips of fabric A
31" x 21" piece of fabric A
Six 2½" x 45" strips of fabric B
31" x 21" piece of fabric B
Eight 3" x 45" strips of fabric B (for inner border)
Nine 2½" x 45" strips of fabric C
Eight 4" x 45" strips of fabric C (for outer border)
Six 2½" x 45" strips of fabric D
Six 2½" x 45" strips of fabric E
31" x 21" piece of fabric E
Binding: See binding directions in Chapter 8—
   How to Quilt, on pages 442 to 445.

DIRECTIONS

All construction is done with right sides of fabric facing and ¼" seam allowances.

1. Sew together a 2½"-wide fabric A strip and a 2½"-wide fabric C strip along one long side. Make two more strip pairs the same way. Take one pair, measure down 2½" from the top edge, and cut across both strips to form a two-patch AC unit (figure 1–2). Continue cutting until you have cut forty-eight two-patch units. Now sew two two-patch units together to form a checkerboard (figure 1–3). You'll need twenty-four AC checkerboards. Press them and set them aside.

2. Sew a 2½"-wide fabric C strip to a 2½"-wide fabric B strip on one long side. Make five more pairs of strips the same way. Measure down 2½" from the top of the unit and cut across both strips (figure 1–4). Continue cutting pairs of strips into two-patch CB units; you will need a total of ninety-six. Sew two CB two-patch units into a checkerboard (see figure 1–5). You'll need forty-eight CB checkerboards. Press them and set them aside.

3. Sew a 2½"-wide fabric D strip to a 2½"-wide fabric E strip on one long side. Make a total of six pairs of DE strips. Measure down 4½" from the top and cut across both strips (figure 1–6). Continue until you cut forty-eight pieces. Press them and set them aside.

4. To make two-triangle squares, refer to Chapter 8—How to Quilt, pages 418 to 419. Take your 31" x 21" pieces of fabric A and fabric B. On the wrong side of the lighter fabric, draw 4⅞" squares, six across and four down (see 1–7A). Mark the diagonals, stitch ¼" away on either side of the diagonals, cut the units apart on the square and diagonal lines, and press the units open. They will look like 1–7B. You will need forty-eight AB two-triangle squares.

5. Using the 21" x 31" pieces of fabrics E and F, make forty-eight EF two-triangle squares, in the same way that you made the AB two-triangle squares in step 4.

6. Next, sew the small units together to form rows and then blocks. Row 1 of the block is made up of pieces sewn in steps 2, 3, and 4. Study figure 1–8, row 1. Sew the AB two-triangle square from step 4 so it is on the left-hand side of row 1, with the fabric B triangle in the upper left-hand corner. Sew the AB two-triangle square to a DE unit from step 3, aligned as shown in figure 1–8. Next, add a CB checkerboard (from step 2) at the right of row 1; make sure that the fabric B squares on the checkerboard are in the upper left and lower right corners (see figure 1–8). Make a total of twenty-four of row 1 in the same way.

7. Row 2 (see figure 1–8, row 2) is sewn from pieces made in steps 1, 3, and 5. Place a DE unit from step 3 horizontally with fabric D to the top; sew it to an AC checkerboard from step 1, aligned so the fabric A squares of the checkerboard are in the upper left and lower right-hand corners. Add an EF two-triangle square from step 5; make sure the fabric E triangle is in the upper left-hand corner. Make a total of twenty-four of row 2. Lay out row 1 and row 2 as shown in figure 1–8 and sew the two rows together. Repeat to join all twenty-four of each row. You are two-thirds of the way done with your blocks.

8. Row 3 (see figure 10–8, row 3) is sewn from units made in steps 2, 4, and 5. Sew a CB checkerboard from step 3, with the fabric B squares in the upper left and lower right-hand corner of the checkerboard, to an EF two-triangle square; make sure the fabric E triangle is in the upper left-hand corner. Add an AB two-triangle square from step 4; make sure the fabric A triangle is in the lower left-hand corner. Make twenty-four of row 3 in the same way. Sew row 3 to the two-row units you made in step 7, positioned as shown in figure 1–8. Repeat for all twenty-four blocks.

1–1. Construction diagram for the Queen's Petticoat. Heavy lines divide pattern units.

9. Lay out the blocks made in step 8 for the quilt center. Study figure 1–9. You will see that the three-row blocks are joined in groups of four to make six main pattern units. Place an upside down block (block 1) in the upper left corner of your work surface (see figure 1–9). To its right, the next block (block 2) is rotated a quarter turn (90 degrees). Block 3 is rotated a quarter turn from block 2. Block 4 is rotated a quarter turn from block 3. Pin the four blocks together as shown in the upper left of figure 1–9 and sew them together to make a pattern unit. Make five more pattern units the same way. When completed, join them as shown in figure 1–9 to make the quilt center.

10. Refer to Chapter 8—How to Quilt, page 427, about adding borders. Attach the inner border strips to the quilt center sides. Attach the top and bottom inner border strips across the top and the bottom of the quilt center, and the width of the side inner borders.

11. Attach the outer border strips in the same way.

12. See Chapter 8—How to Quilt, pages 431 to 445, to finish the quilt as you like. Since it is such a busy pattern, a simple quilting pattern, such as outline quilting or tying, might be a good choice.

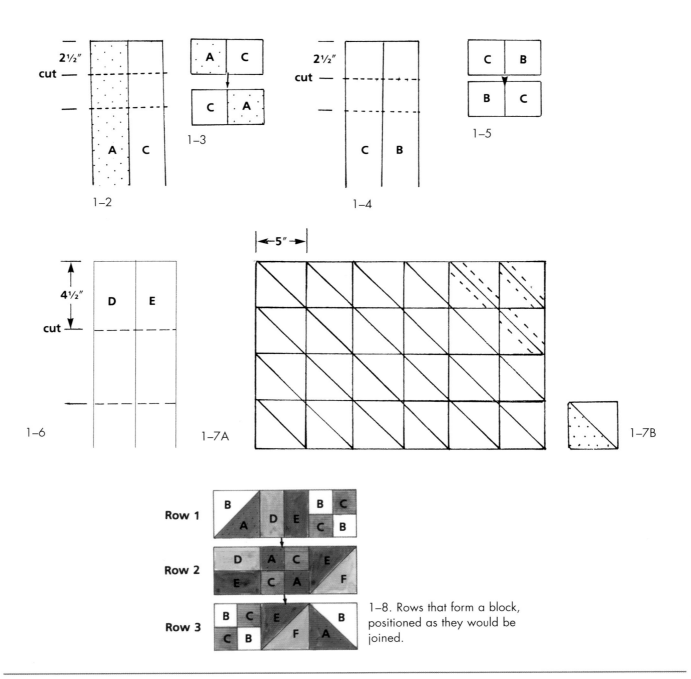

1–8. Rows that form a block, positioned as they would be joined.

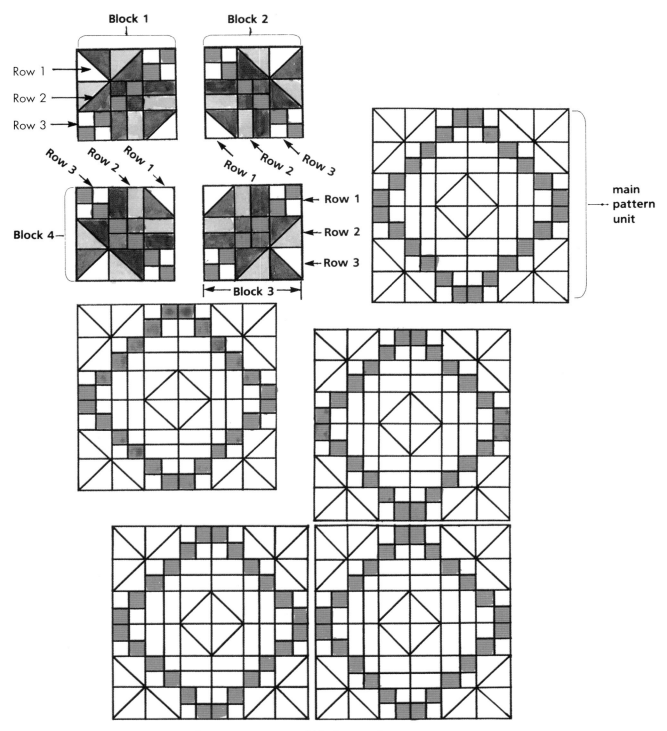

1-9. Diagram showing orientation of blocks to make up a pattern unit, and pattern units to make up the quilt center.

Double Wedding Ring

In colonial America, young girls were taught the art of quilting at a very young age. By the time a girl reached marriageable age, she was expected to have finished at least twelve quilts. The last one had to be her wedding quilt, traditionally made in this pattern.

This quilt would be made by a bride-to-be to cover her marriage bed. The young woman would do the piecing of the quilt top in the time before her wedding, and friends and family would join in to help with the quilting. Quilt pattern given for size: 60" x 72", although the quilt pictured has an added row of rings to make it 72" x 72". This is somewhat challenging due to curved seams, but speed-cutting and strip piecing can greatly cut down assembly time.

YARDAGE

Color A   2¼ yards (should be white)
Colors B–F   ½ yard of each

CUTTING

Please refer to Chapter 8—How to Quilt, pages 414 to 418 before you start.

Color A
Twelve center pieces (use pattern on p. 21, which is one quarter of the total piece).
Thirty-one ovals (use pattern on p. 20).

Colors B–F
Five strips of each at 2½" x 45". When strips are joined, cut sixty-two arches from the striped blocks (use pattern on page 20).
Sixty-two joining squares—12 each from B, C, D and thirteen each from E, F (use pattern on page 21).

SEWING INSTRUCTIONS

1. Sew lengthwise one strip of each of the colors B–F. In any order that you like join together one strip each of colors B–F along lengthwise edges. You will end up with five sets of strips. Press the seams.

2. Use the pattern on page 20 to cut out sixty-two arches from the sheets, making sure to cut out the notched center markers.

3. Match markers on each center piece to an outside marker on each arch. Pin and sew to get units as shown in figure 2–1.

4. Match the inside marker on each arch to the marker on one side of each oval (figure 2–2). Pin and sew.

5. Match center markers on the other side of each oval to corresponding markers on the remaining arches (figure 2–3) and sew them together (figures 2–3 and 2–4 show whole circles but not all your circle blocks will be whole ones).

6. Finally, add a joiner square to each end of the paired arches according to figure 2–4. When you have completed that step, you will be ready to put your quilt together.

7. Use the diagram in figure 2–5 to connect your units to each other. Once your quilt has been pieced together, you can square off the corners and even the sides by adding fabric to fill in around the rings, or you may also choose to bind the edges as they are to produce a scalloped edge.

8. Refer to Chapter 8—How to Quilt, pages 428 to 445 to complete your quilt.

Make 1   Make 5   Make 6

2–1

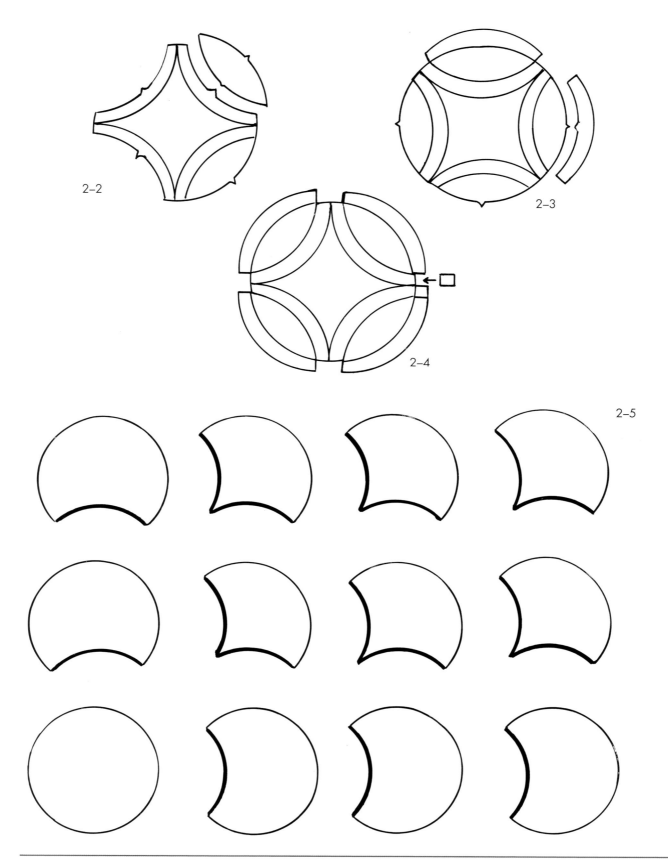

2–2

2–3

2–4

2–5

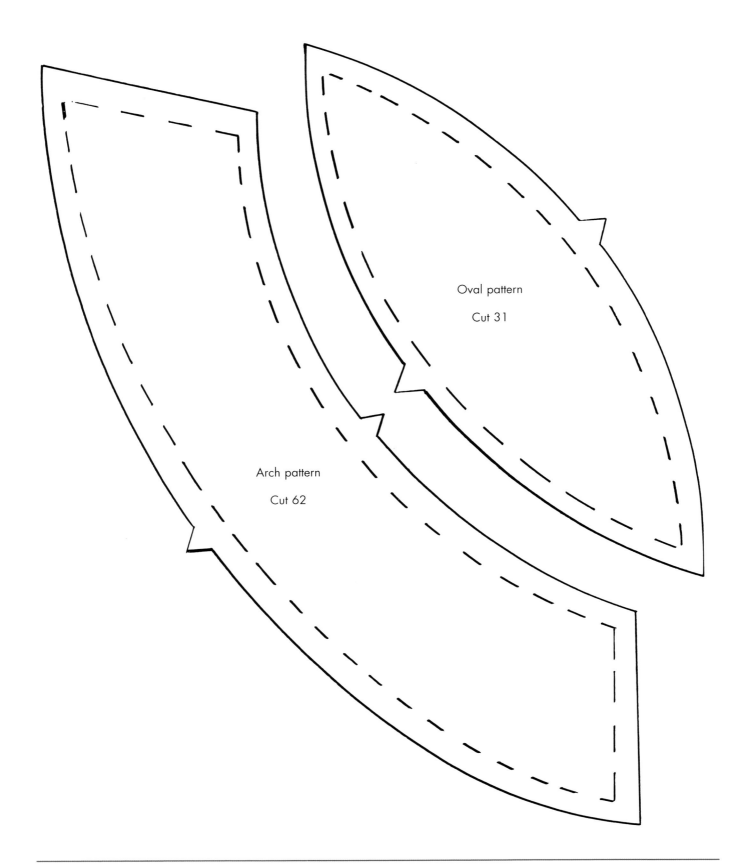

Oval pattern

Cut 31

Arch pattern

Cut 62

Full pattern will look like this.

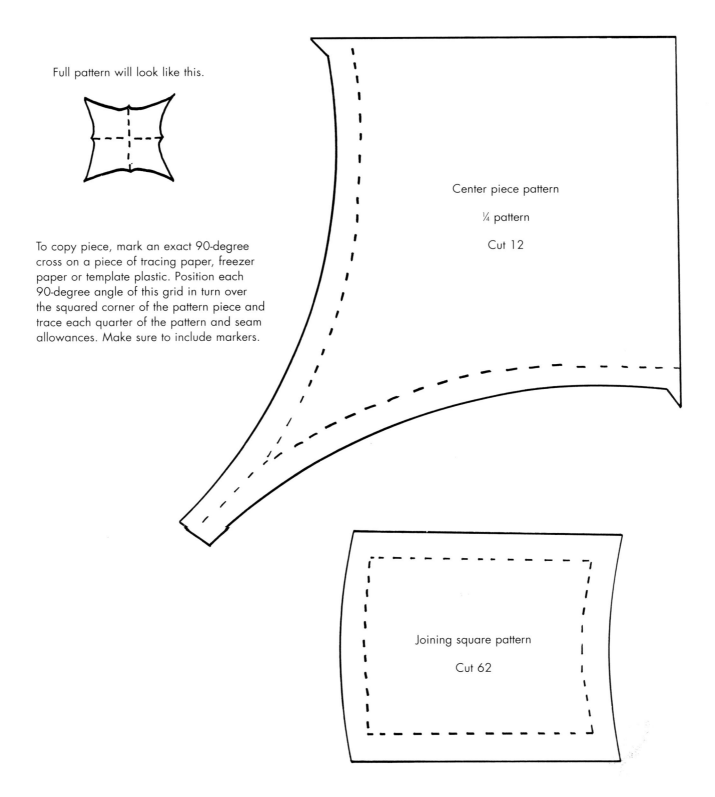

To copy piece, mark an exact 90-degree cross on a piece of tracing paper, freezer paper or template plastic. Position each 90-degree angle of this grid in turn over the squared corner of the pattern piece and trace each quarter of the pattern and seam allowances. Make sure to include markers.

Center piece pattern

¼ pattern

Cut 12

Joining square pattern

Cut 62

Roman Squares

Allover quilts—where a simple unit is repeated all over the quilt top—were among the earliest quilts made by Colonial settlers. There is evidence of their having been made since the 1750s. It wasn't until the 1800s, however, that the allover quilt really came into its own.

The love for European whole-cloth quilts had captured the hearts of many quilters in the early days of our country, but when made with blends of different colors and textures arranged in pleasing geometric patterns, allover quilts can be very beautiful. Roman Squares is such a quilt. Finished size: 78" x 96".

YARDAGE*

3 yards of (dark) (fabrics should be 45" wide)
1½ yards of (light) (fabrics should be 45" wide)
⅔ yard of fabric A (white)
1 yard for the inner border (purple floral)
1½ yards for the outer border (black floral)
5½ yards of backing fabric
5½ yards of batting (45" wide) or equivalent
1¼ yards of fabric to cut single-thickness bias strips
    or 1½ yards for double-thickness bias strips

*Colors in parentheses are the colors in the model.
  Choose whatever colors are pleasing to you.

CUTTING

2½" x 45" (dark) strips: cut 40
2½" x 45" (light) strips: cut 20
7" x 7" squares of fabric A: cut 15; then cut 14
    squares in half on the diagonal into large trian-
    gles; cut the remaining square into quarters on
    the diagonal for the small triangles.
4" x 45" strips for inner border: cut 8
6" x 45" strips outer border: cut 9

DIRECTIONS

Note: All construction is done with ¼" seam allowance and right sides of fabric facing, unless otherwise noted.

1. Take twenty dark and twenty light 2½" x 45" strips. Pair off a dark strip and a light strip, and sew them together lengthwise on one side. Repeat for a total of twenty times to make twenty two-strip units.

2. Place a two-strip piece face up on the sewing machine bed with the light-colored strip closest to the needle. Take another dark 2½" x 45" strip and lay it face down over the light strip, aligned at right. Sew them together along their length at the right (with ¼" seam allowance) to make a three-strip unit. Repeat for a total of twenty three-strip units. Press them open, with seam allowances towards the dark fabrics.

3. Square up the short edge of a three-strip unit. Measure across the top of your three-strip unit. It should measure 6½" across. If it does, measure down 6½" and cut (figure 3–1) across all three strips. (If it doesn't, measure down an equal distance to the strip's width and cut. You want to make a square.) Continue cutting the full length of your strip into squares. Repeat the cutting process for all twenty three-strip units. You will have some extra, which can always be used in other projects (pillow shams, throw pillows, etc.).

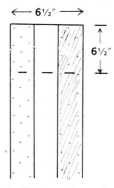

3–1. Cutting strip units

4. Look at the construction diagram (figure 3–2). Follow it as a guide for assembling your blocks and triangles. The rows and corner units are set diagonally from lower right to upper left. Assemble and stitch together the rows as follows in steps 5 through 9.

5. The corner unit (unit **I**) has a small triangle (white in the model) on the top and a large triangle on each side of the pieced block (figure 3–3).

6. Row 1 has three pieced blocks. The first and the third block should be laid in the same direction as the pieced block in the corner unit. Sew one large triangle on each end of row 1.

7. Row 2 has five pieced blocks. Note: Each odd-numbered block in the quilt top will be set with its stripes running in the same direction as the odd-numbered blocks in row 1. Seam one large triangle to each end of row 2.

8. The piecing of the rest of the rows proceeds in the same way (see figure 3–2):
Row 3: large triangle + seven pieced blocks + large triangle
Row 4: large triangle + nine pieced blocks + large triangle
Row 5: large triangle + eleven pieced blocks + large triangle

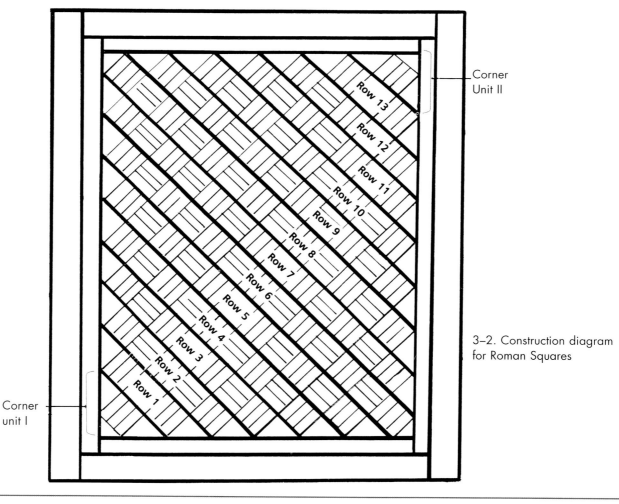

Corner Unit II

3–2. Construction diagram for Roman Squares

Corner unit I

Row 6: large triangle + thirteen pieced blocks
   + small triangle
Row 7: large triangle + thirteen pieced blocks
   + large triangle
Row 8: small triangle + thirteen pieced blocks
   + large triangle
Row 9: large triangle + eleven pieced blocks
   + large triangle
Row 10: large triangle + nine pieced blocks
   + large triangle
Row 11: large triangle + seven pieced blocks
   + large triangle
Row 12: large triangle + five pieced blocks
   + large triangle
Row 13: large triangle + three pieced blocks
   + large triangle

9. The last unit is corner unit II, which is just like corner unit I made in step 5.

10. Read the section on adding borders in Chapter 8—How to Quilt, page 427. When you sew on the first border, remember that the triangles at the end of each row are cut on the bias. As fabric on the bias stretches easily, it is a good idea to stay-stitch these corner pieces before you attach the borders.

11. Proceed to the sections on layering, quilting, and finishing in Chapter 8—How to Quilt, pages 428 to 445.

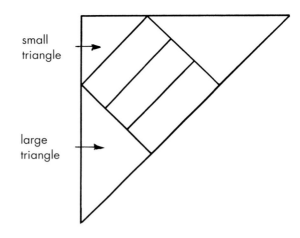

small
triangle

large
triangle

3–3. A corner unit

Framed Quilt Center

During the first half of the 19th century, many quilts were made using a printed quilt center or pillow cover as the center block. This quilt is based on one in The Smithsonian Institute in Washington, D.C. The original, worked in browns and oranges between 1815 and 1830, was made by a Mrs. William Alston.

Mrs. William Alston, the needlewoman who make the original quilt, lived on a plantation near Georgetown, South Carolina. In copying the quilt, the modern day quilter chose green tones. Finding fabrics like the old ones in the original was difficult, so the quilter concentrated on matching print types. Quilt size 88" x 88".

YARDAGE*

18" square center block**

12½" square printed center blocks with a pattern that matches the 18" block or goes with it

1⅔ yards of fabric A (dark green small print)

1¼ yards of fabric B (pink & green print)

1 yard of fabric C (dark green floral)

1½ yards of fabric D (pink & red print)

1¾ yards of fabric E (green & red paisley)

5 yards of fabric for backing

5 yards (45" wide) or equivalent for batting

1¼ yards of fabric to cut single-thickness bias binding or 1¾ yards of fabric to cut double-thickness bias binding

* Colors and patterns in parentheses are those of the model. Choose whatever fabrics are pleasing to you.

** If you can't find an 18" square printed center block, buy a 12½" square one instead, and add a 3½" border around it (the finished border width will be 3"), which will make it 18" x 18". Use it to replace the 18" square.

CUTTING

Cut the two 12½" printed blocks in half on the diagonal to form four triangles

Fabric A
 Four 3" x 45" strips for border 1
 Eight 5" x 45" strips fabric for border 10

Fabric B
 Ten 4" x 45" strips for border 2
 Ten 4" x 45" strips for border 6

Fabric C
 Ten 3" x 45" strips for border 3
 Ten 3" x 45" strips for border 7

Fabric D
 Five 5" x 45" strips for border 4
 Seven 2" x 45" strips for border 8

Fabric E
 Thirteen 4" x 45" strips for border 5
 Thirteen 4" x 45" strips for border 9

Backing: Cut it into two 2½-yard pieces and seam them together on one long side to make a 90" x 90" pieced backing.

Bias binding: Cut 4" wide for single-thickness bias binding or 6" wide for double-thickness bias binding.

DIRECTIONS

All construction is done with right sides of fabric facing and ¼" seam allowances. See the construction diagram (figure 4–1) as a reference for all the steps that follow. Refer to the section on attaching borders in the Chapter 8—How to Quilt, page 427 before starting.

1. Mark the center of the long cut edge of the four printed triangles. Align the center of the triangle with the center of one side of the 18" printed square. Pin the two pieces face to face with raw edges aligned and sew the triangle to the square. Sew the three remaining triangles onto the square in the same way (figure 4–2). Press the unit.

2. Take the four 3"-wide fabric A strips. To attach border 1, stitch one strip to the left side of the quilt center (4–3A); trim off the excess border. Stitch the second strip to the opposite side of the quilt center and trim off the excess. Stitch the third border strip to the top of the quilt center, including the widths of the side borders just added (4–3B); trim any excess border. Stitch the fourth border strip to the bottom of the quilt center in the same way, and trim off the excess. Press the unit open.

3. To attach border 2, sew the four 4"-wide fabric B borders onto the unit made in step 2 (figure 4–4), in the same way you sewed on the fabric A borders.

4. To attach border 3, sew the four 3"-wide fabric C borders to the unit you made in step 3, in the same way you sewed on the fabric A borders.

5. To attach the remaining borders, you will need to piece your border strips, because the borders need to be longer than 45". Piece the border strips

by sewing them together on their short sides. The fabric used for each remaining border is listed below:

> Border 3: four 3"-wide strips of fabric C
> Border 4: five 5"-wide strips of fabric D
> Border 5: five 4"-wide strips of fabric E
> Border 6: six 4"-wide strips of fabric B
> Border 7: six 3"-wide strips of fabric C
> Border 8: seven 2"-wide strips of fabric D
> Border 9: eight 4"-wide strips of fabric E
> Border 10: eight 5"-wide strips of fabric A

6. Finish the quilt as you like, referring to Chapter 8—How to Quilt, pages 428 to 445. For busy prints, using a simple quilting pattern or tying is a good idea.

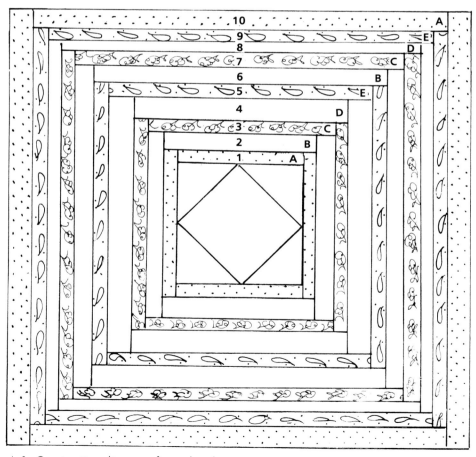

4–1. Construction diagram, framed quilt center

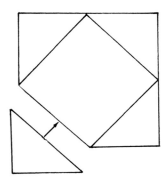

4–2. Attaching triangles.

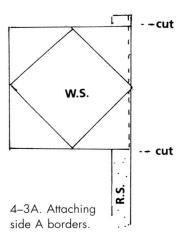

W.S.

R.S.

- - cut

- - cut

4–3A. Attaching side A borders.

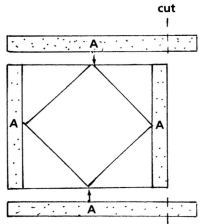

A

A

A

A

cut

4–3B. Attaching top and bottom A borders.

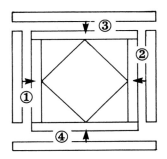

① ② ③ ④

4–4. Order of attaching all borders.

Fan Quilt

The fan quilt was popular between 1800 and the 1850s. Commodore Perry had opened trade with Japan and Japanese motifs were popular. This pattern is a modern version of a traditional fan quilt.

The quilt's black background gives the effect of the black Japanese laquer work that was coming out of Japan. Finished size 76" x 80".

YARDAGE*

Fabric A (black print): 3 yards

Fabric B (light yellow): ⅔ yard

1 yard each of fabrics C, D, E, F, and G (blue, white print, pink, light green, purple)

3 yards of fusible interfacing (18" wide), or equivalent

5 yards of backing fabric

5 yards of batting (45" wide) or equivalent

1 yard of fabric to cut single-bias tape or 1½ yards for double-bias tape

*Colors in parentheses are colors in the model. Choose whatever colors are pleasing to you.

CUTTING

Fabric A, 20" x 45" rectangles: cut 3

Fabric A, 20" x 22" rectangles: cut 3

Fabric B, 4" x 45" strips: cut 4

Nine 3" x 45" strips of each color: fabrics C, D, E, F, and G

Backing: Cut the backing in half to make two 2½-yard lengths and sew them together on a long side to make a 90" x 90" square

Bias strip: See binding directions in Chapter 8— How to Quilt, on pages 442 to 445.

DIRECTIONS

All piecing is done with ¼" seam allowances and right sides of fabric facing, unless otherwise noted.

1. To start, you will be working with four of each color of the 3" x 45" strips of fabrics C, D, E, and G (total twenty strips). Pair the strips off, mix-ing the fabrics, and sew each pair together on one long side. To be consistent, always sew with either the light or the dark fabric on top. Continue until all twenty strips have been sewn into pairs.

2. Trace out or photocopy the fan template (page 34); glue it to stiff cardboard, and cut it out. Stack your sewn C through G pairs of strips in piles of three pairs; they should still be wrong side out and unpressed (figure 5–1). Using the rotary cutter it will be easy to cut through all six layers. Refer to Chapter 8—How to Quilt, pages 414 to 418. Line up the seams. Place the fan section template on top of all the strips; line up the seam on the tem-plate with the seams on the sewn strips, and cut out the fan section through all six layers (figure 5–2). You need to make forty-four two-fabric fan sections. (You will have extras. This is to ensure that you will have enough pieces. You can use the extras in a sampler quilt, a pillow, etc.) Press the sections open, with seam allowances towards the darker fabric.

3. Sew three of your two-fabric fan pieces together on their long sides to form a fan (figure 5–3). Repeat to make a total of twelve whole fans. This will use thirty-six two-fabric fan sections. Pair off the remaining eight fan sections and sew two sec-tions together (figure 5–4) to make a unit of four fabrics. Repeat with the other six two-fabric fan sections to make the corners of the pieced border (see photo). Press all fans well.

4. See Chapter 3—Appliqué Quilt Patterns, pages 145 to 146. Also, see page 59 for a tip on speed appliqué technique. Follow the directions given and back all twelve fans with interfacing.

5. Sew a 20" x 45" fabric A rectangle and a 20" x 22" fabric A rectangle together on their 20" sides to make a panel (figure 5–5). Repeat to make a total of three panels. Number them panels 1, 2, and 3 (figure 5–6).

6. Working with panel 1, pin fan H, face up, in place and cut the fan to align with the edge of the panel (figure 5–6). Do the same with fans I and J. (Save the cut pieces of fan for panel 2.) Press the fans in place on the panels to fuse the interfacing. Sew as directed Chapter 8—How to Quilt, page 425.

7. To make the joiner strips between the panels, sew two fabric B strips together on a short side. Sew another two together the same way.

8. Sew a joiner strip to the right-hand side of panel 1, trim excess, and set the unit aside. Follow figure 5–6 again for panel 2. Pin, press, and appliqué the fans and fan pieces in place. Sew the joiner strip attached to the right side of panel 1 to the left side of panel 2. Sew the second joiner strip to the right side of panel 2. Press and set the unit aside.

9. Panel 3 is done in the same way as the other two. Press and appliqué the last fans and fan pieces in place. Sew the joiner strip attached to the right side of panel 2 to the left side of panel 3. This completes the quilt center.

10. To make the borders, work with the remaining twenty-five 3" x 45" strips of fabrics C through G. Sew five strips together lengthwise into a sheet, using one strip of each of the fabrics. Repeat for a total of five sheets, joining strips in the same order throughout. Square up the top ends of the sheets, across the strips, if they aren't straight. Press.

11. Measure 7" from the top of a pieced sheet (from step 10) and cut across all five strips (see figure 5–7). Continue cutting until all five sheets have been cut into 7"-long pieces. (There are enough of these border pieces to make a complete straight-pieced border, if you do not want to add a fan in each corner, as in the model.)

12. Measure the side of your quilt center. Sew the cut border pieces together on their 7" sides, joining them so that the colors fall into a repeating sequence. Connect enough border pieces to equal the length of the quilt side. Sew the pieced border to the side of the quilt center. Repeat this process for the opposite side of the quilt center.

13. For the top and bottom borders, measure across the top and bottom of the quilt just inside the edge of your newly attached side borders (about $\frac{1}{2}$" down from the edge). This avoids any stretching at the edge that may give you a distorted measurement. Sew enough 7" pieced border units together to make a border that fits across the width of the top and bottom of your quilt center. If you plan to include the fan sections at the corners, do not extend these borders out to the edges of the side borders. Attach the top and bottom borders to the quilt top. This will leave a vacant square in each corner of your quilt top.

14. Working with one of the four corner fan pieces (step 3), place it face down in one of the corners. Line up the center pieced fan seam with the corner angle of the quilt top (figure 5–8). Pin it in place to make sure nothing slides. Stitch around the center curve of the fan, starting $\frac{1}{4}$" from the long edge and ending within $\frac{1}{4}$" of the far long edge (figure 5–8). Remove your pins and flip the fan over so it is right-side up and fills the vacant corner. Turn the raw side edges of the fan under $\frac{1}{4}$". Pin them in place on the border and stitch them in place (figure 5–9). Repeat this process for the remaining three corners.

15. You are now ready to finish your quilt. Refer to Chapter 8—How to Quilt, pages 428 to 445.

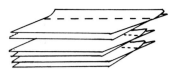

5-1. Three layers of strips, stacked for cutting fans.

5-2. Cutting out fan sections.

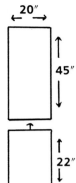

5-3. Piecing fans.

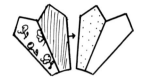

5-4. Piecing corner units.

5-5. Joining panel pieces.

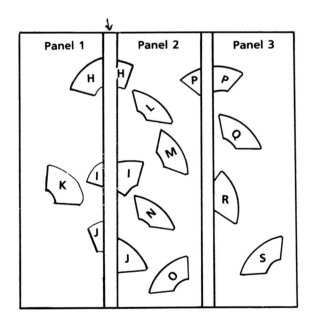

5-6. Construction diagram, quilt center.

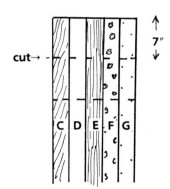

5-7. Cutting border strip units.

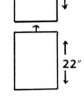

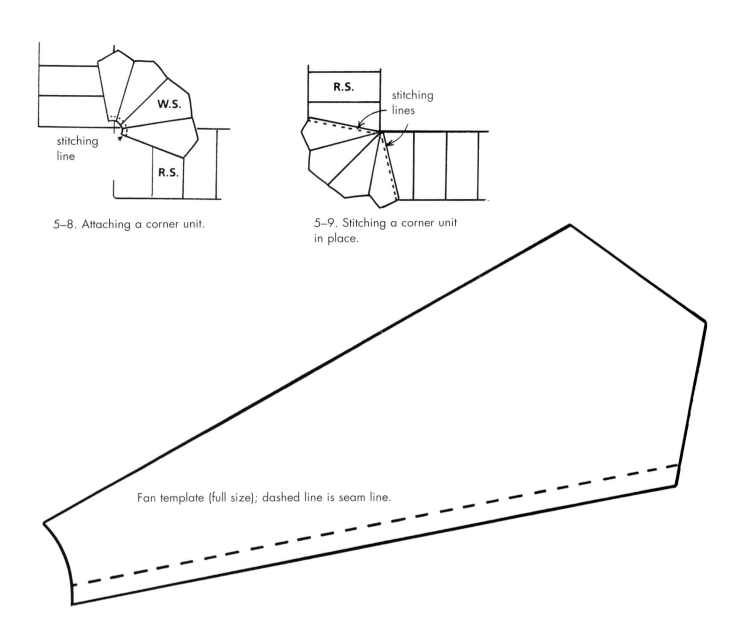

5–8. Attaching a corner unit.

5–9. Stitching a corner unit in place.

Fan template (full size); dashed line is seam line.

Nancy's Windmill

Through The Arts Projects—a part of the WPA that aided artisans and artists during the 1930s Depression—many painters, weavers, quilters, etc. were able to make a living. Renewed interest in quilting meant a need for patterns, so newspapers ran syndicated columns that contained quilt patterns. "Nancy Page" was one.

Most of these columnists were anonymous or used pen names, but "Nancy Page" was an exception. Her byline identified her as Florence La Ganke Harris, an Ohio home economist. Here, her pattern has been revised to utilize speed-piecing. The quilt center is made of 6 rows with 4 blocks in each row. Quilt size: 68" x 89". Finished block size: 11" x 11" without seam allowances (see construction diagram, figure 6–1.)

YARDAGE*

Fabric A (red-and-black print):
 2 yards for the blocks
 3/4 yard for the first border
 1 1/2 yards for the third border
2 yards of fabric B for the blocks (white and dark red print)
1 yard of fabric C for the second border (solid white)
5 yards of backing fabric
5 yards of batting (45" wide) or equivalent
1 yard of fabric to cut single-bias tape or
1 1/2 yards for double-bias tape

*Colors in parentheses are colors in the model. Choose whatever colors are pleasing to you.

CUTTING

Eight 3 1/2" x 45" strips of fabric A
Eight 3 1/2" x 45" strips of fabric B
30" x 45" piece of fabric A
30" x 45" piece of fabric B
Eight 3" x 45" strips of fabric A for the inner border
Eight 4" x 45" strips of fabric C for the middle border
Eight 6" x 45" strips of fabric A for the outer border
Backing: Cut the 5 yards into two 2 1/2 yard pieces. Fold one of these lengthwise and cut on the fold into two lengths of 22 1/2" wide each. Remove selvages and seam one to each side of the 45" wide piece to make a 90" x 90" pieced backing.
Bias binding: Cut 4" wide for single-bias binding or 6" wide for double-bias binding.

6–1. Construction diagram, Nancy's Windmill. Heavy lines are block divisions.

DIRECTIONS

All piecing is done with ¼-inch seam allowances and right sides of fabric facing, unless otherwise noted.

1. Pair off a 3½"-wide fabric A strip with a 3½"-wide fabric B strip. Sew them together on one long side. Make a total of eight AB strip units the same way. Press all seams. Measure down 3½" from the top and cut across both strips to form an AB piece (figure 6–2). Keep cutting AB pieces from the AB strip units until you have made ninety-six AB strips.

2. Next, sew two AB strips (from step 1) together so the squares formed will look like figure 6–3. Press the unit, and cut the square on the diagonal as shown in figure 6–4. Set aside the triangles formed to be used in step 5.

3. See the directions for triangle squares in Chapter 8—How to Quilt, pages 418 to 419. Take the 30" x 45" pieces of fabric A and fabric B and align them with right sides facing. On the wrong side of the lighter fabric, draw out a grid of 4⅞" squares. You will need a grid of forty-eight squares. Mark the diagonal on each square and sew on either side of the diagonal with ¼" seam allowances (see figure 6–5A). Cut the units apart on the drawn square and diagonal lines and press the seams toward the darker fabric side. After all the cutting and sewing is done, you'll end up with ninety-six triangle squares like figure 6–5B.

4. Take two triangle squares and sew them together as a row of two squares, as shown in figure 6–6. Make a total of forty-eight rows the same way. Then take two of the rows and sew them together to form the windmill square, as shown in figure 6–7. Make a total of twenty-five windmill squares.

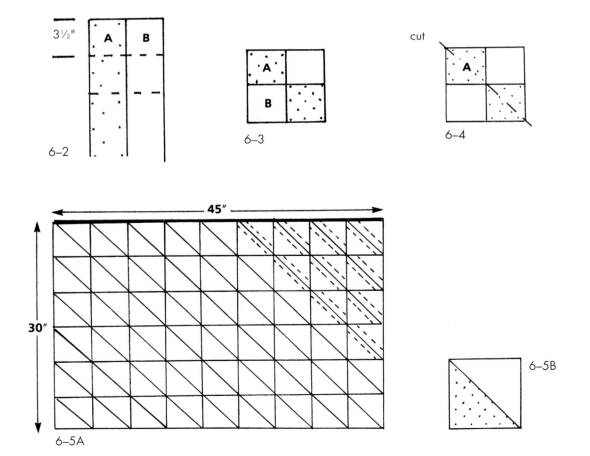

5. Now you are ready to finish the blocks. Sew one pieced triangle from step 2 onto each of the four sides of your windmill square (figure 6–8). If you sew on a triangle and then work your way around the windmill square to attach the other triangles, pressing the seam allowances towards the center as you work, your pieced block will lie well. With all four triangles added, the block will look like figure 6–9. Keep adding pieced triangles to the windmill squares to make all twenty-four blocks.

6. Lay out the blocks in rows on your work surface, four blocks across and six blocks down (see figure 6–1 for reference). Sew the blocks together in rows. Then sew the rows together to complete the quilt center.

7. Read the section on adding borders in Chapter 8—How to Quilt, page 427. Piece the inner border strips, trim the borders to the correct size for your quilt center and add the border.

8. Refer to Chapter 8—How to Quilt, pages 428 to 445, to finish the quilt as you like. Since the piecing pattern is busy, stitching in the ditch or outline quilting might be a good choice of quilting pattern. This is also a good pattern to tie.

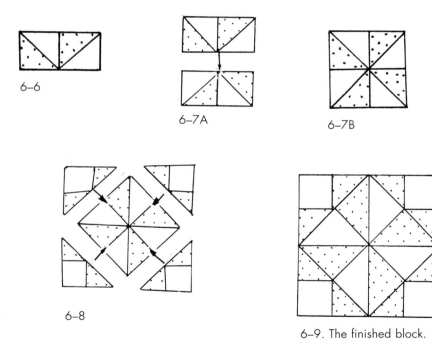

6–6

6–7A

6–7B

6–8

6–9. The finished block.

Star Burst

Star patterns have been popular in many American cultures since the latter half of the 1800s. Dramatic effects can be made with the gradation and placement of colors. This version is a twist on the more traditional rainbow effect, with the very light and very dark calling to mind a snowflake.

Finished quilt size: 66" x 66". You will need fabric in five colors for this project—four for the star burst and one for the background. You should also keep in mind that, if you want your quilt to be larger than 66" x 66", you will have to add borders. For these, you should choose colors that complement your quilt. The lettered colors below indicate yardage for each color from light to dark, with A being the lightest.

YARDAGE

Color A	¾ yard
Color B	½ yards
Color C	1⅞ yards
Color D	1½ yards (center and points of your star)
Background color	2¾ yards
Backing (no borders)	6 yards

Borders for 90" x 90" quilt:

First border	¾ yard
Second border	1 yard
Third border	1½ yards

Borders for 96" x 96" quilt:

First border	1 yard
Second border	1¼ yards
Third border	2 yards

CUTTING

Please read about the use of a Rotary Cutter in Chapter 8—How to Quilt, page 400 and pages 414 to 416, before you start.

Color A	cut eight 2½" x 45" strips
Color B	cut sixteen 2½" x 45" strips
Color C	cut twenty-four 2½" x 45" strips
Color D	cut sixteen 2½" x 45" strips
Background color	cut twenty 11½" squares; cut four 1" squares and cut them in half diagonally

90" x 90" quilt:

First border	cut eight 3" x 45" strips
Second border	cut eight 4" x 45" strips
Third border	cut eight 5" x 45" strips

96" x 96" quilt:

First border	cut eight 4" x 45" strips
Second border	cut eight 5" x 45" strips
Third border	cut nine 6" x 45" strips

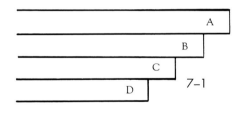

7–1

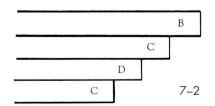

7–2

SEWING INSTRUCTIONS

1. Before sewing your strips, please review page 418 in Chapter 8—How to Quilt. Then refer to figure 7–1 and figure 7–2 to determine the placement of your strips. The illustrations show the amount of space that you should leave from the end of each preceding strip when you add another.

2. Sew strips lengthwise one at a time into sets of four until you have eight sets of each group (figures 7-1 and 7-2). Remember to carefully press all the seams toward the darkest color.

3. Next, cut diagonal strips from the sets that you have just sewn. First mark the sets of strips with diagonal lines, as shown in figure 7–3. The strips should each measure 2½" wide and you should be able to get about 16 strips from each fabric block. This is a generous pattern and you should have leftovers.

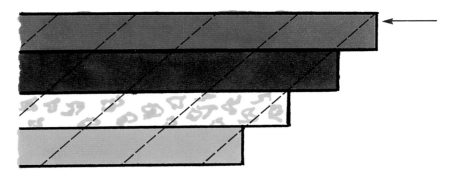

7–3

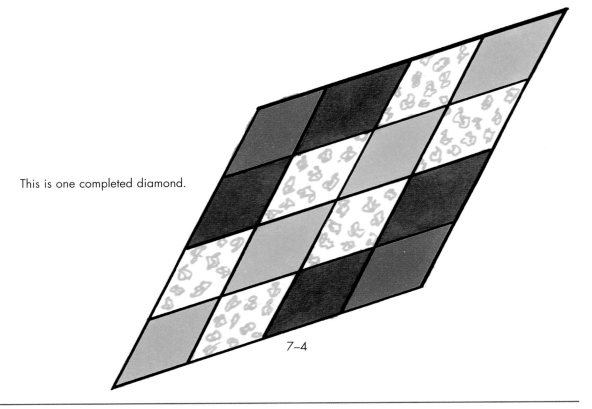

This is one completed diamond.

7–4

4. Join the newly created strips together in sets of four to form diamonds. These will be the points of the star burst. Place the diagonal strips from the two groupings in the combination indicated in figure 7–4.

5. Join four of the diamonds together along their sides, making sure that the seams and colors on each match up, as in the photograph. Join a second set of four diamonds together and then join these to the first set along a central seam. This will form the center star in your quilt.

6. Then sew eight of your squares to the upper sides of your diamonds.

7. Next, sew three diamonds together to form a burst—you should make eight of these. Attach these bursts to the free sides of the squares that you added in the last step.

8. Sew two background-color triangles between the points of the sides, top, and bottom of your star. Then attach your remaining background squares to form the corners of your quilt.

9. Refer to Chapter 8—How to Quilt, pages 428 to 445 to finish your quilt.

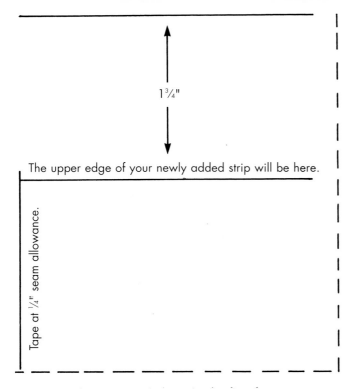

1¾"

The upper edge of your newly added strip will be here.

Tape at ¼" seam allowance.

Photocopy and cut on broken line.

A

B

C

D

Pin a small swatch of fabric next to its letter.

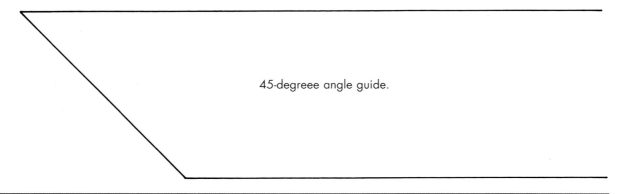

45-degreee angle guide.

Twisted Log Cabin

One of the oldest North American patchwork patterns, Log Cabin is still beloved. According to custom, each block should have both a dark and a light side to represent the darker and lighter sides of life. Red block centers symbolize love, and yellow block centers stand for welcome.

Quilters can create pictures or visual effects with the blocks that are hard to achieve with any other pattern. Twisted Log Cabin is an innovative variation. Finished quilt size: 67" x 87". Block size: 5" x 5", 140 blocks (14 rows of 10 blocks each).

YARDAGE*

$\frac{1}{3}$ yard of fabric A (orange pink)

$\frac{2}{3}$ yard of fabric B (black)

$\frac{1}{3}$ yard of fabric C (green print)

1 yard of fabric D (brown print)

$\frac{2}{3}$ yard of fabric E (dark green solid)

$\frac{2}{3}$ yard of fabric F (light green)

1 yard of fabric G (pink with flowers)

$\frac{2}{3}$ yard of fabric H (yellow)

1 yard of fabric I (white)

1 yard of fabric J for the first border
(floral with dark green background)

$1\frac{1}{4}$ yards of fabric E for the second border
(dark green)

1 yard of fabric to cut single-bias binding or

$1\frac{1}{2}$ yards to cut double-bias binding (light green)

5 yards of fabric for the backing

5 yards of batting (45" wide) or equivalent

*Colors in parentheses are the colors used in the model. Use whatever colors are pleasing to you, but keep their light and dark values the same to preserve the pattern.

CUTTING

All the strips listed below are the same size:
    $1\frac{1}{2}$" x 45"

7 strips of fabric A

11 strips of fabric B

7 strips of fabric C

20 strips of fabric D

12 strips of fabric E

14 strips of fabric F

19 strips of fabric G

14 strips of fabric H

21 strips of fabric I

For the inner border, eight 4" x 45" strips of fabric J

For the outer border, eight 5" x 45" strips of fabric E

Backing: cut into two $2\frac{1}{2}$-yard lengths and sew together on a long side to make a 90" square backing.

DIRECTIONS

Making the Blocks

This quilt may look hard to make, but it isn't; just use the worksheet given here to keep track of the fabrics, and it will go smoothly. The pattern is made with six different blocks (block 1 through block 6). Take a few minutes to look at figure 8–1 through 8–6, so you have an idea of the layout of each block. Photocopy the worksheet given here six times (once for each block), or make your own, and use them as an assembly and fabric guide for each block. Tape the worksheet to your sewing machine or any convenient spot so you can see it while you're working. Each block grows like a snail from the inside out as you add strips.

The directions below are given for block 1.

Note: in parentheses, in numerical order, the number of items to cut or the letter of the fabrics is given for the remaining five blocks. For example, "lay down a fabric B strip (B, F, F, B, H)" means that for block 1 you use a B strip, for block 2 you use a B strip, for block 3 you use an F strip, for block 4 you use an F strip, for block 5 you use a B strip, and for block 6 you use an H strip in this step. You will need to go through steps 1 through 8 six times, once for each block type you are making, choosing the correct fabrics and instructions as you go along. By following the instructions you will make the number or blocks listed below:

Block Type	How Many to Make
Block 1	44
Block 2	27
Block 3	12
Block 4	24
Block 5	21
Block 6	12

All construction is done with right sides of fabric facing and ¼" seam allowances.

1. Place a fabric A (A, A, A, A, A) strip face up on your sewing machine, with a short end towards you. Lay a fabric B (B, F, F, B, H) strip face down over it, and sew them together on one long side. Repeat 1 (0, 0, 0, 0, 0) time. Measure down from the top 1½" and cut across both strips (figure 8–7A) to form a two-square block center (8–7B). You will need to cut a total of 44 (27, 12, 24, 21, 12) of the two-square block centers for this block.

2. Set a fabric B (B, F, F, B, H) strip face up on your sewing machine bed. Top it with a two-square block center from step 1, face down, being sure that the fabric B (B, F, F, B, H) strip is to the top, and sew them together at the right, butting in new two-square block centers until they have all

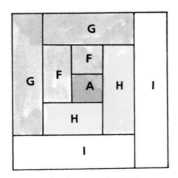

8–1. Block 1 (make 44)

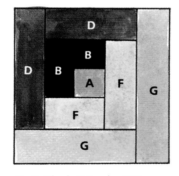

8–2. Block 2 (make 27)

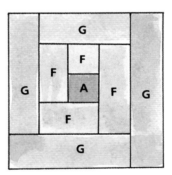

8–3. Block 3 (make 12)

8–4. Block 4 (make 24)

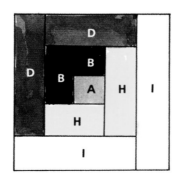

8–5. Block 5 (make 21)

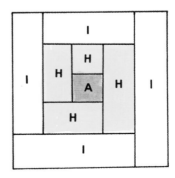

8–6. Block 6 (make 12)

been added to a strip. (Take new strips of the same fabric, as needed.) Cut the units apart across the strip, as shown in figure 8–8A. Press the three-piece units open. They will look like 8–8B.

3. Place a fabric C (F, F, H, H, H) strip face up on your sewing machine bed. Lay your sewn three-piece unit from step 2 face down over the strip, aligned at top and right, making sure that the fabric B piece (B, F, F, B, H) is to the top (A is to the lower right), and stitch them together at the right, butting in new three-piece units until all have been added to a fabric C (F, F, H, H, H) strip. Take new strips as needed. Cut the units apart across the strip as shown in figure 8–9A. Press open the four-piece units (figure 8–9B). Keep checking to see that you are making the right number of blocks (see the block chart given earlier).

4. Set a fabric C (F, F, H, H, H) strip face up on your sewing machine bed. Cover it with a four-piece unit from step 3, with raw edg of the unit and the strip aligned at the right and top, making sure that the fabric C (F, F, H, H, H) piece is to the top (see figure 8–10A). Stitch the four-piece unit and the strip together at the right, butting in new units until they are all attached to a strip. (Take new strips of the same fabric as needed.) Cut across the strip to separate the five-piece units; they will look like 8–10B. Press them open.

5. Now lay a fabric D (D, G, G, D, I) strip face up on your sewing machine bed. Place a five-piece unit from step 4 face down, with the long fabric C (F, F, H, H, H) piece to the top (see figure 8–11A). Align the unit and strip at the top and right. Stitch them together at the right. Attach more five-piece units, taking new strips as needed, until the units are all attached to a strip. Cut across the strip to separate the units, and press the six-piece units open. They will look like figure 8–11B.

6. Place a fabric D (D, G, G, D, I) strip face up on your sewing machine bed. Cover it with a six-piece unit from step 5, face down, aligned at the right, with the just-added fabric D (D, G, G, D, I) piece at the top (figure 8–12A). Stitch them together at

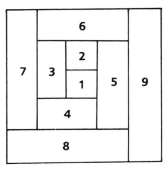

Order of growth of blocks.

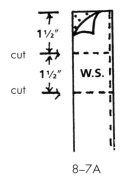

8–7A

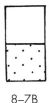

8–7B

the right, butting in new six-piece units, and taking new strips until all the units are attached to a strip. Cut them apart across the strip and press the seven-piece units open; they will look like 8–12B.

7. Lay a fabric E (G, G, I, I, I) strip face up on your sewing machine bed. Place a seven-piece unit over it, face down, aligned at the right and at the top, making sure the longest fabric D piece (D, G, G, D, I) is at the top (figure 8–13a). Stitch the unit and strip together at the right, butting in new units and taking new strips, until all the units are attached to strips of the same fabric. Cut across the strips to separate the eight-piece units, and press them open (8–13B).

8. Add the last fabric strip to your blocks. Put a fabric E (G, G, I, I, I) strip face up on your sewing machine bed. Top it with an eight-piece unit from step 7, face down, aligned at right and at the top, making sure the just-joined fabric E piece (G, G, I, I, I) is at the top. Stitch the strip to the unit at the right, adding in new eight-piece units and taking new strips, until all the units are attached to a strip. Cut across the strips to separate the units, and press them open. See 8–1 through 8–6 for diagrams of the finished blocks.

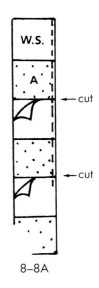

8–8A

8–8B. A three-piece unit.

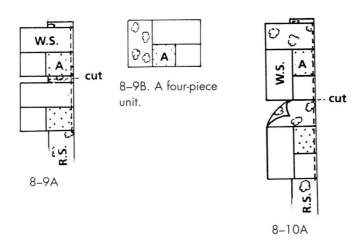

8–9A

8–9B. A four-piece unit.

8–10A

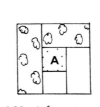

8–10B. A five-piece unit.

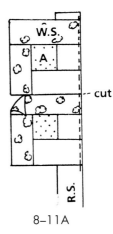

8–11A

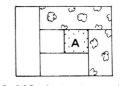

8–11B. A six-piece unit.

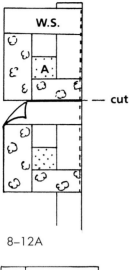

8–12A

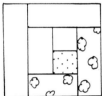

8–12B. A seven-piece unit.

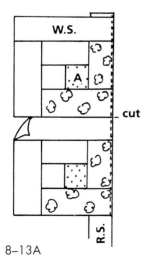

8–13A

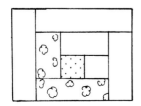

8–13B. An eight-piece unit.

ASSEMBLING THE BLOCKS

9. Assemble the blocks into rows, which will then be sewn together to make the quilt center. Lay out the blocks on a work surface. Make sure that they are arranged correctly (refer to color photo if necessary). The Block Placement and Orientation Chart shows how the blocks should be laid out for each row. The dark L shape in each place in the chart shows how the darker side of the chart should be placed. (A box on the chart means all four sides of the block are the same color.) Make sure the blocks are in the correct order and turned in the right direction. You may want to tag the top of each block with a bit of masking tape to be sure its orientation doesn't get changed as you handle it.

10. Sew each block in the row to the next one, until you have joined all 10 on the row. Repeat for the other 13 rows. After the blocks are sewn into rows, sew the rows together to form the center of the quilt top.

11. Following the directions about attaching borders in Chapter 8—How to Quilt, page 427. Then proceed to pages 428 to 445 to finish your quilt.

Block Placement and Orientation Chart*

For rows 1 and 14	1	1	1	1	1	1	1	1	1	1
For rows 2, 6 and 10	1	2	4	6	5	5	6	4	2	1
For rows 3, 7 and 11	1	2	3	4	5	2	4	6	2	1
For rows 4, 8 and 12	1	5	4	3	2	2	3	4	5	1
For rows 5, 9 and 13	1	5	6	4	2	5	4	3	2	1

* Closed boxes mean that all sides are the same color. Two-sided boxes indicate the position of the darker side of the block.

WORKSHEET FOR TWISTED LOG CABIN BLOCKS

Pin a swatch of fabric next to its letter below. Also glue a swatch of the correct fabric in place on the block diagram, as a guide in visualizing how your block will look and will be pieced. For each of the 6 blocks (1 through 6) make a separate worksheet.

fabric A:

fabric B:

fabric C:

fabric D:

fabric E:

fabric F:

fabric G:

fabric H:

fabric I: Block:_____

Sunbonnet Sue

Starting in the mid-1800s, patterns with little girls began to show up. But Sunbonnet Sue, whose popularity peaked from the 1920s through the 1940s, has become an enduring icon on appliquéd quilts. Loved by young and old alike, her clothes have gone through many modifications and updates as the years have gone by. Finished quilt size: 56" x 69½". Finished block size (not including seam allowances) 11½" x 11½". If you wish this quilt to be larger, add more blocks or more borders.

YARDAGE*

¼ yard (or scraps) of fabric A for sleeves
   (patterned in model)

¼ yard (or scraps) of fabric B for hands

About 1¼ yards total of assorted print and solid
   fabric scraps for hats, dresses, and feet

1½ yards of fabric C (white)

1¼ yards of fabric D for joiner strips and inner
   border (black print with flowers)

1 yard of fabric E for outer border (pink)

4 yards of fabric for backing

4 yards of batting (45" wide) or equivalent

1 yard of fusible interfacing (45") or equivalent

1 yard of fabric for cutting single-thickness bias
   binding or 1¾ yards of fabric for cutting
   double-thickness bias binding

¾ yard of fabric to cut single-thickness bias binding or 1¼ yard to cut double-thickness

*Colors in parenthesis are the colors in the model.
   Use whatever colors are pleasing to you.

CUTTING

3" x 45" strip of fabric A

1½" x 45" strip of fabric B

Twelve 12" squares of fabric C

Six 3" x 45" joiner strips of fabric D

Six 4" x 45" strips of fabric D (for inner border)

Six 5" x 45" strips of fabric E (for outer border)

Backing: cut the fabric into two 72" lengths and
   sew them on a long side to make a 90" x 72"
   pieced backing.

Binding: cut strips 4" wide for single-bias binding
   or 6" wide for double-bias.

DIRECTIONS

All construction is done with right sides of fabric
facing and ¼" seam allowances. See Chapter 3—
Appliqué Quilt Patterns, pages 145 to 146. Also,
see page 59 for a tip on speed appliqué technique.
When sewing Sunbonnet Sue pieces to fusible
interfacing, ⅛" seam allowances are allowed and
have been built into the templates. If you need ¼",
add ⅛" more around each piece as you cut.

1. Trace out the dress, arm, hat, and foot templates onto acetate or tracing paper. If using paper,
back them with stiff cardboard. Make sure that all
pattern templates are face up when you cut, and
placed on the front of the fabric, otherwise some
of the pieces will be reversed.

2. With right sides together, lay the 1½"-wide fabric
B strip (for the hands) over the 3"-wide fabric A
strip (for the sleeves). Sew together along one long
side. Press seams open. Placing the arm template on
this strip, with the marked seam line of the template
over the seam line of the strips so that the template
hand is on fabric B, trace and cut out 12 arms.

3. Cut out twelve of each shape from the fabric
scraps: hats, dresses, and feet, using the templates.
Cut twelve of each shape from interfacing also.
See tip on page 159. Be sure that the pieces will
end up with the adhesive side on the interfacing on
the outside when finished.
Note: The top edge of foot piece is left open.

4. Fold each 12" square of fabric C in half vertically and press; use the crease as the centerline for
positioning. On each 12" square, lay out a dress
with a foot under it and a bonnet and arm over it,
as indicated on the dress template, using the photo
as a guide. Fuse the pieces in place with an iron on
low setting to avoid scorching the fabric. Follow the
specific instructions for pressing given with the
interfacing you use. Once the pieces are fused in
place, hand or machine appliqué them in place.
Complete all blocks in the same way.

5. On a large flat surface, arrange the completed
blocks in four rows of three blocks. Number each
block with a bit of tape to keep track of the order
(see figure 9–1). Set aside blocks 3, 6, 9, and 12.

6. Place a fabric D joiner strip (3" x 45") face up
on the sewing machine bed. Of the remaining
blocks, lay block 1 face down over it, with edges
aligned at top and right. Sunbonnet Sue's head
should be at the top, as shown in figure 9–2A.
Stitch the block to the strip at the right, with ¼"
seam allowance. Continue to sew blocks (about

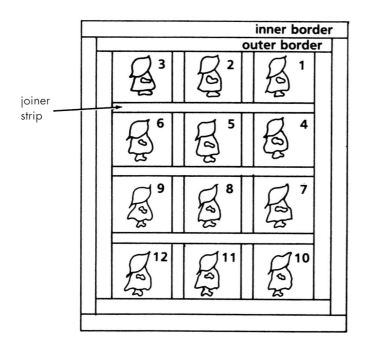

joiner strip

inner border

outer border

9–1. Construction diagram for Sunbonnet Sue.

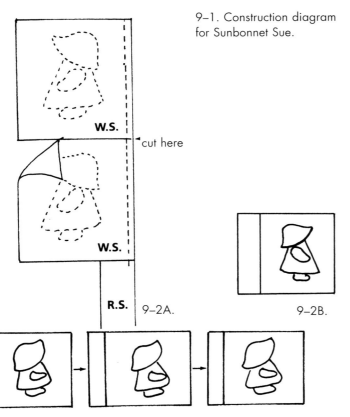

W.S.

cut here

W.S.

R.S.

9–2A.

9–2B.

9–3.

four will fit) to the strip. Take another joiner strip and attach another four, etc. Cut the blocks apart across the strip to separate the units, and press all seams toward the strips. You will now have eight blocks with short joiner strips at the left (see 9–2B).

7. Sew the block 1 + joiner strip unit to the block 2 + joiner strip unit (see figure 9–3). Add block 3 (see 9–3). Make sure Sunbonnet Sue's head is faced in the same direction on all blocks. Complete the other three rows of blocks in the same way, and press all seams toward the strips.

8. Sew a fabric D joiner strip (3" x 45") between row 1 and row 2, between row 2 and row 3, between row 3 and row 4 to complete the quilt center (see 9–1 for reference). Trim off any excess of strip that extends beyond the blocks and press the seams toward the strips.

9. Sew two inner border (4"-wide, fabric D) strips together on a short side, and sew to one side of the quilt center. Repeat for the opposite side of the quilt center. Sew top and bottom inner border strips to the quilt center in the same way, extending them across the width of the side borders. Trim off any excess.

10. Sew two outer border strips (5"-wide, fabric E) on a short side and sew them to the unit made in step 8. Proceed with the outer border as you did for the inner border.

11. Refer to Chapter 8—How to Quilt, pages 428 to 445 for finishing and quilting advice.

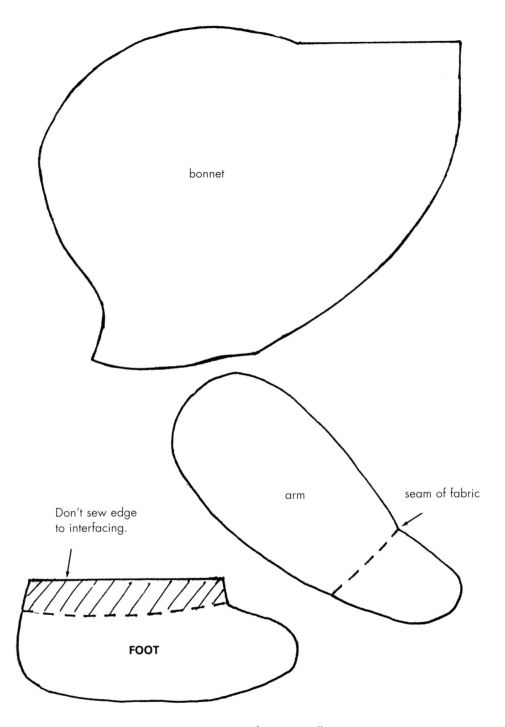

bonnet

arm

seam of fabric

Don't sew edge
to interfacing.

FOOT

Full-size hat, arm, and foot templates; $1/8''$ seam allowances are
included. Shaded area of foot should be placed under the skirt
appliqué before fusing.

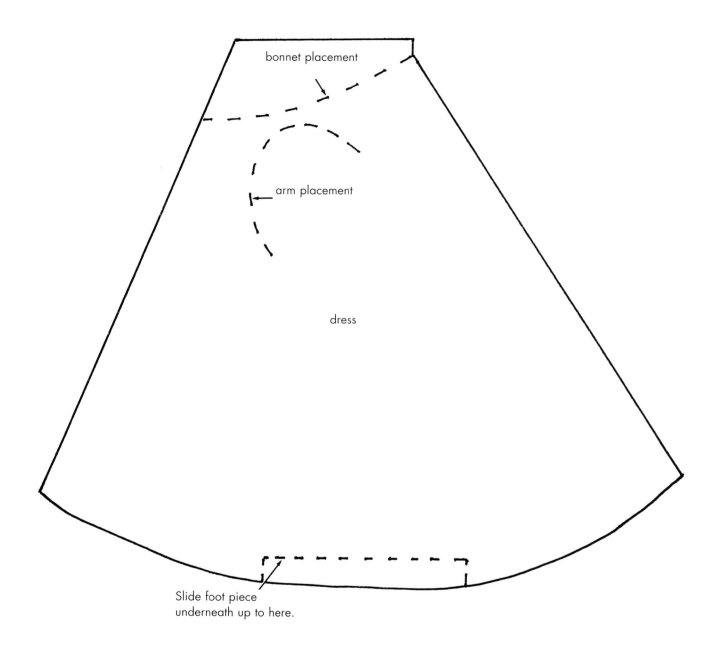

bonnet placement

arm placement

dress

Slide foot piece
underneath up to here.

Full-size dress template; ⅛" seam allowances are included.

Overall Bill

Overall Bill and Sunbonnet Sue first appeared as friends in a primer. They became popular as quilt patterns in the 1920s. Over the years, Bill and Sue have undergone many changes, appearing sometimes as Dutch dolls, colonial ladies and gents, and modern-day children who play football, basketball, and use computers. This is a great pattern for using up those small pieces that you have on hand. Quilt size: 56" x 70". Finished (without seam allowances) block size, 11½" x 11½"; has 12 blocks (see figure 10–1).

YARDAGE*

Assorted print and solid fabric scraps for overalls; scraps should be at least 6" x 7" each

Assorted print and solid fabric scraps for hats and shirts; scraps should be at least 4" x 6" each

1½ yards of fabric A for blocks (off-white)

1½ yards of fabric B for the joiner strips and inner border (blue-green and white print)

1 yard of fabric C for the outer border (solid blue-green)

1 yard of fusible interfacing (45" wide) or equivalent

4 yards of backing

4 yards of batting (45" wide) or equivalent

Binding: 1 yard of fabric to cut single-thickness binding; 1¾ yards of fabric to cut double-thickness binding

*Colors in parentheses are the colors in the model. Use whatever colors are pleasing to you.

CUTTING

Cut a 4"-diameter circle and a 2¼"-diameter circle from cardboard for the hat and hat center templates. Trace the other templates from the book onto acetate or paper. If using paper, back it with sturdy cardboard. Cut out templates and use to make the pieces listed below:

Twelve overalls from fabric scraps and twelve from fusible interfacing

Twelve shirts from fabric scraps and twelve from fusible interfacing

Twelve hats (large circle) from fabric scraps and twelve from fusible interfacing

Twelve hat centers (small circle) from fabric scraps and twelve from fusible interfacing

Twelve 12" squares from fabric A

Six 3" x 45" strips of fabric B (for joiner strips)

Six 4" x 45" strips of fabric B (for inner border)

Six 5" x 45" strips of fabric C (for outer border)

Backing: cut into two lengths of two yards each and seam them together on a long side to make a pieced backing of 90" x 72".

Binding: cut 4"-wide strips for single-thickness binding or 6"-wide strips for double-thickness binding.

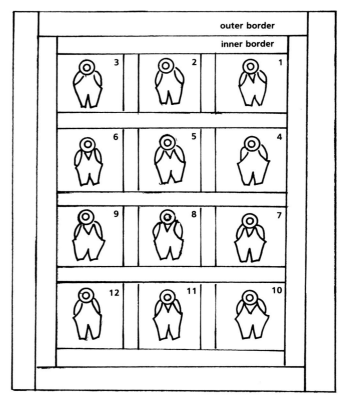

10–1. Construction drawing for Overall Bill.

DIRECTIONS

All construction is done with right sides of fabric facing and ¼" seam allowances. Template patterns include ⅛" seam allowances, which will be used when we sew the appliqué pieces to the fusible interfacing. If you need a ¼" seam allowance for templates, add ⅛ inch".

1. See Chapter 3—Appliqué Quilt Patterns, pages 145 to 146. Also, see page 59 for a tip on speed appliqué technique. Sew all the appliqué pieces for Overall Bill to interfacing. Make sure that they end up with the adhesive side out when you are finished.

2. Fold each 12" square in half vertically and press; use the crease as the center line for positioning. Lay out an overalls, shirt, hat, and hat center on the 12" square. Position the shirt underneath, the overalls over that, the hat next, and the hat center on top. The topmost part of the hat should be about 1½" down from the top edge of the square. Press the positioned pieces in place with an iron on a low setting to avoid scorching the fabric. Follow the specific instructions for pressing given with the interfacing you use. Once the pieces are fused in place, hand or machine appliqué around all edges. For further information, refer to pages 140 to 145 for the various appliqué instructions. Complete all blocks in the same way.

3. On a large flat surface, lay out your blocks in an arrangement that is pleasing to you, in four rows of three blocks across (see 10–1). Set blocks 3, 6, 9, and 12 aside for now (see figure 10–1 for block numbering). Place a 3"-wide fabric B strip face up on the sewing machine bed. Lay the top right block (block 1) face down over it, with Overall Bill standing upright (see figure 10–2); align the two pieces at the top and right, and stitch them together at the right, using a ¼" seam allowance here (and from this point on). Continue to add blocks to 3"-wide fabric B strips until all the eight blocks (1, 2, 4, 5, 7, 8, 10, and 11) are attached to a strip.

(Take new B strips as needed.) Cut across the strip to separate the units (figure 10–2). Now each of the eight blocks has a joiner strip at its left.

4. Sew the blocks with strips together in pairs: 1 and 2, 4 and 5, 7 and 8, 10 and 11 (see figure 10–3) to make a row of two blocks.

5. Place block 3 (from those you set aside earlier) face up on your sewing machine bed. Lay the two-block row of block 1 and 2 face down over it, making sure the joiner strip is at the right (see figure 10–4). Overall Bill's head should be facing in the same direction on all blocks. Stitch them together at the right to complete the first row of three blocks. Repeat this, attaching the remaining two-block rows to the remaining blocks (6, 9, and 12) to complete all four rows.

6. Sew a 3"-wide fabric B joiner strip in between two adjacent rows of blocks (10–4), so when you are done, the quilt center will look like the center in figure 10–1. Trim the strips so they don't extend beyond the width of the row.

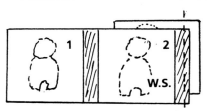

10–3. Joining three blocks to make a row.

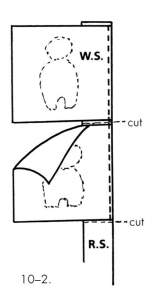

10–2.

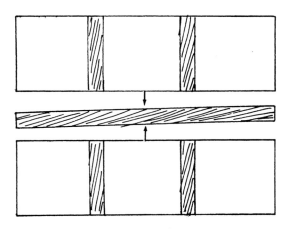

10–4. Adding a joiner strip between rows.

7. Of the six 4" x 45" inner border (fabric B) strips, sew one to the top and one to the bottom of the quilt center made in step 5. Trim any extra border that extends beyond the quilt center width. With right sides together, join two more 4" x 45" fabric B strips along their 4" ends to make a strip for the side border. Make the second side border the same way (see 10–1). Sew these two side strips to either side of the joined quilt center and top borders. Trim off any excess.

8. Piece together the outer border strips on a short side and sew on the outer border in the same way as you did the first border. Finish the quilt as you like.

Full-size overall template, includes ⅛-inch seam allowances.

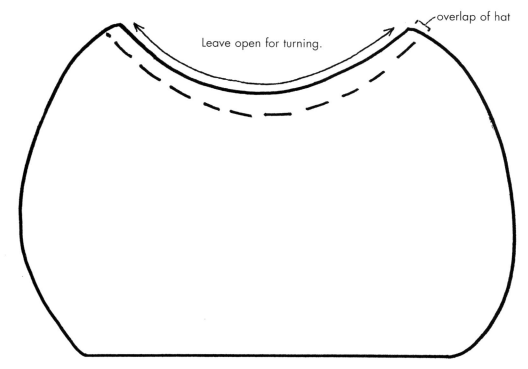

overlap of hat

Leave open for turning.

Full-size shirt template, includes ⅛-inch seam allowances.

TIP ON SPEED APPLIQUÉ

Lay down the fusible interfacing with the adhesive side face up. Place an appliqué piece on top, face down. Cut out the interfacing around the shape of the appliqué piece. Stitch the piece to the interfacing, right side of fabric to adhesive side of interfacing, using a ⅛" seam allowance. Clip any curves or corners. Carefully cut an X in the middle of the interfacing *only*. Be careful not to catch the fabric when you cut. Pull the fabric through the X, turning the piece right side out. Smooth out all edges.

You now have the right side of the fabric on the top, with the glue side of the interfacing on the bottom. Lay the appliqué piece in place on the background fabric and apply it with a warm iron. It will now stay in place for you to stitch around.

A Single Irish Chain in an Amish color palette illustrates how this particular design,
perhaps more than any other, bridges the cultures. The nine-patch quilt block, of which
this quilt is comprised, has almost endless design possibilities, and the simple construction makes
it a good choice for a first quilt. Pieced and quilted by Bettina Havig after an old Amish quilt.

CHAPTER 2
Amish Quiltmaking

by Bettina Havig

A Diamond in a Square quilt. Design, colors, and quilting patterns
all make this a stunning example of traditional Amish quilting.

HISTORY AND BACKGROUND

The Old Order Amish are a religious sect derived from an Anabaptist group called Mennonites. Persecuted in Europe, they sought sanctuary in tolerant Pennsylvania, the earliest groups arriving about 1727. It wasn't until after the American Revolution, however, that significant numbers began to arrive.

Quilting was not among the skills Amish homemakers brought to this country, but one they learned from their new neighbors. The neighbors, whom the Amish referred to as "the English," were often of Welsh or North Country English roots and the women had a rich background of quiltmaking. It was these associations that introduced quiltmaking to the Amish and Mennonites. Many similarities exist between the Amish and traditional Welsh and North Country English quilts. The Bars Quilt designs we associate with the Amish may well have been borrowed from the "strippy" quilts of English tradition.

Amish communities dot the map in the United States. Most are in Ohio, Pennsylvania, Indiana, and Missouri, but communities in Iowa, Illinois, and Kansas also have a long tradition of Amish life.

The Amish strive for simplicity and self-reliance. They reject the fancy fittings of a possession-conscious society. Some timesaving devices, however, were readily absorbed into the lifestyle of the Amish. One crucial to our subject is the treadle sewing machine. As it is powered by the sewer's foot, not by electricity, and because it greatly simplifies and increases output, this piece of equipment was acceptable to the Amish. Traditionally, Amish quilt tops are pieced by treadle machine and then hand-quilted.

AMISH DESIGN CHARACTERISTICS

Practicality is an important factor in the decisions of all Amish quiltmakers. The Pennsylvania Amish designs are generally bold graphics created by large uncut pieces of fabric—termed whole cloth—such as Amish Bars, Amish Diamond, and Diamond in a Square. Avoiding much tedious cutting and piecing produced finished tops in a shorter time. Time and energy was channeled into the quilting—essential for the coverlet to be sturdy and serviceable—which imparted the intricate stitching texture so admired in Amish quilts. In general, appliqué work is not used by the Amish. Layering of fabric is not considered good stewardship of fabric resources.

Midwestern Amish incorporated more pieced patterns in their designs as an efficient use of scraps. Baby Blocks, Double Wedding Ring, Ocean Waves, and Star of Bethlehem are one-patch in concept—designs created from a single template used over and over and usually set together by strips or blocks of a background fabric. The Irish Chain and Churn Dash patterns are among many others that use basic four-patch or nine-patch combinations. Strip quilts, such as Roman Stripe and Log Cabin, also meet the needs of these practical quiltmakers.

Characteristically, Amish quilts have borders—a practical solution of course—quickly adding size to a pieced top. The first border frames and encloses the design. The second, usually at least twice as wide as the first, completes the overall design and provides space for fine quilting. Borders are cut to be conservative of fabric. Often, borders are interrupted at the side seam and a square is used at the corner. Mitering of corners (joining at a 45-degree angle) is rare, as is the use of bias binding for edging, because of the extra trouble and waste involved when fabric is cut on the bias. Quilts are bound either by folding over and stitching the extra backing edge all around, or with narrow, straight strips cut to fit each side.

A distinction must be made between Amish quilts and Amish-made quilts. Amish-made quilts are commissioned—an Amish woman makes the quilt for a fee, to supplement the family income. Amish quilts are made by the Amish for use in their own homes, where restriction to the use of solid-colored fabrics and simple piecing distinguish them from the more flamboyant patterns and designs that an Amish woman might employ for a customer's home. Print fabrics are considered too worldly for the Amish. Depending on the tone set by the leadership of their local religious community, tiny prints might be found on a quilt lining or backing, but it is a concession that is fairly rare.

Amish quiltmaking is as timeless as other factors of their lifestyle. The Amish do not justify or rationalize their work. They accept it for what it is. More than once during my research, my questions of "why" were received with a patient expression and the comment, "It is just so." What I learned about Amish quiltmaking from my Amish friends is folk history, passed to me as it was to them, in oral tradition.

We can learn from the effective placement of dark and light, somber and gay. We may borrow the simple techniques that make these quilting designs so integral to Amish quilts. However, with all this, we still are not able to duplicate the heritage of Amish quilts. I believe it is important not to corrupt the identity of Amish quilting. For this reason I urge you to sign and identify your work. I fear confusing collectors in the future, since quilts made of solid colors are difficult to document. By signing your work, complete with date and place, you will help confirm their origin for future quilt historians.

COLOR

The most striking aspect of Amish quilts, and a key factor in their success as graphic art, is the use of color. The juxtaposition of bright and dull hues and the masterful contrast of light and dark illuminate the quilts. But there are no easy rules.

Contrary to popular conception, there are no color restrictions imposed on the Amish quiltmaker. As I researched Amish quilt construction, I always asked about the use of white in quilts. The answer was always the same: white is difficult to keep clean and therefore is used sparingly. Nor is black an essential color, either for dress or for quilts. It is, however, the traditional color for items such as capes, shawls, and bonnets.

Keep in mind that Amish quilts are made from the leftover fabrics used in their clothing. Almost all clothing is made at home. An Amish woman will select dark colors for herself, usually with a tint of blue—blue green, deep plum, magenta, burgundy, forest green, deep teal—or rich chocolate browns, dark gray, or black. Younger members of the family may be dressed in lighter and brighter colors, including bright hot pink, sky blue, warm tan, yellow, grass green, and even bright red. All this sewing generates many scraps and remnants useful for quilts.

Typically, a quilt features at least two dominant colors, often three. Designs for scrap quilts can use remnants that originally were used for garments, gleaned over an extended period of time. Be willing to try the surprising and unexpected.

For scrap quilts, you need a color that unifies your quilt visually. Backgrounds and borders can pick up hues included in the central design, or you may introduce contrasting colors. Amish quilts are actually sparked by subtle variation. Given two borders, each with separate color blocks at the corners, it is possible to include four colors in the border of your quilt (inner border, inner corner squares, outer border, outer corner squares). Refer to the chart of color groupings (table 1) for suggestions, or construct the pieced section and then take it to your local quilt or fabric shop to try it with various border choices. You will find some intriguing character changes when different colors are laid side by side.

If you select a range of cool, dark colors, try to add a dab of a color that seems out of character. For instance, plan a quilt of slate blue, black, and deep plum—a typical grouping, but rather dull. The Amish are not dull. To spark your selections try a touch of bright aqua or light mauve. The accompanying table (table 1) gives suggested groups of colors and accents.

I make color suggestions, but they are only suggestions, based on experience viewing and appreciating Amish work and on the advice and counsel of my Amish friends. Amish quiltmakers have a wonderful sense of color and harmony, a warm sense of humor, and a balanced perception of their work.

QUILTING STITCH DESIGNS

The fine stitching on Amish quilts is a hallmark of their work, elegant and elaborately executed. Just as some piecing patterns are favored, a few quilting stitch motifs are most often chosen. Feathers form wreaths or flow in graceful curves to fill squares, bars and borders. Cables are popular, as is the Pumpkin Seed border. Fiddlehead quilting motifs appear almost exclusively on Amish quilts. The graceful curves with slender leaves fanning outward are like fiddlehead fern fronds, but are also reminiscent of a fiddle (violin) neck. As a repeated motif, this is used by both the Pennsylvania and Midwestern Amish to line the wide borders of their quilts.

Other life forms that appear on Amish quilts are stylized tulips and roses (possibly acquired from their early Pennsylvania Dutch neighbors), grape clusters, leaves, and twisting vines. But such motifs as birds and butterflies, which frequently appear on English quilts, are rarely used by the Amish.

Quilting stitch patterns and instructions are provided on pages 512 to 530 so you may custom design your quilting. No two Amish quilts are identical—no two feathered circles, no two cable borders can be made exact copies of each other. Specific quilting instructions are not given with each project, so see the section on quilting when you are ready to quilt.

WORDS TO THE WISE

- 100 percent cotton fabric, broadcloth weight, is recommended. Prewash all fabrics (see Chapter 8—How To Quilt, pages 412 to 413)
- All yardages given in this section are based on 45" wide material.
- When ⅛ yard is suggested, you may have an equivalent piece such as 12" x 17", 10" x 20", 9" x 22" that will be sufficient.
- All measurements given provide for and include ¼" seam allowances. Patterns for templates also provide for ¼" seams.
- Templates have a seam line and a cutting line and can be used by those who prefer either method of cutting: (1) marking the template sewing line on the material and then adding your preferred seam allowance on all sides to get the cutting line; or (2) marking the template cutting line and lining up the machine sewing foot to sew ¼" in from the cutting line.
- When templates are not given for triangle pieces in this section, right (90 degree) triangle sizes are given by length of the two short sides (legs).
- Construction in projects is done with right sides of material facing each other unless otherwise noted, and diagrams all show the right side of the fabric unless otherwise noted.
- For machine piecing, verify your seam allowance to be sure of accurate construction. A very small error can result in a major deviation in final size.
- Press seams as you work. Do not steam press.
- Generally, borders are added to the sides of the quilt and then to the top and bottom. An inside border is completed before another border is added. Always check the size of the inner panels and inner borders before cutting fabric for the next border. Small variances in seam allowances can cause finished sizes to vary.
- Cotton batting was the most frequent filler choice until the advent of polyester batting. Now polyester batting is preferred because it is fairly easy to quilt and requires less quilting to stabilize it.
- Batting dimensions given are generally 2" larger on each side than the expected size of the top (trim only after quilting). Batting is usually sold prepackaged.
- Backings (or linings) for Old Order Amish quilts use solid-colored fabric, though Mennonites will sometimes use small prints. If you are not considering the Amish restrictions, feel free to use prints, plaids, or stripes.
- The Amish sometimes quilt with black thread—but not always. You may even use white and off-white threads. The Amish often select thread to match the backing of the quilt, so that it may be used—in practical Amish fashion—reversed as a whole-cloth design, doubling the life of the quilt.
- Background quilting (quilting to fill background areas and give emphasis to motifs) is recommended for use behind any feathered designs.
- Always complete the quilting before binding or finishing the edges.
- The choice of bindings is left to your discretion. For some projects a suggestion is made. The two types of binding most frequently used on Amish quilts are the Self-Binding and the Separate Straight Binding, detailed in the section on binding on page 442. Yardage given for backings generally provides enough for either choice.
- Amish quiltmakers, especially in the first half of the 20th century, often used lightweight wool challis for quilts. It is lovely to work with. Although good, solid-colored wool challis can be expensive, difficult to find, and must be dry-cleaned, you may want to consider its use in a special project.
- Save all your solid-colored scraps!

Amish Diamond in Square Quilt

Traditionally, the Amish Diamond in Square design is identified as typical of the Pennsylvania Amish. It is a bold design, possibly copied from leather-covered prayer books. The bold graphics allow for very lovely quilting designs. 36" x 36"

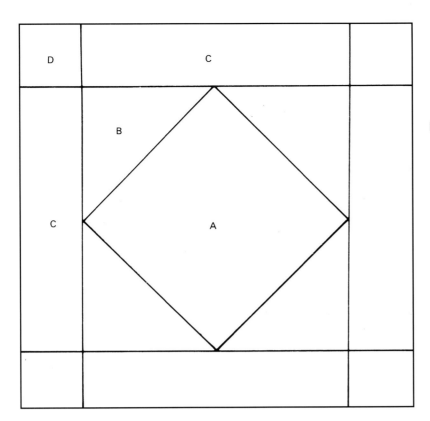

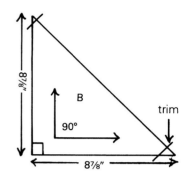

Diagram of finished Amish Diamond in Square

1-1. Diagram of piece B. Arrows indicate straight grain of fabric.

YARDAGE FOR DIAMOND IN SQUARE

Piece	Color	Amount
A	1	½ yard
B	2	⅜ yard
C	3	¾ yard
D	4*	¼ yard
Backing	—	1⅛ yards (trim to 40" x 40")
Batting	—	40" x 40"

* If color for D is repeated from Colors 1 or 2, no additional yardage is required.

CUTTING FOR DIAMOND IN SQUARE

Piece	Color	Quantity	Size
A	1	1	17½" x 17½"
B	2	4	12⅞" x 12⅞" right triangles*
C	3	4	24½" x 6½"
D	4	4	6½" x 6½"

*The short sides of the right triangles are each 12⅞".

CONSTRUCTION: VARIATION I

Each piece is to be measured and cut without a template. This emulates the construction procedure used by an Amish quiltmaker. All measurements include ¼" seam allowance. After cutting a triangle, trim the acute points back ⅜" at a right angle to the longest side of the triangle, to eliminate excess fabric. Press all seams toward the darker fabric as you work.

1. Stitch triangles B to each side of square A (figure 1–2).

2. Stitch a strip C to two opposite sides of the center panel (figure 1–3).

3. Join corner pieces (D) to each end of the remaining two C strips to make the final border units (figure 1–4).

4. Join the border units to the top and bottom of the center panel (figure 1–5). This completes the quilt top.

5. See quilting stitch section on pages 512 to 530. A feathered circle in the center square is graceful and flowing (see figure Q4 on page 521).

6. For quilting and binding see Chapter 8—How to Quilt, pages 428 to 445 to finish the project.

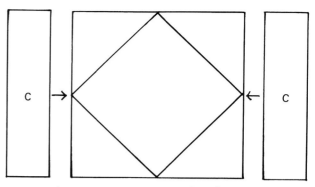

1–3. Stitch strips (C) to opposite sides of center panel.

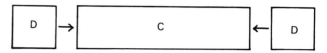

1–4. Join corner pieces (D) to short ends of each remaining strip C.

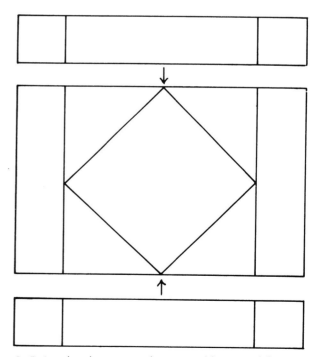

1–5. Join border units to the top and bottom of the center panel.

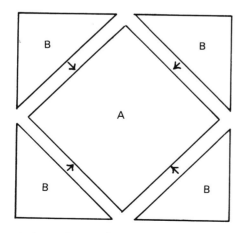

1–2. Stitch triangles (B) to each side of square A.

CONSTRUCTION: VARIATION II

1. Follow construction for Diamond in Square.

2. Measure sides of completed square and cut two strips E of that length and desired width. Attach strips to opposite sides of square.

3. Measure long sides and cut two more strips F to that length and same width as E. Attach F strips.

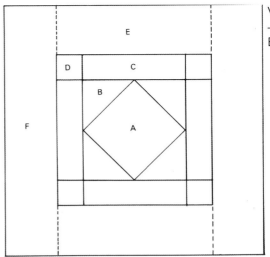

Variation II —Double Border

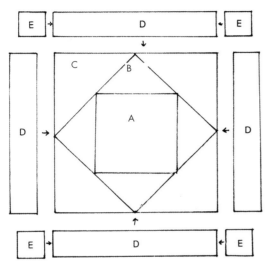

Variation III—Square in Diamond in Square

CONSTRUCTION: VARIATION IV

1. For center unit, construct as for Diamond in Square on page 68. Measure from the exact center of this completed square to the point of one of the corners. Cut four right triangles E with short sides (legs) equal to that measurement.

2. Attach E triangles to all sides of Diamond in Square unit. Measure sides of this completed square to get length for strips F.

3. Using a width of your choice, cut four strips F to the length arrived at in Step 2.

4. Using the width measurement chosen for your F strips, cut four corner squares G whose sides all have that same measurement.

5. Attach border as on page 68.

CONSTRUCTION: VARIATION III

1. Instead of putting a border on an A plus B square, measure from the exact center of this square to the point of one of the corners. Cut four right triangles C with short sides (legs) equal to that measurement.

2. Attach C triangles to all sides of A plus B. Measure sides of this completed square to get length for strips D.

3. Using a width of your choice, cut four strips D to the length arrived at in Step 2.

4. Using the width measurement chosen for your D strips, cut four corner squares E whose sides all have that same measurement.

5. Attach border as on page 68.

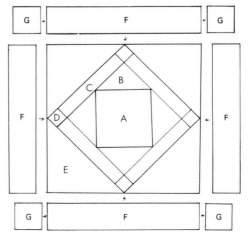

Variation IV —Double Diamond in Square

Amish Bars Quilt

The Amish Bars design is attributed to the Pennsylvania Amish of Lancaster County; however, it may have its roots in English quiltmaking tradition. The construction is very simple and the bars allow for a variety of quilting motifs. No templates are provided for the bars—we are still working in the Amish tradition, so the measurements are given for you to cut the pieces. 24½" x 24½"

D	C							D
C	A	B	A	B	A	B	A	C
D	C							D

Diagram of finished
Amish Bar

YARDAGE

Piece	Color	Amount
A	1	¼ yard
B	2	¼ yard
C	3	¼ yard
D	4*	¼ yard
Backing	Your choice	¾ yard
Batting	—	27" x 27"

*D may be made with Color 2 from scraps of
B instead.

CUTTING

Piece	Color	Quantity	Size
A	1	4	2" x 17"
B	2	3	4" x 17"
C	3	4	4½" x 17"
D	4	4	4½" x 4½"

CONSTRUCTION

1. Piece the center panel (A's and B's) as shown in figure 2–1.

2. Sew two border pieces C to opposite sides of the center panel you made in step 1, attaching them to A strips, as shown in figure 2–2.

3. Sew corners D to each of the two remaining C borders at the short ends. This order of piecing allows for seam adjustments, if necessary, to the length of the top and bottom C borders.

4. Attach border units D-C-D created in step 3 to the top and bottom of the unit created in step 2 (figure 2–2).

5. Press the finished quilt top.

6. For quilting and binding see Chapter 8—How to Quilt, pages 428 to 445 to finish the project.

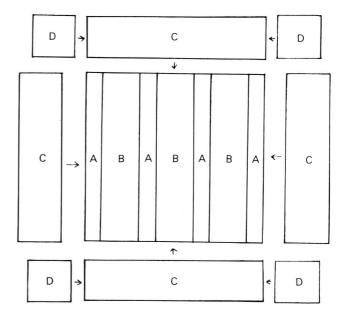

2–2. Piecing borders and corners, Amish Bars

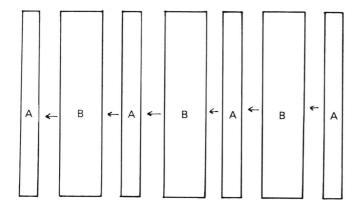

2–1. Piecing stripes in Amish Bars

Double Irish Chain Quilt

Irish chains are used often in Amish designs. This pattern is one of those most obviously learned by the Amish from their "English" neighbors. The construction is simple, and a nice open area allows for a pretty quilting motif. 25½" x 25½"

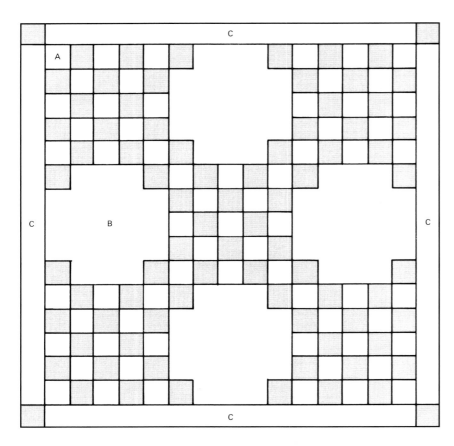

Diagram of finished Double Irish Chain Quilt

YARDAGE

Piece	Color	Amount
A, B, and C (inner border)	1	¾ yard
A	2	⅜ yard
Outer border (optional)*	Your choice	⅝ yard
Backing	Your choice	⅞ yard
Batting	—	28" x 28"

*Not shown in photo or diagrams.

CUTTING

Piece	Color	Quantity	Size
A	1	65	2" x 2"
A	2	80*	2" x 2"
B	1	4	8" x 8"
C	1	4	2" x 23"
Outer border strips (optional)	Your choice	4	4½" x 26"
Outer border squares (optional)	1 or 2	4	4½" x 4½"

*Four are reserved for borders.

CONSTRUCTION

1. Overview: There are two basic units or blocks to be pieced. Unit I (figure 2–5) is composed of 25 squares in a checkerboard pattern. Unit II is an alternate block with a small square appliqued (i.e., sewn on top of the big block) at each corner. You will construct five of Unit I (figure 2–5) and four of unit II (figure 2–6).

2. Chain piecing: What often takes so much time when piecing small units by machine is starting and stopping and cutting threads. Chain piecing eliminates a few steps by avoiding cutting threads at the end of each seam. For your Double Irish Chain, sew two small squares A, one each of colors 1 and 2, together and, without stopping to cut the threads, slip another pair of squares under your needle (see figure 2–1). Continue until you have completed 60 pairs. There will be just a couple of stitch lengths of thread between pairs. Cut the threads to separate the stitched pairs.

3. Now you have 60 pairs like those in figure 2–2 and you're ready to connect the pairs to make a rectangle or strip of four squares as shown in figure 2–3. Press the seams of each strip toward the darker colors. You can chain piece these strips of four squares. You will need 30 strips of four squares to make all the unit I blocks.

4. You have 5 lonely A squares of color 1 left when you complete the strips of four squares. Take a strip of four squares and attach a color 1 A square to the color 2 end of it as shown at the bottom of figure 2–4. Repeat this four more times to make 5 units of five squares. Each goes across the bottom of the checkerboard pattern in Unit I when it is assembled.

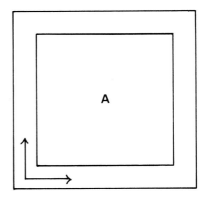

Full-size template A for Double Irish Chain. Outer line, cutting line. Inner line, seam line. Arrows indicate straight grain of fabric.

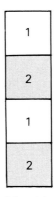

2–3. A strip of four blocks for unit I in the Double Irish Chain Quilt.

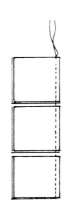

2–1. Chain pieceing (right sides of material are together)

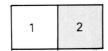

2–2. A pair of A blocks for the Double Irish Chain Quilt. Numbers indicate colors.

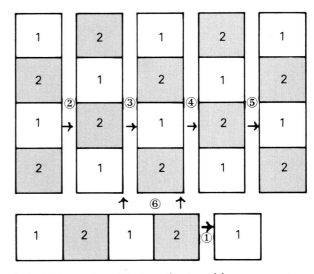

2–4. Order and positioning of strips of four squares to form one unit I in the Double Irish Chain Quilt. Circled numbers indicate order of piecing.

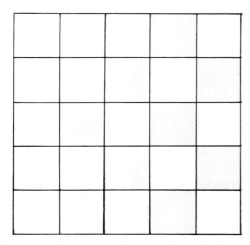

2–5. Diagram of unit I, Double Irish Chain Quilt

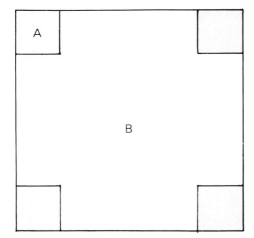

2–6. Diagram of unit II, Double Irish Chain Quilt

5. To make unit I, assemble five strips of four squares and the one strip of five squares, following the positioning of the strips given in figure 2–4. The circled numbers indicate the order of construction. Seam the five strips of four squares together vertically as shown. Then add a strip of five squares across the bottom to complete the unit I checkerboard (figure 2–5).

6. Repeat step 5 four more times until you have made five checkerboard unit I's.

7. Constructing unit II (figure 2–6): Appliqué four small A squares of color 2 to the corners of each 8"

B square. Start by turning under two sides of the two small squares ¼" and pressing them. Position each A square so that the cut (unfolded) edges of the small square are on top of the cut edges of the corners of square B. Appliqué A onto B using a blind stitch and colored thread matching color 2.

8. Repeat step 7 until you have made four unit II's (see diagram of finished quilt).

9. Arrange units I and II as shown in Figure 2–7 and stitch them together, first joining them in rows and then completing the design by joining the rows together.

10. Attach two border strips C to two opposite sides of the central pieced panel that includes all the units I and II, which you created in step 9. Sew an A square of color 2 to the short end of the remaining two C borders to make an A-C-A unit.

11. Attach the A-C-A border units to the top and bottom of the central pieced panel you made in step 10. This completes the Double Irish Chain quilt top. Press the quilt top.

12. For quilting and binding see Chapter 8—How to Quilt, pages 428 to 445 to finish the project.

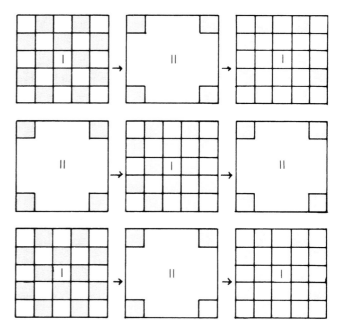

2–7. Order of joining units I and II for Double Irish Chain Quilt.

Sawtooth Bars Quilt

This pattern was taken from an old quilt that had long since worn out. Note the characteristic use of a pumpkin seed quilting motif on the inner border and the fiddlehead design on the outer border. Often the actual plant leaf becomes the model or template. 28" x 38"

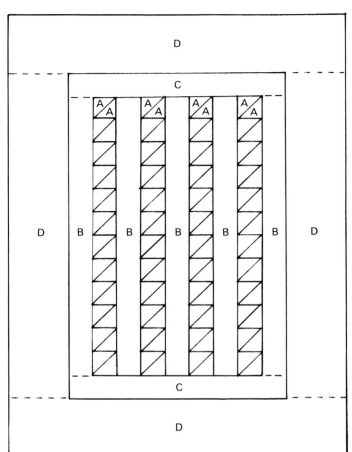

Diagram of finished
Amish Sawtooth Bars.

YARDAGE

Piece	Color	Amount
A	8 to 12 varying colors	⅛ yard of each color, or scraps totaling 1 to 1½ yards
B and C	1	½ yard
D	2	¾ yard, cut on cross grain (from selvage to selvage)
Backing	Your choice	1 yard
Batting	—	32" x 42"

CUTTING

Piece	Color	Quantity	Size
A	Varying	96	Template A
B	1	5	2½" x 24½"
C	1	2	2½" x 18½"
D	2	4	5½" x 28½"

CONSTRUCTION

1. Sew four sawtooth bars by taking 24 triangles of size A and constructing 12 squares; each is made of two A's (figure 3–1a). (Do not use two identical color triangles together in a square.) When joining the triangles in pairs, you may chain piece to save time (figure 3–1b). Join the squares into sawtooth strips (figure 3–1c).

2. Beginning with a plain bar B, sew a plain bar B to a sawtooth bar, followed by a plain bar B, followed by a sawtooth bar, and so on, ending with a last plain bar B (figure 3–2). Press the entire unit.

3. Sew border strips C to the top and bottom edges of the bar unit created in step 2 (figure 3–3). Press.

4. Sew two outer border strips D to the opposite sides of the unit created in step 3 (figure 3–3).

5. Sew the remaining two outer border strips D to the top and bottom of the unit created in step 4 (figure 3–3).

6. Press the finished quilt top.

7. For quilting and binding see Chapter 8—How to Quilt, pages 428 to 445 to finish the project.

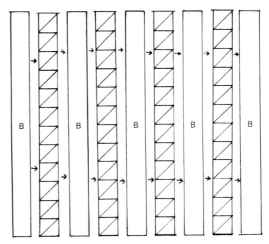

3–2. Piecing order for attaching plain and sawtooth bars.

Template A, for piecing sawtooth bars (full size). Outside line is cutting line. Inside line is seam line. Arrows indicate straight grain of fabric.

3–1. Piecing diagrams for making sawtooth bars: (a) joining two triangles; (b) chain piecing; (c) make pieced strips 12 squares in length for each sawtooth bar.

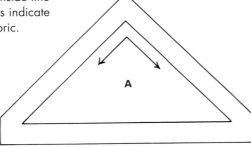

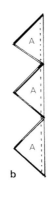

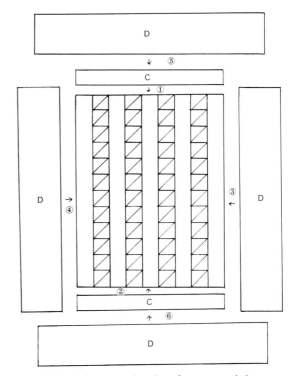

3–3. Order of piecing borders for sawtooth bars.

Basic Diamond in Square Pillow Construction

12" x 12"

The following pillow patterns are scaled-down layouts of Amish quilts, having a center pieced panel, and inner and outer borders with corner squares.

Here are templates and instructions for the basic pillow. All the other pillows, with the exception of Whole Cloth Pillow, follow this same Diamond in a Square construction. Variations in pattern are contained in the central panel, and full-size templates are given for each.

You may also make pillows using a plain center panel, if desired. In that case you would use template A for the center piece. For the other patterns, you can use template A as a sizing guide for your finished pieced panel.

The small scale of these center designs make them good candidates for hand-piecing, and there is little room for more than shadow quilting. Cable quilting or small motifs can be worked in the borders.

As most furniture in Amish homes is constructed with straight, simple lines and is rarely upholstered, pillows like those shown on the next few pages are made for use on rockers, chairs, or dining benches. None of the pillows suggests the use of a ruffle (not very Amish—too fancy!)

YARDAGE, Basic Pillow

Piece	Color	Amount
A	1	⅛ yard
B	2	⅛ yard
C	3	⅛ yard
D	1 or 2	½ yard
E	1, 2, or 3	1½" x 6"
F	1, 2, or 3	⅛ yard
G	1, 2, or 3	2" x 8"
Pillow Back	1, 2, or 3	⅜ yard
Batting	—	16" x 16"
Muslin or batiste	—	16" x 16"

CUTTING, Basic Pillow

Piece	Color	Quantity	Size
A	1	1	Template A
B	2	4	Template B
C	3	4	Template C
D	1, 2, or 3	4	1½" x 7½"
E	1, 2, or 3	4	1½" x 1½"
F	1, 2, or 3	4	2" x 9½"
G	1, 2, or 3	4	2" x 2"
Pillow Back	1, 2, or 3	1	12½" x 12½"
Batting	—	1	16" x 16"
Muslin or batiste	—	1	12½" x 12½"

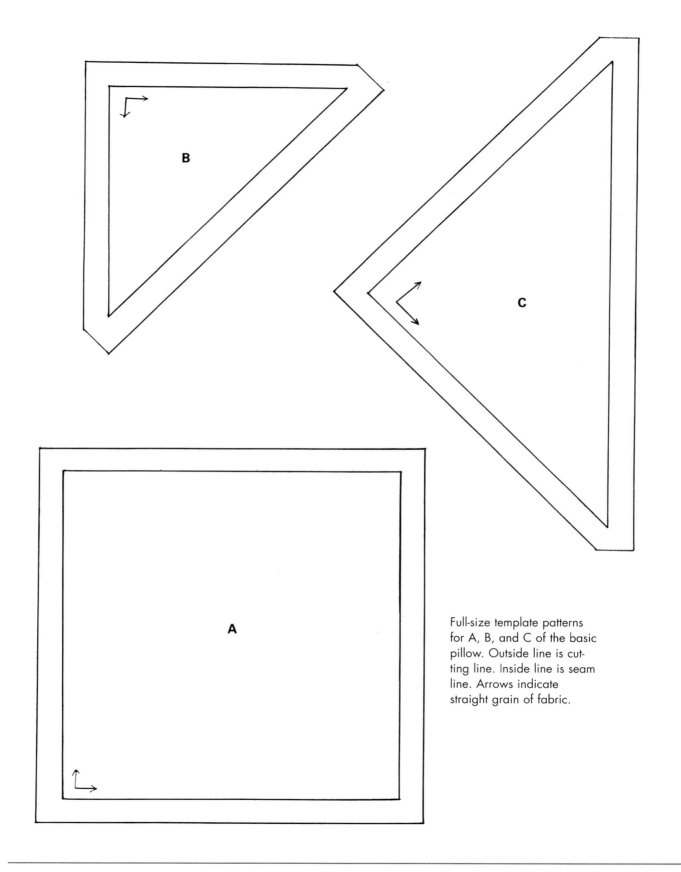

Full-size template patterns for A, B, and C of the basic pillow. Outside line is cutting line. Inside line is seam line. Arrows indicate straight grain of fabric.

CONSTRUCTION

1. Stitch B triangles to central square A, as indicated in figure 4–1. Press seams toward outside.

2. Stitch C triangles to center pieced panel created in step 1, as shown in figure 4–2.

3. Attach two side inner D borders to opposite sides of the center unit created in step 2.

4. Stitch E squares to both short ends of the remaining two inner D borders (figure 4–3). Press seams.

5. Stitch E-D-E inner border units to top and bottom of the center unit created in step 3 (figure 4–3).

6. Attach two side outer F border strips to opposite sides of the center unit created in step 4 (figure 4–4).

7. Stitch G squares to both short ends of the remaining two inner F borders (figure 4–4). Press seams.

8. Stitch G-F-G inner border units to top and bottom of the center unit created in step 5 (figure 4–4).

9. Press the whole pillow top. See quilting instructions on pages 428 to 439, then proceed to Completing and Stuffing a Pillow on page 85.

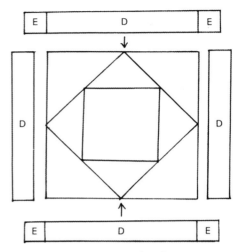

4–3. Attaching inner borders

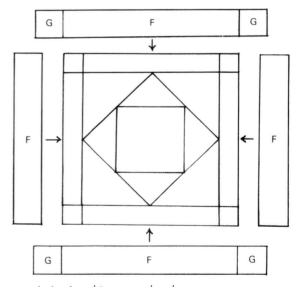

4–4. Attaching outer borders

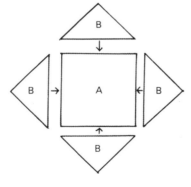

4–1. Attaching B triangles to central square

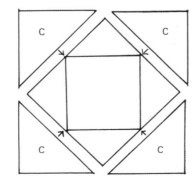

4–2. Attaching C triangles to central unit

Churn Dash Pillow

The Churn Dash design is based on a nine-patch central square. It is one of the older Amish patchwork arrangements, named after the part of a butter churn that agitates cream until butter forms. 12" x 12"

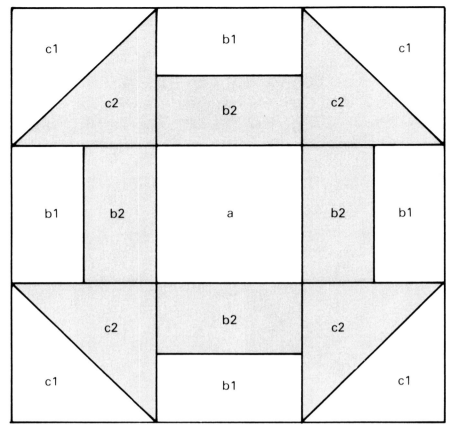

Diagram of completed Churn Dash block (3½" x 3½"), which replaces piece A in Basic Pillow. Numbers indicate colors.

The Churn Dash block given here will be 3⅛" x 3½" when finished and can be substituted for piece A in the Basic Pillow.

YARDAGE

Piece	Color	Amount
a, b1, c1, E	1 (pale gray)	⅛ yard
b2, c2, C, G	2 (dark gray)	⅛ yard
B, F	3 (pinkish orange)	⅛ yard
D	4 (black)	⅛ yard
Pillow back	Choose one of above	⅜ yard
Batting	—	16" x 16"
Muslin		
or batiste	—	16" x 16"

*Colors in parentheses are colors in model.

CUTTING

Piece	Color	Quantity	Size
A	1	1	Template a
b1	1	4	Template b
c1	1	4	Template c
b2	2	4	Template b
c2	2	4	Template c
B	3	4	Template B*
C	2	4	Template C*
D	4	4	1½" x 7½"
E	1	4	1½" x 1½"
F	3	4	2" x 9½"
G	2	4	2" x 2"

*Use Template B and C from basic pillow project.

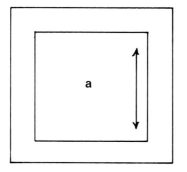
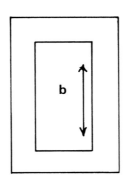

Churn Dash Pillow

Full-size template patterns for Churn Dash block. Inside line is seam line. Outside line is cutting line. Arrows indicate straight grain of fabric.

CONSTRUCTION

1. Take four c triangles of color 1 (we will call these triangles c1) and four triangles of color 2 (c2). Sew them together to make four squares; each is made of one triangle c1 and one triangle c2 (See figure 5–1, corners). Chain piecing will save time and thread.

2. Take four b rectangles of color 1 (b1) and 4 rectangles of color 2 (b2). Assemble them in four squares, each having a b1and b2 rectangle (see figure 5–1, middle of top). You can chain piece them also.

3. Press the squares created in steps 1 and 2.

4. To complete the nine-patch grid for the Churn Dash block, sew the squares together in three columns, as shown in Figure 5–2. Be sure to turn the squares in the correct direction to make the pattern. Then sew the columns together to complete the block.

COMPLETING AND STUFFING A PILLOW

1. Cut your pillow top backing, muslin, and batting 2" larger in each dimension than your pillow top's unfinished size (14½" x 14½"). Hand baste the pillow top, batting, and muslin together, making a sandwich with the right side of the pillow top facing up, the batting in the middle and the muslin on the bottom. Now baste to hold the three layers

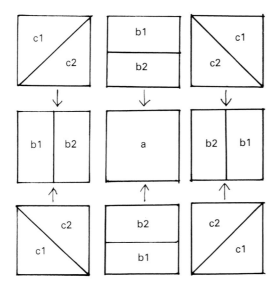

5–1. The eight assembled squares around the "a" center of the Churn Dash block.

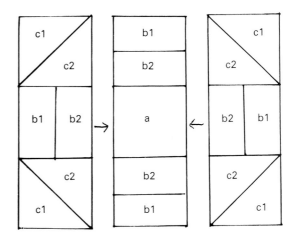

5–2. Assemble the squares in three columns; be sure to position them correctly to make the Churn Dash design. Then assemble the columns to make the block.

flat and snug while you quilt. Baste first in a spiderweb manner, always working from the center to the outer edges, which will ease any excess fullness outward and avoid bunching in the center. Then superimpose a rectangular grid of basting (figure 5–5) to stabilize and reinforce positioning. Finally, run a line of basting completely around the edge about $\frac{1}{8}$" from the outer edge. Do not remove the basting around the edge, even after the quilting is complete. It will keep the layers of the edge securely together while you complete your project.

2. Transfer the quilting pattern of your choice and proceed with the quilting. (See the quilting section on pages 428 to 439.)

3. The Amish way to complete a pillow uses the simplest possible construction. It involves no placket or zipper—never a zipper! Cut a square of fabric for the outside back of your pillow that is $12\frac{1}{2}$" x $12\frac{1}{2}$", using one of the fabrics you chose for the top design. If you want to give the backing body, cut a square of batting $12\frac{1}{2}$" x $12\frac{1}{2}$", and also cut a square of muslin or batiste $12\frac{1}{2}$" x $12\frac{1}{2}$". Make a textile sandwich of the 3 layers: backing-batting-muslin, and hand baste through all 3 layers to hold them together. Otherwise you can simply use the backing by itself.

4. Place the quilted pillow top with right sides together against the outside of the pillow back unit (back-batting-muslin or just backing, whichever you chose). Pin the pillow top to the backing unit along the outer edges of all four sides. About 2" in from a corner, begin stitching (remember that the seam allowances are all $\frac{1}{4}$"). Stitch toward the near corner until you are $\frac{3}{4}$" from it. Turn the fabric to sew across the corner at an angle to the next side (see figure 5–6). Angled corners help soften the sharp points at the pillow corners. Continue stitching , turning all corners in the manner just described, to within 6" or 8" from where you started to sew. Leave that side open and backstitch for 1" to end the seam.

5. Trim off the excess material at the corners of the pillow unit to within $\frac{1}{4}$" of the seam line so that it may be turned easily without bunching up at the corners.

6. Gently turn the pillow cover through the 6" to 8" opening so it is right side out.

7. Stuff the pillow until it is moderately firm, bearing in mind that the stuffing will compact with use.

8. Turn in the edges of the pillow opening and whipstitch them together with matching thread. Note: You may use a 12" pillow form instead of stuffing, but that is not the Amish way. The Amish often use pillows as chair seat cushions. If you wish to use them in this manner, use less stuffing.

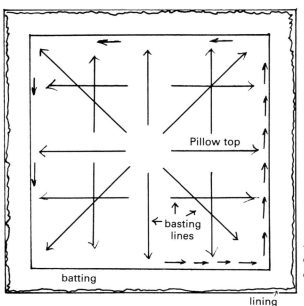

5–5. Basting diagram for any pillow top.

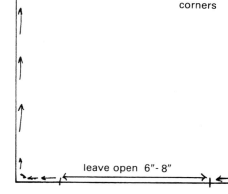

5–6. Sewing line (using $\frac{1}{4}$" seam allowance) for attaching pillow top to back unit.

Ohio Star Pillow

It is fitting for Ohio, which currently has the largest population of Amish, to be represented by a block design. Select three colors for the Ohio Star design. The yardage given is enough for the rest of the Basic Pillow top as well; you can decide which colors to use for each part. 12" x 12"

YARDAGE

Piece	Color	Amount
a1, B, E, F	1 (red in model)	⅛ yard
b2, D, G	2 (black in model)	⅛ yard
b3, a3, C	3 (light orange in model)	⅛ yard
Pillow back	Your choice	⅜ yard
Batting	—	16" x 16"
Muslin or batiste	—	16" x 16"

CUTTING

Piece	Color	Quantity	Size
a	1	1	Template a
b	2	8	Template b
b	3	8	Template b
a	3	4	Template a
B	1	4	Template B*
C	3	4	Template C*
D	2	4	1½" x 7½"
E	1	4	1½" x 1½"
F	1	4	2" x 9½"
G	2	4	2" x 2"

*Use templates B and C from Basic Pillow.

Diagram of finished Ohio Star

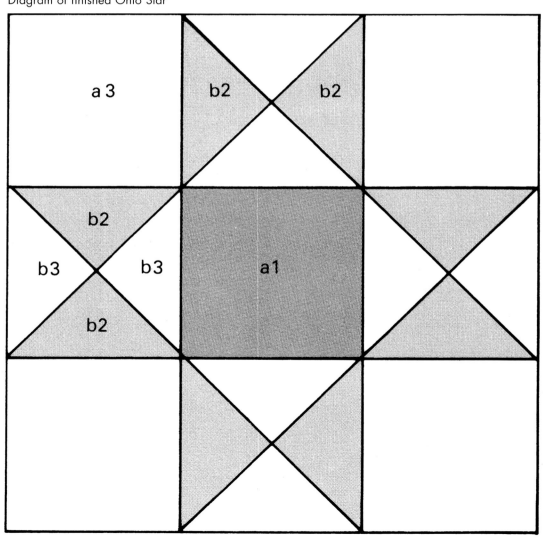

CONTRUCTION

1. With right sides of material together, create eight pairs of triangles (b) by attaching them on one short side (figure 6–1). Each pair has one triangle of color 2 and one of color 3. Chain piecing may be used. Note that the long triangle sides aren't attached to anything in this step.

2. Construct four pieced square units out of the triangles you created in step 1, being sure to follow Figure 6–2 for correct positioning of the colors.

3. Take the five squares of size "a" (four of color 3 and one of color 1) and attach them to the squares you created in step 2, following figure 6–2 for positioning and making three columns of three squares each.

4. Sew the columns of squares together to complete the Ohio Star construction (figure 6–3). Press the block.

5. The Ohio Star substitutes for piece A in the Basic Pillow. For the rest of the Ohio Star pillow top construction, follow the construction steps given in the Basic Pillow project on page 80.

6. To complete the pillow, see instructions on page 85 for "Completing and Stuffing a Pillow."

Templates for Ohio Star. Outer line is cutting line. Inside line is seam line. Arrows indicate straight grain of fabric.

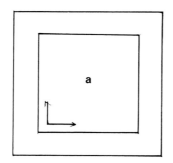

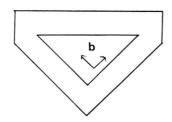

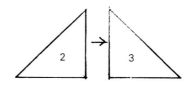

6–1. Attach pairs of triangles on short sides. Numbers indicate colors.

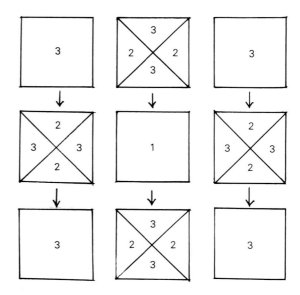

6–2. Guide for attaching squares, Ohio Star. Numbers indicate colors.

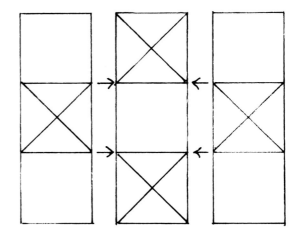

6–3. Attach groups of squares together, matching seams.

Eight-Point Star Pillow

The Eight-Point Star is the basic format of a number of designs, including the Star of Bethlehem. The simple block design is good practice for the more difficult Star of Bethlehem. 12" x12"

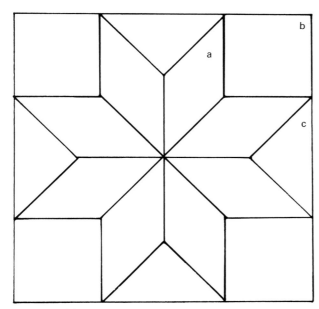

Diagram of finished Eight-Point Star

CONSTRUCTION

The Eight-Point Star block replaces piece A and piece B in the Basic Pillow. A seam allowance of ¼" is used throughout the project.

1. Construction begins with the star itself. You will make two half-stars of four diamonds each. First take two diamonds "a" and stitch them together as shown in Figure 7–1, top left.

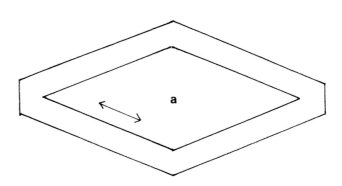

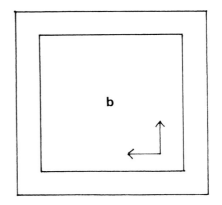

YARDAGE

Piece	Color	Amount
a, E	1 (pink in model)	⅛ yard
b, c, C, F	2 (purple in model)	⅛ yard
D, G	3 (red in model)	⅛ yard
Pillow back	Your choice	⅜ yard
Batting	—	16" x 16"
Muslin or batiste	—	16" x 16"

CUTTING

Piece	Color	Quantity	Size
a	1	8	Template a
b	2	4	Template b
c	2	4	Template c
C	2	4	Template C*
D	3	4	1½" x 7½"
E	1	4	1½" x 1½"
F	2	4	2" x 9½"
G	3	4	2" x 2"

* Use template C from Basic Pillow.

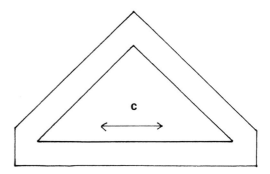

Full-size templates for the Eight-Point Star block. Outer line is cutting line. Inner line is seam line. Arrows indicate the straight grain of fabric.

2. Add a third diamond "a," stitching from the center point out (see figure 7–1), and a fourth diamond "a," also stitched from the center point out. You have now created a half-star.

3. Repeat steps 1 and 2 to make the second half of the star.

4. Now join the halves of the star (figure 7–2), matching the center points carefully. Before sewing, pin or baste the halves together, right sides facing, to secure them. Press the star seams in a clockwise direction so that they lie flat when the unit is joined.

5. Following figure 7–3, attach the four c triangles to the star, and then attach the four b squares. For each piece sewn, position the inner angle (right angle) of the square or triangle to be attached and stitch from the inner angle out on one side. Then go back to the starting point and complete the insertion by sewing the second side (see figure 7–3). This completes the Eight-Point Star block.

6. The Eight-Point Star block replaces piece A and piece B in the Basic Pillow. To complete the Eight-Point Star pillow top, follow the construction steps given on page 82.

7. To complete the pillow, see instructions on page 85 on "Completing and Stuffing a Pillow."

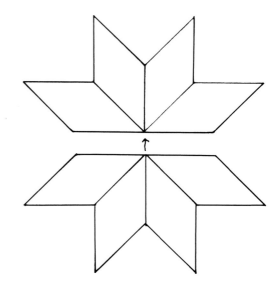

7–2. Attach the two halves of the star to each other, being careful to match the center points.

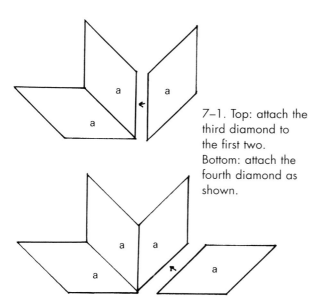

7–1. Top: attach the third diamond to the first two. Bottom: attach the fourth diamond as shown.

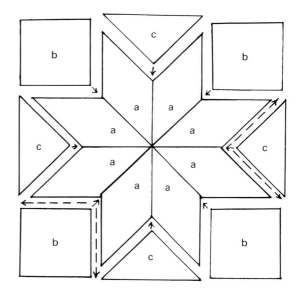

7–3. Attach the four c triangles and the b squares by sewing each side from the innermost point out, then sewing the next side, also from the inner point out. Dashed line indicates direction of stitching.

Whole Cloth Pillow

Whole Cloth refers to a quilt top containing little or no piecing. Sometimes the Amish refer to these quilts as plain quilts. Only a single border is used for this pillow, as the design element comes from the quilting motif. Amish quilts are rich with feathered designs. 12" x 12"

YARDAGE*

Piece	Color	Amount
a and G	1	¼ yard
F and pillow back	2	⅜ yard
Batting	—	16" x 16"
Muslin	—	16" x 16"

* Note: A fabric-safe marker for transferring quilt design also is needed for this project; ½" masking tape is recommended for use in the quilting stage.

CUTTING

Piece	Color	Quantity	Size
a	1	1	9½" x 9½"
F	2	4	2" x 9½"
G	1	4	2" x 2"
Pillow back	2	1	12½" x 12½"

Diagram of finished Whole Cloth Pillow

TRANSFERRING A QUILT MOTIF

Before any sewing is done, transfer the quilting motif given on page 530 to your center panel (piece "a"). Try this:

1. Trace the design, figure Q15 on page 530, with a medium-weight black felt-tip pen onto a 10" square of white freezer paper. (Draw on the side without the coating.) Be sure you have the design well centered on the 10" square.

2. Using an iron set on "cotton," with the coated side of the paper facing the wrong side of the material, press, centering the fabric square on the paper square. The heat of the iron will adhere the paper to the fabric. Now the design is in position and will not slip.

3. Depending on the color you have selected, you may be able to see the design through the fabric with no trouble. If not, you will need to get some light behind it. A lightbox, a tool frequently used by commercial artists, is a good solution. Since most quilters do not have a lightbox—especially not Amish quilters—you may need to improvise. The easiest makeshift lightbox is any good-size clean window during daylight hours.

4. After you have attached your design paper to the cloth panel as described in step 2, hold your prepared center panel "a" with the freezer paper against the window (or tape it there), with the fabric facing you. Trace your design onto the fabric with a fabric-safe marker; this ensures that the lines can be removed, if necessary, when you finish quilting. You will be surprised to see that even very dark colors of material will allow the design to show through if they have the light coming through them. If your material is very dark, a white or silver-colored pencil may work better than a marker.

5. After your tracing of the design onto the material is complete, peel away the freezer paper.

CONSTRUCTION

After you finish transferring the quilting design to the central panel, as described in "Transferring a Quilting Motif," proceed as follows:

1. Complete the pillow top by attaching two border strips F to opposite sides of the central panel "a." Attach squares G to the short ends of each remaining border strip F. Then attach one unit F-F-G to the top of the central panel "a" and one unit G-F-G to the bottom of central panel "a." (See figure 8–1 for layout.)

2. When pressing the pillow top, press the seams only—avoid pressing over your marked design; some markers will be set by heat and will not be able to be removed after that.

3. Cut your pillow top backing, muslin, and batting 2" larger in each dimension than your pillow top's unfinished size (so make them 14½" x 14½"). Hand baste the pillow top, batting, and muslin together. You are making a sandwich with the pillow top facing out, the batting in the middle and the muslin facing out on the bottom. Your basting will hold the three layers flat and snug while you quilt.

Baste first in a spiderweb manner, always working from the central area to the outer edge (see page 86), and then superimpose a further rectangle grid of basting. The "spiderweb" eases the excess fullness out. The grid reinforces the positioning. Finally, run a line of basting completely around the edge of the pillow (or quilt) top about ⅛" to ¼" from the outer edge. Do not remove the basting around the edge, even after the quilting is complete. It will help control the edge while you complete the pillow.

4. Select quilting thread to match or blend with color 1 (the color of piece "a"). Before you complete the rest of your pillow, do the quilting of the central circle, as described in the quilting instructions. Do background quilting as described here in "Adding Background Quilting."

5. Once the quilting is done, follow the instructions on page 85 for "Completing and Stuffing a Pillow," starting with Step 3.

ADDING BACKGROUND QUILTING

This is a good opportunity to see how much background quilting will add depth and enhance your motifs. You can try adding lines across your feathered circle. To do this, you can use ½"-wide mask-

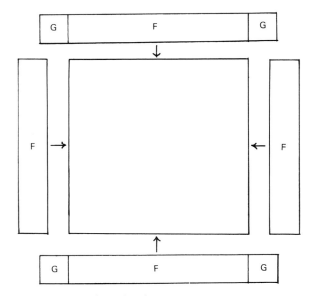

8–1. Attaching border strips to center.

ing tape. That will be the perfect width for quilting the background of the feathered design of the size given in on page 530. Using tape eliminates the need to mark the background lines on the material.

After quilting the circular center design, place a length of masking tape on the diagonal of the center panel and quilt along both sides of the tape (see color photo for reference). Remove the tape, reposition it next to one of the quilting lines you just made, and quilt along the other edge of the tape. You may reuse the tape several times before needing a new piece. Do not quilt through the area already quilted with the feathered motif; add lines only to the outside of the circle. If you quilt inside the circle, make the lines closer together, as in the model.

Because the above design covers a small area, your time in quilting a pillow is minimal; however, I hope that completing the background quilting given here will convince you to spend the extra time necessary to quilt larger projects.

Nine-patch Barn-raising Quilt

This was inspired by an Amish quilt made around 1925. The nine-patch is a simple block to piece, and all the blocks are identical. It is the choice of colors and the arrangement of those blocks that creates the magical illusion of a transparent overlay. 45" x 45"

YARDAGE

Piece	Color	Amount
A, B, backing, border, and binding	1 (pastel pink in model)	3 yards
A and B	2 (black in model)	⅝ yard
A	3 (purple-gray in model)	⅜ yard
A	4 (very bright pink in model)	¼ yard
A	5 (pale purple in model)	½ yard
Batting	—	47" x 47"

CUTTING

Piece	Color	Quantity	Size
A	1	64	Template A
B	1	128	Template B
A	2	64	Template A
B	2	128	Template B
A	3	128	Template A
A	4	64	Template A
Border C	1	2	5" x 36¼"
Border D	1	2	5" x 45"
Backing	1	1	47" x 47"
Binding	1	4	46" x 46"

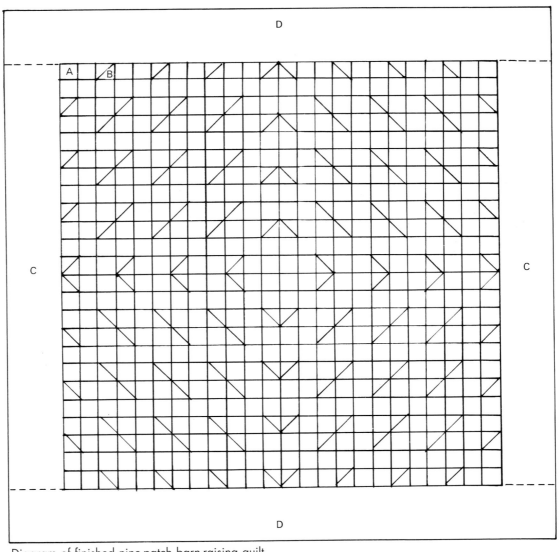

Diagram of finished nine-patch barn-raising quilt

CONSTRUCTION

All construction is done with ¼" seam allowance. The design is made up of sixty-four identical nine-patch blocks.

1. You have 128 B triangles of color 2 (black) and 128 B triangles of color 1 (pastel pink). We will subsequently refer to the black triangles as B2 and the pink triangles as B1. Take one B2 triangle and one B1 triangle and seam them together along their long sides (see figure 9–1). This forms the B2/B1 square. Repeat this process until you have made a total of 128 squares. You can use chain-piecing methods to speed construction. Press the squares open.

2. You are now ready to piece the sixty-four identical nine-patch squares that make up the design. You can use chain piecing to speed things along. To make one square, take the 7 small (A) squares that make up one nine-patch block, along with two of the pieced B2/B1 squares you created in step 1. Follow the color guide in figure 9–2. Piece three columns of three squares each, following the layout in figure 9–3.

3. Once you have finished your three columns, seam them together to form a nine-patch square, as is shown in figure 9–3.

4. Repeat steps 2 and 3 until you have created a total of sixty-four nine-patch squares.

5. Now you are ready to piece the blocks together. You will assemble one-quarter of the entire design at a time (see figure 9–4). Later you will assemble the quarters. Note that the blocks are not all

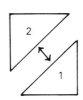

9–1. Join triangles on long sides.

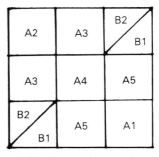

9–2. The nine-patch block. Numbers indicate colors.

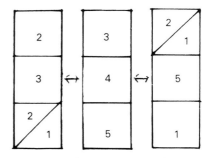

9–3. Seam the columns of 3 squares together to make the nine-patch unit, matching seams. Numbers indicate color.

Left: Full-size templates for nine-patch barn-raising quilt. Inner line is seam line. Outer line is cutting line. Arrows indicate the straight grain of fabric.

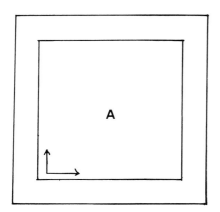

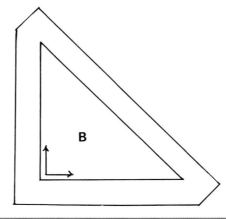

oriented the same way in the quarter. Some have the color 2 square (A2, black in our model), at the upper left, and some have the A2 square in another position (see figure 9–5). Lay out all the blocks for the quarter, verifying their orientation with figure 9–5.

6. Following your quarter-design layout, piece the top left block to the next block in that row, then proceed to join the other two blocks in that row until you have attached all four together.

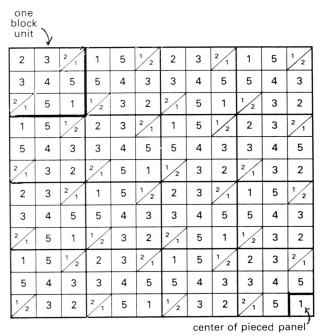

one block unit →

center of pieced panel

9–4. Layout of upper left quarter of nine-patch design. Numbers indicate colors.

7. Piece the next three rows of blocks in the quarter-design layout.

8. Join the four rows to form the upper-left quarter design. Be sure to double-check the rows' orientation.

9. Following the instructions in steps 2 through 8, create three more quarters exactly like the first one.

10. Once you have completed all four quarters, lay them out as indicated in figure 9–6. Note orientation of blocks 1 and 16 and be sure they are correctly placed. (Each quarter is rotated ¼ circle (90 degrees from the previous one to create the pattern.) Seam the quarters together, matching the centers carefully. This completes the central design of the nine-patch barn-raising quilt. Press the central design.

11. For border attachment, take the short borders C and seam them to the sides of the pieced central design (see diagram of finished quilt). Then attach the D borders at the top and bottom of the unit and press the unit. This completes the quilt top.

12. For quilting and binding see Chapter 8—How to Quilt, pages 428 to 445 to finish the project.

9–5. Positioning of nine-patch squares in upper left quarter section of quilt. Note position of block 1 and block 16. "2" refers to color 2.

9–6. Orientation of the four quarters of the quilt design for the nine-patch barn-raising quilt. Note location of block 16 in each quarter.

Ocean Waves Quilt

Ocean Waves is one of the single-template patterns popular with Amish quiltmakers. They cut scraps as they are available and save them up for use at another time. Setting Ocean Waves with black fabric intensifies the jewel-like appeal of the many rich colors. 35" x 35"

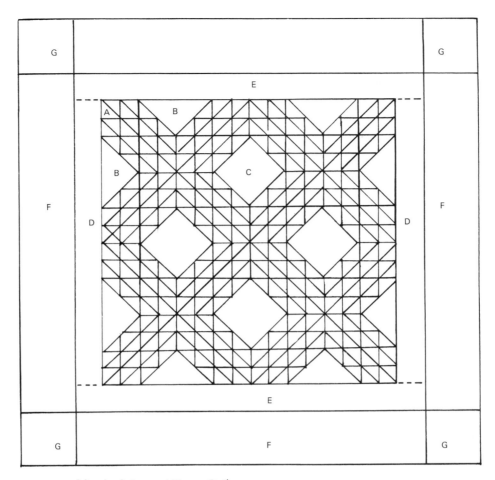

Diagram of finished Ocean Waves Quilt

YARDAGE

Piece	Color	Amount
A	1 through 16	⅛ yard of each color, or scraps that total approximately 2 yards
B, C, F	Black	⅞ yard (31½")
D, E, and G	Your choice (turquoise blue in model)	⅞ yard
Back	Your choice	1¼ yards (trim to 39" x 39")
Batting	—	40" x 40"

Note: a silver pencil for drawing on black is also helpful for this project.

CUTTING

Piece	Color	Quantity	Size
A	1 through 16	384 (24 each of 16 colors)	Template A
B	Black	8	Template B
C	Black	4	Template C
D	Your choice	2	2½" x 23½"
E	Your choice	2	2½" x 27½"
F	Black	4	4½" x 27½"
G	Your choice	4	4½" x 4½"

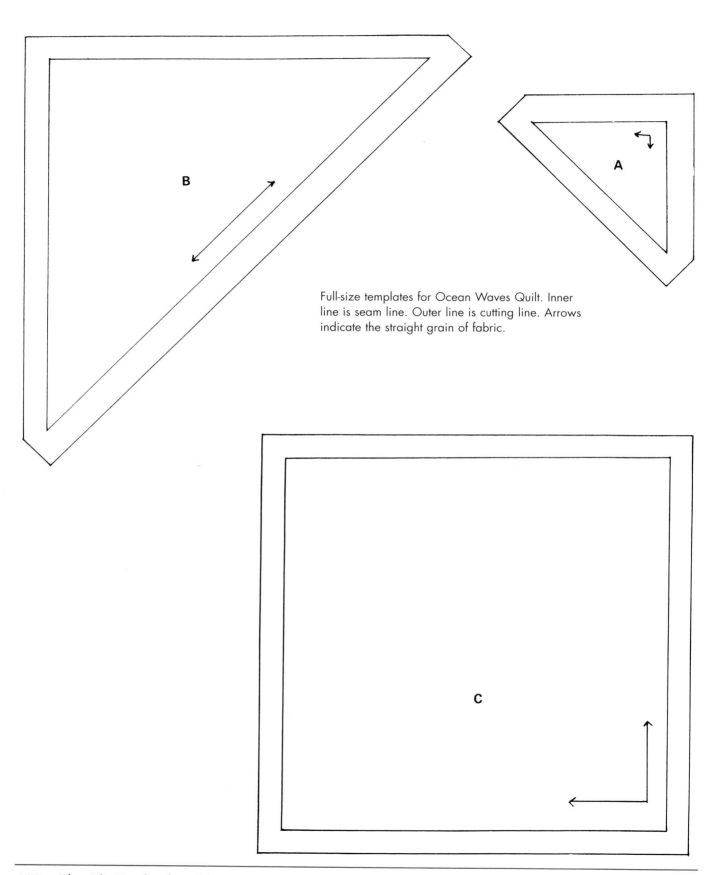

Full-size templates for Ocean Waves Quilt. Inner line is seam line. Outer line is cutting line. Arrows indicate the straight grain of fabric.

A custom quilting motif (figure Q11, bottom) for the C parts (setting squares) of the quilt can be found in the quilt motifs section on page 527. A light box would be helpful for transferring the quilting designs.

CONSTRUCTION

All sewing is done with ¼" seam allowance. First we will create the main wave units, which comprise the Ocean Waves pattern. (You can see the shape of a wave unit in figure 10–2.) Each wave unit is made of 24 A triangles. There are a total of 16 wave units.

MAIN DESIGN

1. Select 24 A triangles at random from your total of 384 A triangles. Make 10 squares by seaming two triangles together on their long sides (see figure 10–1). Do not join two triangles of the same color in a square. Chain-piecing techniques (see description on pages 74–75) will speed up construction. After making your 10 squares, you will have 4 extra triangles left of the 24.

2. Attach the square units you created in step 1 to each other, as shown in figure 10–2. First you need to make two 2-square-long rectangles and two 3-square-long rectangles.

3. Attach an A triangle to one end only of each rectangle you created in step 2 (see Figure 10–2). This uses up the extra triangles you had in step 1. Be sure that each triangle is attached so that its long side is parallel to the long sides of the triangles seamed in the rectangles.

4. Following figure 10–2, lay out and seam together the four units you created in step 3, being sure that the parts are aligned correctly. This completes one entire wave unit.

5. Repeat steps 1 through 4 fifteen times more to create a total of sixteen wave units.

6. Next, seam four wave units to a central setting square C, and then to each other, as shown in figure 10–3. This creates an eight-sided unit, or octagon.

7. Repeat step 6 to form a second octagon unit.

8. Attach the two octagon units created in steps 6 and 7 to each other, as shown in figure 10–4 (next page). Then attach a B triangle to the upper, outer corner of each of the octagons (see figure 10–4, middle). This creates unit II.

9. Take four more wave units and seam them together as shown at top of figure 10–4. Take two B triangles and attach a B triangle in each of the two triangular spaces between the wave units that you just joined together. Attach a C square below the wave units. This creates unit I (see figure 10–4, top).

10. Repeat step 9 to create a second grouping of four wave units, two triangles, and a C unit. Turn it upside down to be the basis of unit III in figure 10–4. Add two more B triangles to the upper, outer corners as shown in figure 10–4, bottom.

10–1. Join two A triangles together on their long sides to form a square.

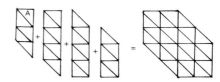

10–2. Join rectangles with triangles at their ends (left) to form a completed wave unit (right).

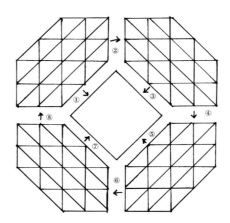

10–3. Join four wave units to a C square and to each other to form an octagon unit. Circled numbers indicate order of piecing.

11. For your final step of work on the central panel, assemble Units I, II, and III, following figure 10–4 as a guide. Be sure to match the seams at pivot points. Do not stitch across the seam allowances.

ATTACHING THE BORDERS

To attach the borders, follow the diagram of the finished quilt.

12. First attach the D border strips to the opposite sides of the central design you completed in step 11 (figure 10–5).

13. Then attach the E borders to the top and bottom of the central design.

14. Sew a G square to each end of two F border pieces.

15. Attach the two remaining F borders to the 2 opposite sides of the unit you created in step 13 (figure 10–6).

16. Attach the G-F-G border units to the top and bottom of the unit created in step 15. This completes the quilt top. Press the quilt top.

17. For quilting and binding see Chapter 8—How to Quilt, pages 428 to 445 to finish the project.

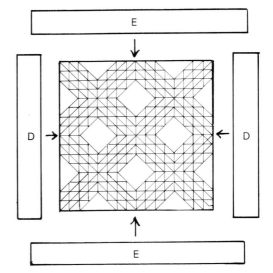

10–5. Attaching inner borders.

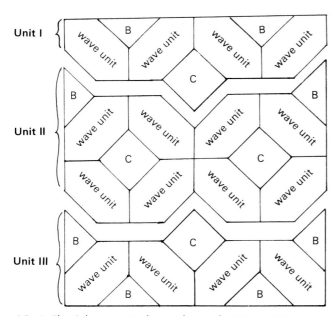

10–4. The 3 large units that make up the Ocean Waves panel.

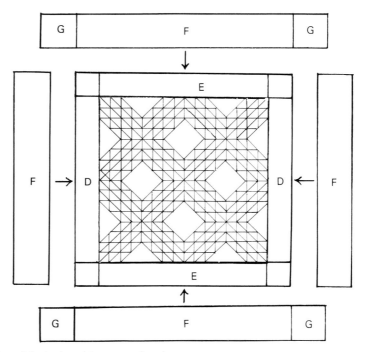

10–6. Attaching outer borders.

Mini Grape Basket Doll's Quilt

This project could also make a stunning wall hanging or large pillow top. As well as each of the nine blocks having a different color basket, more than one black fabric was used, which creates shading and texture. This reflects what might commonly happen when black scraps from different sources are combined. 20" x 20"

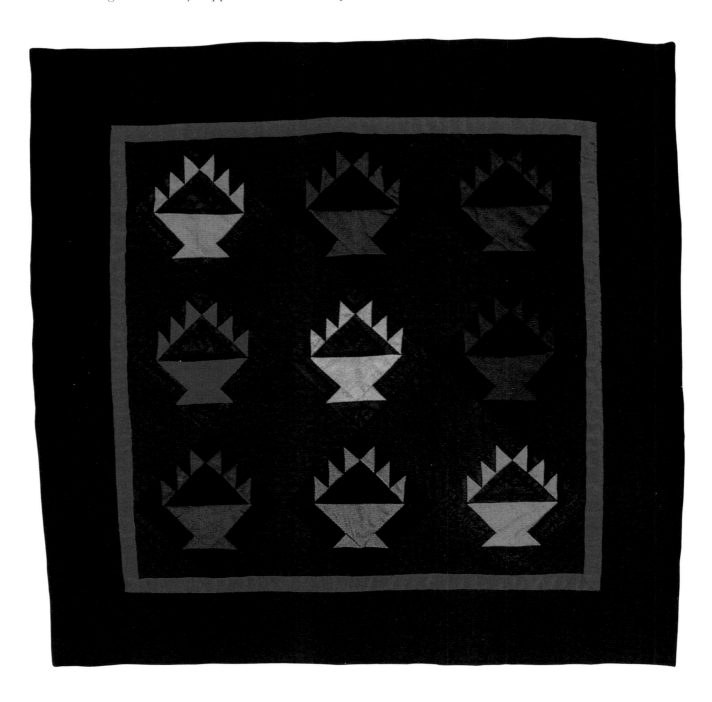

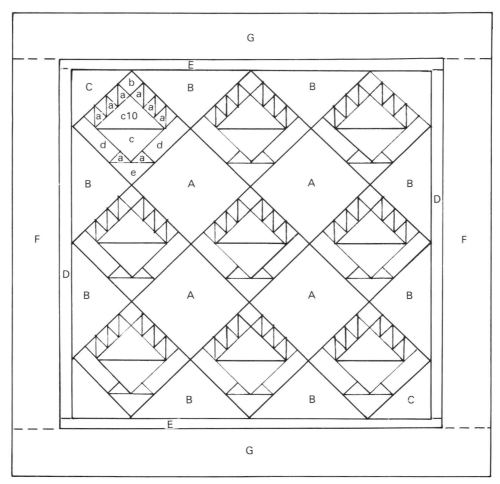

Diagram of finished Mini Grape Basket Doll's Quilt

YARDAGE

Piece	Color	Amount
a (of basket),		at least 9" x 9"
c (of basket)	1 through 9	of each color
a, c, e (background of pieced blocks)	10 (black in model)	¾ yard
B, C, F, G D and E	11* (Electric blue in model)	⅛ yard
Backing	Your choice	24" x 24"
Batting	—	24" x 24"

*Or use the color of one of the baskets, as in the model.

CUTTING

Piece	Color	Quantity	Size
Baskets			
a	1 through 9	8 of each color (total 72)	Template a
a	10	54	Template a
b	10	9	Template b
c	1 through 9	1 of each color	Template c
c10	9	9	Template c
d	10	18	Template d
e	10	9	Template e
Setting Blocks			
A	10	4	Template A
B	10	8	Template B
C	10	4	Template C

Piece	Color	Quantity	Size
		Borders	
D	11	2	1" x 15½"
E	11	2	1" x 16"
F	10	2	2½" x 16"
G	10	2	2½" x 20½"

CONSTRUCTION

All construction is to be done with ¼" seam allowance. Since the pieces are quite small, you may want to piece them by hand. You may also want to trim seam allowances to ⅛" to reduce bulk. Study the finished quilt diagram to get an overall view of the project. First we will piece the 9 Mini Grape Basket blocks.

1. For each basket, take six "a" triangles in the color of that basket (one of the colors 1 through 9, depending on which basket you are working on). We will call these triangles "a". Also take six "a" triangles in color 10 (the background color; we will call these triangles a10). Seam one "a" triangle of the color of your basket and one a10 triangle together on the long side. This creates one of the six pieced small squares you need for each basket (see figure 11–1). Chain piecing may be used (see chain-piecing instructions in Double Irish Chain) if you do not hand piece. Continue to create a total of six "a"/a10 squares in the same manner.

2. Attach three of the squares created step 1 together in a rectangle, following the layout given in figure 11–1, right. Attach a "b" square in color 10 (we will call this b10) to the right end of this rectangle, keeping the "a" triangles at lower right of each square in the rectangle (see figure 11–1). We will call the unit created unit I.

3. Attach the three remaining small pieced squares you created in step 1 together in a rectangle, as shown in figure 11–2. Note that in this rectangle, the "a" triangles are in the lower left of each square. We will call this unit II.

4. Take two triangles of size "c," one of the color of the basket (we will call this triangle "c") and one

of color 10 (triangle c10). Sew them together on the long side with right sides of material facing each other to form a square, which will be placed as shown in figure 11–2, middle.

5. Lay out all the units you made in Steps 2, 3, and 4 as shown in figure 11–2. Double-check their orientation.

6. Attach unit II (the rectangle on the upper right of figure 11–2) to the c10/"c" square, as shown.

7. Attach unit I (on the upper left of figure 11–2) to the unit you created step 6.

8. Now take two of piece "d," color 10 (d10), and two of Piece "a" in the color of the basket. Attach an "a" triangle to the short end of piece d10. Attach a second "a" triangle to the second d10 rectangle on the opposite short end (see figure 11–3, next page). This forms the bottom of the Mini Grape Basket.

9. Attach the d10/"a" unit formed in step 8 to the pieced square formed in steps 1 through 7 (see figure 11–3, next page).

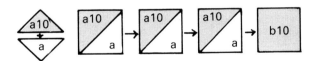

11–1. Left: Pieced square unit for Mini Grape Basket. Right: attaching three pieced squares to a solid square to make unit I. Numbers indicate colors.

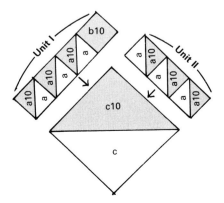

11–2. Attach unit 1 and unit II to pieced c10/"c" square.

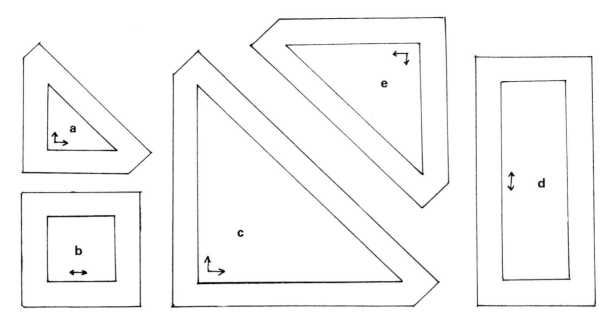

Full-size templates for the Mini Grape Basket block. Inside line is seam line. Outside line is cutting line. Arrows indicate the straight grain of fabric.

11–3. Attach d10/"a" unit to make bottom of basket.

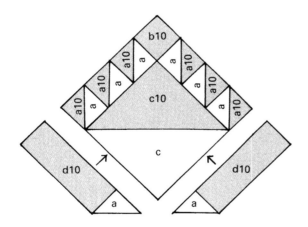

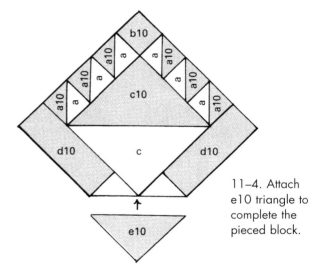

11–4. Attach e10 triangle to complete the pieced block.

10. Take an "e" triangle in color 10 (e10) and attach it to the bottom of the unit created in step 9, as shown in figure 11–4. This completes the first Mini Grape Basket block.

11. Using a different one of the colors 2 through 9 for the "basket" parts of each basket, follow steps 1 through 10 above to create eight more Mini Grape Basket blocks. Press each block.

12. Now take all nine Mini Grape Basket blocks and lay them out as shown in the diagram of the finished quilt. Take eight B triangles, four C triangles, and four A setting blocks (all of color 10) and lay them out as shown in figure 11–5. Seam them together as shown in figure 11–5. This completes the pieced interior of the Mini Grape Basket Quilt.

13. To start working on the inner borders, take the two D strips and attach them to the sides of the center panel, as shown in the diagram of the finished quilt.

14. Take the two E strips. Attach one to the top of the unit created in step 13 and one to the bottom.

15. Take two of the F border strips. Seam one of the F strips to each side of the central unit you have created thus far.

16. Take two G border strips. Attach them to the top and bottom of the unit made in step 15, as shown in the diagram of the finished quilt. This completes the construction of the Mini Grape Basket Doll's Quilt top. Press the entire top.

17. For quilting and binding see Chapter 8—How to Quilt, pages 428 to 445 to finish the project.

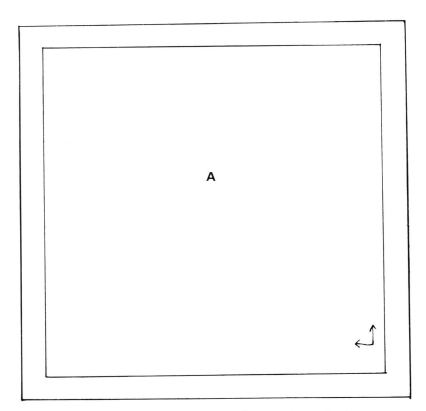

Full-size templates (above and next page) for Mini Grape Basket setting blocks and triangles. Inside line is seam line. Outside line is cutting line. Arrows indicate the straight grain of fabric.

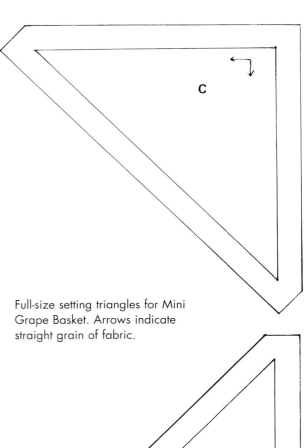

Full-size setting triangles for Mini Grape Basket. Arrows indicate straight grain of fabric.

11–5. Assembling the Mini Grape Basket blocks and the setting blocks. Circled numbers indicate order of piecing.

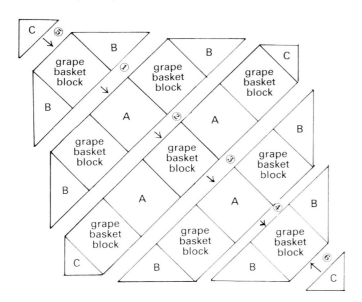

Nine-patch Single Irish Chain Doll's Quilt

This was inspired by an Amish quilt made around 1925. The nine-patch is a simple block to piece, and all the blocks are identical. It is the choice of colors and the arrangement of those blocks that creates the magical illusion of a transparent overlay. 21" x 27"

The nine-patch has almost endless design possibilities. Here it is used in the Single Irish Chain setting arrangement. The color combination is a replica of a full-size Amish quilt made in the 1920's, quilted with hearts and flowers in the large black squares, and cable motifs in the borders.

Use chain-piecing to speed up your work on the nine-patch blocks. See Double Irish Chain Quilt for chain-piecing instructions. Alternatively, you may want to try your hand at the strip-piecing speed method, for which instructions are given here.

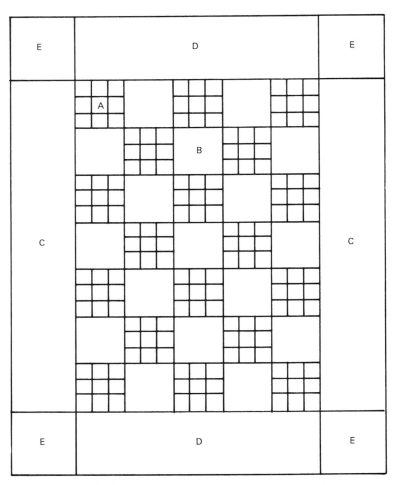

Diagram of finished nine-patch Single Irish Chain Doll's Quilt

YARDAGE

Piece	Color	Amount
A, B, C, D	1 (black)	⁵⁄₈ yard
A	2 (pink)	³⁄₈ yard
A (center of nine- patch block); E, binding	3 (tan)	¹⁄₄ yard
Backing	Your choice	³⁄₄ yard
Batting	—	24" x 30"

CUTTING: TRADITIONAL METHOD

Piece	Color	Quantity	Size
A	1 (black)	72	Template A
A	2 (pink)	72	Template A
A	3 (tan)	18	Template A
B	1 (black)	17	Template B
C	1 (black)	2	4¹⁄₂" x 21¹⁄₂"
D	1 (black)	2	4¹⁄₂" x 15¹⁄₂"
E	3 (tan)	4	4¹⁄₂" x 4¹⁄₂"

CONSTRUCTION: TRADITIONAL METHOD

All construction is done with seam allowances of ¹⁄₄". First you will make the nine-patch blocks, of which a total of eighteen are needed.

1. Take four A squares in color 1 (black); we will call these A1. Take four A squares in color 2 (A2). Take one A square in color 3 (A3). Following figure 12–1 for the color scheme, lay out the pieces as shown. Seam them together into three rectangles of three pieces each. You can use chain piecing to speed up the process (see instructions in Double Irish Chain Quilt).

2. Take the three rectangles you created in step 1. Seam them together into a nine-patch block (see figure 12–2). You now have completed one basic unit of the quilt.

3. Repeat Steps 1 and 2 seventeen more times to make a total of eighteen nine-patch blocks.

4. Take two B squares of color 1 (black) and three of the pieced nine-patch blocks you created in steps 1 through 3. Following figure 12–3, lay out the blocks in a row. Seam the five blocks together

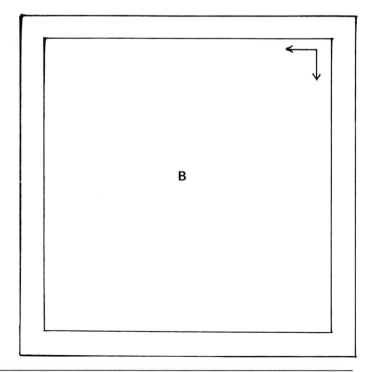

12–1. Seam A squares into three columns, then seam columns together to form a nine-patch unit.

Full-size templates for Single Irish Chain Doll's Quilt. Inner line is seam line; outer line is cutting line. Arrows indicate the straight grain of fabric.

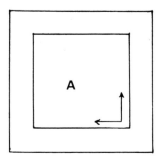

in a row, alternating them as shown in figure 12–3, beginning and ending with a nine-patch block. We will call the row we created Unit I.

5. Repeat step 4 three more times. The four unit I rows made will be used for rows 1, 3, 5, and 7 of the quilt (see the diagram of the finished quilt). Set these aside for now.

6. Take three B squares of color 1 (black) and two nine-patch blocks. Lay out the five squares as shown in figure 12–4. Seam the five blocks together in a row, alternating solid blocks with nine-patch blocks as shown in figure 12–4 , to make unit II.

7. Repeat step 6 two more times. The unit II pieces will be used for rows 2, 4, and 6 of the quilt top.

8. Consulting the diagram of the finished quilt, lay out the seven rows of the central design, which you made in steps 4 through 7. Be sure that the unit I rows alternate with the unit II rows. Seam the seven rows together horizontally, starting with rows 1 and 2 and working your way down. You have now completed the central design.

9. To attach the borders, first take two C borders. Attach them to the long sides of the central panel made in step 8. See the diagram of the finished quilt for reference.

10. Take the two D borders and four E squares. Seam an E square to each short end of each D border piece to create two E-D-E border units.

11. Take the two E-D-E border units you created in step 10 and attach one to the top and one to the bottom of the unit you created in step 9. You have now completed the quilt top. Press the quilt top.

12. To finish the project, see quilting and binding instructions at the back of the book.

CUTTING: ALTERNATE, STRIP-PIECING SPEED METHOD

For the alternate, strip-piecing speed method, cut the strips across the grain of the fabric, from selvage to selvage (see figure 12–5). Instead of cutting individual squares for piecing, you will create strips

first and make your blocks out of them. This will save the time that otherwise would have been needed to sew fifty-four rectangles of three squares each, as is done in the traditional method.

2	1	2
1	3	1
2	1	2

12–2. The completed nine-patch block.

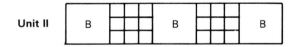

12–3. Seam nine-patch to solid blocks as shown, to make unit I. This is used for rows 1, 3, 5, and 7 of the quilt.

12–4. Seam nine-patch to solid blocks as shown to make unit II. This is used for rows 2, 4, and 6 of the quilt.

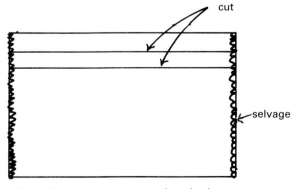

12–5. For strip-piecing speed method, cut strips from selvage to selvage.

Piece	Color	Quantity	Size
A squares	1 (Black)	4	1½" x 45"
	2 (Pink)	4	1½" x 45"
	3 (Tan)	1	1½" x 45"
B squares	1 (Black)	2	3½" x 45"
C	1 (Black)	2	4½" x 21½"
D	1 (Black)	2	4½" x 15½"
E	3 (Tan)	4	4½" x 4½"

ALTERNATE SPEED METHOD OF CONSTRUCTION

1. All construction is done with ¼" seam allowance. First make two bands of three strips each. Take two strips of size 1½" x 45" of color 2 and one strip 1½" x 45" of color 1. Sew them together along their long sides so that color 1 is in the middle, to form band I (figure 12–6).

2. Take two strips 1½" x 45" of color 1 and one strip 1½" x 45" of color 3. Sew them together along their long sides so that color 3 is in the middle, to form band II (figure 12–7). Press both bands, keeping the seam allowance on the side of the dark color.

3. Using your gridded ruler, take band I and check its short edge for squareness, to be sure it is perpendicular to the long edge, that is, makes a square corner like the corner of your right triangle. If it isn't perpendicular, straighten it, by cutting off the part that extends over the square line with your rotary cutter.

4. Now that band l is squared up, make thirty-six 1½"-wide bars by slicing across the three stripes of band I with your rotary cutter. We will call these bars "bar I," since they came from band I (see figure 12–8). Put these bars aside for the moment.

5. Take out band II, which you created in step 2. Straighten the short edge as you did in step 3. Then make eighteen 1½"-wide bars by slicing across the three strips of band II. We will call each "bar II" as they came from band II.

6. Now take two of bar I and one of bar II. As shown in figure 12–9, join them together to make a nine-patch unit. Be sure to observe your ¼" seam allowances.

7. Repeat step 6 until you have made a total of eighteen nine-patch units.

8. Take one of the 3½" x 45" strips you made of color 1 (black, in our model). With your rotary cutter, make twelve 3½"-wide squares from the second ½" x 45" strip of color 1. This will give you the total of seventeen B blocks you need for piecing the quilt top.

9. From here on, you can follow the construction steps given under "Construction: Traditional Method." Begin at step 4 to join the nine-patch squares with solid squares.

Color 2
Color 1
Color 2

12–6. Color arrangement for band I.

Color 1
Color 3
Color 1

12–7. Color arrangement for band II.

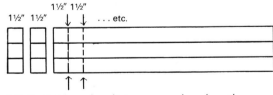

12–8. Cut bars by slicing across bands with rotary cutter.

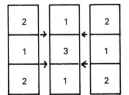

27–9. Seam three bars together to make a nine-patch unit. Arabic numbers indicate colors.

Star of Bethlehem Quilt

The Star of Bethlehem is a favorite of Amish quiltmakers, perhaps because it makes such a striking statement. It looks more complicated than it really is. Relatively small amounts of each color are needed to make the star. There are few Amish quiltmakers who have not used this design. It is generally more popular than the Amish Diamond and Amish Bars. 51" x 51"

Diagram of finished Star of Bethlehem Quilt

YARDAGE

Piece	Color	Quantity
Star pattern	1 (teal blue)*	½ yard
of quilt and	2 (rose)	½ yard
optional	3 (light blue)	½ yard
multicolored border	4 (red)	½ yard
	5 (royal blue)	½ yard
B and C (setting	6 (black	1½ yards
triangles and	in model)	
squares) and border		
Backing	6 (black	54" x 54"
	in model)	
Batting	—	54" x 54"

*Colors in parentheses give choices used in the model.
You can choose any colors you wish, however.

The instructions here are for quick strip-piecing. A rotary cutter, cutting board, and gridded ruler are recommended (see page 414). You will also need a 10" 45-degree right triangle. The swag feather border motif may be found in the section on quilting motifs on page 530, along with other designs suitable for quilting the large squares and triangles.

The Star of Bethlehem is made up of eight large, pieced diamonds. You will make strips that are then sewn together into strip groups of five colors. The groups will be cut into bands and reassembled to complete the diamond sections of your star. When sewing, it will be critical to maintain your ¼" seam allowances.

Try color sketches on copies of figure 13–4 (see page 119) to visualize one unit of the star and try out potential color combinations. The color designated "color 1" will be the center of the star (it is teal in our model). The colors repeat in the same order to the outer parts of the star. Even after you have chosen five colors, there are many color combinations possible for your quilt, depending on your choice of color order. Choose the colors 1, 2, 3, 4, or 5, and set it aside for reference.

CUTTING

1. From each of your five star-design colors (colors 1 through 5), cut five strips, each of which is $2\frac{1}{4}$ x 45". Cut across the straight grain of the fabric from selvage to selvage. These strips will be used to make the star design. (The optional border is made from the remaining sewn diamond strips).

2. The setting squares, triangles, and borders will be cut later.

3. An optional multicolored border inset (see color photograph) may also be cut later (see Optional Border Inset section, page 121).

CONSTRUCTION

Creating the Strip Groups

1. Baste and sew the strips together in groups of five to form strip groups A, B, C, D, and E, as shown in figure 13–1, and as listed below. Be very careful to maintain accurate $\frac{1}{4}$" seam allowances.

Group A: Sew strips in the color order 1-2-3-4-5; press all seams toward color 5.

Group B is pieced in color order 2-3-4-5-1; press seam allowances toward color 2.

Group C is pieced in order 3-4-5-1-2; press seams toward color 2.

Group D is pieced in order 4-5-1-2-3; press seams toward color 4.

Group E is pieced in order 5-1-2-3-4; press seams toward color 4.

2. Press each strip group from the reverse side first; then turn your work over and press it from the right side also, to avoid leaving any hidden

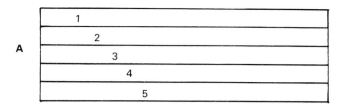

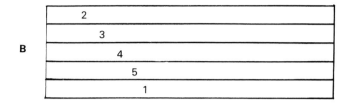

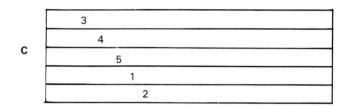

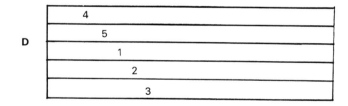

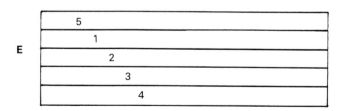

13–1. Assemble five groups of five strips each as shown in A through E. Numbers refer to colors.

tucks. Pressing seam allowances as indicated makes matching the seams easier and cuts down on the bulk under the seam.

Cutting the Strip Groups Into Bands

The next step is to slice across the strip groups to create five-colored bands of small diamonds, which will later be assembled into large diamonds. An example of one band (cut from Group A) is shown in Figure 13–2.

3. Take Strip Group A. Be sure it is laid out on your cutting board with Color 1 at the top. Carefully align the base of your 45-degree right triangle with the long, bottom edge of strip group A. Consult Figure 13–3. You will have some waste at the lower left corner, because in order to make a full band of all five colors, you need to move your triangle in from the left edge 10" to make the first cut. Mark the line with a fabric marker and cut along the line with your rotary cutter, being careful to maintain your 45-degree angle.

4. Using your gridded ruler and rotary cutter, carefully measure and cut 2¼"-wide slices of strip group A. See figure 13–3 for reference. Still using your triangle, make a second cut, also at 45 degrees to the bottom line, as the first cut was. You have now cut out one band A unit.

5. Continue measuring and cutting 2¼"-wide units, until you have cut a total of eight band A units. Label each one at the top with a small piece of paper or masking tape so they don't get mixed up with the other units.

6. Repeat Steps 3 through 5 with strip groups B, C, D, and E, cutting eight bands from each one.

Diamond Construction

Reminder: Be very sure to keep your ¼" seam allowances precisely.

7. Following figure 13–4 as a guide, take a band A unit and a band B unit. Pin them together with right sides facing, being sure colors are positioned as in figure 13–4. When pinned, the band units will not totally overlap each other (figure 13–5). Baste and sew them together. The seam lines will create an X as they intersect.

8. Repeat step 7 until you have created seven more band A/band B units, one for each big diamond that makes up the star pattern.

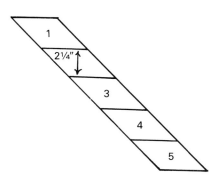

13–2. Example of a band that will be pieced into the large diamond. Not all bands have same color order.

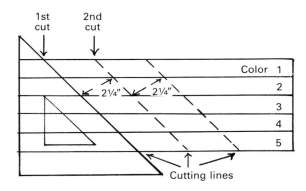

13–3. Cutting strip group A into eight bands, using 45-degree triangle.

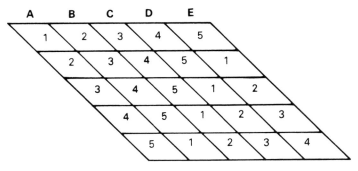

13–4. Order of attaching band units to form a large diamond. Numbers indicate colors. Seam lines form an X where they meet.

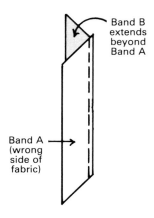

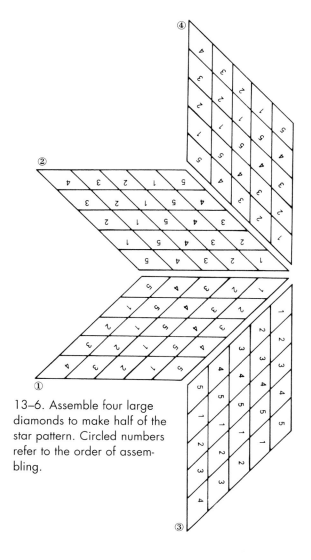

13–5. When two band units are pinned for stitching, they will not totally overlap each other.

13–6. Assemble four large diamonds to make half of the star pattern. Circled numbers refer to the order of assembling.

9. To each of the band A/band B units created in steps 7 and 8, pin, baste, and sew a band C next to Band B, as shown in figure 13–4.

10. To each Band A/band B/band C unit you made in Step 9, sew a band D unit as shown in figure 13–4.

11. To each band A/band B/band C/band D unit you made in step 10, add a band E unit as shown in figure 13–4. This completes all eight diamonds needed to make the star design. The center point will be color 1.

STAR CONSTRUCTION

12. Study figure 13–6. You will see that the large diamonds meet at the center in color 1.

13. Take two of the large diamonds and pin, baste, and seam the sections together along the bands that have colors in order 1-2-3-4-5 (band A), placing color 1 of the first large diamond next to color 1 of the second large diamond, color 2 with color 2, etc., to make the jagged circles that form the pattern (see color figure). Start your seams ¼" from the material's edge, working from the center of the star (color 1) outward. It will make the insetting of the background squares and triangles easier when you come to them later.

14. Take a third large diamond and pin, baste, and sew it in place on the unit you created in step 13, attaching color 1 to color 1, and the other colors to their same colors, as you did for the first two large diamonds. Then attach a fourth large diamond in the same way (see figure 13–6). You now have completed half of the star pattern. Set this half aside.

15. Repeat steps 13 and 14 to create the second half of the star pattern from the remaining four large diamonds.

16. To join the two halves of the star, pin the two halves together starting from the center of the star and pinning outward in each direction. Check to be sure that they are aligned correctly and baste and sew in place. There should not be any gap between the parts.

CORNERS AND TRIANGLES

17. Check the size of the squares C you will need to fill in the corners of the star pattern (see figure 13–7 for placement of squares). Your star should require about 12½" or 13" squares (finished size; cut ½" larger squares to include their seam allowances). However, as your star pattern may have ended up being slightly larger or smaller after it was sewn, we suggest that you cut a paper or cardboard outline of your square, based on the space you have in the corner of your star pattern when you lay it out flat; then add ¼" on each side for a seam allowance and make a cardboard template. Cut out four setting squares from your background material (color 6), using the square template; be sure the right angles are on the grain line of the fabric. This will help prevent stretching along the outer sides of your quilt top. Don't set in the squares yet, however.

18. You can use the cardboard template of the square that you made in step 17 to create a pattern for the four B triangles needed to set the star design. Cut the square pattern template in half on the diagonal, add ¼" seam allowances to each of the three sides of one cardboard triangle, and cut a new cardboard template. Then cut out the four setting triangles from the background material (color 6), using the new cardboard template, with the straight grain of fabric on the long edge of the triangle (which will be the outer edge of the star block).

19. Take your four setting triangles. Insert the triangles along the middles of the four sides of the star (see figure 13–7), by pinning and basting them in place, matching the sides to the sides of each adjacent diamond, and then sewing them from the inner point outward on one triangle side and repeating the process on the other triangle side.

20. After you have set in all four triangles, you can complete the central design block by setting in the squares. Pin and baste them in place in the corners, as shown in figure 13–7. Stitch from the right angle of each star outward to attach the square. Go back to the right angle where the square joins the star to stitch the second side of each square.

FINAL BORDERS*

21. The border quilting design shown in the model fits on a 5" wide border nicely. For a 5" border, cut strips of 5½" x about 48" for the top and bottom border and 5½" x about 58" for the side borders. The exact length may be checked across the center of the quilt. Piece borders if necessary.

22. Mark the middle of the border length of each side and align it with the middle of the unit you created by joining the star pattern and the squares and triangles. Pin, baste, and sew the top and bottom borders in place.

23. Then pin the side border units to the unit you created in step 22, matching the middle of the design with the middle of the border length and working outward in both directions. Try not to stretch the border pieces. To be true to Amish design, do not miter the corners.

OPTIONAL BORDER INSET

24. The thin, striped border shown in the color photograph is stitched in place as a strip. The bands that form the optional border are cut from leftover strip groups A, B, C, D, and E, which were used to make the star. As the recommended width of the optional border is 1", you need to cut bands that are 1½" wide. Cut them on a 45-degree angle as you did earlier when you created the bands to make the star pattern (steps 3 through 6), only these are narrower. You need to cut about 16 bands, of any strip groups you choose.

25. Join four bands end to end for each side of the border inset, measuring the perimeter of the large pieced square to see exactly how long you need to make the border inset, and adding on ½" to each border for seam allowances. The border units probably will be about 48" long each. As they are cut on the bias, the individual bars are very stretchy, so be careful not to pull and stretch them while you are attaching them to the borders of the quilt top.

*If you intend to make the optional striped borders, see steps 24 to 26 before making the final borders.

26. Attach the border insets to the top and bottom and then to the right and left sides of the center panel. To attach the outer borders, see steps 21 to 23 above.

27. To prepare to quilt, first transfer the designs to your quilt top, using the swag feather border, figure Q7, shown on page 524, if you wish to. You can transfer the design using a lightbox or light table. Tape a dark copy of the pattern onto the lightbox and then draw the pattern onto the quilt top with dressmaker's chalk or a fabric marker. Another method is to make a cardboard or plastic template of the design and trace around it on the quilt top. See the general quilting and binding instructions at the back of the book to finish the project.

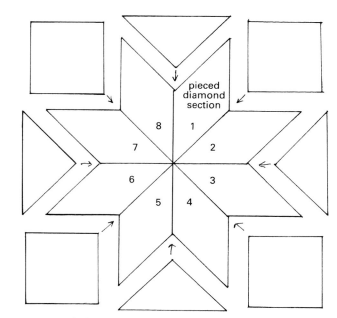

13–7. Attach the setting triangles and squares around the star pattern.

Rainbow Log Cabin Quilt

The Log Cabin design in the photograph is of the variety known as Barn Raising. There is almost no wasted fabric from yardage cut into strips for Log Cabin piecing. The Amish-style Log Cabin block cleverly allows for reduced consumption of very light fabrics. While it is not immediately apparent, there is one-third less light fabric used in the Amish block construction than there is in an English block. Since the Amish use light colors sparingly in clothing for practical purposes, this design may enable the Amish quiltmaker to complete the quilt from scraps on hand. 68" x 76"

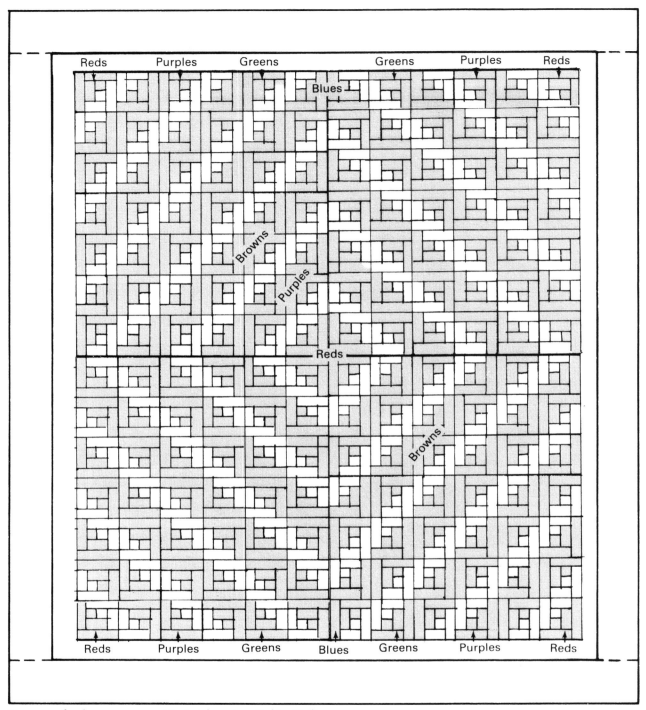

Diagram of color arrangement in Rainbow Log Cabin Quilt

For the quilt shown here you will need to make 168 blocks (12 across and 14 down). You can use the template patterns A, B, C, and D provided here or speed-cut strips with a rotary cutter. Cutting instructions are given for both.

YARDAGE

Each block has a light (L) and dark (d) side to make up the pattern (figure 14–1). For the light side (done entirely in light gray in our model), you can use light to medium-light shades of gray, green, blue, tan, or taupe. The total "light" yardage should be approximately four yards. It is almost always the case that an Amish quiltmaker doesn't consider yardage for inner and outer borders until they are actually needed. By that time she'll know what colors she wishes to emphasize. Border yardages are given in the yardage chart. However, you also may wish to wait until the main design is pieced before you choose colors for the borders.

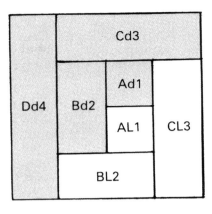

14–1. Basic Log Cabin block, Amish style. A, B, C, D are template sizes. "d" colors are the dark colors of the block. "L" colors are light colors (gray in the model).

Full-size templates for the Rainbow Log Cabin Quilt. Outer lines are cutting lines. Inner lines are seam lines. Arrows indicate the straight grain of fabric.

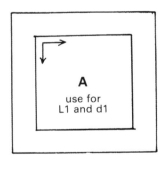

A
use for
L1 and d1

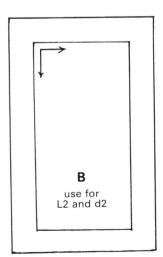

B
use for
L2 and d2

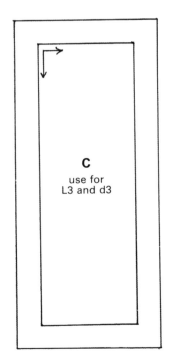

C
use for
L3 and d3

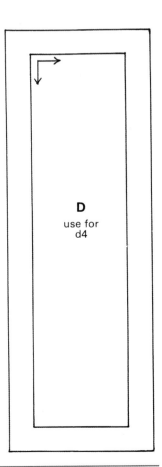

D
use for
d4

YARDAGE: EITHER METHOD

Piece	Color	Quantity
Reds		
Dark sides of red blocks	Very dark red, medium dark red, bright red, dusty rose	$\frac{1}{8}$ yard of each
Purples		
Dark sides of purple blocks	Very dark bluish purple, burgundy (very dark wine), periwinkle, light purple	$\frac{1}{8}$ yard of each
Greens		
Dark sides of green blocks	Very dark blackish green, dark bluish green, olive green, light olive green	$\frac{3}{8}$ yard of each
Blues		
Dark sides of blue blocks	Very dark blue, medium cobalt blue, medium purplish blue, light blue	$\frac{3}{8}$ yard of each
Browns		
Dark sides of brown blocks	Very dark brown, medium reddish brown, yellow ochre (yellowish tan), orange-pink (coral)	$\frac{1}{4}$ yard of each
Light sides of all blocks	Your choice of: light to medium-light gray, green, blue, tan, taupe, or other light shades (light gray in model)	Total about 4 yards
Inner Border	Your choice (dark blue in model)	$\frac{3}{4}$ yard
Outer Border	Your choice (light gray in model)	$2\frac{1}{4}$ yards
Backing	Your choice	4 yards
Batting	—	72" x 80"

*Colors given are those used in the model. You can vary them by using four varieties of any five colors for the "dark" colors.

For the pattern shown, you will make the following number of blocks (identified by dark color only): Reds: 8 blocks. Purples: 40 blocks. Greens: 36 blocks. Blues: 48 blocks. Browns: 36 blocks.

CUTTING

Cutting charts are given for both the pieced method (in which each block is cut separately) and speed cutting. Refer to figure 14–1 to see the position of the dark (d) colors and the light (L) colors in each block.

CUTTING: PIECED METHOD (USING TEMPLATES)

Piece & Size*	Color**	Total Quantity for Quilt
Red Blocks		
A, B, C, D (dark side)	Vary colors of pieces among 4 reds	8 of each size
A, B, C (light side)	Vary colors of pieces among light colors	8 of each size
Purple Blocks		
A, B, C, D (dark side)	Vary colors of pieces among 4 purples	40 of each size
A, B, C (light side)	Vary colors of pieces among light colors	40 of each size

Green Blocks

A, B, C, D (dark side)	Vary colors of pieces among 4 greens	36 of each size
A, B, C (light side)	Vary colors of pieces among light colors	36 of each size

Blue Blocks

A, B, C, D (dark side)	Vary colors of pieces among 4 blues	48 of each size
A, B, C (light side)	Vary colors of pieces among light colors	48 of each size

Brown Blocks

A, B, C, D (dark side)	Vary colors of pieces among 4 browns	36 of each size
A, B, C (light side)	Vary colors of pieces among light colors	36 of each size

Borders†

Inner Borders	Your choice (blue in model)	2 long, 2 short
Outer Borders	Your choice (light gray in model)	2 long, 2 short

* For A, B, C, and D use Templates A, B, C and D, respectively.

** Light colors are all gray in model.

† For border cutting see step 31.

SPEED-CUTTING STRIP METHOD

Instead of cutting individual rectangles for piecing, create strips first and make pieces out of them. This saves cutting time. Cut 1½"-wide strips across the grain of the fabric from selvage to selvage. The amounts to cut are given in the accompanying tables, "Cutting Guide for Speed-Cutting Strip Method." The dark sides of the blocks are given first. If you want to vary the colors of the blocks so that not all A squares in the blue blocks, for example, are light blue, you can cut some strips of the light blue color and some of another blue; however, the total number of A blocks of some color of blue is still 48.

CUTTING FOR SPEED-CUTTING STRIP METHOD: DARK SIDES

Piece	Strip Size	Number of Strips	Length of Strips	Quantity of Pieces
Red Blocks				
d1	1½" x 15"	1	1½"	8
d2	1½" x 20"	1	2½"	8
d3	1½" x 28"	1	3½"	8
d4	1½" x 36"	1	4½"	8
Purple Blocks				
d1	1½" x 45"	1	1½"	40
	1½" x 15"	1		
d2	1½" x 45"	2	2½"	40
	1½" x 10	1		
d3	1½" x 45"	3	3½"	40
	1½" x 15"	1		
d4	1½" x 45"	4	4½"	40
Green Blocks				
d1	1½" x 45"	1	1½"	36
	1½" x 10"	1		
d2	1½" x 45"	2	2½"	36
d3	1½" x 45"	3	3½"	36
d4	1½" x 45"	3	4½"	36
	1½" x 30"	1		
Blue Blocks				
d1	1½" x 45"	1	1½"	48
	1½" x 30"	1		
d2	1½" x 45"	2	2½"	48
	1½" x 30"	1		
d3	1½" x 45"	4	3½"	48
d4	1½" x 45"	3	4½"	48
	1½" x 38"	1		

Brown Blocks

d1	1½" x 45"	1	1½"	36	
	1½" x 10"	1			
d2	1½" x 45"	2	2½"	36	
d3	1½" x 45"	3	3½"	36	
d4	1½" x 45"	3	4½"	36	
	1½" x 30"	1			

The following chart gives the number and size of strips needed for the light (L) parts of all blocks (light gray in the model).

CUTTING FOR SPEED-STRIP METHOD: LIGHT SIDES

Piece	Strip Size	Number of Strips	Length of Strips	Quantity of Pieces
L1	1½" x 45"	6	1½"	168
L2	1½" x 45"	10	2½"	168
L3	1½" x 45"	14	3½"	168

Slice across the strips with a rotary cutter to create individual pieces. First square up the corners of the strips, measuring them on a ruled board or with a right-angle triangle, and cutting off the excess that isn't square with your rotary cutter. (See figure 14–2 for reference in cutting pieces.)

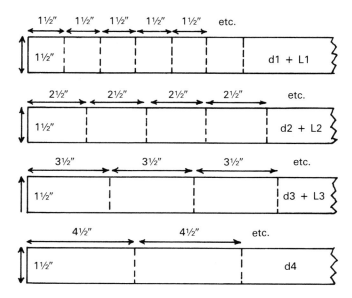

14–2. Cutting for speed-strip method. Take each strip and slice across it with a rotary cutter to make pieces of widths indicated.

CONSTRUCTION

All construction is done with a seam allowance of ¼ ". The 168 blocks are pieced in exactly the same way, using the range of the 4 dark shades (d1, d2, d3, and d4) of the base color for that particular square (red, green, purple, brown, or blue in the model). In the model, all the light (L) pieces are light gray; however, as you may have chosen other light colors, we will refer to these as L1, L2, L3 (see figure 14–1 on page 125).

PIECING THE BLOCKS (FIGURE 14–3)

1. To piece one block, take one each of the four sizes of rectangle (A, B, C, and D) in one dark base color and one each of the 3 light rectangles A, B, and C (gray in the model). Take an A square of color d1 (Ad1) and an A square of color L1 (AL1). Attach them on one side.

2. Attach a B rectangle in color d2 of your base color (Bd2) to the long side of the unit made in step 1 (see figure 14–3).

3. Attach a B rectangle of the light color L2 (BL2) to the unit made in step 2.

4. Attach a C rectangle of the light color L3 (CL3) to the unit make in step 3.

5. Attach a C rectangle in color d3 of your base color (Cd3) to the unit made in step 4.

6. Attach a D rectangle of base color d4 (Dd4) to the unit made in step 5. This completes one block.

7. Repeat steps 1 through 6 to make each of the remaining 167 blocks for the quilt top. When you have completed them, press the square, with the seam allowances to the dark sides.

ASSEMBLING THE BLOCKS

8. As the quilt top is large, assemble quarters of it individually and then join the quarters together. The upper left and lower right quarters are assembled in exactly the same way. Study the color photo for guidance.

UPPER LEFT QUARTER AND LOWER RIGHT QUARTER (FIGURE 13–7)

9. The upper left quarter of the quilt top (without borders) is made up of seven rows of six squares each. Seam the blocks together in order for each row (illustrated in figure 14–4). Assemble the blocks one row at a time and set each row aside as it is finished. Be sure to match the dark sides as indicated, to keep the pattern. You might label each row with a piece of masking tape that you can easily tell which is which later.

10. Seam the blocks of row 1 together in the following order from left to right: red-purple-purple-green-green-blue.

11. For row 2 seam the blocks together in the order: purple-purple-green-green-blue-blue.

12. For row 3 seam the blocks together in the order: purple-green-green-blue-blue-brown.

13. For row 4 seam the blocks together in the order: green-green-blue-blue-brown-brown.

14. For row 5 seam the blocks together in the order: green-blue-blue-brown-brown-purple.

15. For row 6 seam the blocks together in the order: blue-blue-brown-brown-purple-purple.

16. For row 7 seam the blocks together in the order: blue-brown-brown-purple-purple-red.

17. Lay out the rows you just made for the upper left quarter of the design and compare the result with figure 14–4 to be sure the rows are placed and oriented correctly.

18. Sew the rows together in order, matching seams lines, until you have finished the whole quarter. Press.

19. Repeat steps 9 through 18 to make the lower right quarter, which is exactly the same as the upper left quarter; later it is turned upside down when the quarters are assembled.

20. See figure 14–5 for layout of rows and blocks in the upper right quarter, which is made of seven rows of six blocks each. Assemble the blocks one

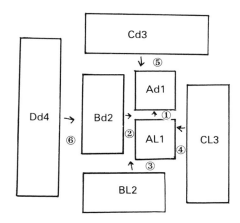

14–3. Order of piecing of single block. Circled numbers indicate order of piecing. d1, d2, d3, d4, and L1, L2, and L3 indicate colors. A, B, C, and D are template sizes.

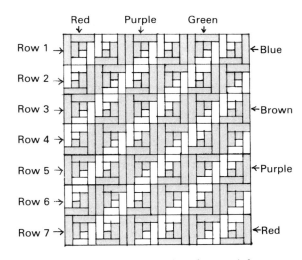

14–4. Assembly order of upper left quarter and lower right quarter.

row at a time, matching dark sides of the blocks to make the pattern. Label and set aside each row as you make it.

21. For row 1 of the upper right quarter, seam the blocks together in the order: blue-green-green-purple-purple-red.

22. For row 2 seam the blocks together in the order: blue-blue-green-green-purple-purple.

23. For row 3, seam the blocks in the order: brown-blue-blue-green-green-purple.

24. For row 4, seam the blocks together in the order: brown-brown-blue-blue-green-green.

25. For row 5 seam the blocks together in the order: purple-brown-brown-blue-blue-green.

26. For row 6 seam the blocks together in the order: purple-purple-brown-brown-green-green.

27. For row seven seam blocks in the order: red-purple-purple-brown-brown-blue.

28. Lay out the rows you just made for the upper right quarter and compare with figure 14–5 to be sure they are placed and oriented correctly.

29. Sew the rows together in order until you have finished the whole upper right quarter. Press.

30. Repeat steps 20 through 29 to create the lower left quarter, which is the same as the upper right quarter (it will be turned upside down in assembly). Label it to avoid confusion later.

ASSEMBLING THE QUARTERS

31. Lay out all four quarters. Compare them with the diagram of color arrangement for the whole quilt to be sure that they are all oriented correctly. Matching seamlines and edges, sew the quarters together. This completes the Rainbow Log Cabin part of the top.

BORDERS AND FINISHING THE QUILT TOP

32. Cutting and attaching inner borders. All borders are cut on straight grain of fabric. Measure across the top and sides of the Rainbow Log Cabin panel. It should be about 48" x 56". To make the inner borders, you need to cut two short strips for the top and bottom and two long strips for the sides. Make the long strips the length of the central panel, plus ½" of the seam allowances (about 56½") x 2½" wide. Make the two short, inner border strips about 52½" (this includes ½" for seam allowances) x 2½". Piece fabric if necessary.

33. Take the two long inner border pieces and sew one to each side of the center Rainbow Log Cabin panel. Take the two short inner border strips and sew one across the top and one along the bottom of the center Rainbow Log Cabin pane.

34. Cutting and attaching outer border strips: Measure your quilt along the side, including the inner borders you just attached. It should be about 60½". Cut outer border sides (long) strips the length of the side plus ½" x 7½". On the sides of the panel, attach the long outer border strips to the inner borders. Measure the quilt across the width, including the inner borders and side outer borders, at the top. It should be about 68". Cut two outer border short strips 7½" x the width of the quilt top plus ½". Attach the outer border short strips to the top and bottom of the quilted panel you created thus far. This completes the quilt top.

35. For quilting and binding see Chapter 8—How to Quilt, pages 428 to 445 to finish the project.

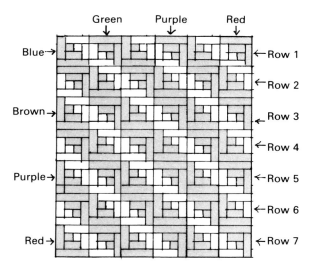

14–5. Assembly order of upper right quarter and lower left quarter.

CHAPTER 3
Appliqué Quilt Patterns

by Maggie Malone

Flower Garden, appliquéd and quilted by Irene Goodrich
from patterns by Ruby Short McKim.

INTRODUCTION

Appliqué can truly be an art form, whether cozy folk art or artistic collage done with fabric and thread. But you needn't be an artist to create a stunning appliqué quilt. Most of the quilters whose work is pictured in this section have had no formal art training, yet they have created quilts with wonderful design and workmanship that also invite you to wrap up in them on a cold winter night. These examples are provided to show the endless possibilities of appliqué and to serve as inspiration for your own development as a quilter.

The basic instructions in this section will give you a good start if you are new to appliqué. Some of the techniques may even be new to the experienced quilter, or will serve as helpful refreshers. The patterns presented here are a good starting point—here are traditional old familiar favorites, as well as some more unusual designs. But don't stop there! Just about everything under the sun can be successfully interpreted in appliqué.

APPLIQUÉ BASICS

Appliqué is the simple technique of sewing a fabric cutout onto a larger piece of fabric, or background block. The major difficulty encountered is in learning to turn under the seam allowances of the appliqué pieces smoothly. In the following pages you will find several techniques that will make this task a little easier. Select one or a combination of techniques, or make up your own. There is no right or wrong way to do appliqué. Choose the most comfortable method for you that achieves the results you want with the least amount of hassle. Quilting is supposed to be a fun and enjoyable pastime.

CHOOSING AND PREPARING FABRIC

As with all quilting, the best choice is 100 percent cotton. It is soft and pliable and forms a sharp crease when the seam allowances are pressed under. I would also recommend a blend of 65 percent cotton and 35 percent

Flower Garden, Detail (Nasturtium block).

polyester. The high cotton content makes the fabric more pliable. But you also get the advantage of the colorfastness and durability of polyester. I know I sound like a heretic when I recommend polyester, but it has been my experience that 100 percent cotton does not hold up well to frequent washing. You will begin to see

Flower Garden, Detail (Chrysanthemum block).

wear within three or four washings. Avoid a higher polyester percentage in the fabric. The more polyester, the harder the fabric is to work with, and it will not hold a crease. Also avoid percale (the fabric many sheets are made of) because it is so closely woven that it is very difficult to hand sew through.

All fabrics used should be washed, dried, and ironed before cutting, as they shrink in washing, especially the first washing. Test each fabric for colorfastness by swishing a small piece of it around in warm soapy water. If a fabric "bleeds" (the color comes out in the water), do not use it in your quilt. Trim off the selvages and discard them, as they are difficult to quilt through.

HAND APPLIQUÉ OR MACHINE APPLIQUÉ?

Traditionally, appliqué was done by hand and was frequently used for very formal, elegant quilts. I think hand appliqué is the best choice, although there are some machine techniques that can be almost as invisible as hand appliqué. If you find the process of sewing to be a very enjoyable part of quiltmaking, and you don't become frustrated at the slow pace, hand appliqué is for you. Interesting textures can be achieved by hand appliqué using crochet cotton or lightweight yarn and a blanket stitch or other decorative hand stitch to appliqué some of the simpler patterns.

Before you start cutting out your appliqués, you need to decide how you're going to attach them. This will affect whether you need to cut them with a seam allowance or not. If you never have tried appliqué before, make up a sample block using each method described, to see which you prefer. An experienced quilter can make almost invisible stitches by hand appliqué; however, hand appliqué takes longer than machine appliqué. Machine appliqué has the advantage of being faster to do and stronger. For a quilt that is going to be washed frequently, or if you need to finish a project quickly, machine appliqué might be the answer. Decorative stitches, such as satin stitch, can be done by machine appliqué.

Mimbres Turtles was designed, appliquéd, and quilted by Fran Soika.

Machine Appliqué Overview

In machine appliqué, the pieces are sewn on the background by machine. Machine appliqué using a satin stitch or a hem stitch adds a homey touch to casual designs like the sunbonnet patterns. Floral designs with large, simple pieces also look good with machine appliqué.

There are several methods of machine appliqué. You could cut the appliqués with no seam allowances, fuse them to the background fabric with fusible webbing, and satin stitch the pieces in place. Another machine appliqué possibility is to cut the appliqués with seam allowances, turn the seam allowances under, and machine blindstitch the appliqué pieces in place with colorless nylon monofilament. Or you could use a decorative stitch with contrasting color of thread. Machine appliqué will be discussed in more detail later on. You will need a sewing machine that can sew zigzag stitches to do machine satin stitch, and one that can do machine blind stitch, if you want to attach the appliqués that way.

Hand Appliqué Overview

If you are doing hand appliqué, you will need to add seam allowances around the templates in this book before you cut out your pieces. Seam allowances of ⅛" to ¼" are commonly used. If you're just learning to appliqué, cut out a few sample appliqué pieces with ¼" seam allowances, some with ³⁄₁₆" seam allowances, and some with ⅛" seam allowances, and try sewing them on a sample block to see which is most comfortable to you. There are several ways to do hand appliqué, which will be discussed in more detail later on. The stitches may be hidden or decorative. It's probably a good idea to cut out pieces for a block just before you're ready to sew them on, rather than cutting out the pieces for all the blocks at once. This keeps the edges from fraying and keeps them from getting lost.

TOOLS AND SUPPLIES

In addition to fabric, and basic supplies as listed on pages 400 to 405, you will need the following supplies for some of the special techniques presented:

- Graph paper and colored pencils: for planning quilt designs and calculating sizes and yardages.
- Freezer paper: This is ordinary translucent white freezer paper that is coated on one side with polyethylene. Also available in quilt shops is a special freezer paper that has graph lines printed on it. Freezer paper can be used in several ways. For instance, you can trace a pattern onto the freezer paper and then adhere it to the fabric, and cut out the appliqués. Freezer-paper templates can be used to hold the turned-under seam allowances before you appliqué a piece in place.
- Fabric glue stick: for temporarily adhering appliqués to the background block and for turning under seam allowances before stitching.
- Spray starch: used to hold seam allowances in place for hand appliqué. Makes a very sharp crease when the seam allowances are turned under and pressed. It can get rather messy; the iron should be cleaned frequently when you use spray starch.

Thunderbird, appliquéd and quilted by Anne Doherty. Design by Fran Soika based on a traditional Pueblo image.

The following tools and supplies are nice to have but not essential:

- Lightbox: This tool is wonderful if you do a lot of quilting or other types of crafts. It is a box with a translucent top, illuminated from below by fluorescent lights. Good for tracing patterns onto fabric. Place your pattern on top of the box, lay the fabric over the pattern, and trace it onto the fabric. Lightboxes are available at quilt supply shops or art supply stores. The same effect can be achieved by taping the pattern to a window and taping the fabric over the pattern, but it's not nearly as convenient.
- Bias press strips: These narrow, metal or heat-resistant plastic strips are a big time- and finger-saver when preparing long, narrow pieces of fabric for appliquéing, such as stems and vines.

HOW TO MAKE A COMPLETE PATTERN

Choose the appliqué pattern you want from Chapter 9—Quilt Templates, page 147. In most cases the patterns, although they are given full size, are a fraction of the full pattern, as the full pattern is much larger than the page. On the pattern page it indicates what fraction of the full pattern is shown—for example, ⅛, ½, or ¼. Color plates of the finished appliqués are given at the beginning of the chapter, so you can see how the fraction relates to the whole design.

How do you get the full pattern to work with? The patterns are symmetrical, which means that the pattern fraction you are given is reflected (mirrored) without change around an imaginary line called the line of symmetry or rotated around a point (see figure 1 for more about symmetry).

Half Pattern

For a reflected pattern that is given as ¹/₂, take a piece of tracing paper at least as big as your background block will be, fold your tracing paper in half; then trace the pattern in the book, including its center line, in indeli-

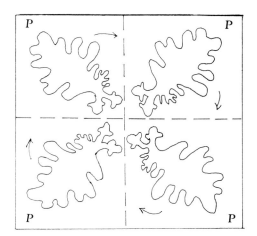

a.

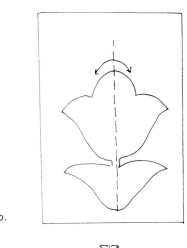

b.

Simple criss-cross quilting sets off this Rose Wreath detail from Cheryl Pedersen's Baltimore Sampler Quilt (see also page 155).

ble ink onto one half of the piece of tracing paper. Flip the paper over and trace the first half again on the other side of the tracing paper in pencil, aligning the two halves on the center line. Then ink in the drawing of the second half on the front of the tracing paper.

Folded Paper Pattern for Simple ¹/₄" and ¹/₈" Patterns

For a simple reflected pattern, you can probably avoid tracing the entire pattern by just tracing the fraction and cutting a template from folded paper as follows: Cut a sheet of lightweight tracing paper a few inches

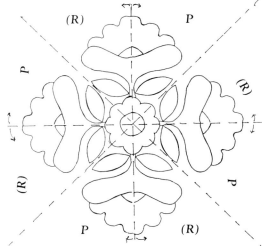

c.

3–1. From partial pattern to block pattern. a: Quarter pattern rotated around a point of symmetry. b: Half pattern reflected across one line to make the full pattern. c: Eighth pattern reflected across 4 lines to make the full pattern. P = pattern; (R) = revised pattern.

bigger than the size of the finished block. For example, assume we are working with a quarter reflected pattern, like the Harrison Rose pattern (page 463). Fold the tracing paper square into fourths. Open the paper and lay the crease lines along the dashed lines of the pattern in the book, matching the centers of the paper and the design. Trace the pattern onto a quarter section of your paper (omit the stems and buds, just trace the central rose and leaves). Refold the paper. Staple all four thicknesses of paper together to keep them from shifting. Cut out the pattern from the paper along the outermost edges of the design, through all four thicknesses of paper (figure 3–2). Remove the staples and open out your whole pattern template. Use it to trace your main pattern onto the background fabric block.

For a simple eighth pattern, you can cut the pattern out on folded tracing paper in the same way as discussed above for the quarter pattern; just fold your paper on the diagonal after you fold it in quarters to make eight sections. Trace the pattern from the book onto a one-eighth section of your tracing paper, aligning the pattern's dashed lines with the paper's folds. Then refold the paper, staple it through all eight layers to hold it, and cut around the outermost lines of the pattern through all eight thicknesses at once. When you remove the staples and open the paper out, you will have a template of the complete pattern (although it won't have all the inner lines drawn in).

Complex Patterns
If a complicated pattern is given as an eighth, use an indelible black pen to trace out the eighth pattern (P)

3–2. Cutting a pattern from folded paper.

from the book onto a piece of tracing paper or template plastic the size of the eighth pattern. (In this section R indicates a reversed pattern, P indicates an unreversed pattern.)

Then take a square of tracing paper at least as large as your planned appliqué block. Fold the paper into quarters and on the diagonals into eighths. Mark the intersection of the lines (the center of the paper) with a black dot.

Take your traced-out eighth pattern, align the eighth pattern beneath the large tracing paper so the dashed pattern lines fall on the folds and the centers line up. Trace the entire eighth pattern, including the guidelines, onto the large tracing paper with indelible pen.

For the section to the right of the eighth pattern you just traced, you usually need to reverse the eighth pattern. Turn the eighth pattern over and align it under the large tracing paper next to the section you just traced. Trace the reversed eighth pattern onto the block-size tracing paper.

Continue tracing each eighth of the pattern, alternating reversed with unreversed eighths, until you are done (figure 3–3).

PREPARING AND MARKING THE BACKGROUND BLOCK

The block size given on the pattern is the smallest square on which the pattern will fit. You may want to add more space around the pattern to improve the way it looks, or to make your quilt a certain size. Before you cut all your blocks, do some test sketches of your quilt top with your graph paper or full-size sketches of a block to be sure the block size and design go together well. See the section on Calculating Quilt Size also, before you choose a block size. You can reduce or enlarge a pattern if necessary. In that case, reduce or enlarge your block size by the same percentage you use to change the pattern size.

When cutting your blocks, add at least 1" or 2" more than your desired finished block size (without seam allowances) to your block. For a block whose finished size will be 16", cut an 18" square, for example. This extra fabric gives you a little leeway to match blocks if they do not line up properly when it comes to assembling the quilt top later on.

Next, fold the block in half top to bottom and press. Open the block out and fold in half from side to side. Press. Open the block and fold on the diagonal in both directions, pressing each fold. Your block is now divided into eighths. The folds are guidelines for placing the appliqués, which may be all that is needed for positioning a simple appliqué pattern.

For a simple pattern, you can mark the pattern onto the background block by tracing around the pattern template that you have traced and cut out by the folding method (see above). Place the templates on the background fabric block, matching guidelines and block centers, using the photo of the completed block for reference. Trace around the templates, using a fabric marking pencil that shows up well on your fabric or a

Miniature Hanover Tulip was appliquéd and quilted by Leita E. Shahan from a reduced version of Hanover Tulip, a pattern by Beverly Cosby.

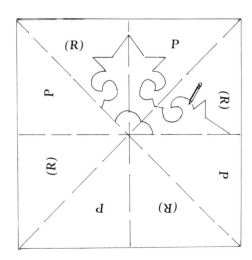

3–3. Tracing a whole pattern from an eighth pattern. Trace the eighth pattern (P) onto a piece of tracing paper the size of the eighth pattern. Trace the pattern on one-eighth of your large tracing paper. With reversed eighth pattern (R) underneath, line up the dashed lines and trace the reversed pattern. Continue tracing eighths, alternating the pattern and reversed pattern until you trace all eight sections.

#2 pencil. Use thin, light lines for this and all fabric marking.

For a complicated pattern with many parts, it's probably better to trace the entire pattern onto your background block. You probably already have made a copy of the whole pattern on tracing paper: If not; trace one as described above in Complex Patterns. Tape the background block over the complete pattern, aligning the guidelines on the folds in the block. A lightbox comes in handy at this point, or lacking one, tape the fabric and pattern to a window. Use a fabric marking pencil or similar tool and trace the pattern onto the background fabric.

If the design consists of multiple layers of appliqué, such as a flower with a center circle, the bottom appliqué (flower) is the only one you need to mark, because you won't be able to see the center markings once the bottom shape is basted down anyway.

Accuracy in appliqué work is not nearly as important as it is when doing patchwork, but there are exceptions. A few patterns are designed in such a way that they form a continuous design line from block to block. When working with these patterns, it is essential that the design lines meet properly. In this case, it is a good idea to mark the full pattern onto the background block.

CUTTING THE APPLIQUÉ PIECES

Although the block pattern is given in the book on one piece of paper, when you look at the photograph of the appliqué, you see that it is usually made up of two or more smaller appliqué patterns.

Let's assume you've already prepared the background block fabric as described above. The next step is to make templates of the appliqué pieces. If you have made a copy of your whole pattern, it's easy to trace out each appliqué shape individually, glue it to cardboard, and cut out each appliqué shape from the cardboard for a template. (Plastic template material can be used instead.) Label the front and reversed side of each template. (Some quilters also number each appliqué template and number the pieces correspondingly on their block pattern.)

The patterns in this book are given without seam allowances. For hand appliqué, you need to add seam allowances around each piece after you trace it. About ³/₁₆" to ¼" is optimal. Some people add seam allowances for machine appliqué also. Keep in mind that the wider the seam allowance, the more likely you will have to clip it in various places to get it to lie flat.

Because many pieces are small and fray easily, it's a good idea to cut them as you need them. Cut all the pieces you need for a block, but not more. However, you can trace the others onto your appliqué fabrics all at the same time if you wish, leaving space around each for seam allowances. After you have made a block and seen how well your seam allowances worked, you can adjust them when you cut the rest of the pieces. How you trace and cut your appliqués depends on what

Heirloom Appliqué, appliquéd and quilted by Betty Nye; pattern by Pat Andreatta.

method of appliqué you will use, so see the individual sections under Turning the Seam Allowances and Attaching the Appliqués for specific details.

Many appliqués are made of several layers of fabric stitched on top of each other. For ease of cutting and assembly, it is a good idea to plan how you will cut and sew appliqués. When an appliqué will be built up of two

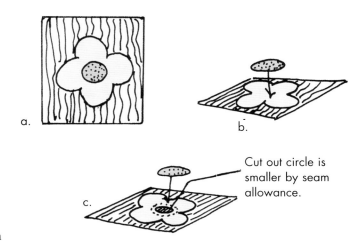

3–4. Cutting an appliqué. The finished flower (a) could be cut with a solid underneath shape and a circle of the second fabric superimposed (b); or it could be cut as a flower with a reduced circle cut out and a circle of the second appliqué fabric placed over the cutout (c).

or more layers, you can cut the underneath shape as a solid piece of appliqué fabric and cut the shape from the second fabric to go over it as shown in figure 3–4a and b. If you get several layers on top of each other, it is possible to trim them from the back of the block to reduce bulk so they won't be hard to quilt through. This is explained later under Reducing Appliqué Thickness. Another method is to cut the bottom shape from the first appliqué fabric with a hole under where the next layer will be. Then cover this space with the shape from the second appliqué fabric (see figure 3–4c).

To do this, position the center appliqué template on the outer fabric shape and trace around it. Reduce the size of the central shape marked on the outer shape by drawing in a seam allowance on the outer shape, inside the traced central shape, and cut away the reduced central shape from the outer shape's fabric. Trace, cut, prepare, and position the center appliqué over the outer shape, and baste both in place on the block, or otherwise secure it.

General Appliqué Cutting Instructions

Be sure there is enough room around each piece for a seam allowance, if you need one. Trace the appliqué template, using a fabric marking pencil or pen. Move the template over on your fabric, far enough to provide for two seam allowances, and trace again. Repeat for as many appliqués as are needed.

If there are any reversed pieces you need to cut, be sure to flip the template over to the other side (reversing it) before tracing them. You do not have to align the template with the straight grain of the fabric, as in patchwork. In fact, putting the appliqué on the bias will enable it to stretch and it will be easier to work with. If you are planning to use a machine satin stitch to sew on the appliqué, it may not be necessary to add seam allowances around the pieces as you cut, because the raw edges of each shape will be protected by the stitches, which are very close together. You may prefer to add a seam allowance even when doing machine satin stitch

if your machine is an older model that doesn't sew as fine a satin stitch as some of the newer models. There are always stray threads that pop through the satin stitching and there is a certain amount of fraying as time goes by. Do a test appliqué without seam allowances on your sewing machine to see if the results are good before you cut your project pieces; if they aren't good, add seam allowances to each piece when you cut.

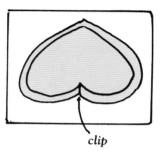

3–5. Clipping a seam allowance on an inward point

TURNING SEAM ALLOWANCES AND ATTACHING THE APPLIQUÉS

The goal of all methods of turning seam allowances is the same: to get the correct seam allowance turned under so it will stay while you stitch it in place. No matter what method you use, if an edge of an appliqué piece will be covered by another piece in the final design, leave the seam allowance unturned along the edge to be covered. You will have to clip the seam allowance to make it lie flat when turning a seam allowance on an inward (concave) curve or point (see figure 3–5). Clip perpendicular to the seamline, up to a few threads from the seamline. Outside (convex) curves also may need to be clipped at intervals.

Designs should be sewn down, starting with the bottom center pieces and working outwards. It is best to position all the pieces for a block and baste them in place before sewing anything on permanently. (If you use fusible webbing, however, you don't need to baste. See the section on fusible webbing on page 141.)

The basic method of preparing and attaching appliqués, which our forebears used and many people still do use, is to trace the appliqués onto the right side of their respective appliqué fabrics, add seam allowances, cut out the pieces, and turn the seam allowances over to the wrong side of each appliqué piece. Seam allowances are clipped as needed, and then each piece is basted in place onto the background block and sewn down by hand appliqué. In the next few pages, several other methods of turning seam allowances and attaching appliqués are described.

Moss Rose, appliquéd and quilted by Irene Goodrich, using patterns by Nancy Cabot.

Needleturning Method of Hand Appliqué

The seam allowances can be turned under with your needle as you sew. First, trace the appliqué shapes onto the right sides of their respective fabrics, and cut them out, adding seam allowances as you cut. Baste the appliqués into position on the background block, keeping your basting stitches near the center of each piece. Using the middle of the needle (the shank), tuck the

seam allowance under the appliqué, making sure you have turned it exactly on the traced seam line. Take a few tiny tacking stitches, then turn under some more of the seam allowance. Start turning the seam allowance under at a place on the appliqué that isn't near a point, if possible. (See the section on Hand Appliqué Stitches for more details.)

Freezer Paper on Top Method of Hand Appliqué

One alternative to the basic method of hand appliqué is to trace out the appliqué piece on the dull side of freezer paper (the white kind with a polyethylene coating) and cut it out of the paper to use as a template. Then, using a hot iron and no steam, iron and baste the freezer paper template, shiny side down, to the front of the fabric piece from which you will cut the appliqué. Cut the appliqué out of the fabric, adding seam allowances all around (figure 3–6a), but leave the template in place as a sewing guide and stabilizer. Then baste the template and appliqué in place on the front of the background block, positioning it correctly by using a lightbox or using the pressed lines as a guide (figure 3–6b). Thread your sewing needle with hand sewing thread that has been run through beeswax to keep it from tangling. Using the middle part of the needle, simply turn the seam allowances under as you go, using tacking stitches to hand stitch the appliqué in place (figure 3–6c). You may need to clip the seam allowances at the curves in some places. When you're done, snip the basting thread and peel off the freezer paper.

Starch Method of Turning Seam Allowances

This method may be used for machine or hand appliqué. Trace the reversed appliqué shape onto the wrong side of the appliqué fabric, and cut out the appliqué, adding a seam allowance as you cut. Take your cardboard template of the appliqué shape and place it face down on the wrong side of the cut-out appliqué piece. Take some liquid starch on a brush or cotton swab, and dab it on the seam allowances

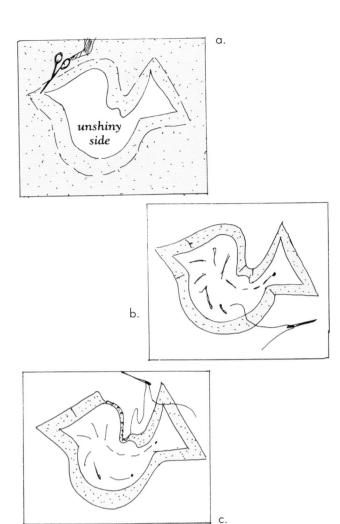

a.

unshiny side

b.

c.

3–6. Freezer paper on top method of hand appliqué. a: Freezer paper pattern piece, shiny side down, is fused to right side of the appliqué fabric. Cut out, adding seam allowances as you go. b: The cut-out appliqué, with freezer paper still in place, is basted in place on the background block. c: Seam allowances are needle-turned under, using the freezer paper pattern as a guide. Clip seam allowances as necessary.

(figure 3–7a); then iron them down around the template (figure 3–7b); clip seam allowances as necessary. Use a toothpick or other stick to hold the seam allowances in place as you iron, to avoid burnt fingers. Remember that you do not need to turn any seam allowance that will lie under another appliqué. After the seam allowances are ironed in place, gently remove the template. Baste the appliqué shape right-side up onto the front of your quilt block and appliqué it in place, clip-

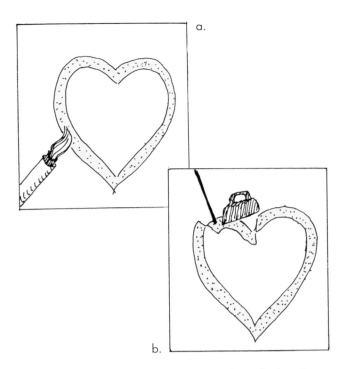

a.

b.

3–7. Starch method of preparing an appliqué for hand appliqué. a: Reversed template of pattern is positioned on wrong side of cut-out appliqué; seam allowances are wet with liquid starch. b: Seam allowances are ironed in place around the template, which is then removed.

ping any curves or adjusting any edges, if necessary, to smooth it out.

Fabric Glue Method

Another method of turning seam allowances, one that is particularly useful for simple designs with moderate curves, is to use fabric glue to hold the turned-under seam. Just run the fabric glue stick along the seam allowance and turn the seam allowance over to the wrong side of the appliqué. Baste or fabric-glue the appliqué in place and stitch the appliqué to the background block by hand or by machine appliqué.

Fusible Webbing Method

Fusible webbing is particularly useful for machine appliqué. You can use it to attach appliqués with seam allowances or appliqués without seam allowances.

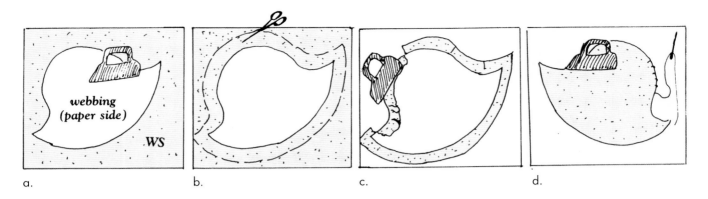

a.   b.   c.   d.

3–8. Fusible webbing for machine or hand appliqué, with seam allowances. a: Fuse the cut-out reversed webbing shape on the wrong side of the appliqué fabric. b: Cut the appliqué out of the fabric, adding seam allowance as you go. c: Peel the paper off the fusible webbing and tack the seam allowances in place with an iron or fabric glue. d: Position the appliqué on the background fabric and fuse in place with an iron. Then sew on the appliqué.

Choose a lightweight webbing so it isn't difficult to sew through. To make appliqués with seam allowances, trace the reversed appliqué onto the paper side of the webbing. Cut the shape out of the webbing along the traced lines without seam allowances. Fuse the webbing shape to the wrong side of the appliqué fabric (figure 3–8a). Cut out the appliqué, adding a seam allowance around the shape as you cut (figure 3–8b).

Remove the backing paper from the webbing. Clip the seam allowances of curves at sharp indentations to achieve a smooth turning of the seam allowance. To tack down the seam allowances to the uncovered side of the webbing, use the very tip of the iron and press, following manufacturer's directions, until the seam allowance fabric adheres to the webbing (figure 3–8c). If the iron touches the uncovered webbing, the adhesive makes the iron sticky and it will require cleaning. Continue around the appliqué until all seam allowances are adhered to the webbing.

Position the prepared appliqués in the appropriate places on the background block and press them in place, starting with the layers that are closest to the block. The appliqué will stay put without pins, which can distort or shift the piece. The edges are not stuck down, so you can slip other appliqué pieces under the appliqué if need be. If you make a mistake in positioning, the appliqués can be lifted and repositioned with many types of webbing. The webbing becomes a permanent part of the appliqué, but it is light enough to quilt through with a sewing machined.

To make appliqués without seam allowances for machine appliqué using fusible webbing, trace the reversed appliqués onto the paper side of fusible webbing, leaving a little space between each shape, and cut each appliqué out of the webbing with some extra webbing around it. Fuse the webbing piece to the wrong side of your appliqué fabric. Carefully cut the appliqué shape out through the webbing and fabric on the appliqué's outline, without adding any seam allowance. Peel off the paper. Fuse the shape in place on the background block and satin stitch down, using thread that matches each appliqué fabric, changing threads as necessary.

Place a piece of tear-away stabilizer or tracing paper under your block before starting to appliqué, to keep the block from getting pulled into the sewing machine. Work from the center of the block outwards.

Freezer Paper Inside Method of Hand Appliqué
In this method, freezer paper is used to adhere the appliqué piece to the background block. The polyethylene coat of the shiny side of freezer paper temporarily tacks the appliqué in place. You can also baste them in

place if you find they tend to fall off. Trace the unreversed appliqué piece on the dull side of freezer paper (figure 3–9a), without adding seam allowances, and cut out the shape as a template. Place the appliqué fabric wrong-side up and position the reversed freezer paper template on the fabric, shiny side up, and trace around it (figure 3–9b). Adding a seam allowance of fabric around the traced shape as you go, cut out the shape from the fabric (figure 3–9c). Clip the seam allowances to within a few threads of the seam line at inward curves. Replace the template, shiny side up, on the wrong side of the fabric. Turn the seam allowances over the freezer paper and tack them in place by ironing them onto the freezer paper (figure 3–9d), or glue them in place with fabric glue. Then iron the appliqué in place on the background block with a hot iron, shiny paper side down, and appliqué it in place, without removing the freezer paper (figure 3–9e). To remove the paper, turn the block over to the back. Cut a slit in the background fabric in the center of the appliqué piece (being careful not to cut through to the front), and pull the freezer paper out through the slit. Use a tweezers if necessary. Close up the slit with hand overcast stitch.

Turning Under Sharp Points
Leaves are frequently features of appliqué designs, and the sharp points they have need special attention for turning seam allowances. (See figures 3–10a through 3–10f.)

HAND APPLIQUÉ STITCHES

Basic Tacking Stitch
Select hand-sewing thread, preferably 100% cotton, to match the appliqué piece. This is thinner than regular sewing thread and so is more easily hidden. If you can't find the exact color, a grayed or slightly darker version of the appliqué color is usually good.

Cut an 18" piece of thread. Run the thread through your beeswax to keep it from tangling. Knot

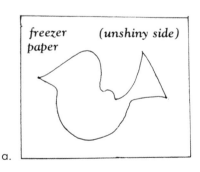
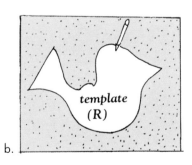
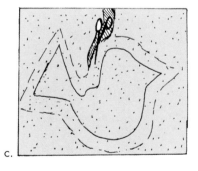

3–9. Preparing an appliqué, freezer paper inside method. a: Trace appliqué on non-shiny side of freezer paper. Cut out shape. b: Trace reversed pattern on wrong side of fabric. Set paper pattern aside. c: Cut out shape from fabric, adding seam allowance as you go. d: Replace paper pattern, shiny side up, on wrong side of fabric. Tack seam allowances in place on the paper with hot iron. e: Tack shape by ironing it in place on background block. Hand appliqué in place.

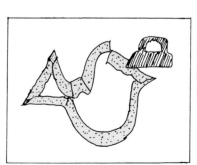

Miniature Sunbonnet Sue appliquéd and quilted by Leita E. Shahan.

the thread and sew through the back of the block; bring the needle up just under the folded edge of the seam allowance. Taking the smallest stitch possible, take the thread down immediately in front of the place you came up, over and perpendicular to the edge of the appliqué, going into the block (see figure 3–11).

Decorative Hand Appliqué Stitches
Patterns such as Sunbonnet Babies were often sewn down using a decorative buttonhole or blanket stitch to outline the pieces. A thread heavier than hand-sewing thread, such as crochet cotton or three strands of embroidery floss, was used to execute the decorative stitch so that it would stand out and frame the appliqué.

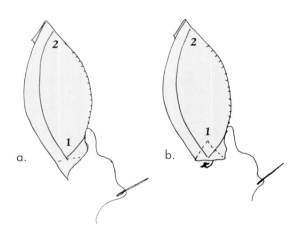

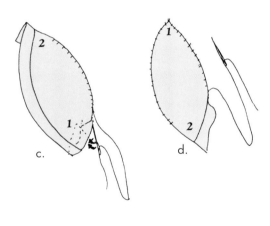

3–10. Hand appliquéing a leaf. a: Beginning on a side, about ½" from a point, turn under the seam allowance and tack in place until you are about ½" from the next point. b: Fold under the seam allowance at the point so the point of the leaf lies on the base of a triangle that is turned under; finger press it in place. c: With the side of your needle, tuck under the remaining right seam allowance and tack it in place. Tuck under the left seam allowance at the first point (1) and tack it in place. Then rotate your work (d) so the unfinished seam allowance is at your right, and tack down the side seam until you are about ½" away from the second point of the leaf (2). e: Fold up the second corner as you did the first corner, and tuck the seam allowance to the right of the point in place. Then tack it. Tuck the seam allowance at the left of the point in place, and finish tacking around the point to complete the leaf (f).

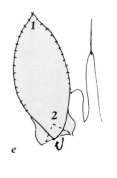

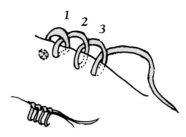

3-12. Close-up of blanket stitches (widely spaced) and button-hole stitches (close together).

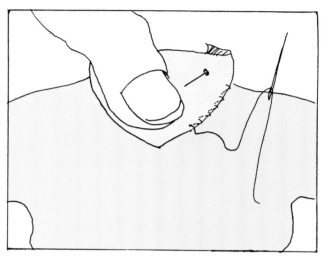

3-11. The tacking stitch, hand appliqué. The needle comes up through the background fabric and through the seam allowance and top layer of the appliqué just under the seam allowance fold of the appliqué. The needle goes down into the background fabric right next to where it came up. The "traveling" (dashed line) is done underneath the two fabrics, and you emerge again in the appliqué seam allowance, just below the fold of the seam allowance. About 7 to 10 stitches to the inch, or every ⅛" is sufficient.

Choose a color of thread that contrasts with the appliqué, and attach the appliqué with the buttonhole stitch or blanket stitch; the blanket stitch is simply the buttonhole stitch done with the stitches spaced farther apart (see figure 3–12).

MACHINE APPLIQUÉ STITCHES

The satin stitch is the stitch most commonly used for machine appliqué, and is described at right. If you plan to use other stitches, it is best to add seam allowances on your appliqué pieces when you cut them, and turn the seam allowances under, because other stitches won't protect the appliqué edge from fraying.

Position each appliqué piece in its proper place on the background block. If you are not using fusible web-bing, baste, pin, or glue (with fabric glue) each piece in position on the background block. If you are using fusible webbing, fuse the pieces in place, starting with the layer that is directly touching the background block and working up.

Straight Stitching

For this method, you can use thread to match each appliqué color or you can use nylon thread, which will be almost invisible. If you use nylon thread, fill the bobbin with regular sewing thread. Set the stitch length for 8 to 10 stitches to the inch. Position the appliqué so that the needle just catches the edge of the fabric. Sew it in place. If your sewing machine has the capability, you could also use a hemstitch or blindstitch to sew down the appliqué.

Satin Stitch

With the satin stitch, you may be able to cut the appliqué without seam allowances, as the closely spaced stitches cover the raw edge. This depends on your sewing machine; the newer models can do much finer satin stitch than the older ones.

stop and turn here

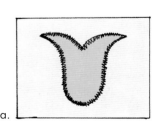 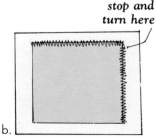

a.   b.

3-13. Machine appliqué, using satin finish. a: Taper the width of the stitch before a point and gradually increase it again after the point. b: To stitch a corner, stop stitching a bit before the corner with the needle in the background fabric, and turn the fabric. Then resume stitching.

Set the machine for satin stitch; do a test stitch on some scrap fabric to get the correct width and length of stitch for the effect you want. The wider stitch, the more prominent the stitching will be. The idea is to hide the raw edge of the appliqué, so it will look pretty and to prevent fraying of the fabric. If you want a really thin line of stitching, I would recommend that you cut your appliqués with a seam allowance.

To prevent puckering of the background fabric when satin stitching, place a sheet of tear-away stabilizer or tracing paper under the block. Sew through the stabilizer and when the sewing is complete, tear it away. To execute a smooth inward curve, stop the machine frequently with the needle in the appliqué fabric and turn the block slightly. For an outward curve, stop the machine with the needle in the background fabric and turn the block.

When sewing leaves or other tapering shapes, as you come to the point, gradually decrease the width of the satin stitch until you reach the point. With the needle down in the background block, rotate the fabric to its new position; gradually increase the stitch width as you sew away from the point on the other side (figure 3–13a).

To turn a right-angle corner, stitch up to a short distance before the corner and stop, with the needle down in the background fabric, then rotate the block until you are lined up to sew the second side of the angle (figure 3–13b).

STEMS AND VINES

Stems and vines are used frequently in appliqué designs. If the pattern has straight seams, the fabric can be cut on the straight grain of the fabric. For curved stems, you will need bias strips. When cloth is cut on the bias, it is more easily stretched, making it easier to form into smooth, flat curves. Purchased bias tape can be used, but it is more economical—and easier to get the exact color you want—if you make your own bias strips, as described at right. These may be used for either hand or machine appliqué.

Appliqué detail from Adams Friendship Quilt, designed by Vicki Skemp, appliquéd and quilted by the Madison County, NC Community Quilters.

Cutting Bias Strips

To cut bias strips, take an on-grain square of fabric and spread it out on a flat surface. Fold the upper left corner down on the diagonal until the left edge of the fabric lines up with the lower edge of the fabric (figure 3–14a). The diagonal fold is the bias of the fabric, 45 degrees from the straight grain. Press the fold and cut along the fold. Measure out the needed width of your bias strip perpendicular to the cut edge and mark the other long side of your bias strip (figure 3–14c). Cut the strip. Continue cutting as many strips as you need. Many quilters usually cut a long strip and trim it to the necessary length just before they apply it to the block.

Preparing and Applying Bias Strips: Method 1

Cut a bias strip three times wider than the finished width of the stem (figure 3–15a). With the right side of fabric facing out, fold one long raw edge in to the center of the strip (figure 3–15b). Press. Fold the second long raw edge over so its raw edge is just short of the first fold (figure 3–15c). Press. Turn the strip over and press it again on the top, but do not push the iron along the strip; just set it down, then pick up the iron and

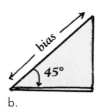

a. **fold over**   b.   c.

3–14. Cutting bias strips. a: Fold the square in half on the diagonal so its long side is the bias of the fabric (b). c: Cut strips whose sides are parallel to the bias fold, of whatever strip width you need.

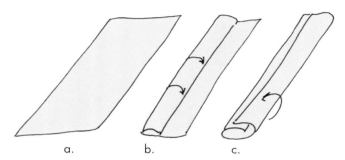

a.   b.   c.

3–15. Making bias strips, Method 1. a: The strip is right-side up. b: Fold one raw edge in. c: Fold the second raw edge in so its raw edge is short of the outside fold.

move it to the next section. Pushing the iron will stretch the strip. Baste the strip in place with its raw edges face-down on the block.

Preparing and Applying Bias Strips: Method 2.
This method is suitable for very thin stems. Mark the stem position on the background fabric. Cut a bias strip four times as wide as the width of the finished stem. Fold the strip in half on its length, with the right side of the fabric facing outwards (figure 3–16a). Press the fold to make a crease. Fold the strip in half on its length again, and press the fold (figure 3–16b). Open out the second fold. The crease you made when you pressed the strip the second time is your sewing line (figure 3–16c). To apply the bias strip, lay the raw edges of the folded strip along the guideline for the stem. Keep the raw edges of the strip even with the guideline, and sew along the crease by machine or by hand, using a small running stitch (figure 3–16d). Then fold the loose long edge of the strip over again along the sewing line and bring the fold over the raw edge along the guideline (figure 3–16e). Be sure the raw edges of the strip are covered. Appliqué stitch the fold in place along the guideline.

Preparing and Applying Bias Strips: Method 3.
Cut a bias strip to a width two times plus ½" wider than the finished appliqué. (For example, if you need a finished appliqué of ½" width, cut a bias strip that is 1½" wide.)

Fold it in half on its length, with the right side of the fabric facing out (figure 3–17a), pin the long edges together, and stitch the raw edges together ¼" in from the edge (figure 3–17b). (This may be done by machine, regardless of whether you will do machine or hand appliqué.)

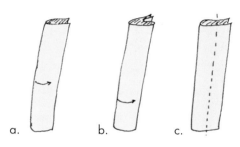

a.   b.   c.

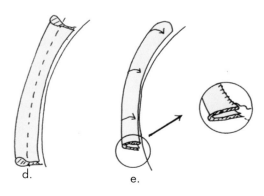

d.   e.

3–16. Making bias strips, Method 2. a: Fold strip in half on its length and press. b: Fold on its length again, press, and open the second fold out again. c: Stitch together the edges of the bias strip on the most recently made fold line. d: Stitch the bias strip in place with the raw edges on the guideline. e: Fold over the unattached (folded) long edge, and tack or machine stitch it in place.

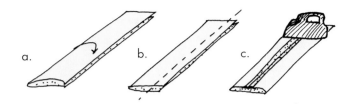

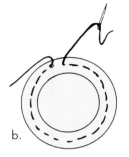

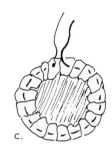

3–17. Making bias strips, Method 3. a: Fold the cut strip in half, right-side out. b: Stitch ¼" in from the raw edge. c: Bring the seam allowances to the center of the strip and press.

Center the seam allowances on the width of the strip and press them (figure 3–17c). Trim any seam allowances back if they extend beyond the edges of the strip. The strip is now ready to apply to your design, with the seam allowance facing the block fabric.

The pressing task may be made easier by inserting a bias press strip or bias bar (a long strip of heat-resistant plastic) into the strip after you sew the long edge. Fold the seam allowance under the strip and press the whole unit. Press strips are sold at quilting stores and are available in varying widths. Choose a strip that is just a bit narrower than the width of your finished stem, so it will fit in easily.

REDUCING APPLIQUÉ THICKNESS

If the finished appliqués are several layers thick, you may find that it is very difficult to quilt through them. To solve this problem, turn the quilt block over to its back and, using a pair of embroidery scissors or special appliqué scissors, trim away the center of the background fabric that lies immediately underneath the appliquéd area (figure 3–19). Be sure to leave at least ¼" uncut between the stitching of the appliqué to the background and the cut edge, to be sure that the background fabric doesn't unravel. Where there are several layers of appliqué, some of the bulk of the bottom layer of appliqué (where it is covered by another layer) may be reduced in the same way.

3–18. Preparing circles for appliqué. a: Mark and cut out fabric circle, adding seam allowance. b: Run a line of basting ⅛" in from raw edge. c: Reposition the template on the wrong side of the fabric and pull the basting stitches to fit the fabric around the template; then press.

CIRCLES

It is often difficult to turn under and sew the seam allowances of circles evenly and smoothly. The following method will give you perfectly round circles every time.

Trace a circle of the correct size onto template cardboard, and cut it out. Trace the template and cut out your fabric appliqué circle, adding a ¼" seam allowance around the template circle as you go. (See above.)

3–19. Reducing the thickness of an appliqué. The shaded area is cut out of the background fabric and removed.

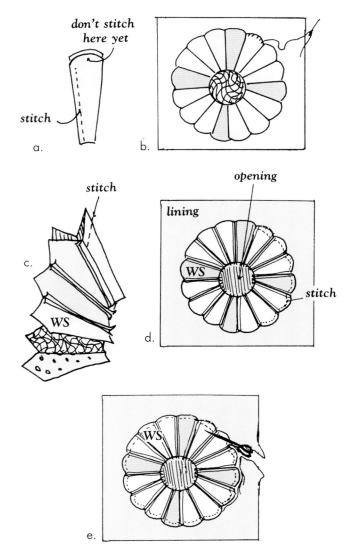

3–20. Dresden Plate. a: Stitching together the round-ended segments. b: Appliquéing the round-ended plate to the background block. c: Hemming the edges of the angular segments. d: Stitching a round-ended "plate" to a square of lining fabric. e: Trimming off the excess lining fabric.

DRESDEN PLATE

The Dresden Plate pattern is given in three versions in the pattern section of the book: with rounded segments, with angular segments, and in a version that uses both types of segments. The latter is generally known as Fancy Dresden Plate. The pattern is given without seam allowances; add ¼" seam allowances around all pieces before cutting. The number of segments can vary from 12 to 16. The pattern is usually made up as a scrap design, but you can use a planned color scheme if you desire. Stitch the individual sections to each other with right sides of fabric facing (figure 3–20a) and ¼" seam allowances, but do not stitch into the curved (or pointed) top seam allowance. Press the joined seam allowances of the segments open to reduce bulk.

The plate is then appliquéd to a background block (figure 3–20b). For the angular version of Dresden Plate, you can turn under the seam allowances of the points after you have stitched the segments together and before appliquéing as follows: Select one of the angular segments and fold it in half down the middle, with right sides of fabric facing (figure 3–20c). Sew along the top seam line from the side seam to the point with ¼" seam allowances. Trim the seam allowances, turn the segment right-side out and press. Repeat this process for all angular segments of the angular version. Then appliqué the entire plate in place as a unit, appliquéing on the center circle last (see earlier instructions on preparing a circle appliqué).

The traditional way of attaching the Dresden Plate is to baste it to the background block and turn under each segment's outer edge as you come to it, stitching it in place with tacking stitches. Here's an alternative to the usual method of turning under seam allowances on the versions of Dresden Plate that have curves on the outer edge of the segments. The method that follows, although it does use more fabric than other methods, makes the job easier. It is done after the individual segments of the plate are assembled, but before the center circle is added. Cut a square of lining fabric bigger than the circle formed by the assembled plate. Since this fabric square will not show, it is a good place to use up some of those ugly pieces of fabric you know you will never use in any of your quilts.

Lay the assembled plate right-side down on top of the lining fabric square. Following the seam lines, stitch all around the outside edge of the plate (figure 3–20d). Trim off the excess lining fabric, even with the plate's edges. Clip the seam allowances at the curves and trim the seam allowances to reduce bulk. Turn the entire plate right-side out by pulling the lining fabric through the hole in the center of the plate. Smooth out the seams and press. Trim away excess lining fabric in the center circle and appliqué the plate to the background block. Appliqué the center circle over the plate after turning under the circle's seam allowance.

ADVANCED APPLIQUÉ TECHNIQUES

STUFFED APPLIQUÉ

Padding or stuffing areas of the design with loose batting is the most common way of adding depth to your block. There are several methods that can be used to accomplish this.

Method 1

Sew the appliqué in place as usual. Turn the block over to the back and carefully cut a small slit in the background block fabric only, in the center of the appliqué you want to stuff. (You will have your appliqué stitches to guide you.) Insert loose batting through the slit, pushing it into the space between the background and appliqué fabrics until you achieve the effect you want. Do not overstuff the appliqué or you will distort the background block. A blunt needle, a knitting needle, or a pencil back is helpful in pushing the stuffing exactly where you want it to be (figure 3–21). Sew up the slash in the back with a whipstitch when you are done stuffing.

Detail of Dresden Plate Quilt, designed by Vicki Skemp, appliquéd and quilted by the Madison County, NC Community Quilters.

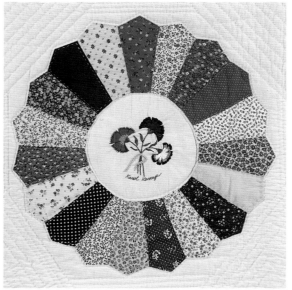

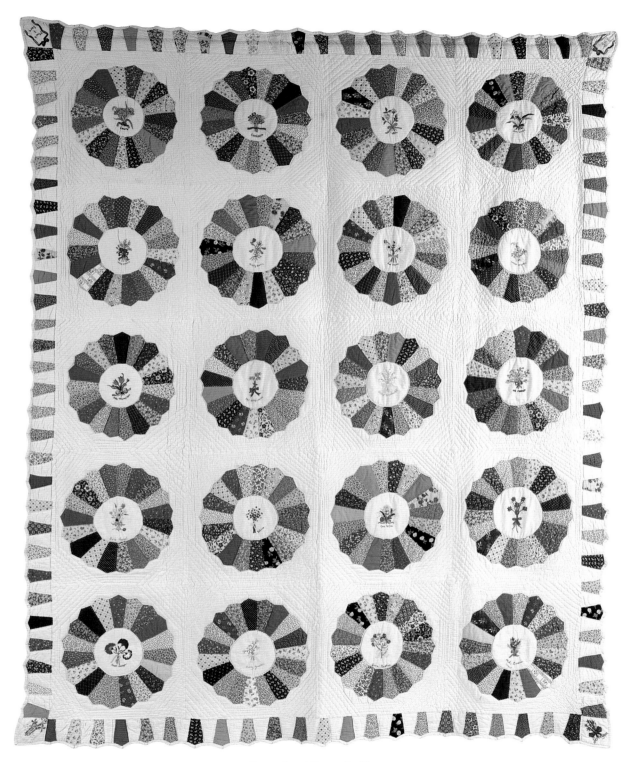

Dresden Plate Quilt

72" x 90" • Designed and organized by Vicki Skemp

Traditional Dresden Plate quilt with a non-traditional touch of embroidered nosegays in the center of each plate.
Pieced, embroidered, and quilted by the Madison County, NC Community Quilters.

Method 2

Sew the appliqué in place, leaving an opening of ½" to 1" as you come to the end of the stitching. Insert batting through the opening, tamping it into any corners and distributing it evenly, until you have reached the thickness you want (figure 3–22). Sew the opening closed.

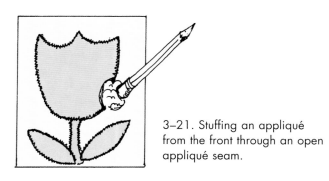

3–21. Stuffing an appliqué from the front through an open appliqué seam.

Method 3

This method is especially useful when stuffing a large appliqué piece. Cut a sheet of batting in the shape of the appliqué, but slightly smaller all around. You can cut one or two layers of batting, depending on the depth you want to create. Position the batting on the block front, lay the appliqué over the batting, face up, and baste everything in place. Sew the appliqué down.

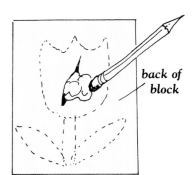

back of block

3–22. Stuffing an appliqué from the back through a slit in the background fabric, which is later stitched closed.

SHADOW APPLIQUÉ

This appliqué technique imparts a soft, shimmery, muted finish to the appliqué. It is achieved by placing a square of translucent fabric such as organza or voile over the appliqué block. The fabrics chosen for the appliqué shapes should be fairly bright, because the overlay will mute the colors. The appliquéing and quilting are best done by hand. Proceed as follows:

1. Cut out the background block of fabric, with seam allowances added. Press the block in quarters or eighths to make fold lines to aid appliqué positioning. If necessary, trace the outline of the pattern lightly onto the background block to aid you in placing the appliqués.

2. Then cut the appliqué shapes out of their respective fabrics, without seam allowances, and glue them in place on the background block with fabric glue (figure 3–23a). Extend any edges of shapes that will be overlapped by about ¼" before cutting. (You may cut the reversed appliqué shapes out of fusible webbing, then fuse the webbing shapes to the wrong side of the appliqué fabric that is needed for each appliqué shape. Cut the shapes out of the appliqué fabrics, and fuse them in place with an iron on the front of the block instead of using glue.)

3. Cut a block of translucent fabric, such as voile or organza, the size of the background block plus seam allowance. Position the translucent block over the appliqué block and baste overall and around the outer edges of the block to hold it in place (figure 3–23b). Cut and baste one translucent square for each shadow appliqué block.

4. Sew the appliqués on with hand running stitches all around their shapes through all three layers of fabric (translucent fabric, appliqué, and backing), just inside the cut edges of the appliqués (figure 3–23c). With a washable pen or pencil, mark quilting lines around your appliqués in whatever design you like.

5. Prepare all the shadow blocks in your project the same way as described in steps 1 to 4. Cut any plain setting blocks out of the backing fabric, if you are using setting blocks around the shadow blocks, and mark their quilting lines also. Baste and sew the quilt blocks together to form the quilt top, first in rows, then joining the rows together in the usual way.

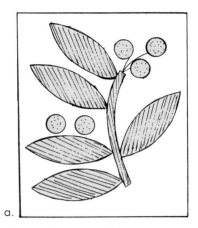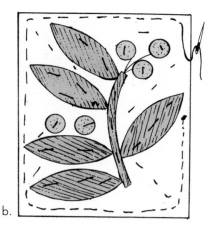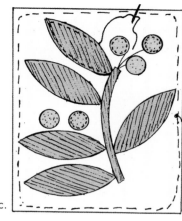

3–23. Shadow appliqué. a: The appliqué pieces glued in place on their block. b: Translucent layer of fabric basted over the block. c: Individual appliqué pieces are sewn through all three layers in the running stitch.

6. Lay out your quilt backing and batting, put the quilt top face up over them, and baste the three layers together in the usual way.

7. To quilt, follow the lines you have drawn on your quilt blocks, and quilt through all the layers, one block at a time, starting in the center of the quilt.

CREATING NEW PATTERNS

Once you have completed several appliqué blocks, you will be ready to try your hand at designing your own block. Don't be timid. The nice thing about appliqué is that anything and everything can be turned into a pattern. Here are some suggestions to get you started.

Rearrange the elements in some of the blocks in this book. See how many different ways you can arrange the various appliqué pieces to come up with new designs. Combine elements from two or three blocks to create a new one.

Children's coloring books are ideal sources for patterns. The pictures are simple line drawings that can be used as is, enlarged or reduced to fit your needs.

Children's books are also useful sources of design ideas. Select a picture you like and enlarge it on the photocopy machine, or by the grid method. (Make a grid of small squares on the original picture. Draw a grid of enlarged squares on a separate paper, and copy the design onto the enlarged grid, square by square.) If the pattern is too detailed, eliminate some of the detail in your enlargement. To do this, draw around the outline, then draw in lines to delineate the major sections of the picture.

Adapt patterns from other forms of needlework.

Embroidery, needlepoint, and cross-stitch patterns are easy to convert to appliqué patterns. In many instances, embroidery patterns can be used as is. At other times, you may want to enlarge a pattern and eliminate some of the detail. To convert a cross-stitch or

Closeup of a block from Creatures of the Night by Nola Eschedor.

needlepoint design, trace around the outer edge of the pattern. Add a few detail lines to fill out the shape. Garden books and catalogs are picture sources for fruit, vegetables, and flowers. You don't need to make an exact botanical copy. All you need do is convey the impression of a particular flower or fruit, so eliminate any unnecessary detail.

Museums, art books, and artwork of all kinds should be studied for design ideas. There are many, many books available with patterns for decorative painting. These make great appliqué patterns. In fact, check out the patterns provided for other crafts also. Greeting cards, quilting magazines, in fact, all printed material can provide fodder for your quiltmaking.

Detail of Victorian Ladies, designed, appliquéd, and quilted by Betty Nye.

Explore your surroundings. Wallpaper may inspire a new design or translate a carpet pattern into a matching quilt. Cookie cutters may be used to create a winter scene. Fabrics have many patterns, texture, and color variations. Sometimes seeing a certain fabric can spark a wonderful idea.

CALCULATING QUILT SIZE
AND BLOCKS NEEDED

The patterns provided here do not give a suggested quilt size, just the final block size. Before you can figure the amount of fabric to buy, you must know how many blocks you need to complete the quilt top. When you know how many blocks you need, you can determine how much fabric will be required for the appliqués. See Chapter 8—How To Quilt, pages 408 to 412, to help you plan your quilt.

AMOUNT OF FABRIC
NEEDED FOR APPLIQUÉS

1. Count how many appliqué units of a particular fabric you need per block. For example, in block A there are 4 light pink tulip shapes that will be cut from the same fabric (figure 3–24).

2. Multiply the number of units per block by the total number of blocks; for our purposes, let's assume the quilt has 35 blocks. That would mean we need 35 blocks x 4 tulips per block, or 140 pink tulips for the quilt top.

3. Measure the tulip, add $\frac{1}{4}$" seam allowances around it, and determine from what size rectangle the tulip block could be cut. Let's say the tulip will fit on a 3" x 5" rectangle, including seam allowances.

4. Divide the width of the rectangle into the width of the fabric you have. In this case, let's say we have 45"-wide fabric. Then 45" divided by 3" = 15, so we know 15 tulips can be cut across the width of the fabric.

5. Divide the length of the appliqué's rectangle into one yard (36") of fabric to calculate how many units will fit on one yard of fabric. In our example, that's 5" divided into 36" = 7; 7 tulip rectangles can be cut down the length of the fabric.

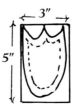

3–24. Block A, which has 4 tulip shapes (left). Right: the rectangle of appliqué fabric from which a tulip shape, including seam allowances, can be cut.

6. Multiply the number of units that can be cut across by the number of units that can be cut down the length of one yard (36") to determine how many units can be cut from 1 yard of fabric (45" x 36"). In our example, that's 15 units across x 7 down = 105 units per yard.

7. Divide the total number of units you need in the quilt top (calculated in step 2) by the number of units you get per yard to determine the total yardage required to make those units. In our case we need 140 tulips, but we get 105 per yard, 140 divided by 105 = about 1.3 yards; round up to about 1½ yards. We therefore need 1½ yards of fabric to make the tulip appliqués. Repeat this process to estimate the yardage for each appliqué fabric.

You also need background fabric of course, which can be calculated by multiplying the size of one block (adding in 2" on the sides for safety's sake) times the number of blocks in the quilt. Calculate how many blocks will fit across 45". For example, if you need thirty-five 6" x 8" blocks, divide 45" by 8 (6" + 2") to get 5; five

Pomegranate detail of Baltimore Sampler Quilt, appliquéd and quilted by Cheryl Pedersen from her original block designs and others.

Baltimore Sampler Quilt, appliquéd and quilted by Cheryl Pedersen from her original block designs and others.

blocks can be cut across the width of the fabric. To calculate what length of background fabric you need, take the length of the block, 8", add some extra (2") to get 10" long. We will need 7 rows of blocks because we can only cut 5 across the fabric. Seven x 10" per block length = 70", or about 2 yards. We'll therefore need 2 yards of background fabric.

To choose from a collection of appliqué templates, see Chapter 9—Appliqué Templates, page 447.

A Single Irish Chain embellished with flower appliqué. The little green squares were cut one by one using a transparent template in order to center a little pink flower in each square. Note the leafy vine quilting around the border and the centered medallions used to date and personalize the quilt. Designed and organized by Vicki Skemp, appliquéd and quilted by the Community Quilters of Madison County, NC.

CHAPTER 4
Community Quilting

by Karol Kavaya and Vicki Skemp

A painting by Vicki Skemp of the Community Quilters of Madison County, NC,
working at a quilt frame on their "Starry Night" quilt.

It is often difficult to find, let alone build and nurture, community. And it is even harder to find a group activity that feeds the creative spirit. From our own personal experience, we have found that group quilting meets these needs. In joining together to make a quilt for a chosen recipient, we extend an embrace that acknowledges the elements of life from joy to grief, welcome to farewell, noteworthy accomplishments to everyday milestones.

You could say we built our community stitch by stitch. To this day, the bonds we share create a fabric that is strong and true. In fact, the more we think about it, a community comes together like the pieces of a quilt—some pieces are bright, others subtle, but all of them bring out the best in each other when melded together into a harmonious whole.

Though you may think that group quilting is a quaint, country tradition from a bygone era, indeed, it is a vital activity that is practiced as much today in big cities and sprawling suburbs as it is in isolated rural areas. Whatever your situation or lifestyle, no matter where you live, you can make a group quilt. All you need are a few people interested in quiltmaking, even if only one of them has a rudimentary knowledge of sewing. If you think you don't have the skill, we encourage you to not let that thought hold you back from this joyful, sharing endeavor. We did it, and so can you! Read through this section—and then do it!

To find potential quilt mates, look to your activities and lifestyle: your office or work associates, your book club, P.T.A. parents, fellow church members, acquaintances from the gym, your Girl Scout troop, garden club members, or your own family. Many people would like to be a part of quiltmaking, but are timid about leaping into it on their own. For these, an invitation to work on a quilt with others will give them their start. One advantage of group quiltmaking is that one person doesn't carry the entire load.

If your new group consists mainly of people who don't know each other very well, a fund-raising quilt may be a good choice for your first project. For instance, women from the P.T.A. might make a quilt to auction or raffle off as a fundraiser for new library books, or church members could make one to benefit their outreach program. Our group has made raffle quilts for the animal shelter, the library, and a local peace group. On the other hand, if your group consists of close acquaintances, then occasions such as weddings, new babies, friendship, major birthdays, or anniversaries all give you plenty of opportunities to make a group quilt.

This section will help you design, organize, and make a group quilt. It is a practical manual that will lead you step by step. The process is very simple. Since the quilt is to be given away, a recipient is chosen. The quilt is designed in block fashion, with individual blocks pieced together to make the quilt top. Participants receive kits for making their blocks, then send the finished blocks back to the organizer. The organizer pieces the top together, then gathers a group to do the quilting in a series of quilting bees. Finally, the quilt is presented to the recipient at a special surprise party.

Whether you begin your quilt with a group of ready-made friends, or are gathering new acquaintances together, the process of making a group quilt will soon begin to work its magic. Before you know it, you'll feel a bond with your quilt mates and find yourself part of a new and growing fellowship. It's hard to say who benefits most from group quilting, the recipient or the quilters. The recipient receives a true labor of love, a gift that warms the heart and one far superior to any you can purchase, while the quilters experience the deep joy found in sharing, creating, and giving.

ORGANIZING A GROUP QUILT

We have tried to distill the knowledge gained from our varied experiences in order to pass along ideas, systems, and patterns that have worked well for us. We have also remembered our past mistakes and problems in the hope that we can help you avoid certain pitfalls. Though every group and each quilt will be different, we

Maple Leaf Quilt

Size: 88" x 96" • Designers & Organizers: Laura Ball, Betsy Love, Vicki Skemp, Libby Woodruff

This quilt was our first group effort. Since the wedding of the recipients was to be in October, with the ceremony under a big tree, the Maple Leaf pattern seemed perfect. The organizers sent templates of the pattern with instructions for assembly to a list of the couple's friends. Participants were told to choose cotton fabric, using blue for the background and autumn colors for the leaves.

believe these time-tested methods will be useful to anyone beginning this exciting and rewarding endeavor.

SELECT AN ORGANIZER

The organizer is the one who will see the quilt through from beginning to end, delegating work where possible, filling in the gaps when necessary. The organizer is usually, though not always, the person who has the idea to make a quilt for a certain event and is, therefore, the one laden with the most responsibility. She is the one who makes sure all jobs get done. Ideally, the organizer has some sewing skills, or has a good friend who can provide this help.

The organizer may be the one who plans the quilt. Then she contacts the potential participants, purchases the fabric, and assembles and distributes the kits for the blocks. She calls and reminds people to get their blocks finished, assembles the completed blocks into a quilt top, and prepares the top for quilting.

She may host, or get others to host, quilting bees. She makes sure the quilting gets done on time, binds the edge of the quilt, and sees that a party is planned to present the finished masterpiece. The organizer doesn't have to do all these things herself. With any luck, she will find responsible helpers among her quilting friends.

If you are making a group quilt for the first time, we advise it be a team endeavor. Most of our quilts have had one or two organizers. Once you have a pool of experienced organizers, they can easily work together with first timers who then become organizers-in-training.

THE ORGANIZER, or, Somebody Has To Be the Bad Guy…

"The quilters had just presented a beautiful wedding quilt to friends immediately after their ceremony. As one of the bride's friends was enjoying gazing at the quilt she had organized, filled with the lovely sense of a job well done, the husband of one of the other quilters came up to her.

'You all have really done a good job! What does it take to put something like this together?'

'Well, you kind of have to keep after people to make sure they get their stuff done on time, and then you have to make sure everyone gets a chance to quilt…'

'Somebody has to be the bad guy, huh?'

"Once when I was in charge of a particular quilt, the blocks were very slow in coming back. A few weeks past the deadline I was shopping in a local hardware store, and, from the corner of my eye, saw a woman whose block was not yet returned slip quietly out of sight behind a nail bin. No one likes to be nagged or to do the nagging, but sometimes it's in the job description for the organizer."

—V.S.

"Keep enough contact so that the project can be completed on time; be prepared to beg, be prepared to fix a block that comes back to you wrong. Buy enough fabric. Have enough commitment from others when you start the project to see it through (sometimes that means a few very dedicated people). Provide complete kits. Give clear instructions. Give accurately cut pieces of fabric so no one has to curse you when she's at her machine. Assure the group that it's all right to call with questions. When they get weary, remind them how much the quilt will mean to the recipients. When you ask for a certain size block, tell them that a $1/4$" variation is allowed." —K.K.

"Make sure that all instructions are clearly given, even for experienced quilters, because not everyone does things the same way. I have given instructions that all seams should be $1/4$" and even explained how to measure that on the sewing machine…and still gotten back ten different size squares from twenty people. The bottom line is to have fun and spend time with good friends in a special communal effort!" —L.W.

you want to present the quilt to the expectant mother, or to the mother and the new baby. We generally opt for the latter, because, in part, it provides us with an opportunity to meet the newest member of our community, but mostly because it gives us extra time to work on the quilt!

Remember, in setting your deadline, to allow plenty of time for all steps. Be especially mindful of the deadline for getting the pieced blocks back from the participants. We find that the more time you give participants to complete the blocks, the more time people will take; the sadly human tendency to procrastinate is alive and well among quilters.

In general, we think it is a good rule to allow participants no less than two weeks for completing and returning an easy pieced block, and no more than six weeks for a difficult block involving fine embroidery. When you give participants more time than that, blocks seem to get forgotten, lost, or eaten by the dog. The

Be Realistic!

"Make sure that each person is willing to help and that she can meet the deadlines. Be prepared to call and double check on your participants if they pass the time schedule. If time is not critical, this isn't so important, but the project may only be the priority that you are willing to make it."   —L.W

MAKING A GROUP QUILT STEP-BY-STEP
Step 1

Establish a Time Frame, or, She's Having a Baby!
You want to make a group quilt, and you have a recipient in mind. Now what? First, think time frame. No matter what kind of quilt you are planning, you should have some general date of completion in mind.

A wedding quilt, anniversary quilt, or going-away quilt provides its own logical date of presentation. A friendship quilt, one done "just because," can be timed to suit the organizer. For a baby quilt, ask yourself if

A one-patch pattern is used in this block.

organizer should also build in a generous buffer zone of time that is allotted to calling (and hassling, if necessary) people who haven't returned their blocks.

You will also need to factor in time for sewing the blocks for the top together, for basting the top, batting, and backing together, and especially for quilting. Don't forget to allow time for binding the edge and for sewing on an optional sleeve and I.D. panel. (Too often, we have done these final tasks in the wee, dark hours of the morning of the surprise party.)

Step 2

Contact and Enlist Participants

Your next concern is to determine how many folks are willing to work on the quilt. Contact all the friends and relatives of the recipient who you think may be interested in your project. If you wish, include out-of-town people. Working long distance has the potential for added aggravation, but it can be very special for the recipient if you include close friends and relatives in this way.

When talking with potential participants, try to get some idea of their skill level—can they piece a block by hand or on the sewing machine, can they quilt, embroider, appliqué, or are they willing to learn? Can they get the work done on time, or are they planning to be in Nepal for the next 6 months?

Remember that your goal is to be as inclusive as possible and to give everyone who wants to participate a chance to help in some way. Occasionally, we've had people who are totally unable to sew give money to help with the cost of the materials, thereby entitling them to have their names on a quilt as a participant.

Step 3

Choose Your Design

All quilts are made from individual blocks that are pieced together to make the quilt top. Sometimes one person will do several blocks, sometimes two people will work on one. Sometimes people will not do a block, but will help with the quilting.

A Texas Star block.

The number of participants for your quilt and their skill levels will directly influence your design choice. We have done baby quilts with only nine or ten participants, and bed quilts with as many as 40. We have even done a few small wall hangings with only two or three participants.

Once you have a fair understanding of the group with whom you'll be working, you can begin to design your quilt. We generally begin by first deciding on the size of the quilt, whether it will be a square or rectangle, and the number of blocks it will contain. When deciding on the size of your quilt, keep the standard sizes of batting in mind:

Crib	45" x 60"
Twin	72" x 90"
Full	81" x 96"
Queen	90" x 108"
King	120" x 120"

The batting should be approximately 3" larger on each side than your quilt top.

The following illustrations offer some basic ideas you can use for designing your quilt.

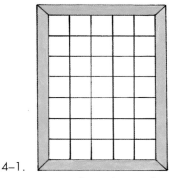

4–1.

A. Border with mitred corners.

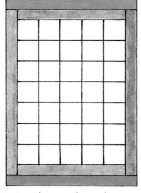

B. Border made with strips of fabric.

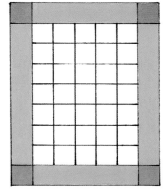

C. Border with blocks at the corners.

As shown in figures 4–1A, B, and C, you can add to a quilt's size, within reason, by adding a border.

Notice in figures 4–2A and B, that if you are alternating two patterns or colors in your blocks, and you want to end up with corners that are the same, you will need to use an uneven number of blocks up and down. We usually opt for the uneven number, feeling that it results in a more pleasing balanced look.

When designing a quilt, one of the things you'll have to decide is the placement of the blocks. Figures 3A and B show two examples. Will they be separated from one another by solid blocks or sashing, or will they be sewn directly to each other? Simple blocks look fine when they are next to each other. More complex or fancy blocks look good when separated by plain blocks or sashing. Sashing forms a sort of frame around the individual blocks and also lessens the number of pieced blocks needed to achieve a given size quilt.

As shown in figures 4–4A and B, you will need to decide whether to place each block on point or square.

THINKING ABOUT YOUR DESIGN

In addition to taking into consideration the skill levels of the participants, consider the personal tastes of the recipient (or the recipient's parents in the case of a baby quilt). Sometimes it just takes thinking about the recipient and imagining what he

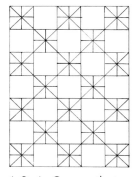

4–2. A. Corners that are the same.

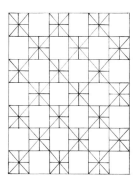

B. Corners that are different.

4–2. A. Simple blocks next to each other.

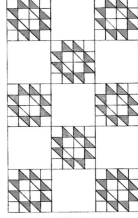

B. Pattern blocks separated by plain blocks.

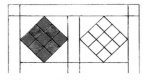

4–2. A. Block "onpoint."

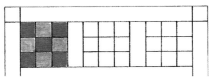

B. Block positioned "square."

or she might like. (It helps to look around their home, if possible.) Sometimes the designer already has a pattern or motif she's been itching to use.

Colors are usually chosen to reflect the recipient's (or the designer's) taste, and sometimes people are simply seduced by fabrics they see in the store. If you don't know a person's taste, a traditional pattern in traditional colors is usually a safe choice. (For more color ideas see Chapter 8—How to Quilt, page 406.)

What Makes a Design Easy?
In picking a geometric quilt pattern, look for one using few pieces worked in straight lines. Unless you are working with fairly good seamstresses, avoid choosing designs with curves; down that road lies frustration and heartbreak.

Squares are very simple, and a one-patch, four-patch, or nine-patch design is perfect for beginners or quilters in a hurry. An Irish Chain (see pages 60, 73, 111, 156, and 187) can be extremely elegant and still very easy to accomplish. Triangles aren't difficult to work unless their points are long and thin with stretchy bias edges. Shoofly (see page 201) is a personal favorite of ours, as is Ohio Star (see page 87). Pinwheel (see page 200) is another pattern suitable for first-time quilters.

As a rule of thumb, the fewer the pieces and seams in a patchwork block, the less chance there is for error and for size variation. However, be prepared for variations on the returned blocks. Though you instruct your participants to sew with ¼" seams, you'll be amazed at how differently people measure the same ¼".

One of the simplest solutions for a group of mostly inexperienced participants is to use squares or rectangles of a background fabric on which each quilter embroiders or appliqués a design. Then the blocks are joined together using a simple sashing. (See pages 204 and 205.)

COLOR DRAWING
Making a color drawing of your potential quilt is very useful. It can be a precise diagram on graph paper or

An example of an individual block embroidered with flamingos.

just a rough sketch; either way, it will be an enormous help in visualizing your project. It's surprising to find how many times you'll want to refer to this clear picture as you go through the steps of quiltmaking. Also, if you want to share your vision with your helpers, that picture will instantly convey your idea.

Step 4
Choose Your Quilting Pattern
Now is the time to consider quilting patterns. You can wait until the top is complete for a final decision; but if you know that you want to feature the quilting, be sure that your quilt's design incorporates sufficient areas of solid colors or subtle monochrome prints to show off your careful stitching. On the other hand, "busy" fabric will camouflage uneven stitches. Think about your group's abilities, and plan accordingly.

The simplest choice for a quilting pattern is outline quilting (see figures on page 439), where you stitch around an image or around the elements of a pieced pattern. The quilting is usually done either ¼" away from the seam line or in the ditch, which is in the seam line itself. Another traditional approach suitable for beginners is an allover quilting pattern. This can be superimposed on a simple pieced pattern and provides an exciting counterpoint (see Chapter 8—How to

Quilt, pages 436 to 439).

If your idea of quilting runs to fancy wreaths and feather plumes, cable borders and Celtic knots, see Chapter 10—Quilting Patterns, page 511, or visit a quilt store and see what they have to offer in the way of templates. Templates are the easiest way to mark a quilt with a beautiful pattern, and they make it possible to re-mark lines easily if your pattern becomes hard to see. If you have a template you want to use, make sure that there are suitably sized areas in the quilt design to accommodate the template's size.

RANDOM PLACEMENT AND MAVERICK SQUARES

Sometimes we deliberately choose to vary a quilt design simply by using fabric that is almost, but not quite, like the others. We like to imagine an old-time quiltmaker who has used up all of one particular fabric in her scrap bag and has had to substitute something similar.

Another trick is to make a "mistake" in putting together a block. For example, in a quilt of nine-patch blocks, if your pattern calls for five darks and four lights, one or two blocks with four darks and five lights can look more interesting.

Even though these mistakes are not always readily apparent at first or even second glance, a quilt with a few such "errors" can be more visually interesting and more alive than a quilt that repeats itself with machine-like precision.

Step 5
Choose Fabric, Batting, Backing, and Binding

FABRIC

After you've chosen your quilt design, unless it is to be a scrap quilt where the participants choose their own fab-rics, you will need to select the fabric. If you know the recipient's color preferences or wish to coordinate the quilt with the decor of their home, your color choices will be obvious and easy to make. Otherwise, the organ-

izers get to pick the colors they like!

It helps to have someone with a good eye for color combinations be part of the decision-making process at the store. We advise that no more than three women go to the store to choose fabric—more than that is cumber-some, since too many personal tastes get into the mix.

Use 100 percent cotton fabric. You'll be putting a great deal of time and work into this project, so be careful with imported fabrics, since they may not be colorfast. Also avoid "bargain" fabrics that may be flimsy, may have too much sizing, or may run when washed. We like to buy a little extra fabric to allow for miscalculations or disasters. ("Mikey put my quilt pieces in the blender! Can I have another kit?") This may be one of the reasons some of our organizers have amassed such a collection of scraps.

Remember that your quilting stitches will show

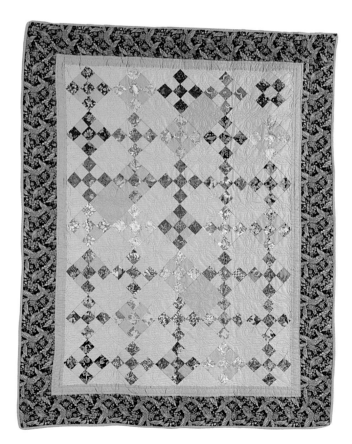

An example of maverick squares in a simple nine-patch.

more clearly on solid-colored fabric. If you are not sure of the quilting skills of the participants, choose prints that will mask uneven stitches.

BATTING, BACKING, AND BINDING

You may choose to buy your batting, backing, and binding when you purchase your fabric, or later, if desired. Since we live an hour away from any good fabric stores, we often try to do all our shopping at once.

Furthermore, if you buy these items when you purchase your fabric, it will give you a better idea of your expenses. This is an important consideration if you are asking participants to contribute toward the cost of material for the quilt.

BATTING

A look at your fabric store or quilting catalogue will reveal a dazzling array of batting—polyfill, cotton, silk, wool, and blends in a range of sizes and prices. Our personal preference is for a low loft (not too fat and puffy), which allows the quilting stitches to show well.

We have not had a good experience with 100 percent cotton batting, finding it difficult to needle, though there are newer versions that promise easier quilting. Avoid the cheapest polyester batts; the fibers can migrate through the fabric of your quilt, producing an unpleasant hairy look. Our favorite batting, though slightly pricey, is a blend of cotton batting with 20 percent polyester.

Read the instructions that come with your batting and follow them carefully, especially if you must prewash your batting. Note also quilting directions; some batting calls for very close quilting to keep it in place, others need far less. See Chapter 8—How to Quilt, pages 431 to 432.

How Wide is 45"?
When determining fabric yardage, remember that so-called 45" fabric may not actually measure 45" across, even as it comes straight off the bolt. Plus, the fabric

Play with fabric scraps or samples until you find a combination that is pleasing.

may shrink when you prewash it. Also, we recommend that you remove the selvages before use. For these reasons, we figure our yardage based on an assumed usable fabric width of 40" to 43".

BACKING

If your quilt top is 100 percent cotton, your backing

should be the same. In choosing backing, be sure to select fabric that, while not flimsy, is easy to needle. A large bedsheet, though tempting because of its size, is usually difficult to quilt because its material is so closely woven.

Though reason tells you that the backing should be measured to the same size as the finished top, the fact is that the quilting sometimes draws up the backing fabric. For this reason, we allow a generous extra 3" to 5" per side when buying backing fabric. Believe us, it's worth the extra expense to avoid the sinking feeling that comes when you realize, near the end of your quilting, that your backing isn't quite reaching the edge, and that you somehow have to piece a strip onto it. Also, if you think you will hang your quilt on the wall, buy enough extra backing fabric to make a sleeve on the back of your quilt to accommodate a hanging rod (see Chapter 8—How to Quilt, pages 445 to 446).

Determining the Amount of Backing

As beginning quilters, we often opted for a busy print for our backing so that the unevenness of our stitches (usually worse on the back) wouldn't show. As we became surer of our quilting skills, we sometimes chose a solid backing in a color that contrasted with the top and allowed the quilt to be displayed on either side. Refer to Chapter 8—How to Quilt, page 412, for measurements and advice on how to figure yardage.

BINDING

When we first began to make quilts, we did as many old-time quilters did and simply made our backing a few inches larger all around. When the quilting was finished, we pulled the backing up around the quilt's edge, then turned it under and blind stitched it into place on the quilt top. Over time, we learned that using a bias strip rounds the corners more smoothly and also wears much better. We've seen older quilts using the backing-as-binding method in which the only worn places were along the edge. Now we recommend bias binding.

While many experienced quilters prefer to make

their own bias binding for a custom look, we usually choose to buy packaged single or double-fold bias tape. It comes in many colors, is easy to use, and is usually packaged in 3-yard lengths. When figuring the amount you need, remember to add extra for joining lengths and for corners. You can buy the binding when you purchase your fabric, or wait until the top is pieced or

Top example shows self-binding of a quilt. Bottom example shows contrasting custom-made bias binding.

even until it's quilted.

For some quilts, an unobtrusive color of binding that matches and blends with the border may be preferable, while other quilts may demand the little jolt of color that a contrasting binding can provide. Since binding is one of the last steps, you may find that it is easier to make this final design choice once you've completed all the quilting.

Step 6

Prepare the Top and Backing Fabric

Please refer to the steps for this in Chapter 8—How to Quilt, page 422.

Step 7

Make the Kits

We believe that we achieve the most consistent results when two or three people cut out all the pieces for the blocks to be sewn and put them into kits. If this isn't feasible, or the quilt is to be made scrap style, where each worker provides her own fabric, we make templates and send them out with our instructions. In this step we will cover both methods.

PRECUT KITS

These kits will have all the pieces, cut correctly and ready to assemble, for a chosen quilt block. Also included are detailed instructions. To make the kits, the organizer(s), will cut out all pieces for all blocks in the quilt (these can easily number in the hundreds).

If your pattern pieces are squares, triangles, or rectangles, and you are familiar and comfortable with the use of the rotary cutter, you can speed your cutting and eliminate the step of pencil marking. Otherwise, marking with pencil and using scissors works just fine. When marking fabric for cutting, we've used two methods: measuring and templates.

MARKING BY MEASURING

We can best explain this by offering an example. If you're making a nine-patch (a quilt block made of nine equal squares) or a Pinwheel (all triangles), you can use a straightedge to mark a straight line along the selvage edge of the fabric (having first remembered to remove the selvage as instructed in step 6). With a metal or a plastic square, mark a perpendicular line along the adjoining edge. Now you can work with a 90-degree

Precut block pieces and instructions.

angle and straight lines (see figure 4–5). Using a ruler you can measure and mark your fabric at the correct intervals (e.g., $3\frac{1}{2}$" intervals across each edge). Then, connect your marks and you will have your squares ready for cutting (see figures 4–6 and 4–7).

You can mark triangles in this same manner. First, determine the size of square that will produce two triangles of the desired size. Then be sure to mark the diagonal at the exact corner, as shown in figure 4–8, to achieve triangles of identical size.

Note: If you want to cut triangles from a square (and we do), measure the length of one triangle leg (one of the shorter triangle sides). Add $\frac{7}{8}$" to that measurement and cut a square that size.

MARKING BY TEMPLATE

You will be repeatedly placing the template on the fabric and tracing around it. (Yes, this is slow….but so meditative.) Use a shared line wherever possible and try to get the most out of your fabric (see figure 4–9).

House Quilt

91" x 91" (detail) • Designers & Organizers: Vicki Skemp and Susan Adams
The School House pattern used in an imaginative way and framed with Window Pane sashing.
Some original antique feedsack fabrics are included in the construction.

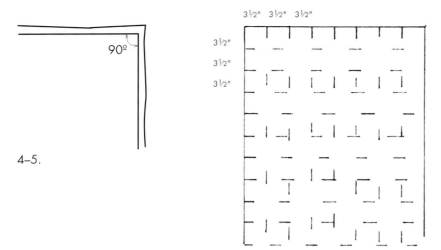

4-5.

4-6.

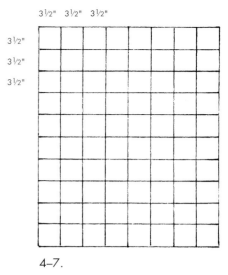

4-7.

4-8.

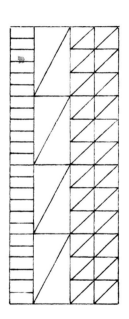

4-9.

TIPS FOR MARKING AND CUTTING

Be extremely careful in all your marking and cutting. Always try to hold your pencil at the same angle. Always cut on the line, not to one side or the other. It's best to not do your marking and cutting when you're feeling rushed. Seemingly minute errors, when multiplied many times, can mean trouble later on. A key difference between a quilt made by one person and a quilt made by a group is that when one person does all the marking, cutting, and sewing, you're assured of more overall consistency.

Note: Your templates and/or precut pieces should include a ¼" seam allowance on all sides of each piece. Please remember to include this allowance when marking the fabric or making a template. If some of your participants will be sewing by hand, instruct them to measure an exact ¼" inch from each edge, then mark this sewing guideline with a pencil.

TEMPLATE KITS

These kits will contain templates and instructions. They may include the fabric to be used or they may ask that the participants provide some or all of their own.

MAKING YOUR OWN TEMPLATES

You can easily make your own templates. If you are using templates from a book or other source, trace your template shapes onto clear plastic template material (this is our recommended choice, which is readily available at craft or quilting shops) or thin cardboard or poster board (this is economical, but templates made from these materials tend to wear away and lose precision with much use).

name, letter of the piece, and size of the finished block on each template—this is helpful when using the templates again. A final optional touch is the use of a product such as gritty dots that you stick on your template to keep it from sliding around on the fabric when you are marking your shapes.

NITTY GRITTY

A board covered with a fine-grit sandpaper can be a great help when marking the fabric with a template. The fabric's annoying tendency to slide around under the template is eliminated, making your job less tedious. These boards can be purchased from quilting suppliers or made at home.

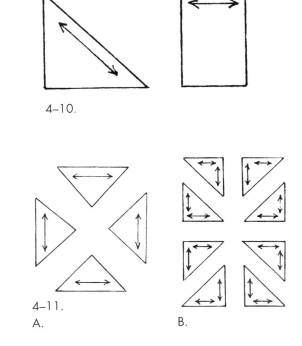

4–10.

4–11.

A.   B.

ASSEMBLING THE KITS

Now that you've cut out your quilt pieces or made your templates, the next step is to assemble the kits. The kits will contain the instructions and the correct pieces needed to complete the assigned block. When all the kits are assembled, double-check them to make sure each one contains what it should.

Jenny's Flowers and Starry Night hang on the line.

If you are designing your own pattern, first draft a precise pattern on paper. Remember to include the ¼" seam allowance on all sides of each piece. Next, transfer the various pieces of the pattern to your template material. Use a sharp pencil to make a thin, clear line. For maximum precision, hold the pencil as near to vertical as is comfortable.

Mark your template with an arrow showing where the straight grain of the fabric needs to be on each piece (see figure 4–10).

Tip: When marking triangles with a template, you can avoid stretchy bias edges by placing the edge of the triangle that will be on the outside of the block on the straight of the grain (see figures 18A and B).

When you cut out your template, be as accurate as possible. Use a good sharp pair of scissors and cut on the line, not to one side or the other. Write the pattern

The makings of a template kit.

Always save some extra templates and extra fabric. (You did get extra fabric, didn't you?) Inevitably you will need replacements—a kit will have been lost in the mail; or you will get back a block so badly done that you will choose to make a new one.

Write your instructions for the least-skilled non-quilter you can imagine—in other words, the more detail the better. Remember, what is obvious to you may not be obvious to another. When you have completed writing the instructions, have someone else read them, checking for clarity. Don't omit this important step or you could have many phone calls from confused quilters. Experience has taught us to try to avoid the sheepish feeling we get from handing out incomplete or unclear instructions.

To help you write your own instructions, we've provided the guidelines below. Don't be discouraged by this lengthy list. We have tried to anticipate all the problems you may encounter. Of course, if your workers won't read or don't follow the instructions, they will have trouble, but you, at least, will have done your part. Right?

Remember and remind your participants (and yourself) that making a quilt is not a life or death matter. Most mistakes can be fixed, and your goal is not a perfect quilt but a quilt made with love and joy (and at least some attention to detail).

Instruction Guidelines

1. On the outside of the envelope containing your kit, tell your participant to immediately check the contents to make sure all needed pieces are included.

2. Begin your instructions with an inventory of what should be in the kit and how many blocks the participant is being asked to make.

3. Give the name and provide a sketch of the block(s) to be done, including the size.

4. Make a color chart, if necessary (see figure 4–12).

5. Provide the recipient's name. If the quilt is to be a surprise, note that in BIG LETTERS.

6. Include notes on the ¼" seam allowance.

7. If necessary, provide instructions to hand-sewers on marking a sewing line that is ¼" from the raw edge.

8. Explain the importance of pressing, not ironing, at each step, and of pressing the seam allowances to the dark-fabric side.

9. If each block is to be signed, include instructions for this. Embroidery or indelible ink are good choices. Indicate to the participant where you want the signature placed on the block (see figure 4–13).

10. Include a diagram for assembly and order of procedure, with instructions to measure at each step and redo if necessary.

11. Remind participant to avoid stretching the pieces if they need to remove or pick stitches from badly sewn units. Taking apart and resewing the unit too many times can damage the fabric.

12. Did we mention the importance of the ¼" seam allowance? If you are working with people who sew clothing, they may be accustomed to a ⅝" seam allowance. Stress, and stress again, that the pieces for the quilt use a ¼" seam allowance!

13. Tell participants to press and measure the finished block. Remind them of the exact size of the block. If necessary, note any allowable variation, e.g., that ¼" smaller or larger is okay.

14. Include the deadline for returning the block.

15. Include the address for returning the block.

16. Provide phone numbers for a help line, giving the participants people to call if they need help with the block.

17. If known, give the date of the quilt presentation and any party plans.

■ green
▨ blue
▩ red
▥ yellow
□ muslin

4–12.

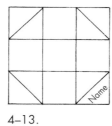

4–13.

18. Request money to help pay for quilt materials. (We only ask for small amounts based on the cost for that quilt.)

PREPARING FOR THE NEXT STEP

Your kits have gone forth. Aside from sewing together your own block or blocks, you can breathe easily for a few weeks until it's time to start getting the finished blocks back. Or you may want to use the time to help some novice seamstresses to sew together their blocks.

A get-together for your beginners may solve a lot of problems, as nothing replaces hands-on help for the inexperienced.

Step 8
The Blocks Come Back

One of the most exciting parts of group quiltmaking is when the blocks start to come in. With special blocks involving appliqué, embroidery, crazy quilting or quilter's choice, it's fun to see what the needleworkers' imagination and skill have produced. There is curiosity as to whether the seamstresses did their job well, and great joy when that's the case. And, there's disappointment when there's a serious goof—or should we say, a challenge?

Be aware that you may have to make some tearful or threatening phone calls before all the blocks are returned. Since making reminder phone calls is much easier than begging, don't wait more than a couple of days after the deadline to contact the errant participants. Occasionally we've had to ask that a block be returned, finished or not, so that we can get on with assembly of the top. Usually though, we've planned ahead and set a deadline with a buffer zone, which allows us to be patient and wait for all finished blocks to be returned.

Shoofly block in process of assembly.

Once all the blocks are completed and returned, your first job is to press and measure each one. In a perfect world, if you asked for 8½" blocks, that's what you'd get. But it's not a perfect world and human error can affect measuring, marking, cutting, and piecing. One way or another, we've dealt with every block that has come back to us in the past 20-something years. Most of them have been just fine; others have required various fixes.

HOW TO FIX BLOCKS THAT NEED FIXING

This section includes some of the most common problems you will encounter with the block and how to fix them. If none of these fixes are appropriate for your problem blocks, you will need to make a new block, using that extra fabric you should have on hand.

THE BLOCK IS TOO BIG

If you can do it without affecting the pattern, trim each edge to obtain the desired size.

Note: As an example, this will work for Pinwheel blocks, but not for Shoofly blocks (figures 4–14 A and B).

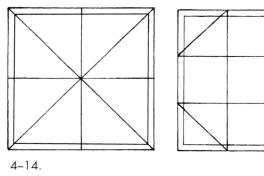

4–14.
A. Pinwheel.   B. Shoofly.

THE BLOCK IS TOO SMALL

If the block is no more than ¼" off, use a pin to mark the edge with the incorrect seam allowance. This will remind you to use a ⅛" seam allowance when joining it to another block. (See Chapter 8—How to Quilt, page 422, for joining instructions.)

If the block is off by ½" or more, you can try to sew strips of fabric to the edges to reach the desired size. This works best if you have some fabric that matches the overall background of the offending block.

Step 9

Decide on the Layout

If you are following a predetermined layout, such as our pattern for the Starry Night quilt on page 189, you will sew your blocks together according to the given pattern. If you have chosen a random or scrap pattern, lay all your blocks on the floor or on a bed where you can look at them and shift them around to balance the colors (or unbalance them) to your liking. As shown in figures 4–15 and 4–16, different effects can be achieved with different color placements.

Step 10

Sew the Top Together

For all next steps of construction, refer to Chapter 8— How to Quilt, pages 417 to 445.

HOOP ALTERNATIVE

If you absolutely have no room to set up a quilting frame, even large quilts can be quilted using hoops. In fact, many quilters prefer using hoops when quilting fancy patterns such as feather plumes and wreaths which involve frequently changing the direction of your stitching. The great big hoops can be tiring to hold and unwieldy unless on a stand. A good size hoop for group work is approximately 14".

To use hoops with a group, first make sure your quilt is closely basted. Then drape the quilt over a big table and seat the quilters around. Each quilter will have her own hoop. You probably can't seat as many quilters around the quilt at a time as you could with a frame. Each quilter will require extra room, since she will be twisting her hoop around as she works.

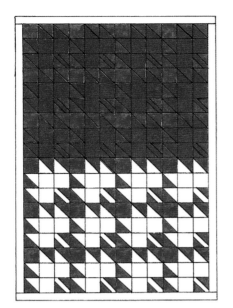  

4–15. Positioning the same Maple-Leaf block in different ways provides a variety of effects.

 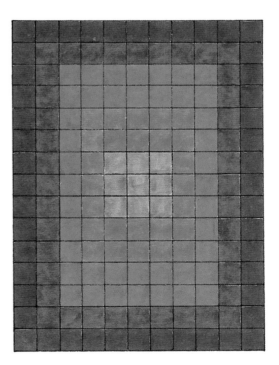

4–16. Two different effects using a one-patch pattern.

A fine example of an Ohio Star quilt.

SET UP THE QUILTING FRAME

A quilting frame with a base which you purchase or build yourself is ideal. You will tack or stitch the top and bottom edges of your quilt to the two longer rails. You will then roll the quilt onto the rails and quilt in sections, rolling the quilt as necessary to expose the unquilted areas.

If you don't have a quilting frame, you can easily make one using four 2 x 2s, four 4" or 5" C-clamps, and four ladderback straight chairs. First cut two of the 2 x 2s into 46" lengths (or have them cut for you at a lumberyard or home store). Then cut the other two into 98" lengths. These lengths will make a frame that will accommodate quilts up to 86" x 100".

As with a ready-made frame, you will first tack or stitch the quilt to the two longer rails, roll the quilt, then C-clamp the long rails to the two shorter ones, which will rest across the tops of the chairs. This is not the greatest quilting frame, but it has the advantages of being cost effective, easy to make, portable, and easy to store. We have quilted many of our quilts using this type of frame.

Step 11

Put the Quilt on the Frame

Cut two strips of fabric, such as cotton, muslin, or lightweight denim, each 6" wide and almost as long as the longest rails. Fold the strips in half lengthwise. Using a staple gun or thumbtacks, tack one strip along each of the long rails. Make sure you tack the two raw edges to the wood. You will baste your quilt to these strips, the top edge to one strip, the bottom edge to the other.

QUILTING-FRAME PATTERN

If you are inclined to build things, or have someone to do it for you, here is a dandy frame we have all enjoyed using. It's very solid and works well for a large group of quilters.

You will need:

One 2 x 4, ten feet long (cut into four 30" sections for risers and racks for the rails)

One 2 x 6, six feet long (to be cut in half crosswise for the "feet" of the frame)

Two 2 x 2s, each eight feet long (for the rails)

8 carriage bolts

Use a stable lightweight wood, such as a good grade of white pine. (This will make it easier for one person to move the quilt frame around.)

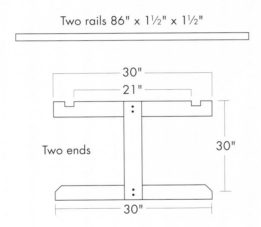

Begin basting in the center; baste to one side, then go back to the center and baste to the other side. Keep the edge you are basting parallel to the rail.

You can omit using the strips. Instead, use thumbtacks to tack the top edge of the quilt directly to one of the long rails, pushing the thumbtacks through all three layers of fabric. If you do this, be sure to place the thumbtacks close to the edge of the quilt where the holes will be hidden by the binding. Start tacking at the center of the rail, then work toward the ends, smooth-

ing the edges as you go. Do the same for the bottom edge of the quilt to fix it to the remaining long rail.

We prefer using the fabric strips. Pushing thumbtacks into wood through the two layers of fabric and batting can be difficult. Putting the strips on the rail is a one-time job, since you will keep the strips on the rails when the quilt is finished and removed. The strips also provide you with the advantage of quilting closer to the ends when the quilt is on the frame.

ROLLING THE QUILT

Once the quilt is attached to the rails, it is helpful to have at least one other person work with you. Not only are you trying to prevent massive wrinkles in the quilt, you are trying to get it wound squarely and evenly on the frame. If one end of the quilt is wound more tightly than the other, the quilt will be off-kilter. An equal amount of quilt on each rail at the start ensures that you can begin quilting in the very center of the quilt. We highly recommend making this a two- or four-person job.

To start, stretch out the quilt that you have attached to the rails—do not pull it taut. Begin rolling toward the center, rolling the quilt under, onto the rails. Keep a steady tension as you roll. When only the central two or three rows of your quilt top are showing, stop rolling and secure one long rail to the two short rails.

If your quilting frame is one that rests on chairs, secure one long rail to the short rails with two C-clamps. Once one long rail is secured, tightly pull the quilt, then secure the other long rail. You want the quilt to be stretched but not taut; if the quilt is under undue strain, the tension can pull out the stitches.

Place your quilters' chairs around the quilt, and get ready to work. Many of us find we quilt more comfortably if the quilt frame is slightly higher rather than lower, but there are always individual preferences. Sometimes we put the frame in front of a sofa to accommodate the "low" sitters and arrange dining chairs on the other side for the "high" sitters.

Regardless of the quilt's size, always begin your quilting in the center. First quilt the center row of your pattern. Then, preferably with help, unclamp the frame and roll the quilt toward one end, keeping the tension even. Reclamp the frame, and continue quilting from where you left off. You will gradually be quilting toward one end of the quilt. Re-roll as often as necessary till you reach the upper or lower end of the quilt. At the end, quilt as close to the secured edge as you can, while still maintaining a decent stitch. Now roll the quilt all the way back to the center and quilt toward the other end. When you have done all the quilting that it is possible to do on the frame, remove the quilt from the frame and complete any unfinished bits using hoops. At this stage, since the rest of the quilt is already quilted, you may not need to use hoops.

Step 12

Arrange the Quilting Bees

Quilting is a mixture of work and fun. Unless someone really dislikes needlework, the lure of socializing with friends and acquaintances, as well as the promise of good food and drink, will bring people to the quilting

frame. A full-size quilt takes many hours to finish, but most people say that the quilting is the most satisfying part of the whole process for them.

First, some planning. Determine how many people can fit comfortably around the quilt when it is on the frame. Usually, for a large quilt, three people per each long side is the most comfortable arrangement. It is seldom possible to quilt at either short end of the frame.

Using masking tape to mark a straight line for quilting.

Next, contact your quilters. Give them a choice of different days, then ask them to choose one. Plan both week and weekend days to accommodate a variety of schedules. Don't just say, "Come if you can," or you may end up with too many or too few quilters. Try to get people to commit to the day they've chosen—if they don't show up, there's a space someone else might have filled.

Tell your quilters you plan on working most of the day—our usual plan is 10 a.m. to 4 p.m. with a lunch break. Remember, it takes time to warm up and get into the rhythm of quilting, even for the most experienced quilters. Also, the good stories never get told until later in the day! We usually ask everyone to bring food to share for lunch; if this is too much trouble or special diets are involved, quilters can bring a bag lunch. The hostess usually provides the beverages. She should also make sure there is plenty of light to quilt by and comfortable seating around the frame. Elbowroom may be a different story!

The hostess should have these items on hand:
- Extra pairs of small scissors for cutting thread
- Two or three spools of quilting thread in the correct color
- Good-quality quilting needles in two or three sizes
- Adhesive bandages
- A few thimbles (though really everyone should bring her own)
- Masking tape if used for marking
- A spare pair of reading glasses and a needle threader aren't a bad idea if any of your quilters are over 50.

Step 13

Quilting

The major objective in quilting is to keep the batting from shifting around between the top and bottom fabrics. What we mostly see is the attractive solution to this utilitarian problem—the stitching pattern on the top of the quilt. Good quilting takes practice, but even beginners can do a respectable job.

To begin, mark your pattern if you haven't done so already (refer to Chapter 8—How to Quilt, pages 428 to 430). Buy thread that is specifically designated for quilting. Traditionally, you use the same color thread for all the quilting, but the choice is up to you. If most of your quilters are beginners, you may want to use a color that blends with the background in order to camouflage crooked stitches.

Quilting takes practice; be patient and forgiving with yourself and others. The motion and rhythm of quilting can be very relaxing. Sometimes we choose to listen to music we enjoy if only a few of us are working. Books on tape are good when you are quilting alone. Refer to Chapter 8—How to Quilt, pages 434 to 441 for detailed instructions on quilting methods.

A few of the items you may need for quilting. Clockwise from top: pattern template, masking tape, marker, thread, thimble, finger guard, scissors.

Step 14

Bind the Quilt

Refer to Chapter 8—How to Quilt, pages 442 to 445 for binding instructions and suggestions.

Step 15

Finishing Touches

You're almost there! Remove all basting threads, and trim off any stray thread ends. Be careful! At this stage, we've seen overexcited quilters make small holes with the points of their scissors while hurriedly trimming threads. Needing to mend a just-finished quilt is really depressing.

Check once more for forgotten pins or needles. If the quilt has gotten dusty or has collected cat hair (cats adore napping on quilts that are on the frame), try tumbling it (the quilt, not the cat) in the dryer on the no-heat setting. Vacuuming with low suction can also help. One way to avoid having this sort of problem is to cover the quilt on the frame with an old sheet or dust cover between quilting sessions.

Of course, if the quilt does actually get soiled (blood, sweat, tears), you may need to wash it in the machine (only if the quilt is washable, of course). Use cold water with a mild soap (one made specially for woolens or for quilts) on a gentle cycle. Then tumble dry on low heat.

NAMES ON QUILTS

Please don't omit this identification step. We did when we first began, and now, 20 years later, there's a lot we don't remember about some of our quilts. It often happens that some people do a great deal of work on a quilt while others do very little. Someone may even do a block so badly that it has to be taken apart and redone by the organizer. But the loving intention is the same, and the names on a quilt represent the participation of the community in a group expression of friendship. For this reason, the names are very important to the recipient(s) and we have always tried to involve as many people as possible in a quilt, even if some only do a few symbolic stitches.

Some of our group quilts have had the names of each participant embroidered on the block she sewed, or around the outer border of the quilt. On some of our later, more consciously artistic efforts, the designers felt that the names detracted from the overall design. On these quilts, the names were written in indelible ink on a cloth panel, which was then sewn to the back of the quilt.

For a panel, we generally use unbleached muslin or pastel cotton, prewashed and ironed, to make our panel. Make your panel large enough to hold all necessary information. We write with indelible ink, using a fine-point pen intended for marking fabric, first testing the pen on the fabric to make sure it doesn't bleed.

Information to include may be the name of the quilt, recipient(s), date of presentation, occasion for the quilt (wedding, birth, etc.), where it was made, name(s) of designer/organizer, and names of all participants. Turn the edges of the panel under and hand-stitch the panel to the bottom of the back of the quilt, taking care not to let your stitches show on the top.

CONGRATULATIONS!!!

Rejoicing and Hurrahing!!! Dancing in the Streets!!! You've finished!!! Put the quilt somewhere you can enjoy looking at it for a while. Right now this may feel like one of your grandest accomplishments, not unlike giving birth. This is a good time to take a picture of the quilt. When you've given it away, you'll be glad to have a record of it.

PLANNING YOUR SURPRISE PRESENTATION

Your party plans will depend on you, your quilters, and your recipients. If the party is a surprise, do remind your party guests not to leave invitations where the quilt recipients might see them.

We present our baby quilts at the end of a regular baby shower. Wedding quilts are presented at the wedding party or at a party scheduled for a later date. We usually reveal friendship quilts at parties ostensibly created for some other purpose. Surprise! Keep in mind that someone has to make sure the honorees actually show up—you don't want an even bigger surprise!

We often hang the quilt up rather than gift wrap it. This provides for a wonderful shock effect for the people, receiving the quilt, and the guests are able to enjoy and admire the quilt all through the party.

SIMPLE PATTERNS SUITABLE FOR GROUP QUILTING

Here are patterns for three quilts with variations. They range from a small quilt with only nine blocks, to an ambitious, bed-covering quilt with 99 pieced blocks.

Each pattern will give the yardage requirements (where applicable), the cutting and piecing instructions, possible variations (ways to make the quilt larger, smaller, simpler, more complicated), as well as quilting suggestions.

Karol's Food Quilt

44" in diameter • Designer & Organizer: Libby Woodruff

A thank-you made for the woman who managed our food co-op for many years. Notice all the participants'
names around the edge. The shape reflects the name of the co-op, The Circle. Round quilts not being easy to hang,
our solution was to sew a semi-circle of fabric on the back, and cut a strong piece of corrugated cardboard
to fit the pocket. It stabilized the top half of the quilt so that its sides hang correctly.

GENERAL INSTRUCTIONS

Though you should already have read the detailed step-by-step instructions in the How-to section, we want to stress again five important basics:

1. Before you begin to sew, mark your sewing machine so that you will be sewing with a consistent ¼" seam. To mark the machine, place the needle near the down position. With a ruler, measure ¼" from the needle to the right (including the needle in the ¼" measurement.) Place a piece of masking tape on the stitch plate at that measurement, to the right of the measurement. As you sew, you will guide the edge of your fabric along the edge of the masking tape. Practice on a piece of scrap fabric. Sew your seam, take the fabric out of the machine, then measure the seam allowance. It should be just ¼". The stitches of the thread should be on or just inside the ¼" measurement, or what we call a "scant" ¼". Always use an exact ¼" seam allowance.

2. Remember that pressing is different from ironing. In pressing, you use less back and forth movement, which causes the fabric to stretch and will distort your pieces.

3. Press your fabric at each step.

4. Press all seams to the side and toward the darker fabrics where possible. Do not press the seams open, as you

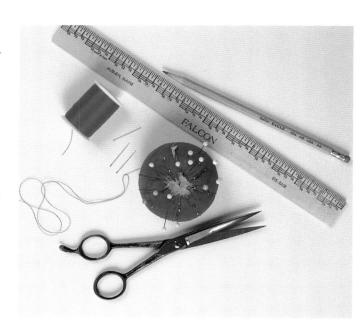

Anyone can make a quilt with a few basic tools and notions.

would do in dressmaking. (Pressing the backing is an exception to this rule. See Chapter 8—How to Quilt, page 417.)

5. Note that when we give measurements for cutting strips, we assume the width of your fabric is 40". It may measure a few inches more and that's fine. Don't bother to cut it down to 40".

Beginners' Favorite

This is the all-purpose quilt—our favorite for beginners—and what could be easier? Squares (or rectangles) separated by a contrasting sashing, afford a blank palette for quilting, appliqué, embroidery, stencils, fabric paint—whatever you and your group choose. Or, you can let the fabric itself steal the show; just use a variety of interesting fabrics with a coordinating sashing to unite them. We have even used this pattern when working with very young children, making the squares of felt and letting each child decorate his own square by gluing cutout felt shapes to the squares.

We offer two variations of this pattern. The first, which we call Bottom-Line Easiest of All, has only nine blocks, a single border, and a small amount of quilting. It could be a nice baby quilt, as in our example, or, with more sophisticated fabrics and different quilting, it could be a charming wall hanging.

The second variation is still simple to construct. (The embellishments, however, are more complicated.) The Alphabet Baby Quilt requires 30 blocks, 26 for the letters and 4 for the corners. We chose reproduction feed sack material with its nostalgic tiny prints and soft colors. (The same quilt done in bold primary colors would be a vibrant adaptation.) We appliquéd the letters (patterns cut freehand from freezer paper) onto the background squares, further securing them with decorative blanket stitching. The embroidered motifs representing each letter are an eye-catching but optional extra. You'll find other examples of one-patch quilts identified throughout this book.

VARIATION 1

Bottom-Line Easiest of All
Finished Sizes
Block size: 10"
Border width: 4"
Quilt size: 38" x 38"

FABRIC

Blocks and surrounding strips: ¼ yard each of nine different fabrics
Border: ⅔ yard
Backing: 1¼ yards
Bias tape for binding: 5 yards

CUTTING DIRECTIONS

From each ¼ yard of the nine different colors cut the following:
8½" squares, one from each color
18 strips, two from each of the colors, each measuring 1½" x 8½"
18 strips, two from each color, each measuring 1½" x 10½"
From the border fabric, cut:
Four strips, two measuring 4½" x 30½"
Two measuring 4½" x 38½"

ASSEMBLY

1. Following figure 4–17, piece your nine blocks, following the color placement in the photo. Remember to press, not iron, the seams.

2. Following figure 4–18, join the blocks in three horizontal rows of three blocks each. Press the seams. Now join the three horizontal rows, pinning to match the seams. Press.

3. Following figure 4–18, add your side borders. Press the seams. Then add the top and bottom borders. Press the seams.

4. Layer the top, batting, and backing. Baste the layers together.

5. Quilt as desired. (We used simple concentric hearts in the squares and straight lines in the narrow strips and in the wide border.)

6. Finish the edge with bias-tape binding. And don't forget your identification panel! (Hanging sleeve is optional.)

4–17.

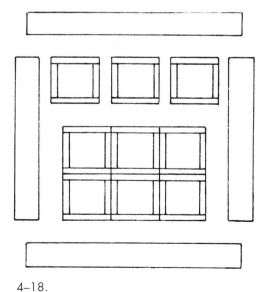

4–18.

Alphabet Baby Quilt

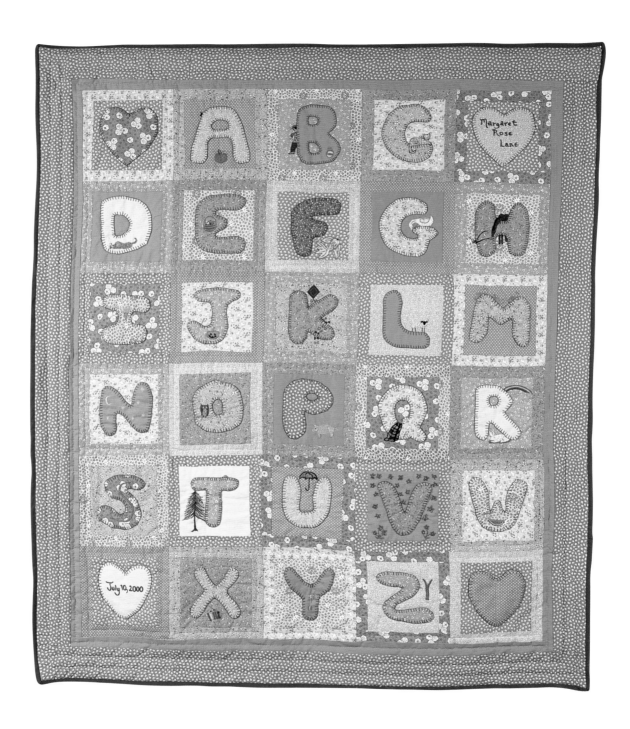

VARIATION 2

Alphabet Baby Quilt
Finished Sizes
Block size: 8"
Inner border width: 1"
Outer border width: 3"
Quilt: 48" x 56"

FABRIC

Blocks: Fifteen ½ yard pieces of assorted fabrics*
Inner border: ⅓ yard
Outer border: ⅔ yard
Backing: 3⅓ yards
Bias binding: 6 yards
Alphabet Letters: Use leftover fabric

*This will make 30 blocks. You can cut two blocks and eight edging strips from each ¼ yard. This quilt would also work as a scrap quilt, with each participant choosing her own fabric for the blocks and the organizer providing the border fabrics.

CUTTING DIRECTIONS

From the assorted colors, cut:
Thirty 6½" squares, two from each fabric
Sixty 1½" x 6½" strips in pairs of assorted colors
Sixty 1½" x 8½" strips in same pairs of assorted colors
From the inner-border fabric cut:
Six 1½" x 40" strips. From these strips, piece two 1½" x 42½" strips, and two 1½" x 48½" strips.
From the outer-border fabric cut:
Five 3½" x 40" strips. From these strips piece two 3½" x 50½" strips, and two 3½" x 48½" strips.

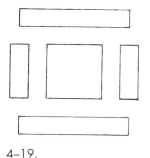

4–19.

ASSEMBLY

1. Following figure 4–19, piece the 30 blocks.

2. Add appliquéd letters and other desired embellishments before joining the blocks together.

3. Following figure 4–20, join the blocks in six horizontal rows of five blocks each. Press the seams. Join the horizontal rows, pinning to match the seams. Press.

4. Add the narrow border, sewing on the side borders first. Press the seams.

5. Add the outer border, sewing on the side borders first. Press the seams.

6. Seam the backing together and press.

7. Layer the top, backing, and batting. Baste the layers together.

8. Quilt as desired. (We outlined the letters and put straight lines in the borders.)

9. Finish the edge with bias-tape binding. Add the identification panel and sleeve (optional).

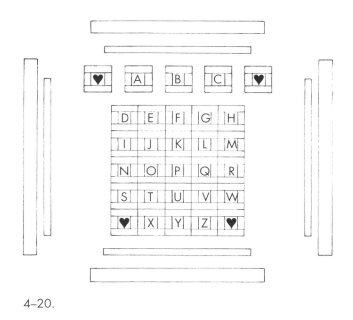

4–20.

Single Irish Chain

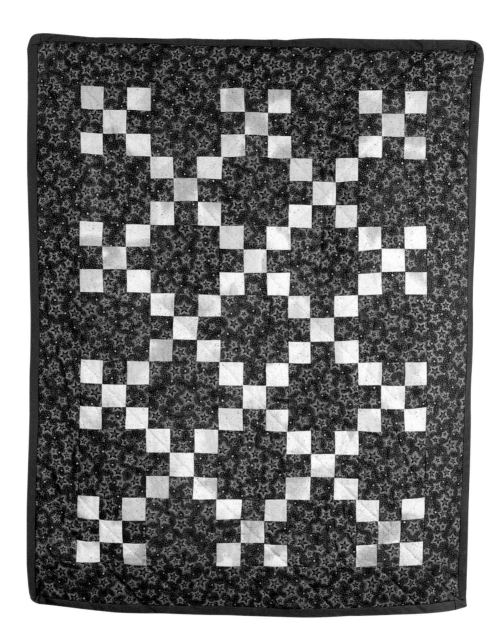

Alternate a basic nine-patch block composed of darks and lights with solid squares of dark or light, and you have achieved a Single Irish Chain. You can make this simple quilt with print fabrics and minimal quilting, or you can use solids, which afford ample space for elaborate quilting—whatever suits your fancy. This pattern is for a crib quilt, but you could easily expand it to make a bed-size quilt.

FINISHED SIZES

Block A (nine-patch): 6"
Block B (solid): 6"
Border width: 3½"
Quilt: 37" x 49"

FABRIC

Note: The figures given are for rotary cutting or for careful measuring and marking. If you use templates to cut your small squares, you will probably need a little extra fabric.

Block A: ½ yard dark fabric (¾ yard if using templates)
Block A: ½ yard light fabric (¾ yard if using templates)
Block B: ⅔ yard dark fabric
Border: ⅔ yard dark fabric
Backing: 2 yards
Bias Binding: 5 yards

4-21.

CUTTING DIRECTIONS

For Block A:

From the dark fabric, you will need seventy-two squares, each measuring 2½" x 2½". To get them, cut five 2½" x 40" strips. Each strip will yield sixteen squares measuring 2½").

From the light fabric you will need ninety squares, each measuring 2½" x 2½". Cut six 2½" x 40" strips.

Each strip will yield sixteen squares measuring 2½".

For Block B:

From the dark fabric, you will need seventeen squares, each measuring 6½" x 6½". To get them, cut three 6½" x 40" strips. Each strip will yield six squares measuring 6½".

FOR THE BORDERS:

From the dark fabric, cut five 4" x 40" strips. From these five strips, construct two 4" x 37½" strips by trimming two of the five strips cut above. Then construct two 4" x 42½" strips by adding the necessary lengths.

ASSEMBLY

1. Following figure 4–21, piece eighteen nine-patch blocks. Press the seams toward the dark fabric.

2. Following figure 2, join the blocks in seven horizontal rows of five blocks each. Press the seams. Now join the horizontal rows, pinning them to match seams. Press seams.

3. Add the border strips, sewing the side strips on first. Press the seams toward border.

4. Seam the backing together and press.

5. Layer the quilt top, batting, and backing. Baste the layers together.

6. Quilt as desired. (For our example, we made a template of a free-form star to quilt in the solid blocks. We quilted diagonal lines through the light squares of the nine-patch blocks, extending these lines into the border.)

7. Finish the edge with bias-tape binding. Add the identification panel and hanging sleeve (optional).

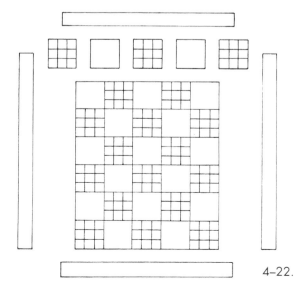

4-22.

Starry Night

This pattern looks complex, but actually is composed of two very easy blocks—the Pinwheel and Shoofly. As shown, our example uses 99 blocks (36 Shoofly and 63 Pinwheel blocks). This may seem like quite a lot unless you have a large and enthusiastic group with people willing to piece multiple blocks. We chose to use Pinwheels in various shades of blues and purples (and a few deep reds) to lend motion and vibrancy to the background surrounding the yellow Shoofly blocks.

Alternatively, you could make the quilt much easier by substituting solid blocks for some or even all of the Pinwheels, and by using a solid border as directed in the 31-block variation of this pattern. You would still have a beautiful quilt with room for fancy quilting on the blank blocks and borders. We'll give yardage for both options.

FINISHED SIZES

Shoofly and Pinwheel blocks: 8"
Narrow border: 2"
Outer Border: 8"
Quilt size: 76" x 92"

FABRIC

Yellow(s) for Shoofly blocks and narrow border:
   1¾ yards*
Medium-dark blue(s) for Pinwheel and Shoofly
   blocks, and eight small rectangles in the border:
   4½ yards
Medium-light blue for Pinwheel blocks:
   2¼ yards **
Deep red for eight Pinwheel blocks: ½ yard
Backing: 9 yards***
Bias-tape binding: 10 yards

   *Our yellow yardage was unequally divided
   among four very similar yellows.
  **Again, as with the yellow yardage, we used sim-
   ilar shades of blue in unequal amounts.
***This may seem very generous if you are follow-
   ing the guidelines in step 5 on page 165, but if
   you try to get by with only 6 yards, you will be
   awfully close to coming up short.

CUTTING DIRECTIONS

Note: If you are using various shades of one color,
you will divide your cutting among them.

Shoofly Blocks
The following will make 36 Shoofly blocks 31 for
the body of the quilt, and five for the border:

Pattern piece A
You will need a total of thirty-six squares:
   From the yellow(s), cut three strips, each meaur-
ing 2½" x 40". Each strip will yield sixteen squares
measuring 2½".

Pattern piece B
You will need a total of 144 rectangles:
   From the medium-dark blue(s), cut nine strips,
each measuring 3½" x 40". Each strip will yield
sixteen rectangles measuring 2½" x 3½".

Pattern piece C:
You will need a total of 288 triangles:
   From the medium-dark blue(s), cut eight strips,
each measuring 3⅞" x 40". Each strip will yield
ten squares measuring 3⅞". You will need a total
of seventy-two squares. Following figure 4–23, cut
the squares on the diagonal to yield 144 triangles.
   From the yellow(s), cut eight strips, each measuring 3⅞" x 40". Each strip will yield ten squares.

4–23.

measuring 3⅞". You will need a total of seventy-
two squares. Following figure 1, cut the squares on
the diagonal to yield 144 triangles.

PINWHEEL BLOCKS

The following will make sixty-three Pinwheel
blocks: thirty-two for the body of the quilt and 31
for the border:
   From the medium-dark blue(s), cut sixteen strips,
each measuring 4⅞" x 40". Each strip will yield
eight squares measuring 4⅞". You will need a
total of 126 squares. Cut each square on the diagonal to yield 252 triangles.
   From the medium-light blue(s), cut fourteen
strips, each measuring 4⅞" x 40". Each strip will
yield eight squares measuring 4⅞". You will need
a total of 110 squares. Cut each square on the
diagonal to yield 220 triangles.
   From the red fabric, cut two strips, each measuring 4⅞" x 40". Each strip will yield eight squares
measuring 4⅞". You will need sixteen squares. Cut
each square on the diagonal to yield thirty-two triangles.
   You will need eight medium-dark blue rectangles to go near the corners of the border. Cut two
strips, each measuring 2½" x 40". Each strip will
yield four rectangles measuring 2½" x 8½".

For the narrow yellow border, cut seven strips, each measuring 2½" x 40". You will need to piece the strips to attain the proper lengths for the sides and the top and bottom. For the sides, you will need two pieced strips, each with a length of 72½". For the top and bottom you will need two pieced strips, each with a length of 60½".

ASSEMBLY

Note: See Sample Organizer's Instructions, pages 194 and 195, for more detailed instructions.

1. Following figure 4–24, piece the 36 Shoofly blocks together.

2. Following figure 4–25, piece the 63 Pinwheel blocks together.

3. Following figure 4–26, join the blocks in nine horizontal rows of seven blocks each. Press the seams. Now join the horizontal rows, pinning to match the seams. Press.

4. Add the narrow yellow borders, sewing on the side borders first, then the top and bottom borders. Press the seams away from the yellow.

5. Referring to figure 4–26 piece the outer side borders. Note that the side strips begin and end with blue rectangles. Press the seams. Next, sew the side borders to the quilt. Try to eyeball the blocks to get the horizontal seams to match up, even though they are separated by the yellow border. Press the seams.

6. Referring to figure 4–26, piece your top and bottom borders. Note the changed placement of the blue rectangles. Sew the top and bottom borders to the quilt. Again, try to line up the blocks visually. Press the seams.

7. Seam the backing together and press. Layer the top, batting, and backing. Baste the layers together. (see detailed instructions in Chapter 8—How to Quilt, pages 431 to 433.)

8. Quilt as desired, or follow figure 4–27 for a suggested quilting pattern.

9. Finish the edge with bias-tape binding. Add the

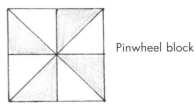

Pinwheel block

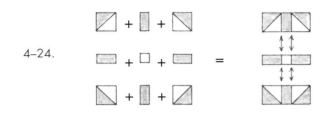

4–24.

4–25.

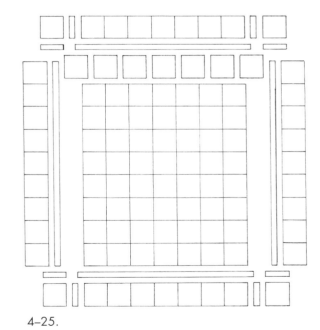

4–25.

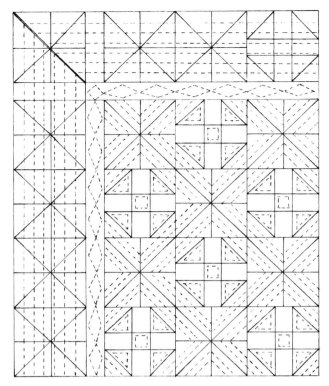

4–27.

identification panel and sleeve (optional).

Variation

31-BLOCK VERSION FABRIC

Yellow for the Shoofly blocks and narrow border:
  1½ yards
Blue for the Shoofly blocks: 1¾ yards
Blue for the solid blocks: 2 yards
Blue for the border: 2¼ yards
Backing: 9 yards
Bias binding: 10 yards

CUTTING DIRECTIONS

The following will make 31 Shoofly blocks:

Pattern piece A
From the yellow, cut two strips, each measuring 2½" x 40". Each strip will yield 16 squares measuring 2½". You will need 31 squares.

Pattern piece B
From the blue, cut eight strips, each measuring 3½" x 40". Each strip will yield 16 rectangles meas-

uring 2¼" x 3½". You will need 124 rectangles.

Pattern piece C
From the blue, cut seven strips, each measuring 3⅞" x 40". Each strip will yield 10 squares measuring 3⅞". You will need 62 squares. Cut each square on the diagonal to yield 124 triangles.

Also pattern piece C:
From the yellow, cut seven strips, each measuring 3⅞" by 40". Each strip will yield 10 squares measuring 3⅞". You will need 62 squares. Cut each square on the diagonal to yield 124 triangles.

For your solid blocks, you will need 32 squares: From the blue, cut eight strips, each measuring 8½" x 40". Each strip will yield four squares measuring 8½".

For the narrow yellow border, cut seven strips, each measuring 2½" x 40". You will need to piece the strips to attain the proper lengths for the sides and the top and bottom. For the sides, you will need two pieced strips, each with a length of 72½". For the top and bottom, you will need two pieced strips, each with a length of 60½".

For the outer blue border, cut four strips, each measuring 8½" x 76½". Note that you are cutting your fabric lengthwise this time rather than across its width.

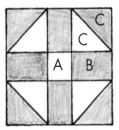

ASSEMBLY

Note: See page 195 for more detailed instructions.

1. Following figure 4–28, piece the 31 Shoofly blocks together.

2. Following figure 4–29, join the Shoofly and solid blocks in nine horizontal rows of seven blocks each. Press the seams. Now join the horizontal rows, pinning to match the seams. Press.

3. Add the narrow yellow borders, sewing on the side borders first, then the top and bottom. Press the seams away from yellow.

4. Add the wide, blue outer borders, sewing on the side borders first, then the top and bottom borders. Press the seams.

5. Seam the backing together and press. Layer the top, batting, and backing. Baste the layers together. Quilt as desired.

6. Finish the edge with bias-tape binding. Add the identification panel and sleeve (optional).

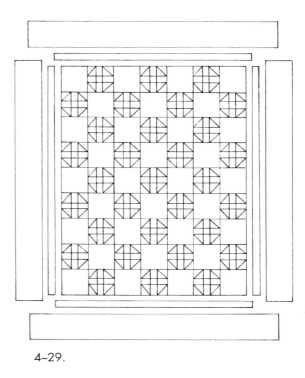

4–29.

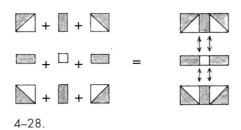

4–28.

Organizer's Instructions to the Participants

NOTE TO THE ORGANIZER:

Following are the step-by-step instructions for pattern III, Starry Night, the ninety-nine block version, which we enclosed in the kit to the participants. Though these are specific to a particular quilt, the format illustrates how to organize the information and the amount of detail you will need to provide to the participants. Use these as a guideline for writing your own instructions, modifying them to suit your project.

As the organizer, be aware of the number of kits you will need to send out. For this particular quilt we needed to make up 99 kits, one for each block. We made 63 Pinwheel kits and 36 Shoofly kits. Of the Pinwheel kits, eight kits consisted of four red triangles and four blue triangles, and 55 kits consisted of four medium-dark and four medium-light triangles. The 36 Shoofly kits consisted of one yellow pattern piece A square, four blue pattern piece B rectangles, four yellow pattern piece C triangles, and four blue pattern piece C triangles.

When writing your instructions, keep a few general principles in mind. Always include a direction to read the directions! You cannot remind participants enough about the ¼" seam allowance. In the instructions you will see illustrations. You will need to provide thumbnail sketches of the blocks in various stages of assembly to give your participants a visual aid. Even experienced quilters appreciate these, and they will save you from receiving squares that are assembled incorrectly. Include a list of what the kit contains (see step 2 below).

SAMPLE INSTRUCTIONS FOR PINWHEEL KIT

Important: Read directions thoroughly before beginning. It's very important that you use an accurate ¼" seam allowance. The finished quilt contains many small seams, and if they are off a little, the finished quilt will be off a lot.

1. This is what your finished block will look like. Be sure to place your darks and lights as they appear in the drawing.
2. This kit contains eight triangles of equal size, four dark and four light. (Red, if you have it, is considered a light.)
3. Press all the pieces, then lay them out as in the illustration of the block in step 1.
4. Match up each light triangle with a dark triangle, right sides together (facing). Sew each pair together along the long, diagonal edge. (This is a bias edge and will stretch if you pull on it, so try not to!)

5. Carefully press the sewn-together triangles open to form a square, making sure to press the seam toward the darker fabric. Be careful not to stretch the square as you press! After pressing, you will have four squares.
6. Measure each square. It should be 4½" x 4½". If the square is more than ⅛" off, please carefully pick out your sewing and redo.
7. Assemble your Pinwheel as shown:

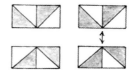

Note: Press and measure for accuracy at each step. If your finished block measures ¼" under or over the desired 8½", that's allowable.

SAMPLE INSTRUCTIONS
FOR THE SHOOFLY KIT

Important: Read directions thoroughly before beginning. It's very important that you use an accurate ¼" seam allowance. The finished quilt contains many small seams, and if they are off a little, the finished quilt will be off a lot.

1. This is what your finished block will look like:

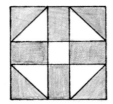

2. This kit contains one small yellow square, four blue rectangles, four yellow triangles, four blue triangles.

3. Press all the pieces, then lay them out as in the illustration of the block in step 1.

4. Match up each yellow triangle to one blue triangle, right sides together (facing). Sew each pair together along the long diagonal edge. (This is a bias edge and will stretch if you pull on it, so try not to!)

5. Carefully press the sewn-together triangles open to form a square, making sure to press the seam toward the darker fabric. Be careful not to stretch the square as you press! After pressing, you will have four blue and yellow squares.

6. Measure each square. It should be 3½" x 3½". If the square is more than ⅛" off, please carefully pick out your sewing and redo.

7. Assemble your Shoofly as shown.

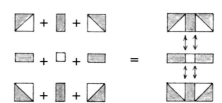

Note: Press and measure for accuracy at each step. If your finished block measures ¼" over or under the desired 8½", that's allowable.

Quilts for Kids

By the Community Quilters of Madison County, NC

Kendel's Celestial Baby Blocks

Size: 35" x 38" • Designers & Organizers: Vicki Skemp and Peggy Barnes
A stacked pyramid variation of the classic one-patch Baby Block pattern, appliquéd to a starry-sky background.
Letters were assigned to participants, and they were asked to add motifs on the other two diamonds.
The narrow border is made from strips of various harmonious solid colors pieced together on the diagonal.

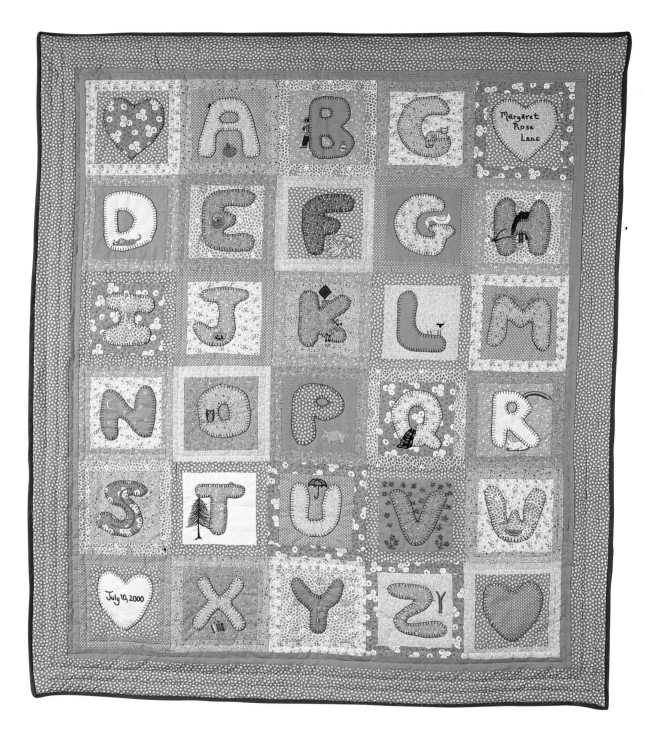

Alphabet Baby Quilt

Size: 48" x 56" • Pieced, appliquéd, and quilted by the Community Quilters of Madison County, NC
ABC quilts are perfect for babies. They will spend countless hours staring at the bright colors and designs associated with the letters. As they learn to talk, you can use them to help the child learn not only the names of the letters, but the things that start with that letter's sound. Directions for making this quilt are on page 185.

Lily's Baby Blocks

Size: 45" x 57" • Designer & Organizer: Laura Ball

Here is a traditional Baby Block pattern, with embroidery and appliqué on the blocks.
The organizer chose the soft colors and tiny print fabrics. The skill of the participants ranged from
a practicing fiber artist to the delightfully well-executed labor of a first-time embroiderer.

Noah's Pinwheels

Size: 40" x 49" • Designer & Organizer: Karol Kavaya

This quilt was made in the traditional, easy four-patch Pinwheels pattern of timeless charm. The organizer gave participants templates and instructions to use blues, greens, or pinks—one solid, one print. There is a narrow border and it is outline quilted ¼" from the seams.

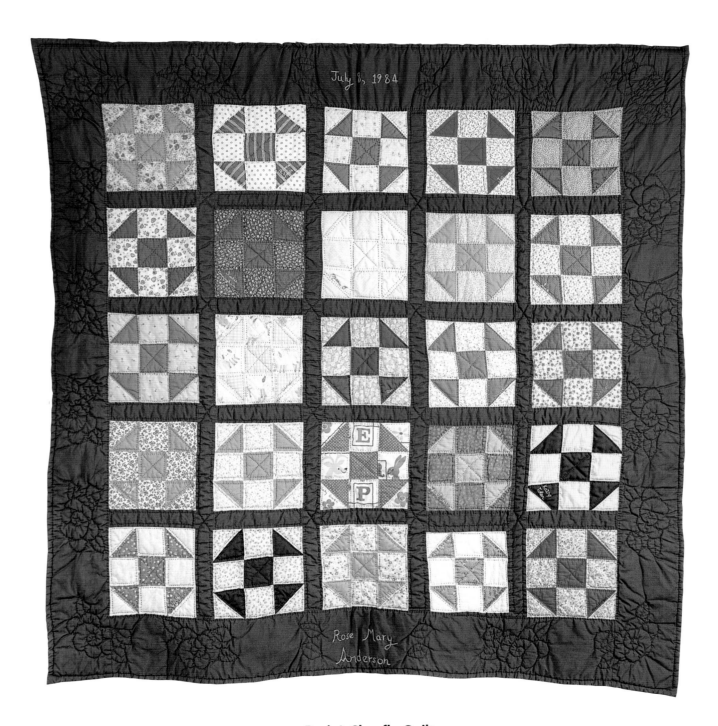

Rosie's Shoofly Quilt

Size: 54" x 54" • Designer & Organizer: Vicki Skemp
The Shoofly pattern, like the Pinwheel, is a very traditional and very easy nine-patch.
Participants received templates for the square and the triangle, and were told to use fabrics in basic
crayon colors. The quilting pattern included roses in the border in honor of the baby, named Rose Mary.

Ryan's Nine Patch

Size: 46" x 50" • Designers & Organizers: Cindi Kulp and Ruth Uffelman
A group of young mothers, most of whom had not done much quilting, produced this lively
quilt using bright contemporary fabrics with novelty prints to bring a fresh new look
to the reliable old Nine Patch. Clamshell quilting was used on the pieced center.

Sailboats

Size: 46" x 47" • Designers & Organizers: Libby Woodruff and Susan Adams
A Pinwheel block alternates with one that begins with a four-patch for the sails, to which strips of "sky"
and "boat" are added. The vintage cloth used in the pinwheels was from a grandmother's collection.
She had made her (now grown) grandson's pajamas from the fabric.

Celestial Quilt

Size: 38" x 59" • Designer & Organizer: Libby Woodruff

The designer decided on a celestial theme, then chose the background, border, and sashing fabric.
She sent out the blue background pieces with sketches of the images she wanted each
participant to reproduce. They were free to use embroidery, appliqué, or both.

Anna's Animals

Size: 38" x 50" • Designer & Organizer: Vicki Skemp

Participants were given precut green fabric and told to embroider and/or appliqué a familiar animal.
Blue squares at the sashing intersections are embroidered with insects. Stymied by depicting hooves,
one needleworker sewed strips of fabric to be meadow in which the horse and cow are standing!

Kate's ABC Quilt

Size: 38" x 47" • Designers & Organizers: Katie Cunningham and Libby Woodruff
This quilt was a challenging one to plan and piece as it is fashioned of squares and rectangles
in a variety of sizes and configurations. The X block shows Raggedy Ann having
an X-ray, but little Kate has "loved" off all the red yarn hair.

Circus Quilt

Size: 29" x 38" • Designer: Vicki Skemp • Organizer: Glenda Jones

This cheery circus quilt is another designed with a variety of rectangles. The designer controlled the finished appearance of the work by giving participants exact patterns and materials. Several of the figures—the ringmaster, the clown and balloons—are appliquéd and stuffed for a 3-D effect.

Noah's Ark

Size: 47" x 56" • Designer & Organizer: Vicki Skemp

The idea for this design came from a hooked rug seen in a magazine. Note the background quilting
of ocean and sky behind the ark. This quilt shows the range of the group's skills—from fairly clumsy
first-time appliqué to incredibly beautiful embroidery—all of them adding up to a charming whole.

Tilson's Fantasy Quilt

Size: 38" x 51" • Designer & Organizer: Rita Hayes

For this tell-me-a-bedtime-story quilt, navy blue diamond patches were sent to participants with
a request to apply a favorite fantasy figure. The large central diamond and corner triangles went to the
more experienced needlewomen. Outline quilting and simple straight lines highlight the figures.

Jesse's Farm Quilt

35" x 52" • Designer & Organizer: Libby Woodruff

The group calls this a "jigsaw-puzzle" quilt. An overall picture was drawn on freezer paper, then divided
into different areas. A scene or object was assigned to each participant, then the designer reassembled them.
It requires careful planning and an accomplished seamstress to piece it all together.

Maggie's Cats Quilt

Size: 39" x 50" • Designers & Organizers: Libby Woodruff and Susan Adams
Maggie's family had many cats, so this quilt grew around an idea and some
cat patterns. It is another example of the jigsaw-puzzle assembly, put together in horizontal
sections with lots of embroidery, appliqué, and straight background quilting.

PART II

Quilting in
Today's World

CHAPTER 5
Weekend Quilting

With material by Karol Kavaya and Vicki Skemp

An Amish-inspired lap quilt, whose beauty and impact is in no way diminished
by its simple construction and the speed with which it can be made.

Celestial Potpourri Bags

These delightful little confections feature shadow quilting. Be sure to select a sheer fabric to appreciate the beauty of this technique. Use these bags to scent your drawers, or as quick-and-easy party favors.

YOU WILL NEED (per bag)

¼ yard of chiffon or similar transparent material
Templates (page 470)
Batting scrap
Paper
Pencil
Gold metallic quilting thread

Potpourri mix
⅛ yard of narrow gold ribbon

Use ¼" seams throughout.

MEASURE AND CUT

Chiffon: one rectangle, 7" x 22"

1. Fold the chiffon in half vertically so that it is now 7" x 11". Stitch along the short raw edge and one long raw edge. Turn right side out and press.

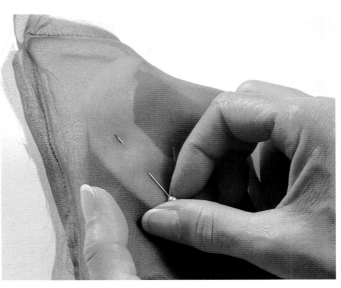

2. Trace the desired template and cut it out; then pin the pattern to the batting scrap, and cut out the shape. Center the batting shape on one half of the rectangle, between the layers of chiffon. Pin in place.

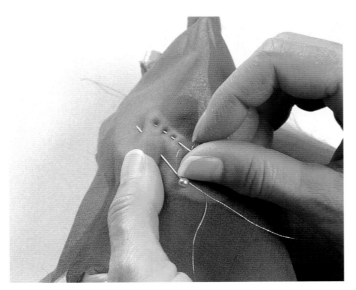

3. Quilt around the batting shape with the gold thread, first working along the edges of the design to hold the batting in place. Then, fill up the image with echo quilting as desired. Leave the trailing ends of the threads, if you want.

4. Fold the rectangle horizontally, right sides together, and stitch the side and bottom. Turn the bag right side out. Fill it with a potpourri mix of your choice, and tie the bag closed with the gold ribbon.

Delicates Travel Pouch

Here is an elegant way to pack and safeguard fine hosiery, silk scarves, jewelry, etc. This bag can be packed flat or rolled up to fit in a corner of a suitcase. You will learn to mark both straight and curved lines for quilting when you create this project.

YOU WILL NEED

¹/₃ yard of pale green fabric
¹/₃ yard of cream or white satin
1 package of craft-size batting
Purchased cable stencil or
    quilting pattern (page 471)
Fabric marking pen or pencil
Paper

Black permanent marker
³/₄" masking tape
Pale green quilting thread
2 yards of lavender ribbon

Use ¹/₄" seams throughout.

MEASURE AND CUT

Pale green fabric: one rectangle, 10" x 26"
Cream fabric: one rectangle, 10" x 26"
Batting: one rectangle, 10" x 26"

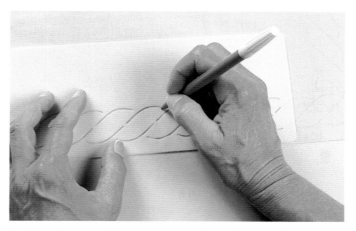

1. Transfer the cable pattern onto the perimeter of the pale green fabric, as shown in the photo. If you prefer to use the pattern on page 471, trace it onto a piece of paper with the permanent marker, and then place the paper under the fabric. Now, trace the design onto the fabric with a marking pen or pencil. Pin or baste together the green rectangle and batting. Quilt the cable motif.

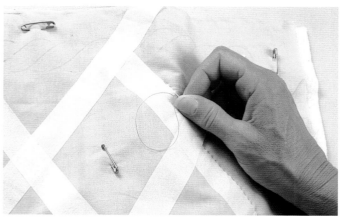

2. Use the masking tape to create the lattice pattern shown, and quilt along both sides of the tape. Remove the tape and basting when your quilting is completed. If there are any markings remaining from step 1, remove them as directed.

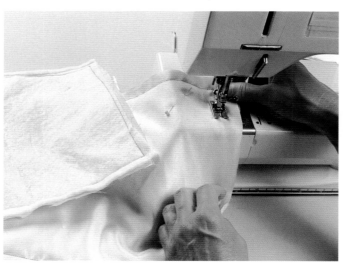

3. Pin the satin rectangle to the quilted layers, right sides together. Stitch around the edges, leaving a 4" or 5" opening in the middle of one end. Turn right side out and slipstitch the opening closed.

4. With the right side of the bag facing you, fold to create a pocket with a depth of 9½". The right sides will be together, so now is the time to stitch the sides of the pocket.

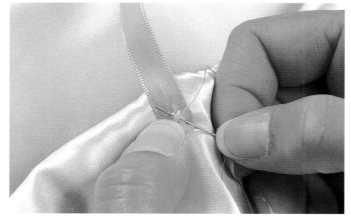

5. Turn the bag right side out. Cut four 18" ribbon ties, and tack them onto the bag.

Brightly Colored Bunting

Don't worry about the cold on a winter outing when baby is tucked into this bunting. It is simple to construct and quilt, and the quilting pattern will give you a good opportunity to perfect your stitch. It will make an excellent present for a newborn.

YOU WILL NEED

1 yard of lime green print fabric
1 yard of royal blue fabric
1 package of craft-size batting
¾" masking tape
Fabric marking pencil
Royal blue and lime green quilting thread
Quilting hoop
Silver snaps, sizes 1/0 and 2/0

MEASURE AND CUT

Lime green print fabric: one rectangle,
    24½" x 33½"
Royal blue fabric: one rectangle, 24½" x 33½"
Batting: one rectangle, 26" x 35"

Use ¼" seams throughout.

2. Trim the batting almost to the seam line, being careful not to cut the fabric. Trim the corners. Turn the bunting right side out; turn the unfinished seams under, and blindstitch the gap closed. Measure 7" from the bottom edge, and mark each side with masking tape. Then topstitch around the top and sides as shown, ⅛" from the edge, starting and stopping at the marked spots. Remove the tape.

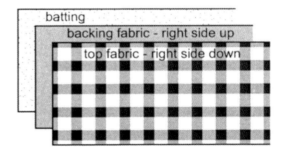

1. Sandwich the layers as shown above. Place the lime green and blue fabrics with their right sides together and edges aligned. Then, place these fabrics onto the piece of batting. (The batting will be slightly bigger all the way around.) Pin the three layers together along the edge, pinning well to keep all the layers in place when stitching. Sew around the edge, but leave a gap on one short edge for turning right side out.

3. Mark the bunting for quilting with a wavy freehand design that runs both horizontally and vertically. Baste. Place the bunting into the hoop and quilt, using royal blue thread for the vertical lines and lime green for the horizontal lines. Remove the marks and basting.

4. Fold the sides of the bunting toward the center, overlapping the front by $^3/_4$", as shown in the photo. Pin along the overlap, and put a piece of masking tape $6^1/_4$" from the bottom of the bunting.

5. With the bunting face up, stitch the front closed about $^3/_8$" from the edge of the overlap, starting at the bottom of the bunting and sewing to your mark. Sew the top row of stitching several times to reinforce, as shown. Remove the tape. Now, pin the bottom of the bunting with the wrong sides together, and sew $^1/_4$" from the edge, backstitching at the beginning and end. Run another line of stitching near the first one for added strength.

6. Mark places to sew 5 size 1/0 snaps on the front of the bunting, to be hidden by the overlap; sew on the snaps. Fold the front corners down about $7^1/_2$" to form the collar of the bunting. Mark a spot for a size 2/0 snap underneath each point of the collar; sew on the snaps.

Batik Tablecloth

Liven up your dining area with this exotic table covering. The quilted patterns in the border complement the design of the batik print; you could quilt the border simply at first and add more stitching at your leisure.

YOU WILL NEED

1½ yards of batik fabric
¼ yard of turquoise fabric
2 yards of khaki fabric
1 package of crib-size batting
¾" masking tape
Light yellow quilting thread

MEASURE AND CUT

Batik fabric: one square, 42" x 42"
Turquoise fabric: two strips, each 1½" x 42"
   two strips, each 1½" x 44"
Khaki fabric: two strips, each 13" x 44"
   two strips, each 13" x 55"
Batting: two pieces, each 5" x 54"
   two pieces, each 5" x 44"

Use ¼" seams throughout.

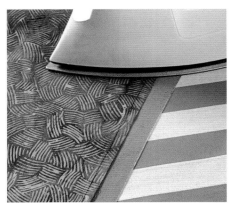

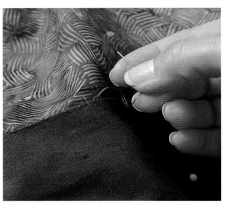

1. Stitch one of the 42" narrow turquoise strips to a side of the batik square, right sides together. Repeat on the opposite side of the square with the other 42" strip. Sew the 44" turquoise strips to the remaining sides of the square. Press the seam allowances outward, as shown.

2. Pin the 13" x 44" khaki strips to the narrow turquoise strips on two opposing sides, right sides together. Stitch and press the seam allowance toward the outer edge. Press the outer edge under ¼". Next, fold and press the wide khaki strip so the exposed seam on the back of the tablecloth will be covered by the pressed edge of the strip. Unfold the strip and place the 5" x 44" batting strip along the crease; pin if desired, and then baste as shown, below left. Remove the pins.

3. Fold the khaki strip back over to cover the seam once again, and blind-stitch as shown. Repeat steps 2 and 3 with the opposite side.

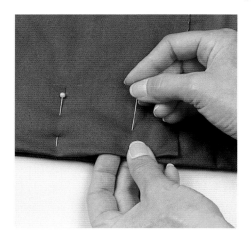

4. Now, using the 13" x 55" khaki strips, repeat steps 2 and 3 on the remaining two sides. These strips will extend ½" on either end. Fold in the unfinished ends, pin in place as shown, and whip-stitch the ends closed.

Tip: Make a set of matching napkins for this piece. You will need an additional yard of fabric; we chose the turquoise cloth. Cut four 16½" squares, and machine hem the unfinished edges. You don't have to use this project for dining, necessarily; it will also adorn (or hide) any nondescript table.

5. Use the masking tape to create a weave pattern in the border. Quilt along one side of the tape for your basic line, and then the other side of the tape for your second line. Now pull up the tape and lay it along the second line; quilt along the other side to create a third line. Repeat this procedure as necessary, and remove all tape and basting when you have completed the quilting. This photo illustrates the possibilities of simple and/or more complex quilting in the border.

Tangy Table Runner

This piece will spice up any meal—not to mention the table. Add one part good food, one part good company, mix well, and savor. Measure, cut, and piece with precision, for there are lots of seams in this project.

YOU WILL NEED

1¾ yards of lime green fabric

¼ yard of yellow fabric

⅛ yard of teal fabric

1¾ yards of orange fabric

1¾ yards of print fabric

1 package of crib-size batting

Quilting pattern (page 473) or purchased stencil

Fabric marking pencil

¾" masking tape

Quilting hoop

Lime green quilting thread

MEASURE AND CUT

(See figure 5–1.)

Lime green fabric: two strips, each 5½" x 56½"
  two strips, each 3½" x 6½" inches
  four strips, each 5½" x 6½" inches

Yellow fabric: three squares, each 4" x 4"
  two squares, each 3" x 3"

Teal fabric: six strips, each 1" x 4"
  six strips, each 1" x 5"
  four strips, each 1½" x 3"
  four strips, each 1½" x 5"

Orange fabric: two strips, each 2¼" x 56½"
  two strips, each 2¼" x 20½"

Print fabric: one rectangle, 17½" x 57½"

Batting: one rectangle, 17½" x 57½"

Use ¼" seams throughout.

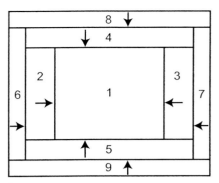

5–1. Block piecing sequence

1. You will begin by assembling the pieced blocks from the small strips of lime green, yellow, and teal fabrics, as shown in the photo. Lay out a total of five blocks, three with the larger yellow blocks at the center and two with the smaller yellow blocks at the center.

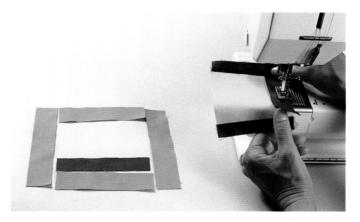

2. Assemble each block, starting with the center and sewing in the sequence indicated in figure 5–1, with the right sides of the fabric together. (Note that the sewing sequence will be correct for each style of block, despite a difference in the size of the pieces.)

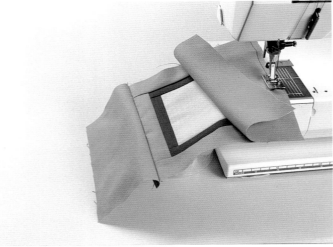

3. Sew the blocks together into a row as shown, alternating the lime rectangles with the pieced blocks. After you have sewn the row of blocks together, stitch the 3½" x 6½" lime green strips to either short end of the row, right sides together. Then, sew the longer lime green strips to each long edge of the row, right sides together. Lastly, with right sides together, sew on the orange borders, first the long edges, then the short ends. Center the short borders so you will have an equal amount of fabric to turn over at each end.

4. Mark the top for quilting, drawing a freehand design. Use masking tape for the straight lines. Next, sandwich the layers: first the top, right side down; then the batting, centered; and finally the print backing, right side up. Make sure the orange border extends equally on all four sides, as shown, as you will use the excess to create the border.

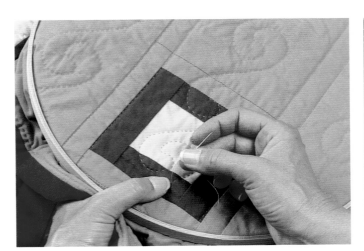

5. Carefully pin along all four edges of the table runner, making sure to catch all three layers. Baste. Quilt, following the motif in the long lime borders and the center. Then quilt in the ditch along the seams of the pieced blocks and lime borders, along the long borders, and along a straight line formed by the teal edges of the pieced blocks. Remove the basting stitches and the tape.

6. Fold the front borders over to the back, turn the raw edges under ¼", and blindstitch. Stitch the two short ends first, then the two longer sides, to form square corners.

Mrs. Mondrian's Potholder

Let modern art assume a traditional use in your kitchen. This project uses a different application of strip piecing, based on the time-honored Log Cabin square. The preparation is super fast and simple with a rotary cutter.

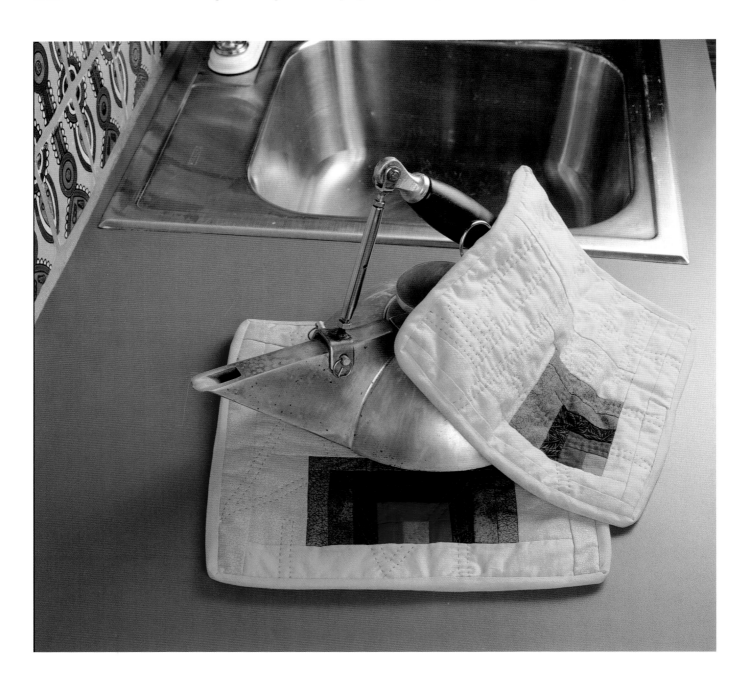

YOU WILL NEED

(for three potholders)
½ yard of print fabric
1 package of craft-size batting
½ yard of denim
½ yard of unbleached muslin
¼ yard of each: pink, red, brown, dark green,
    medium green, and yellow print fabric
¼ yard of yellow fabric
Rotary cutter
Rotary mat and ruler
¼" quilter's masking tape
Red quilting thread
1 package of yellow wide single-fold bias tape
1 metal D-ring

Use ¼" seams throughout.

MEASURE AND CUT
FOR THE POTHOLDER

Print fabric: one square, 10" x 10"
Batting: one square, 9½" x 9½"
Denim: two squares, each 9½" x 9½"
Muslin: one square, 12" x 12"

MEASURE AND CUT FOR
THE PIECED TOP

(See figure 5–2.)
Pink fabric (no. 1): one square, 1" x 1"
Red fabric (nos. 2 and 3): one strip, 1" x 4"
Brown fabric (nos. 4 and 5): one strip, 1" x 5"
Dark green fabric (nos. 6 and 7): one strip, 1" x 6"
Medium green fabric (nos. 8 and 9): one strip, 1" x 8"
Yellow print fabric (nos. 10 and 11): one strip,
    2" x 10"
Yellow fabric (nos. 12 and 13): one strip, 3½" x 15"
Yellow fabric (nos. 14, 15, 16, and 17): four strips,
    each 1" x 10"

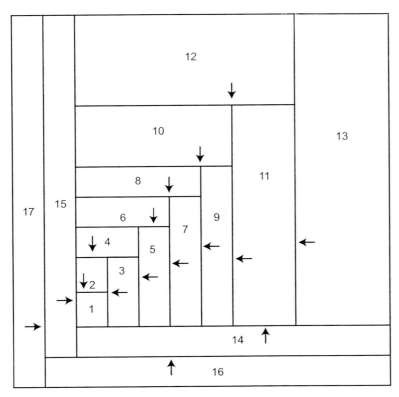

5–2. Potholder piecing sequence

1. Align the pink square about 3" from the lower left-hand corner of the muslin square, right side up. Place the dark red strip on the pink square, right sides together, aligning the top, bottom, and left sides. (You will have excess fabric on the right side.) Stitch along the top.

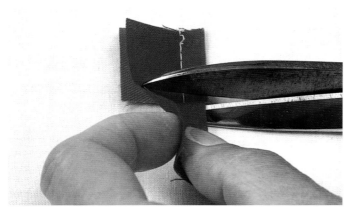

2. Trim off the excess fabric even with the pink square, as shown in the photo. Open and press. Now lay the remaining red strip over pieces 1 and 2, align the right edges, and stitch along the right side. Open and press. Continue sewing in this fashion, following the order shown in figure 5–2; the arrows will indicate which edge to stitch first. (Note that each strip will be cut and the remainder used for the second strip in that color, as in steps 1 and 2, except for strips 14 through 17.) When you finish, measure to be sure that your piece is square. If it isn't, trim to a square.

3. Use the masking tape to make random geometric shapes. Pin or baste the batting square to the back of the strip-pieced square. Quilt along both sides of the tape, removing it when you are finished.

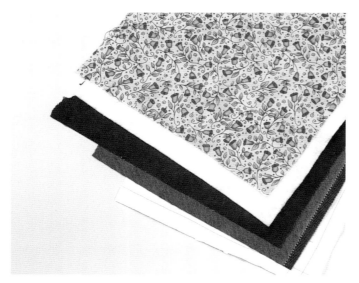

Variation: Once you have perfected this technique, you can vary it to create your own designs. For example, alter this piecing design to create a companion potholder to this project. You can also increase the dimensions of the potholder and make a complementary hot pad; because of the small amounts of fabric needed for this project, you will have enough left over to create both of these accompanying pieces.

4. Pin together the quilted square (right side down), two denim squares, and backing print square (right side up). (If you prefer extra insulation, add another square of batting, as shown.) Open the bias tape, fold over the raw end 1/2", and pin to all four sides, placing the right side of the bias tape against the right side of the front. Stitch the bias tape to the potholder, overlapping the ends. Fold the tape over and blind-stitch in place on the back, mitering at the corners. Attach the D-ring with needle and thread.

Evening Star Place Mat

Elongated pieces are a slight challenge, but the effect is worth the effort. To achieve the best results, follow the instructions closely. Use an assortment of off-white fabrics to create this simple ornamentation for your table; it's beautiful, functional, and patterned after the traditional evening star motif.

YOU WILL NEED

(For four place mats)
¼ yard of off-white gingham fabric
⅓ yard of green fabric
¾ yard of off-white print fabric
1 yard of off-white print fabric (for the back)
1 package of craft-size batting

Templates (page 472)
Fine-point pen or pencil
One sheet of quilter's template plastic
¾" masking tape
Quilting hoop
Off-white quilting thread
Quilting pattern (page 473)

MEASURE AND CUT

(For one place mat)

Gingham fabric: one rectangle, 4" x 5½"

Green fabric: four triangles from template A
four triangles from template B

Off-white print fabric: four triangles from template A
four triangles from template B
four rectangles, each 4" x 5½"
two strips, each 2" x 11"
two strips, each 2" x 18½"

Off-white print fabric (for the back): one rectangle,
14" x 18½"

Batting: one rectangle, 14" x 18½"

Use ¼" seams throughout.

1. Trace template patterns A and B onto the quilter's template plastic and cut out on the line. Next, place these templates onto the fabric, align the arrow on the template with the straight grain of the fabric, and cut according to the list above. Trace the templates onto the fabric carefully, and then cut on the marked lines precisely.

2. Placing the right sides together, pin all the green A pieces to the off-white B pieces, and pin all the off-white A pieces to all of the green B pieces. Note that the A and B pieces will be offset and should not meet exactly; when pinning, make sure that the B piece extends ¼", as in the photo. This offset creates the seam allowance that will allow the four triangles to meet to form a rectangle. Stitch all the pieces together and press the seam allowances to the darker side.

3. Next, you will make rectangles by sewing together the bicolored triangles. To make sure you will have the proper seam to allow the triangles to form a rectangle, place the bicolored triangles together (right sides facing), and hold them up to a light source. At the point where the two diagonal seams meet, there should be a ¼" seam allowance, as shown in the photo. Stitch all the triangles together to form four rectangles.

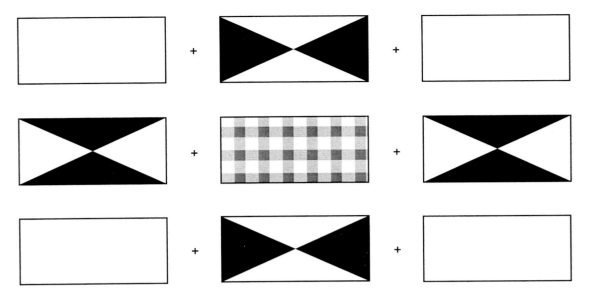

4. Piece the rows as illustrated, adding the off-white print rectangles. Now, line up the seams and sew the rows to one another; press. Sew the shorter off-white strips on the sides for borders, and press. Then stitch the remaining strips onto the top and the bottom, backstitching at the beginning and end of each border. Press the top of the place mat.

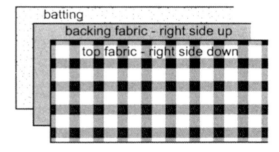

5. Sandwich the layers and pin together: batting at the bottom, then the backing, right side up; and last the top, right side down. Sew together, leaving a gap at one end. Trim the corners and trim the batting close to the seam line. Turn right side out and gently push the corners out to a point. Turn the unfinished raw edges inward and blindstitch the gap closed.

TIP: Remember—you have enough fabric left for three more place mats!

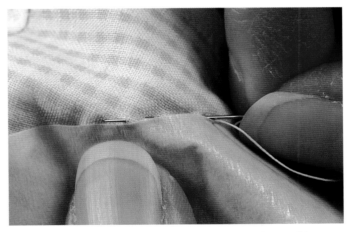

6. Baste. Then mark the top for quilting with the masking tape, finding the midpoint on each side of the center rectangle; form a central diamond here. (See the quilting pattern on page 473 for reference.) Extend the lines through the border, but do not quilt through the green fabric. Put your place mat into a hoop and quilt, working from the center out. Outline quilt around every green piece, extending into the border. Now, quilt around the entire place mat, $1/4$" from the outer edge. Remove the tape and basting.

Crazy Quilt Evening Bag

This bag is a jewel of an accessory for a simple cocktail dress, combining sumptuous fabrics with romantic embroidery. It may use crazy quilt construction, but the effect is dazzling—definitely not crazy.

YOU WILL NEED

Templates (page 474)
⅛ yard of unbleached muslin
Permanent marker
Scraps of silk, satin, and velvet fabrics
Skeins of embroidery floss in
     various colors
Embroidery hoop
Embroidery needle
¼ yard of pink silk
¼ yard of black velvet
1 package of craft-size batting
1 yard of black medium round cord
6" of black thin cord
Decorative button

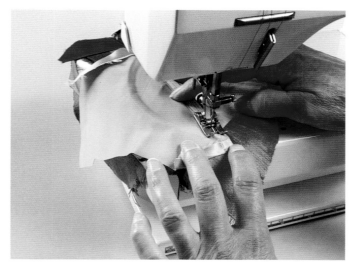

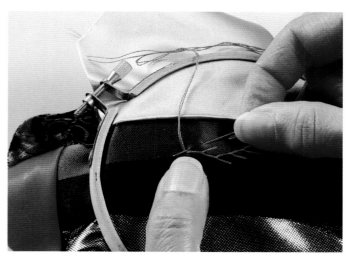

1. Transfer the templates onto paper, enlarge 200 percent, and cut them out. Use the pocket template to cut one piece from the muslin. Sew the silk, satin, and velvet scraps to the muslin in random fashion, using crazy quilt piecing (see page 420). Begin with one scrap right side up. Then add the second scrap, right side down on the first scrap, and stitch along one edge through all layers. Open and press. Continue in this fashion as shown until the entire piece of muslin is covered. Trim the sewn scraps even with the muslin edge. Staystitch around the pocket a scant ⅛" from the edge.

2. Embellish the pocket with embroidery, but use only two strands of the embroidery floss to fit the small scale of this project. (See page 475 for embroidery stitches.)

3. Next, cut one pocket from the pink fabric. Pin the pink lining to the completed crazy quilt pocket, right sides together. Stitch across the top only. Turn the pocket right side out and press. As before, staystitch the raw edges together with a scant ⅛" seam.

4. Using the templates, cut one front and one back from the black velvet. Repeat for the batting. Baste the batting pieces to the back of each velvet piece. Lay the velvet/batting back piece on your work surface, velvet side up. Now place the embroidered pocket on the back piece, embroidered side down, aligning the straight bottom edges. Place the velvet/batting front piece on top, velvet side down. Align the bottom edges. (Note that the curved top of the bag is pictured at the bottom of this photo.)

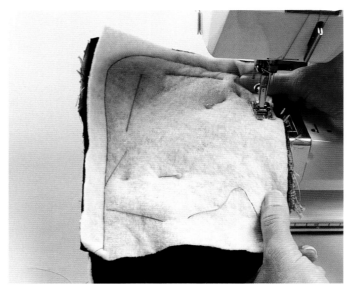 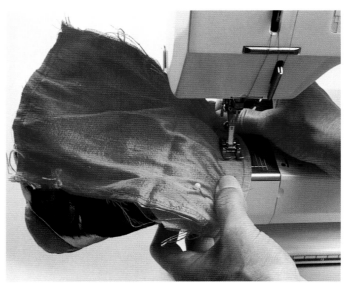

5. Pin; stitch the sides and the bottom, through all layers. Turn right side out.

6. Using the templates, cut the front and back pieces from lining fabric. Placing right sides together, pin and sew. Leave the lining wrong side out, and stitch the front top edge of the lining to the front top edge of the velvet bag, right sides together. Push the lining into the velvet bag.

7. Cut the medium black cord to the desired length for a shoulder bag. Tack each end between the lining and the velvet bag at the side seams, as shown. Turn the raw edges of the black velvet flap and the lining flap under about $\frac{1}{8}$". Pin together and hand stitch to finish the top. Cut the thin black cord to the desired length, and make a loop by sewing the two ends together in the center of the underside of the flap. Sew the decorative button onto the center of the front pocket to complete the closure.

Silk Pillbox Hat

This stylish headgear is special because it is made of silk. When determining your hat size, be sure to measure and calculate carefully so you get a good fit.

YOU WILL NEED

Drafting compass
¼ yard of teal fabric
¼ yard of teal print fabric
⅓ yard of pink fabric
1 package of craft-size batting
Gold metallic quilting thread
Quilting pattern (page 471)
  or purchased stencil
Fabric marking pencil

TO DETERMINE
YOUR HAT SIZE

Measure your head at the point where you will wear the hat. This measurement—plus ½" seam allowance—will be the length of your band. The band's width will be 4". To draft a circle of a suitable size, refer to the chart below. If your head measurement differs from those given, choose the next size up for your circle's diameter. You can then ease it in to fit the band that is your correct size.

Head Measurement in Inches =
Circle Diameter in Inches

Head Measurement in Inches	Circle Diameter in Inches
22	7
22⅜	7⅛
22¾	7¼
23⅛	7⅜
23½	7½

Use ¼" seams throughout.

1. Measure and cut a circle of the appropriate size from the solid teal fabric and a circle from the pink lining fabric. Referring to your head measurement, cut a 4"-wide band from the teal print fabric and the pink lining fabric, being sure to add the ½" seam allowance to your head measurement. Staystitch all edges to prevent the silk from fraying. Cut a circle from the batting. Fold the two fabric circles into quarters, and press lightly to make four equidistant marks.

2. Place the ends of the outer band right sides together and stitch. Press the seam to one side. Fold and press to find four equidistant points, with the seam being one point. Transfer the quilting pattern onto the right side of the teal fabric circle; draw a freehand design based on our pattern, or use a purchased stencil. Pin the batting to the teal circle, and quilt. Now, pin the quilted top to the teal outer band as shown, right sides together, matching the four equidistant points. Stitch all the way around, easing in any fullness.

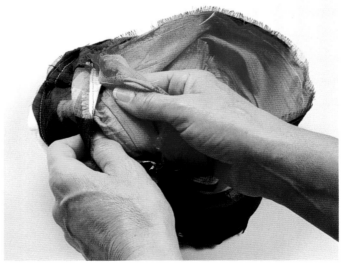

4. Turn the hat right side out, pulling carefully through the 4" gap. Press. Blindstitch the gap closed.

Variation: Add batting to the band, and quilt it in addition to the top. Use a star or spiral for the quilting pattern on top.

3. Carefully trim the batting to the seam line. Turn the outer shell right side out. Repeat step 2 with the lining fabric, but omit the batting and quilting. Pin the outer shell (turned right side out) inside the inner shell (turned inside out), matching seams and equidistant points. Pin along the edge and stitch as shown, leaving a gap of about 2" on either side of the seam.

Quilted Vest

Transform a simple garment into a one-of-a-kind fashion statement. You will appreciate the versatility of this reversible design, though the project does involve a fair amount of both sewing and quilting.

YOU WILL NEED

An easy vest pattern
Red fabric
Print fabric
1 package of crib-size batting
Custom bias binding (page 443) to fit pattern, 1½" (wide, or packaged bias tape
¾" masking tape
Red quilting thread
Button(s), thin silk cord for fastening loop (optional)

MEASURE AND CUT

Two fronts and one back in red fabric, print fabric, and batting, per pattern requirements

Note: Buy a pattern that is one size larger than your usual size, as the quilting will draw up the fabric. Ignore the sewing instructions and extraneous pieces in the pattern; you just need the pieces for the front and the back. Take the yardage requirements from the pattern, and when you are selecting fabrics, choose a solid fabric for the outside to highlight the quilting.

Use the standard ⅝" garment seam, except when applying bias binding.

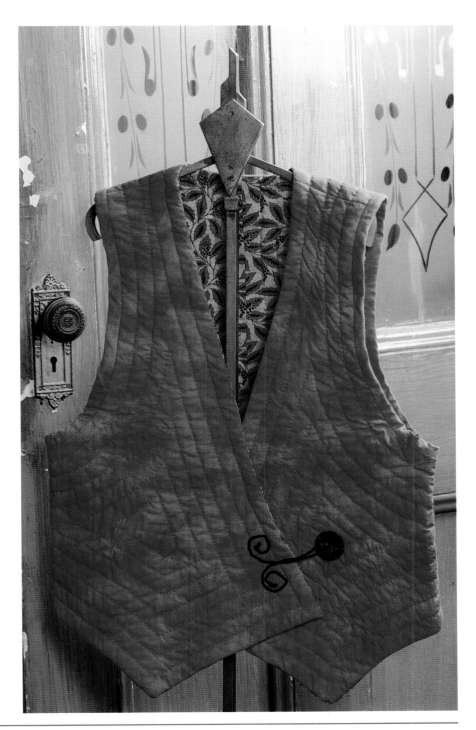

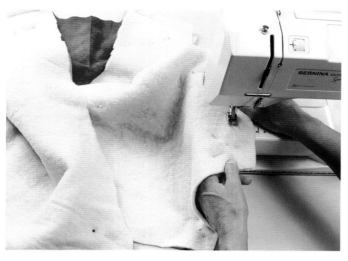

1. Beginning with the print fabric, place the vest fronts and the back right sides together, and stitch at the shoulders and sides. Press the seams open. Next, pin the batting pieces to the wrong side of the red fabric. As shown, stitch the red fabric together at the shoulders and sides, right sides together, as with the print fabric. Trim the batting close to the seams; press open. Place the print and red vests right sides together, and stitch the neck and the outer edges. Do not stitch the armholes.

2. Clip the curves at the neck. Turn the garment right side out through one armhole. Press, concentrating on the edges so they look crisp.

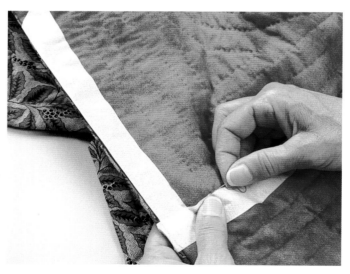

4. Using the masking tape, establish a quilting line along the edge and side seams of the vest, as shown. Quilt, filling up the body of the vest with echo quilting. Remove the tape when you are done. Add fasteners or ties, if desired.

3. To bind the armholes, measure and cut bias strips (see page 443) according to the circumference of the armholes, adding 1" for overlap. Fold the raw end of the bias binding over ½" and pin in place, with the right side of the binding against the outer side of the armhole. Sew the binding on with a ¼" seam; continue stitching until the raw end of the binding overlaps your starting point. Fold the binding over, turn the raw edge under, and blindstitch to the inside, as shown. Repeat for the other armhole. (You may also use packaged bias tape in this step, if you prefer.)

Tips: Use metallic quilting thread—or a contrasting color—for more drama. Instead of a solid for the outer fabric, choose a bold stripe or distinctive print and use it as your quilting guide.

Hawaiian Quilting Appliqué

This heritage quilting technique from the islands makes a unique adornment for a shoulder bag. This method can also be used to create other decorative items for your home—a throw pillow or a wall hanging, perhaps.

YOU WILL NEED

¼ yard of red fabric
¼ yard of turquoise fabric
1 package of craft-size batting
Template (page 475)
Paper
Ballpoint or marking pen
Quilting hoop
Fabric shoulder bag, homemade or
   purchased
Red and turquoise quilting thread

MEASURE AND CUT

Red fabric: one square for the background, cut to your desired measurement, plus ½" on each side
Batting: one square, cut to the same size as the red fabric
Turquoise fabric: one piece, cut to the instructions in steps 1 and 2

Use ¼" seams throughout.

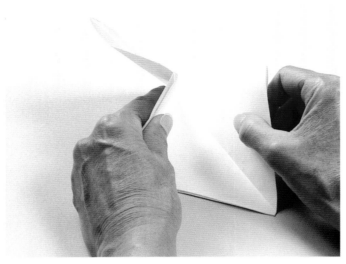

1. Trace the template for the appliqué onto a piece of paper, and cut it out. If you prefer, you can create your own template: Cut a paper square about 1" smaller than the finished size of the background square. Fold the paper in half top to bottom. Fold in half again side to side. Finally, fold in half diagonally. (This is like those snowflakes you cut out as a child.) Experiment by cutting along the edges until you have a pleasing pattern when you unfold the paper. Keep it fairly simple and make your cuts rounded, as sharp angles are harder to appliqué well.

2. Fold the turquoise fabric as described above (fold in half top to bottom, fold again in half side to side, and then in half diagonally). Use our paper template or the one you made in step 1, and place it against the fold of the fabric; then trace around it. Cut it out, open, and press.

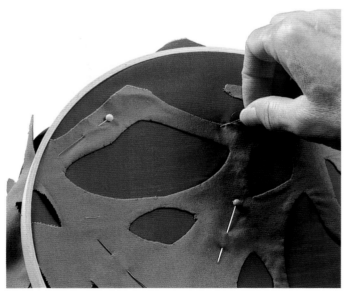

3. Center the fabric appliqué on the background fabric, and pin in place. Place into the quilting hoop and appliqué with a blindstitch, turning under the edges of the appliqué as you go. (See page 425.)

4. Pin or baste the appliquéd fabric to the batting. Echo quilt as desired. Turn the raw edges under and press. Pin the square to the bag and blindstitch in place.

Lazy Day Pillow

The soft colors and simple lines of this pillow evoke a summertime feeling, and illustrate the possibilities of easy four-patch block construction. It would be wonderful in a hammock, wouldn't it?

YOU WILL NEED

1/3 yard of cream fabric
1/3 yard of yellow fabric
3/4 yard of green fabric
1 3/4 yards of blue fabric
One package of craft-size batting

Fabric marking pencil
Ruler
3/4" masking tape
Cream, yellow, green, and blue quilting thread
20" pillow form

Use 1/4" seams throughout.

MEASURE AND CUT

Cream fabric: one square, 10½" x 10½"

Yellow fabric: one square, 10½" x 10 ½"

Green fabric: one square, 10½" x 10½"
  two strips, 2½" x 28"

Blue fabric: one square, 10½" x 10½"
  two strips, 2½" x 28"
  two rectangles, 20" x 24½"

Batting: one square, 25" x 25"

1. Stitch the fabric squares together as in the photo, and then press the seams to the darker side. Find and mark the horizontal center of one of the blue strips, which you will use for the border. Match this center mark to the center seam of the pillow front, and pin the blue strip to the pillow front, right sides together. Stitch, starting and stopping ¼" from each end. Sew the other blue strip onto an adjacent side, and then sew the green strips onto the remaining sides of the pillow front, being sure to stop stitching ¼" from each end.

2. To miter the corners (see page 442), fold the pillow front horizontally. Place a ruler along the fold at one corner, extending over the border strips. Mark the border, as in the photo, and sew along the marked line. Trim the mitered seam to ¼", and press to one side. Press the border seams outward. Repeat for each of the remaining corners.

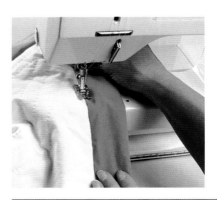

3. Mark the center of each side of each square with a straight pin. Follow the design in the photograph to place the masking tape for marking the basic diamond shape. Pin or baste the pillow front to the square of batting. (A backing is not necessary.) Quilt the diamond shapes, and then quilt the rest of the square as shown, moving the tape to mark successive outlines on the pillow front. Remove all tape when finished.

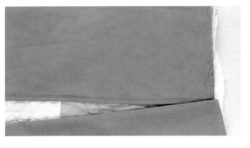

4. After the front of the pillow cover is quilted, add the pillow back. Begin by machine hemming one long edge of each blue rectangle. Then, pin the long raw edge of one rectangle to the top of the quilted front, placing right sides together. Pin the second rectangle to the bottom of the pillow front, right sides together. The second piece will overlap the first. (The photo shows the first rectangle as it is being covered by the second rectangle.) Stitch around all four sides of the pillow cover.

5. Turn the pillow cover right side out. Press. Topstitch as closely as possible along the border seam—not in the border. Lastly, insert the pillow form.

Lap Quilt

This Amish-inspired project is a soft and cuddly throw for a winter's day…snuggle under its flannel backing and watch the snow fall. Don't forget the hot chocolate. If you want to learn to use a rotary cutter, this quilt provides a good opportunity to practice that skill.

YOU WILL NEED

½ yard of royal blue fabric
½ yard of squash fabric
½ yard of red fabric
½ yard of black fabric
½ yard of purple fabric
1 yard of olive fabric
1½ yards of mauve fabric
1½ yards of navy blue fabric
3 yards of gray flannel fabric
1 package of crib-size batting
Rotary cutter (optional)
Rotary mat and ruler (optional)
Paper or cardboard
White fabric marking pencil
¾" masking tape
Quilt hoop
Royal blue, squash, red, black, purple, and olive
    quilting thread
2 packages of black extra-wide double-fold bias tape

MEASURE AND CUT

Royal blue fabric: three squares,
    each 11½" x 11½"
Squash fabric: two squares, each 11½" x 11½"
Red fabric: two squares, each 11½" x 11½"
Black fabric: two squares, each 11½" x 11½"
Purple fabric: one square, 11½" x 11½"
Olive fabric: two squares, each 11½" x 11½"
    two strips, each 3½" x 39¼"
Mauve fabric: two strips, each 1½" x 35½"
    two strips, each 1½" x 44¾"
Navy fabric: two strips, each 2" x 46¾"
Flannel: two pieces, cut selvage to selvage at the
    midpoint of the entire yardage
Batting: one piece, 45" x 58"

Use ¼" seams throughout.

1. Sew the squares into rows, right sides together, according to the design shown in the photo. Press the seams to the darker side. Then sew the rows to one another, right sides together. Next, sew on the borders, all with right sides together, in this order: the longer mauve strips on the sides; the remaining mauve strips on the top and the bottom; the navy strips on the sides; and finally the olive borders on the top and bottom. Press the completed top. Sew the two pieces of flannel together along their longer edges, right sides together. Press the seam open. Now sandwich the layers: flannel on the bottom, right side down, and then center the batting on the flannel. Now add the top, right side up, also entered. Smooth the wrinkles and baste. You will have more flannel than you'll need; for ease of handling, trim it so you have an excess of only 3" all the way around—after basting.

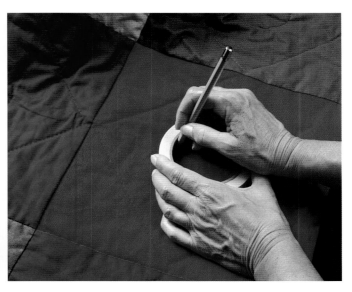

2. Measure and cut a 7³⁄₈" square paper or cardboard template. Center the paper template on a middle quilt square. Carefully place masking tape around the perimeter of the template, as shown. Remove the template, and quilt along the inside of the square of tape.

3. Use the roll of masking tape as the other template. Place it in the center of the quilted square, and trace along the inside with a fabric marking pencil. Quilt along these markings. Continue in this manner to finish quilting inside the squares.

4. Quilt around each block in the ditch. Continue until you have quilted the entire top. Mark straight lines on the borders with masking tape, and quilt. Remove the basting thread and tape when you finish. Trim along all four sides of the quilt to align the three layers. To apply bias tape, first sew the two lengths of tape together in a ¼" seam. Then, fold over the raw end of the bias tape ½" and pin to the quilt, right sides together. Stitch, overlapping at the end. Fold the tape over to the back of the quilt, and blindstitch down by hand; be careful not to catch the quilt top with your stitches.

Embroidered Window Valance

Add an elegant touch to your window with this valance, constructed of brushed denim in rich colors. You will enjoy the lush texture of this fabric; it is the perfect backdrop for quilting and embroidery.

YOU WILL NEED

¼ yard of maroon brushed denim fabric
¼ yard of dark green brushed denim fabric
¼ yard of medium green brushed denim fabric
⅔ yard of black fabric
Fabric marking pencil
1 skein each of cream, blue, light brown, moss
   green, gold, and silver-gray embroidery floss
Embroidery needle
Embroidery hoop (optional)
1 package of crib-size batting
Black quilting thread
Quilting hoop (optional)
Wooden dowel (to fit valance)

MEASURE AND CUT

Maroon fabric: four squares, each 5⅞" x 5⅞"
Dark green fabric: four squares, each 5⅞" x 5⅞"
Medium green fabric: two strips, each 3" x 40½"
Black fabric: one piece, 10½" x 40½"
   one strip, 3" x 40"
Batting: one rectangle, 12" x 43"

Use ¼" seams throughout.

1. Cut the maroon and dark green squares on the diagonal, yielding eight triangles of each color. Match each maroon triangle with a green triangle, being sure to place the softer, brushed right sides together. Sew the pairs of triangles together along the diagonal to make eight two-color squares. Press the squares open, with the seams to the darker side. Sew the squares together to form a row. Placing the right sides together, sew a medium green strip to each long edge of the row. Press the seams outward; press the top.

2. Using the fabric marking pencil, draw a freehand design onto the top; embroider along your design, using only two strands of floss. (You can use an embroidery hoop if desired, but the denim has so much body that you may not need one.) Remove the marks when finished. Note the gradation of colors.

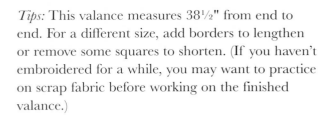

Tips: This valance measures 38½" from end to end. For a different size, add borders to lengthen or remove some squares to shorten. (If you haven't embroidered for a while, you may want to practice on scrap fabric before working on the finished valance.)

Variation: For a more rustic look, use a branch from the woods to hang this valance.

3. To sandwich the valance: Place the batting on a work surface and smooth; then place the black piece of backing on top, centered, with its right side up. Place the pieced top on the backing, right side down, aligning the edges of both fabrics. Pin well around the edges. Stitch with the fabric side up, being sure to catch all three layers. Leave a 6" gap at one short end for turning the valance right side out. Carefully trim the batting, as shown.

4. Trim the corners. Turn the valance right side out. Fold the edges of the gap inward, and blindstitch closed. Quilt around the inside of each triangle and along the edge of each long border. (Use a quilting hoop if desired.) With your machine, topstitch around the valance, ⅛" from the edge, as shown. Make a hanging sleeve (see page 445) from the black fabric strip, and attach using a blindstitch. Insert a wooden dowel through the sleeve to hang.

African Women Wall Hanging

Your quilting skills and your imagination can enhance a piece of unique fabric. Here, a design featuring African women carrying gourd vessels is enhanced with quilting and beads. There are many pictorial fabrics available; choose one that captures your fancy and embellish as your heart desires.

YOU WILL NEED

²/₃ yard of pictorial print fabric
¹/₂ yard of maroon fabric
¹/₂ yard of green fabric
²/₃ yard of black fabric
1 package of craft-size batting
Assorted small beads: black, wooden, and colored
Black quilting thread
Quilting hoop
Fabric marking pen or pencil
1 package of black extra-wide double-fold
    bias tape
Dowel or rod

MEASURE AND CUT

Print fabric: one rectangle, 10³/₄" x 18"
    one rectangle, 9¹/₂" x 18"
Maroon fabric: one rectangle, 6³/₄" x 18"
    one strip, 2⁵/₈" x 18"
Green fabric: one rectangle, 7¹/₂" x 18"
    one strip, 2" x 18"
    one strip, 3" x 38"
Black fabric: one rectangle, 19" x 37"
Batting: one rectangle, approximately 21" x 40"

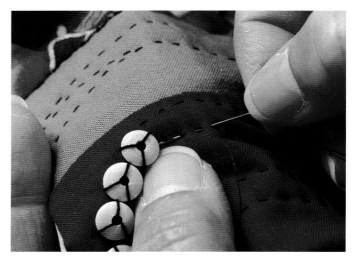

2. With the marking pen or pencil, draw a freehand quilting design on all the solid-colored fabric. Sew the wooden beads on to complement these designs. Now sandwich the layers: black fabric on the bottom, right side down; batting in the center; then the multi-colored panel on top, right side up. Baste. Place the hanging into the quilting hoop (careful of your beads!). Quilt along the design of the print fabric in several places on each panel to secure the batting; quilt the solid panels.

1. Sew the 18"-wide fabric pieces together in the following order, from left to right: wide maroon, wide print, narrow green, narrow maroon, narrow print, and wide green. Press the seams to one side. (Be sure to do it now, because you can't press after the beads have been sewn on.) With quilting thread and needle, add the colored beads to the print fabric, making all of the knots on the back of the fabric.

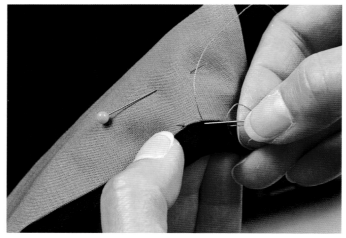

3. Remove all marks and basting thread. Trim the batting and backing fabrics to the size of the top, if necessary. Sew the bias tape around the raw edges of the front of the wall hanging, right sides together; fold over and blindstitch on the back. Make a hanging sleeve (see page 445) from the remaining strip of green fabric, and attach, as shown. Insert the dowel or rod through the sleeve.

CHAPTER 6

Contemporary Quilting

With material by Cheryl Fall

The blocks of color and selective piecing used on "Desert Nights" not only cut down
on the time it takes to make the quilt, but contribute to its fresh, contemporary style.

Village Streets Lap Quilt

Reminiscent of New England row houses, this charming quilt works up in a flash. Because there are no bias edges or triangle pieces to worry about, it is an excellent project for a beginner. Change the colors of the houses to suit your own décor, but try to use a nice floral fabric for the borders. Finished size: 40" x 52".

MATERIALS

⅓ yard of fabric in each of 3 colors for the houses: medium blue, medium teal, and medium pink, the model

4" x 33" strip in each of 3 roof colors: mustard, medium rose, and light blue in the model

¼ yard of pale green print fabric for the horizontal "grass" rows

⅔ yard black fabric for the windows, doors, and inner border

2½" x 24" strip of brick red solid fabric for the chimneys

⅓ yard tan fabric for the chimney rows

1½ yards of a coordinating floral print fabric for the outer border

42" x 54" piece of quilt batting

42" x 54" piece of backing fabric of choice

5½ yards of black double-fold quilt binding (folded width, ½"; unfolded width, 2")

All-purpose sewing thread in a neutral color and black

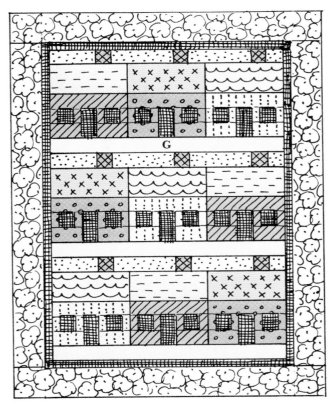

1–1. Construction diagram of the quilt.

CUTTING GUIDE

Quantity	Size	Use
Black fabric:		
Three	2½" x 17"	windows (W)
One	2½" x 30"	doors (K)
Two	1½" x 42½"	inner border
Two	1½" x 30½"	inner border
Floral border fabric:		
Two	4½" x 40½"	top/bottom outer border
Two	4½" x 44½"	side outer border

Quantity	Size	Use
From each house color cut:		
Two	1½" x 17"	A pieces
One	2½" x 30"	B pieces
One	2½" x 33"	C pieces
Tan fabric:		
One	8½" x 24"	E and H pieces
One	2½" x 8"	F squares
Pale green print:		
Three	2½" x 30½"	G strips

DIRECTIONS

All construction is done right sides of fabric facing and seam allowances of ½", which are included in the given measurements.

1. Cut your fabric strips as indicated in the cutting guides for each fabric.

2. Look at the quilt construction diagram, 1–1, and the house construction diagram, 1–2, to familiarize yourself with the parts of the project.

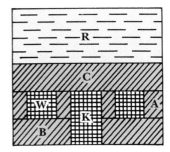

1–2. Construction diagram of a house block

1–4. B piece stitched.

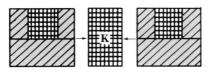

1–5. Joining two AWA window units to a door (K).

5. Take the 2½" x 30" strip of house color 1 and cut it into six 2½" x 4½" B pieces. Do the same for house color 2 and house color 3.

6. Stitch a B piece on its long side below each AWA unit, as shown in figure 1–4, to make an AWA+B unit. The A and B pieces should be of the same color within the same unit. Do this for all eighteen AWA units. Set them aside.

7. Take the 2½" x 30" black strip and cut six 2½" x 4½" doors (K) from it.

8. On both long sides of a K piece (door), sew an AWA+B unit (see figure 1–5). The two AWA+B pieces that are on either side of one door should be of the same house color. The unit formed is the

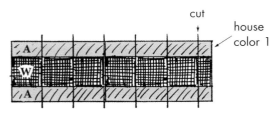

1–3. Cutting the AWA window units.

3. First we'll make the window units (AWA) of the house. Take one black 2½" x 17" strip and two 1½" x 17" strips of the first house color (we'll call it house color 1). Referring to figure 1–3, seam them together on a long side to make an AWA strip and cut across all three strips to make 2½"-wide AWA window units. Make six AWA window units with house color 1. Set them aside.

4. Repeat step 3 with house colors 2 and 3. Set the AWA units aside.

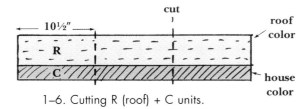

1–6. Cutting R (roof) + C units.

1–7. Joining an RC unit to a windows + door unit to make a house block.

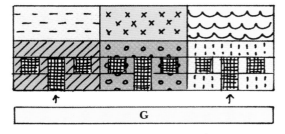

1–8. G strip stitched to the bottom of a house.

windows + door unit. Repeat eight more times. Set the units aside.

9. Take the 2½" x 33" piece of fabric of house color 1 and the 4½" x 33" strip of the roof fabric that goes with that house color (see photo). Seam them together on one long side. Then cut across a two-strip unit to make three 10½"-wide RC units from house color 1, as shown in figure 1–6. Repeat for the other two roof strips and the other two 2½" x 33" strips of house color fabric (house colors 2 and 3).

10. Take each RC unit and match it up with the windows + door unit from step 8 that has the same house color as C. Stitch the RC piece to the windows + door unit as shown in figure 1–7 to make a house block. Repeat for a total of nine house blocks.

11. Referring to the color photo for placement if necessary, stitch 3 of the house blocks together along their sides to form a house row. Press. Stitch one pale green 2½" x 30½" G strip to the bottom of each house row (figure 1–8). Press the seam allowances towards the G strip. Repeat for the other two house rows. Set them aside.

12. Take your 8½" x 24" piece of tan fabric and your 2½" x 24" strip of brick red fabric for the chimneys. Seam them together on a long side and slice across the two strips to make nine 2½"-wide ED units as shown in figure 1–9a. Trim three of them so the tan side becomes 6½" (see figure 1–9b); the trimmed ones are now DH units.

13. Cut three 2½" x 2½" F squares from the tan 2½" x 8" strip. Then stitch a DH unit to two ED units and an F square to make a chimney row, as shown in figure 1–10. Make two more chimney rows the same way and press the seam allowances towards the darker fabric.

14. Stitch one chimney row to the top edge of each house row + G strip from step 11. Press the seam allowances towards the chimney rows (figure 1–11).

15. Stitch together the 3 house + chimney row units made in step 14 to form the quilt center (figure 1–12). Press.

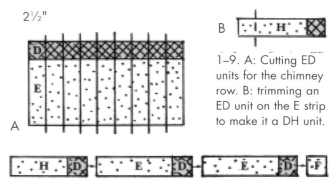

1–9. A: Cutting ED units for the chimney row. B: trimming an ED unit on the E strip to make it a DH unit.

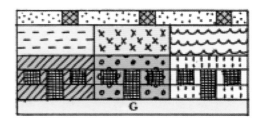

1–10. Stitching together the pieces to form a chimney row.

1–11. A house + chimney row.

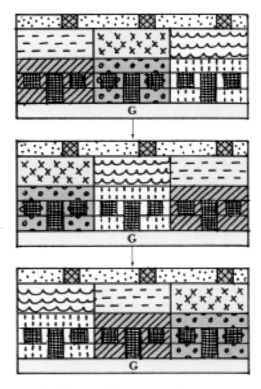

1–12. Assembling the quilt center.

16. See figure 1–13 for all border attachment steps. Stitch one 42½" black border strip to the left and one to the right side of your quilt center. Stitch one 32½" black border strip to the top and one to the bottom of the quilt center.

17. Stitch one 44½" x 4½" floral border strip to the left and one to the right of the quilt center made in step 16. Stitch one 4½" x 40½" floral border strip to the top and one to the bottom of the quilt. This completes the quilt top.

18. Tape the quilt back to your work surface, wrong side up, center the batting over the backing, and center the quilt top right-side up over the batting. Hand-baste or pin-baste the layers together. Referring to Chapter 8—How to Quilt, pages 434 to 441. Hand or machine quilt it as desired.

19. After quilting, baste around the outside edges of the quilt top, about ½" in from the raw edges, and trim away the excess batting and backing fabric that extend beyond the quilt top to prepare the quilt for the binding.

20. Bind the quilt with the bias binding, using black thread; see Chapter 8—How to Quilt, page 443 for more binding information.

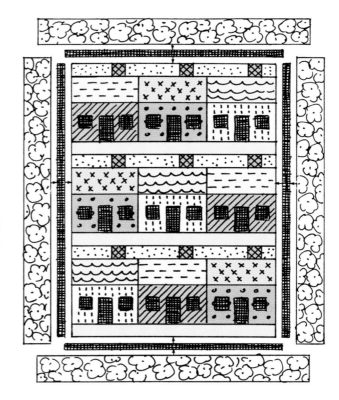

1–13. Attaching borders to the quilt center.

Scandinavian Woods Quilt and Runner

This quick-to-make set would be a lovely Christmas gift for a special friend. Reminiscent of the old German feather trees, it's sure to bring old-world charm to any room. The border, quilted with pearl cotton, adds an extra dimension to the quilting. Finished quilt size: 33" x 33"; finished runner size: 17" x 40"; finished block size: 11" x 11". Ornament size: 4" x 4".

MATERIALS FOR BOTH PROJECTS

½" yard green print fabric

¾" yard red print fabric

2½" yards tan or light brown fabric

All-purpose threads to match fabrics and binding

35" x 35" piece of quilt batting (for the quilt)

35" x 35" piece of fabric (for the quilt backing)

19" x 42" piece of quilt batting (for the runner)

19" x 42" piece of fabric (for the runner backing)

1 skein of green pearl cotton

7 yards of tan or light brown double-fold quilt
binding (folded width ½" ; unfolded width, 2"):
4 yards for the quilt
3 yards for the runner

CUTTING GUIDE

Quantity	Size	Use
Green fabric:		
One	1½" x ½"	A unit
One	2½" x 22"	B unit
One	3½" x 22"	C unit
One	4½" x 22"	D unit
One	5½" x 22"	E unit
Six	1½" x 10½"	trunks
Tan fabric:		
One	4½" x 22"	A unit
One	3½" x 22"	B unit
One	2½" x 22"	C unit
One	1½" x 22"	D unit
Three	5½" x 44"	F strips
Six	1½" x 11½"	G strips
Three	1½" x 25½"	H strips
Two	2½" x 27½"	middle borders, quilt
Two	2½" x 31½"	middle borders, quilt
Four	1½" x 11½"	I side bars, runner
Two	1½" x 13½"	Q strips, runner
One	12½" x 13½"	K block for runner

Red print fabric:		
Six	1½" x 1½"	treetop strips
Two	1½" x 25½"	inner border, quilt
Two	1½" x 27½"	inner border, quilt
Two	1½" x 33½"	outer border, quilt
Two	1½" x 31½"	outer border, quilt
Two	2½" x 36½"	L runner border
Two	2½" x 17½"	M runner border

DIRECTIONS

Construction is done with right sides of fabric facing and seam allowances of ¼", which are included in the given measurements. Always press the seam allowances towards the darker fabrics. Identical blocks (figure 2–1) are made for the quilt and the runner; you need four blocks for the quilt and two for the runner. Cutting guides and directions give cutting and piecing for quilt and runner blocks together; the assembly of each project is given
separately.

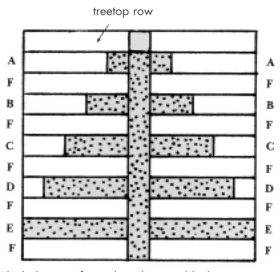

2–1. Block diagram for quilt and runner blocks.

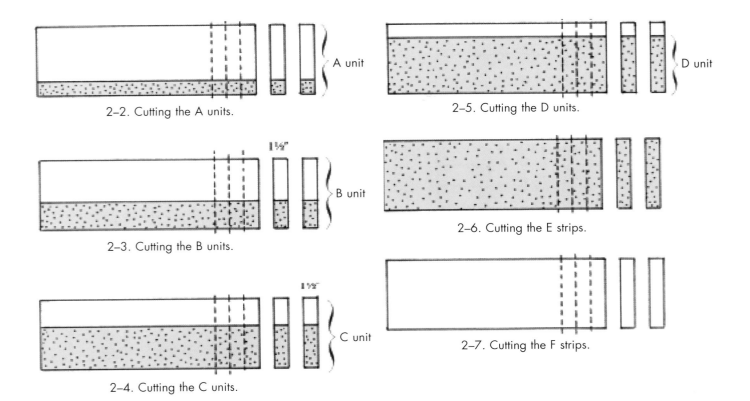

2–2. Cutting the A units.

2–3. Cutting the B units.

2–4. Cutting the C units.

2–5. Cutting the D units.

2–6. Cutting the E strips.

2–7. Cutting the F strips.

MAKING THE QUILT AND RUNNER BLOCKS

1. Following the cutting guides, cut all the strips necessary and tag them with the unit for which they will be used, so you can find them easily. The blocks are assembled from separate units (see figure 2–1), which we'll make next.

2. Take the tan $4\frac{1}{2}$" x 22" strip and the green $1\frac{1}{2}$" x 22" strip. Stitch them together along one long edge. Press the stitch open. Using a ruler and rotary cutter (or a scissors), cut across both strips to make twelve $1\frac{1}{2}$"-wide A units, as shown in figure 4–2. Set them aside.

3. To make the B units, take the $3\frac{1}{2}$" x 22" tan strip and the green $2\frac{1}{2}$" x 22" strip and stitch them together along one long side. Press open. Cut across both to make twelve $1\frac{1}{2}$"-wide B units, as shown in figure 4–3. Set them aside.

4. To make the C units, take the tan $2\frac{1}{2}$" x 22"

strip and the green $3\frac{1}{2}$" x 22" strip and stitch them together along one long edge; press the strip open. Cut across both strips to make twelve $1\frac{1}{2}$"-wide C units, as shown in figure 2–4. Set them aside.

5. To make the D units, take the tan $1\frac{1}{2}$" x 22" strip and the green $4\frac{1}{2}$" x 22" strip and stitch them together along one long edge; press open. Cut across both strips to make twelve $1\frac{1}{2}$"-wide D units, as shown in figure 2–5. Set them aside.

6. To make the E strips, take the green $5\frac{1}{2}$" x 22" strip and slice off twelve $1\frac{1}{2}$"-wide E pieces, as shown in figure 2–6. Set them aside.

7. To make the seventy-two F strips, take the three tan $5\frac{1}{2}$" x 44" strips and cut off seventy-two $1\frac{1}{2}$"-wide pieces (see figure 2–7). Forty-eight F strips are for the quilt; twenty-four are for the runner. Set them aside.

8. Take a red $1\frac{1}{2}$" square. Stitch one F strip to each of two opposite sides of the red square as shown in figure 2–8. Press. This is a treetop row. Make five

2–8. The completed treetop row.

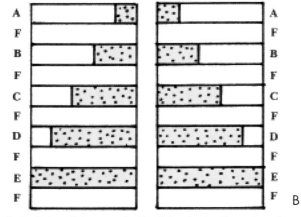

A   B

2–9. Sides of the tree. A. The left side. B. The right side.

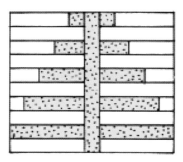

2–10. The tree block without the top row.

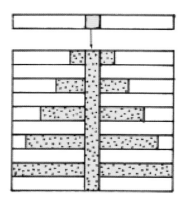

2–11. Stitch the treetop row to the top of the tree.

more treetop rows the same way. Set them aside.

9. To make the left side of one tree block, assemble units A, B, C, D, and E, alternating with five F strips, as shown in figure 2–9A. Press. Make the right side of the tree block as shown in figure 2–9B. It uses the same units as the left side, but they are assembled in a mirror image to the left side. Press. Make a total of six left sides and six right sides of the tree blocks in the same way.

10. Take a green 1½" x 10½" strip for the tree trunk. Stitch one left side and one right side of a tree to the trunk, as shown in figure 2–10. Make a total of six trees the same way. Press.

11. Stitch one of the treetop strips made in step 8 to the top of a tree block, as shown in figure 4-11 to complete the tree block; do the same for the other five tree blocks. Press the blocks.

QUILT ASSEMBLY (FOUR-BLOCK QUILT)

12. Take six tan 1½" x 1½" G strips and three tan 1½" x 25½" H strips. Stitch together three G strips, alternating with two tree blocks, to make a row as shown in figure 2–12A. Make a second row the same way. Press. Stitch the two tree rows to either side of an H strip and add two more H strips on the outer sides, as shown in figure 2–12B. Press. This makes the quilt center (figure 2–13).

BORDER ATTACHMENT OF QUILT AND FINISHING (FOUR-BLOCK QUILT)

13. Refer to figure 2–14 for steps 13 through 15. Take the two red 1½" x 25½" strips and stitch one to the top edge and one to the bottom edge of the quilt center. Press. Take two 1½" x 27½" red strips and stitch these to the sides. Press.

14. For the middle border, take the two tan 2½" x 27½" strips and stitch one strip to the top edge of the quilt center and one to the bottom edge. Press. Take the two tan 2½" x 31½" strips and stitch them to the side edges of the quilt. Press.

15. For the outer border, take the two red 1½" x

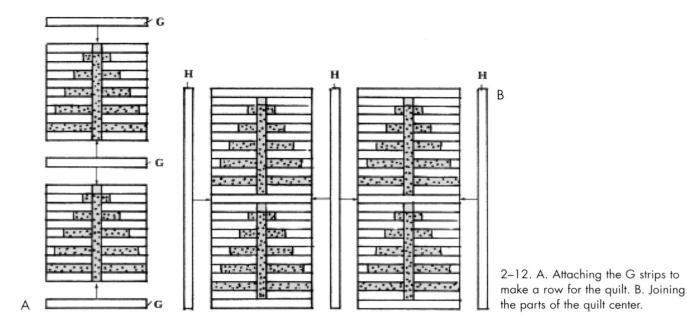

2–12. A. Attaching the G strips to make a row for the quilt. B. Joining the parts of the quilt center.

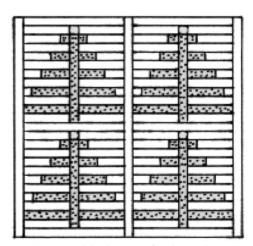

2–13. Assembly diagram for the quilt center.

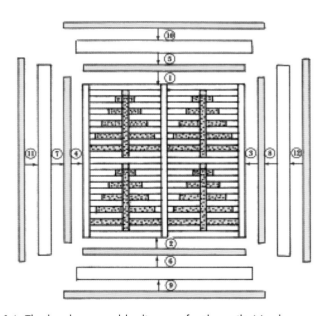

2–14. The border assembly diagram for the quilt. Numbers show order of piecing.

31½" strips and stitch one to the top and one to the bottom edge of the quilt center. Take the two red 1½" x 33 ½" strips and stitch them to the sides. Press. This completes the quilt-top assembly.

16. Choose a border pattern from Chapter 10—Quilting Patterns, page 511. Transfer the quilting pattern lines to the tan border areas of the quilt top, referring to Chapter 8—How to Quilt, pages 428 and 434.

17. Tape the 35" x 35" piece of fabric, face down, to your work surface. Center the batting over it and center the quilt top, face up, over the batting. Hand baste or pin baste the layers together to prepare for quilting. Hand or machine quilt the body of the quilt as desired.

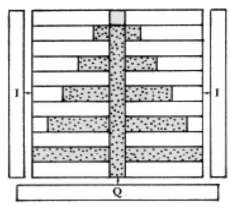

2–15. Stitching the I strips and the Q strips to the tree block for the runner.

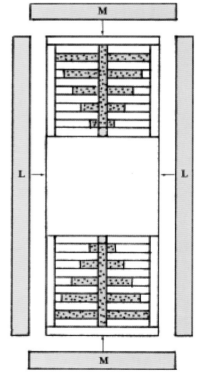

2–16. Assembly of the runner.

18. To quilt the tan border, thread a large-eyed needle with a comfortable length of the green pearl cotton. Hand quilt along the markings in the border.

19. Baste ¼" in from the raw edges all around the quilt top. Trim away the excess batting and backing that extends beyond the edges of the quilt top to prepare the quilt for the binding.

20. Bind the quilt with the bias binding.

TABLE RUNNER ASSEMBLY

21. For the table runner, take the four tan 1½" x 11½" I strips for the side bars. Take two tan 1½" x 13½" Q strips for the bottom bars of the blocks. Stitch the I strips to each side of one block. (Instructions for the blocks were given in steps 1 to 11 above.) Repeat for the second block. Stitch the Q strip to the bottom of each block, as shown in figure 2–15. Press.

22. Take the twelve 1½" x 13½" tan K blocks. Stitch one tree block to each 13½" edge of the tan blocks so that the tops of the trees face the tan block (figure 2–16, center). This completes the runner center. Press.

23. Take the two red 2½" x 36½" L border strips. Stitch one to each long side of the runner center (figure 2–16). Press. Take the two 2½" x 17½" red M strips and stitch them to the two short ends of the runner. Press. This completes the runner top.

24. Transfer a pattern for the hand quilting, centered, onto the K block of the runner.

25. Tape the 19" x 42" runner backing face down on your work surface, and center the batting over that; center the quilt top, face up, over that. Hand baste or pin baste the layers together.

26. Choose a central quilt motif (see Chapter 10—Quilting Patterns, page 511) for the K square. Refer to Chapter 8—How to Quilt, pages 434 to 445, then hand or machine quilt as desired.

27. Bind the runner with the bias binding to complete the project.

MATERIALS TO MAKE ONE ORNAMENT

3½" square of tan fabric or another color
4" square of tear-away stabilizer or tracing paper
Two 1" x 3½" strips red fabric (borders)
Two 1" x 4½" strips red fabric (borders)
4½" square of red fabric for backing
4½" square of low-loft batting
Green all-purpose thread for machine embroidery
One small brown bead
5" length of ¼"-wide green satin ribbon

Make these ornaments in tan, or in your favorite colors to hang on your tree. You can pin them on the quilt or tack them in place with a few stitches. Finished size of ornament: 4" x 4", excluding hanging loop.

DIRECTIONS

Construction is done with seam allowances of ¼" and right sides of fabric facing.

1. Trace the machine embroidery lines from the pattern (figure 4–17) onto the tan piece of fabric. Place the stabilizer against the wrong side of the marked tan square. Using the green thread and a medium-width machine satin stitch, embroider along the marked lines. Pull the thread tails to the back side of the piece and clip. Tear off the stabilizer and press the square.

2. Stitch the 3½"-long red border strips to the top and bottom of the embroidered tan square, as shown in figure 4–18. Stitch a 4½"-long red border strip to each side of the square to complete the ornament front. Press.

3. Baste the 4½" square of batting to the wrong side of the embroidered square, about ⅓" in from the raw edges. Place the ornament front and the backing fabric square together, with right sides facing. Stitch along the side and bottom edges, and stitch along the top edge, leaving a 1" opening along the top edge. Clip the corners of the seam allowances and turn the ornament right side out. Press.

4. Fold the length of ribbon in half to form a loop. Insert the ends of the loop into the center of the opening in the top of the ornament and hand stitch the opening closed, encasing the ends of the loop in the stitching.

5. Hand stitch the bead to the top of the tree as indicated by the small circle on the full-size pattern.

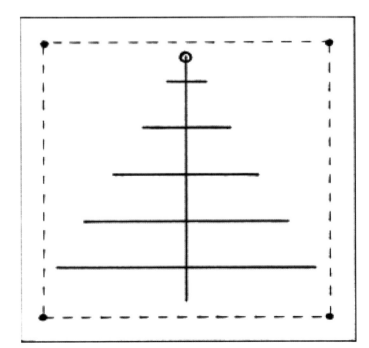

2–17. Full size pattern of the Christmas tree ornament, with embroidery lines (solid lines) and seam allowances (dashed lines). Small circle is bead placement.

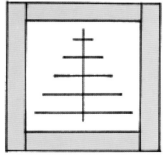

2–18. Stitch the short borders and then the long borders to the center.

Briar Rose Lap Quilt

This is a very simple quilt to construct. It's based on a 2" grid and has no bias edges or triangles. An average stitcher can easily have the quilt top made in less than a day. Finished quilt size: 54" x 54". Finished block size 14" x 14".

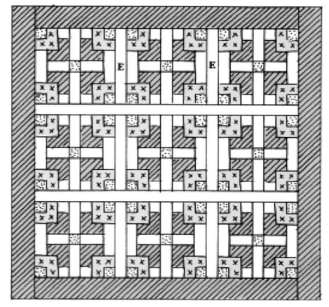

3–1. Construction diagram of the quilt.

CUTTING GUIDE

Quantity	Size	Use
Rose fabric:*		
Nine	2½" x 40"	B units
Two	4½" x 46½"	borders
Two	4½" x 54½"	borders

*Cut all the dark rose strips on the length of the
   fabric (not across)

Quantity	Size	Use
Green fabric:		
Three	2½" x 40"	A units
Three	4½" x 40"	B units

Quantity	Size	Use
Pink fabric:		
Three	2½" x 40"	A units
One	2½" x 25"	center block strip
White fabric:		
Two	2½" x 46½"	sashing*
Nine	2½" x 40"	A units, C units, D strips
Two	6½" x 25"	center block strip
Six	½" x 14"	sashing

*First cut the 46½" sashing strips from the length
   of the fabric; then cut the rest from the width.

MATERIALS

1⅔ yards dark rose print fabric
1½ yards solid white fabric
¾ yard green print fabric
½ yard pink fabric
6¼ yards of white double-fold quilt binding
   (folded width, 1½"; unfolded width, 2")
White all-purpose sewing thread
60" x 60" piece of quilt batting
60" x 60" piece of fabric for the backing

DIRECTIONS

Construction is done with right sides of fabric facing
and seam allowances of ¼", which are included in all
of the given measurements. The quilt center consists
of nine blocks, separated by sashing (see figure 3–1).

1. Referring to the cutting guides, cut the necessary strips of each fabric.

2. Take one pink, one green, and one white strip
of size 2½" x 40". Stitch them together on a long
edge with the green in the center to make a three-
strip unit. Press all the seam allowances in one
direction. Make two more three-strip units the
same way. Referring to figure 3–2, cut across all
three strips in the unit to make 36½"-wide A units.
(You will have some extra three-strip units left over,
which you can use to make an extra block for a pillow, if you wish.) Set the A units aside.

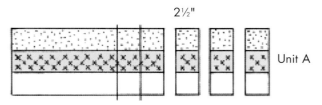

3–2. Cutting A units.

3. Take a green 4½" x 40" strip and a rose 2½" x 40" strip. Stitch the rose strip to the green strip along one long edge to make a two-strip unit. Repeat to make two more two-strip units. Cutting across the two-strip units, cut a total of thirty-six 2½"-wide B units from the two-strip units, as shown in figure 3–3. Set the B units aside.

4. Take the six 2½" x 40" rose strips and three white strips the same size. Stitch a white strip between two rose strips on their long edges to make a three-strip unit (see figure 3–4). Make another three-strip unit the same way. Cutting across the three-strip units, cut a total of eighteen 4½"-wide C units.

5. To assemble the blocks, see figure 3–5 for the block diagram. Referring to figure 3–6A, stitch one A unit and one B unit together as shown to make an AB unit. Repeat to make a total of eighteen AB units. Set them aside.

6. Referring to 3–6B, stitch one A and one B unit together as shown to make a reversed AB unit (henceforth known as ABr). Make a total of eighteen ABr units. Press all units. Set them aside.

7. Take three white 2½" x 40" strips. From each of these strips cut six 2½" x 6½" D strips, for a total of eighteen D strips. Stitch one of these white strips to each of the C units as shown in figure 3–6C to make a D+C unit. Press.

8. Assemble the two halves of the block. Referring to figure 3–7A, make the left unit of the block by stitching together one AB, one ABr, and one D+C unit as shown (figure 3–7B shows the completed left unit). The right unit of the block is simply the left unit rotated 180 degrees (turned upside down), so make a total of eighteen left units the same way. We will turn nine of them upside down to be the right units of the blocks. Set them aside.

9. Take the two white 6½" x 25" strips and the pink 2½" x 25" strip. Stitch one of the white strips to each long side of the pink strip. Press the seam allowances towards the pink strip. Cut across all three strips to make nine 2½"-wide pieces (figure 3–8). These are the center block strips.

2½"

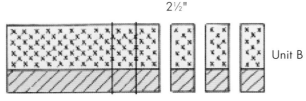

3–3. Cutting B units.

Unit B

4½"

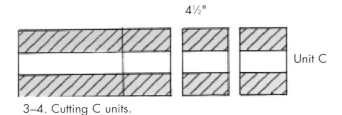

3–4. Cutting C units.

Unit C

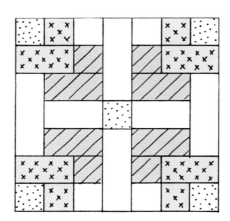

3–5. Block diagram.

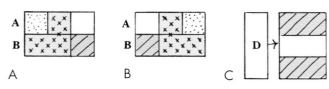

3–6. Assembling units. A. The AB unit. B. The ABr unit. C. The D+C unit.

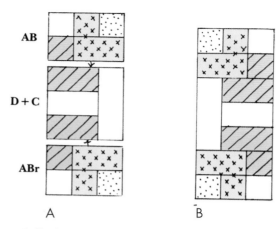

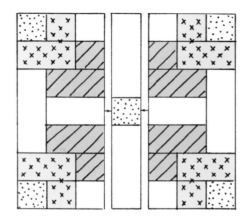

3–7. Assembling a half of the quilt block. A. Assembling the left block unit. B. The completed left block unit. The right block unit is simply the left block unit, rotated 180 degrees.

3–9. Stitching the block halves to the center block strip.

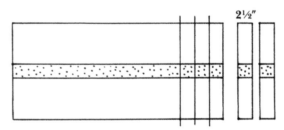

3–8. Cutting the center block strips.

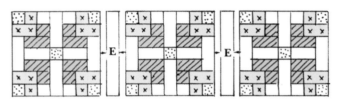

3–10. Stitching blocks and E strips to form a row.

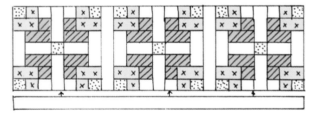

3–11. Stitching a long sashing strip to a block row.

10. Stitch one left block unit and one right block unit (a left unit rotated 180°) to the center strip as shown in figure 3–9. Press. Make eight more blocks the same way.

11. Take the six white 2½" x 14½" E sashing strips. Assemble a row of three blocks, stitching two E strips in between them as shown in figure 6–10. Make two more rows the same way. Press.

12. Assemble the quilt center by sewing a 2½" x 26" long sashing strip to the bottom of two block rows as shown in figure 3–11, and then stitching the rows together as shown in the construction diagram (figure 3–1). The row without the long sashing strip is the bottom row of the quilt center. Press. This completes the quilt center.

13. Take the two rose 4½" x 46½" border strips and stitch one to the top and one to the bottom of the quilt center. Press the seam allowances towards the rose strips. Take the rose 4½" x 54½" border strips and stitch one to each of two opposite sides of the quilt center; press the seam allowances towards the rose fabric.

14. Tape the backing fabric, wrong side up, to your work surface. Center the batting over it, and center the quilt top, right side up, over the batting. Hand-baste or pin baste the layers together. Refer to Chapter 8—How to Quilt, pages 434 to 445.

15. Baste through all three layers about ¼" in from the raw edges of the quilt top. Trim away any excess batting and backing that extend beyond the edges of the quilt top.

16. Bind the quilt with the double-fold quilt binding to complete it.

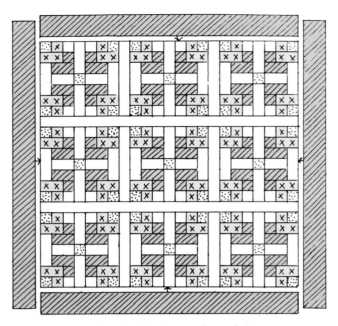

3–12. Stitching the borders to the quilt center.

A finished Briar Rose quilt block.

Potted Topiary Tree Quilts

A bright floral border and lilac ribbons set a romantic tone for these two projects. One of the green fabrics you choose should have just a hint of the same colors of flowers used in the border fabric. Block size: 5" x 13". Finished size of the one-block quilt: 15" x 22". Finished size of the three-block quilt: 28" x 22".

MATERIALS FOR BOTH QUILTS

¼ yard of light green fabric

¼ yard of lilac fabric

¼ yard medium green fabric

½ yard of off-white solid fabric

½ yard of floral print fabric

Two 12" x 15" scraps: one of a light pink and one of a medium pink fabric

6" x 6" scrap of light brown fabric for tree trunks

12" x 18" piece of paper-backed fusible webbing for the bows

All-purpose sewing threads to match the fabrics

17" x 26" piece of quilt batting for one-block quilt

17" x 26" piece of fabric to back the one-block quilt

32 x 26" piece of quilt batting for three-block quilt

32 x 26" piece of fabric to back the three-block quilt

5½ yards of green double-fold quilt binding (folded width, ½"; unfolded width, 2"): 2½ yards for the one-block quilt and 3 yards for the three-block quilt.

DIRECTIONS

Construction is done with right sides of fabric facing and ¼" seam allowances, which are included in all of the measurements. The appliqué bow pattern is given without seam allowances, which are not needed for machine appliqué. To hand appliqué, add ⅛" seam allowance around the pattern. The block in the one-block quilt (figure 4–1) and those in the three-block quilt are pieced in the same way. There is slight variation in the colors of some pieces in the outside trees of the three-block quilt.

ONE-BLOCK QUILT (FIGURE 4–1)

1. See the cutting guides for the one-block quilt and cut and label the strips and pieces. Next, we'll make some two-triangle squares by the speed method.

2. A squares: Take the medium green and the off-white 2½" square. On the wrong side of one of these fabrics draw a 1⅞" square. Draw a diagonal line through this square. Place the two squares of

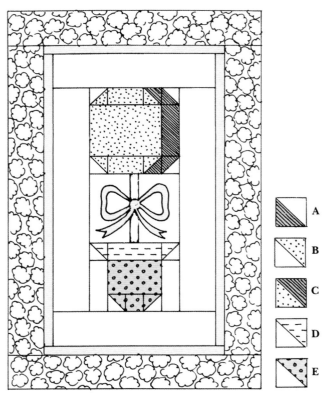

4–1. Construction diagram of the one–block quilt (the tree block is the same as the center block of the three-block quilt).

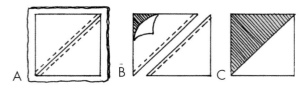

4–2. Making A squares. A. Marked lines and stitching. B. Cutting the units apart. C. The finished A square.

fabric together, right sides facing, and stitch ¼" from each side of the diagonal line (figure 4–2A). Cut out the square along the marked lines, and cut it in half along the diagonal line (figure 4–2B). Press each resulting unit open to form a two-triangle off-white/medium green unit A square, as shown in figure 4–2C. Set them aside.

3. B squares: Repeat step 1 using an off-white and light green square of fabric, as shown in figure 4–3, to make the B squares. Set them aside.

ONE-BLOCK QUILT CUTTING GUIDE

Quantity	Size	Use
Off-white fabric:		
Four	2½" x 2½"	A, B, D, and E squares
Two	4½" x 2¾"	I strips
Two	1½" x 3½"	M strips
Two	2½" x 13½"	N strips (border 1)
Two	2½" x 9½"	O strips (border 1)
Light pink fabric:		
One	2½" x 2½"	D squares
One	1½" x 3½"	J strip
Medium pink fabric:		
One	2½" x 2½"	E square
One	3½" x 2½"	K strip
One	1½" x 1½"	L square
Light green fabric:		
Two	2½" x 2½"	B and C squares
Two	2½" x 1½"	F strips
One	3 ½" x 4½"	G rectangle
Medium green fabric:		
Two	2½" x 2½"	A and C squares
One	1½" x 3½"	H strip
Lilac fabric:		
Two	1" x 17½"	border 2 strips
Two	1" x 10½"	border 2 strips
One	5" x 6"	bow appliqué
Floral fabric:		
Two	2½"x 18½"	border 3 strips
Two	2" x 14½"	border 3 strips
Light brown fabric:		
One	1" x 4½"	tree trunk

4. C squares: Repeat step 1 using a light green and a medium green square, as shown in figure 4–4, to make the C squares. Set them aside.

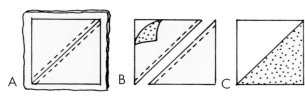

4–3. Making B squares. A. Drawing lines and stitching. B. Cutting the units apart. C. The finished B square.

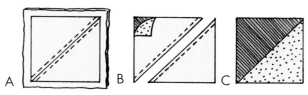

4–4. Making C squares. A. Drawing lines and stitching. B. Cutting the units apart. C. The finished C square.

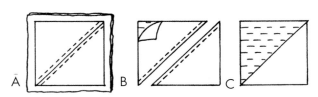

4–5. Making D squares. A. Drawing lines and stitching. B. Cutting the units apart. C. The finished D square.

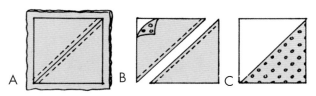

4–6. Making E squares. A. Drawing lines and stitching. B. Cutting the units apart. C. The finished E square.

5. D squares: Repeat step 1 using one light pink and one off-white square of fabric, as shown in figure 4–5, to make the D squares. Set them aside.

6. E squares: Repeat step 1 again, using one medium pink square and one off-white square of fabric, as shown in figure 4–6, to make the E squares. Set them aside.

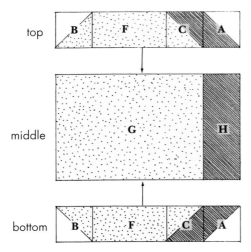

top

middle

bottom

4–7. Assembling the treetop from its three parts (for one-block quilt and inner tree on three-block quilt).

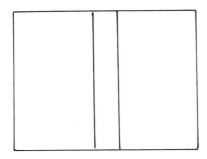

4–8. The center tree unit (bow is not appliquéd in place yet).

4–9. The pot top for the one-block quilt and the central block of the three-block quilt.

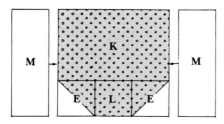

4–10. The pot bottom for the one-block quilt and the central block of the three-block quilt.

7. Treetop: Referring to figure 4–7, assemble and stitch an A, B, and C square along with a light green $1\frac{1}{2}$" x $2\frac{1}{2}$" F strip to make the top section of the treetop. Take another A, B, and C square and an F strip and assemble and stitch the bottom unit, referring to figure 4–7, bottom. Press and set these two sections aside.

8. Middle section of the treetop: Take the medium green $1\frac{1}{2}$" x $3\frac{1}{2}$" H strip and stitch it to the light green $3\frac{1}{2}$" x $4\frac{1}{2}$" G rectangle. Then assemble and stitch the top, middle and bottom treetop sections together as shown in figure 4–7. Press and set aside.

9. Center unit of the tree: Take the 1" x $4\frac{1}{2}$" strip of light brown fabric and the two $4\frac{1}{2}$" x $2\frac{3}{4}$" I strips of off-white fabric and stitch one of the off-white I strips to each side of the brown strip (figure 4–8). Press the seam allowances towards the brown fabric. You now have a tree center unit measuring $4\frac{1}{2}$" x $5\frac{1}{2}$".

10. Bow: First see Chapter 3— Appliqué Quilt Patterns, pages 136 to 146.

(*For machine appliqué.*) Trace the bow shape onto the paper side of the fusible webbing. Fuse the webbing bow to the wrong side of a scrap of the lilac fabric. Cut out the bow, remove the paper backing of the webbing, and fuse the bow in place on the center unit of the tree. Machine appliqué the bow in place using matching thread and a medium-width satin stitch.

(*For hand appliqué.*) Trace the bow onto the right side of a scrap of the lilac fabric with a washable pen or pencil. Cut out the bow, adding $\frac{1}{8}$" seam allowances around the entire bow as you cut, as well as inside the loops. Prepare the bow for hand appliqué. Baste the bow in place on the center unit of the tree and hand appliqué it with lilac hand sewing thread.

11. Pot top: Take the light pink fabric $1\frac{1}{2}$" x $3\frac{1}{2}$" J strip. Stitch one D square to each end of the pink J strip as shown in figure 4–9 to make a DJD units: Press and set aside.

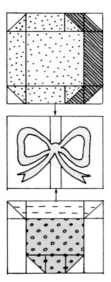

4-11. Assembling a tree block for the one-block quilt and the central block of the three-block quilt. Closeup of block.

12. Pot bottom: Take the 3½" x 2½" medium pink K strip and a 1½" L square of the same fabric, plus two E squares. Stitch one E square to each of two opposite sides of the L square as shown in figure 4–10, and stitch the resulting ELE unit to one long edge of the medium pink K strip. Take two off-white fabric 1½" x 3½" M strips and stitch one of these to each side of the pot bottom (see figure 4–10). Press.

13. Assemble the block: Stitch the DJD unit made in step 10 to the pot bottom made in step 11. Then stitch the center unit of the tree above the pot, and stitch the treetop unit above the center unit (see figure 4–11). Press. This completes the block.

14. Border 1: Take the two off-white 2½" x 13½" N strips and stitch one of these strips to each long side of the quilt block (see figure 4–1). Take two 2½" x 9½" O strips and stitch one to the top and one to the bottom of the block. Press. This makes the quilt center.

15. Border 2: Take the two lilac 1" x 17½" strips and stitch one to each long side of the quilt center. Take two 1" x 10½" lilac strips and stitch them to the top and bottom of the quilt center. (These lilac strips will have a finished width of only ½", hence the 1" cut width). Press.

16. Take the two floral print 2½" x 18½" strips, and stitch one to each long side of the quilt center. Take the two 2½" x 14½" floral print strips and stitch one to the top and one to the bottom of the quilt center. Press.

17. Lay out the backing fabric wrong side up, center the batting over it, and center the quilt top right-side up over the batting. Hand baste or pin baste the layers together to secure them for quilting. See Chapter 8—How to Quilt, pages 434 to 445. Hand quilt or machine quilt the project, as desired.

18. Baste around the quilt top, about ¼" in from the raw edge on all four sides. Trim away the excess batting and backing that extend beyond the edges of the quilt top.

19. Bind the quilt with the green binding to complete it.

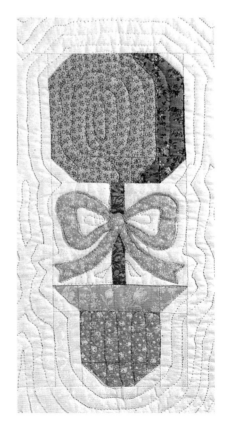

Closeup of Potted Topiary Tree block.

THREE-BLOCK QUILT CUTTING GUIDE

Quantity	Size	Use
Off-white fabric:		
Four	21½" x 6½"	A, B, D, and E squares
Six	4½" x 2½"	I strips
Six	1½" x 3½"	M strips
Four	2½"x 13½"	N strips
Two	2½" x 23½"	P strips
Light pink fabric:		
One	2½" x 6½"	D squares
One	1½" x 3½"	J strip
Two	3½" x 2½"	K strips
Two	1½" x 1½"	L strips
Medium pink fabric:		
One	2½" x 6½"	E squares
One	3½"₂ x 2 ½"	K strip
One	1½" x 1½"	L square
Two	1½" x 3½"	J strips
One	1½" x 14"	corner units
Light green fabric:		
Two	2½" x 6½"	B and C squares
Two	2½" x 1½"	F strips
One	3½" x 4½"	G rectangle
Two	1½" x 3½"	H strips
One	1½" x 14"	corner units
Medium green fabric:		
Two	2½" x 6½"	A and C squares
Two	1½" x 3½"	H strips
Two	3½" x 4½"	G strip
Lilac fabric:		
Two	1" x 23½"	border strips
Two	1" x 18½"	border strips
Three	5" x 6"	bow appliqué
Floral fabric:		
Two	2½" x 18½"	border strips
Two	2½" x 24½"	border strips
Light brown fabric:		
Three	1" x 4½"	tree trunks

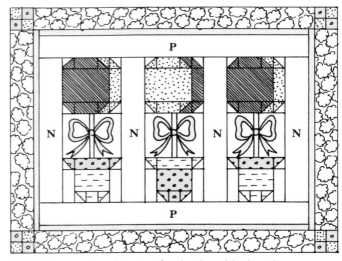

4–12. Construction diagram for the three-block quilt.

THREE-BLOCK QUILT

See the cutting guides for the three-block quilt. Cut and label the strips and pieces. Look at figure 4–12, the construction diagram for the three-block quilt. The center tree block is exactly like the one for the one-block quilt. The outer blocks have some pieces done in varying colors. The F and G pieces in the tree are medium green. The H pieces are light green. Also, the pot colors are varied from the those of the center block. To make the three-block quilt, we will need six each of the A, B, C, D, and E squares.

1. A squares: Take the 2½" x 6½" pieces of fabric in off-white and medium green, and trace out three 1⅞" squares on the back of one piece. Draw a diagonal line through each square. Place the two rectangles of fabric together, right sides facing, and stitch ¼" from each side of the diagonal line (figure 4–13). Cut out the square along the marked lines, and cut it in half along the diagonal lines (figure 4–13B). Press each resulting unit open to form a two-triangle off-white/medium green unit A square, as shown in figure 4–13C. Set aside.

Full-size appliqué pattern for the bow, given without seam allowances. Add seam allowances of ³⁄₁₆" as you cut for hand appliqué only.

4–13. Cutting two-triangle squares. A. Marking and stitching. B. Cutting the units apart. C. Finished two-triangle square.

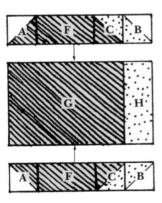

4–14. Assembling a treetop for the outer blocks of the three-block quilt.

2. Repeat step 1 with the remaining 2¹⁄₂" x 6¹⁄₂" rectangles. B squares: Off-white and light green. C squares: Light green and medium green. D squares: Off-white and light pink. E squares: Off-white and medium pink.

3. Assemble the middle tree block as you did the block for the one-block quilt (see steps 7 through 12 of the one-block quilt instructions). Press.

4. Two outside tree blocks: Referring to figure 4–14, assemble and stitch an A, B, and C unit along with a medium green 1¹⁄₂" x 2¹⁄₂" F strip and assemble and stitch the bottom unit, referring to figure 4–14, bottom. Press and set aside these two sections .

5. Middle section of the treetop: Take the light green 1¹⁄₂" x 3¹⁄₂" H strip and stitch it to the medium green 3¹⁄₂" x 4¹⁄₂" G rectangle. Assemble and stitch the top, middle, and bottom treetop sections together as shown in figure 4–14. Make another treetop section the same way for the second outer tree. Press and set aside.

6. Center unit of the tree: Follow the instructions in step 9 of the one-block tree quilt (see figure 4–8). Make two more center units the same way. Press. Machine appliqué or hand appliqué bows in place as you did for the one-block quilt (step 10). Set aside.

7. Pot tops for outer block: Take the medium pink fabric 1½" x 3½" J strip. Stitch one E square to each short end as shown in figure 4–15, top, to make an EJE unit; make a second EJE unit the same way. Press and set aside.

8. Pot bottoms for outer block: Take the 3½" x 2½" light pink K strip and a 1½" L square of the same fabric, plus two D squares. Stitch one D square to each of two opposite sides of the L square, as shown in figure 4–15, and stitch the resulting DLD unit to one long edge of the light pink K strip. Take two off-white fabric 1½" x 3½" M strips and stitch one of these to each side of the pot bottom (see figure 4–15). Make another pot bottom the same way. Press.

9. To assemble the outer tree blocks, first stitch the EJE unit made in step 7 to the pot bottom made in step 8. Repeat for the second outer block. Then stitch the center units of the tree above the pots, and stitch the treetop units above the center units (see figure 4–16). Repeat for the second outer tree. Press. This completes the blocks.

10. Assemble the quilt center by alternating off-white 2½" x 13½" N strips with the three tree blocks, as shown in figure 4–12. Stitch them together and press.

11. Border 1: Take the two off-white 2½" x 23½" P strips. Stitch one to the top and one to the bottom of the quilt center (see figure 4–12 for reference). Press.

12. Border 2: Take the two 1" x 23½" lilac strips and stitch one to the top and one to the bottom of the quilt center. Cut two 1" x 18½" lilac strips and stitch them to the short sides. Press.

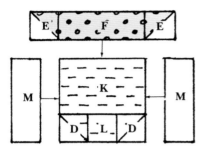

4–15. Assembling a pot for the outer blocks of the three-block quilt.

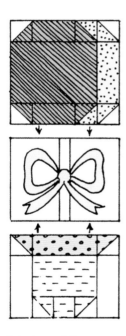

4–16. Assembling a tree block for the outer blocks of the three-block quilt.

13. Take the medium pink a 1½" x 14" strip and the light green strip of the same size. Stitch them together on one long side. Cut eight 1½"-wide two-square pieces across both strips (figure 4–17A). Form the four-patch corner units with two two-square pieces (figure 4–17B).

14. Take two 1½" x 24½" floral strips and stitch them to the top and bottom of the quilt center. Take two 2½" x 18½" strips from the same fabric and stitch one of the four-patch corner units made in step 13 to the short ends of both strips (figure 4–18). Stitch the resulting strips to the sides of the quilt top. Press. The completed quilt top will look like figure 4–12.

15. Lay out the quilt backing wrong side up, center the batting over it, and center the quilt top right side up over the batting. Baste, quilt, and bind the three-block quilt as you did the one-block quilt.

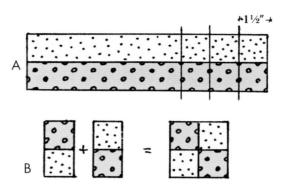

4–17. A. Cutting strips for the four-patch border corners. B. The finished corner.

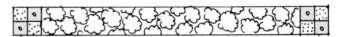

4–18. Two four-patch corners attached to a short floral border strip.

Patchwork Angel Wall Hanging

Grace your walls this Christmas with a smiling patchwork Christmas angel. Stitched from bright Christmas prints, she's a lovely addition to your holiday decor, or stitch her country cousin from your favorite pastels and use her all year-round. Finished size of each wall hanging: 24" x 30".

MATERIALS

Christmas Angel fabrics:

½ yard green print
½ yard red print
½ yard white print
¼ yard off-white solid
5" x 11" flesh-color scrap
4" x 8" deep gold print scrap

Country Angel fabrics:

½ yard blue print
½ yard pink print
½ yard off-white print
¼ yard off-white solid
5" x 11" flesh-color scrap
4" x 8" light brown print scrap

For either quilt:

2 small buttons for eyes (green for the Christmas
    Angel quilt; blue for the Country Angel quilt) or
    black embroidery floss
26" x 32" piece of quilt batting
26" x 32" piece of fabric for the backing
All-purpose sewing threads to match the fabrics
3¼ yards off-white double-fold quilt binding
    (folded width, ½"; unfolded width, 2")
1 skein each of brown, tan, and red/pink 6-strand
    embroidery floss

DIRECTIONS

Construction is done with right sides of fabric facing and seam allowances of ¼", which are included in the given measurements. The instructions are for the Christmas Angel (see figure 5–1). For the Country Angel, use the fabrics in the Country Angel yardage requirements and cutting guides, substituting pink where red is given in the Christmas Angel, etc. Fabrics for Country Angel are given in brackets.

ANGEL QUILT CUTTING GUIDE

Quantity	Size	Use
Green print fabric (Christmas)		
Blue print fabric [Country]:		
Two	2½" x 22"	border strips
Two	2½" x 20"	border strips
Four	2½" x 2½"	M squares
One	4½" x 4½"	N squares
Two	3½" x 3½"	for B and
		D squares
One	6½" x 8½"	P rectangle
Red print fabric (Christmas)		
Pink print fabric [Country]:		
Two	2½" x 26½"	border strips
Two	2½" x 20½"	border strips
One	7" x 17"	for A squares
One	3½" x 10½"	for D squares
One	3½" x 3½"	for E squares
White print fabric (Christmas)		
Off-white print fabric [Country]:		
Two	2½" x 6½"	K strips
Ten	2½" x 2½"	L squares
One	7" x 17"	for A squares
One	3½" x 3½"	for C squares
Two	4½" x 4½"	O squares
Off-white solid fabric (for either):		
Two	4½" x 4½"	G squares
Four	2½" x 2½"	H squares
One	3½" x 10½"	for D squares
One	3½" x 3½"	for F squares
Flesh-colored fabric (for either):		
Three	3½" x 3½"	for B, C, and
		I squares
Deep gold print fabric (Christmas)		
Light brown print fabric [Country]:		
Two	2⅞" x 2⅞"	squares for
		triangles
One	3½" x 3½"	square for
		F square

Cutting Pieces and Making the two-Triangle Squares

1. The quilt is composed of squares, rectangles, and two-triangle squares. The quilt will be assembled in five parts (see 5–1 or 5–2). First, cut out all the pieces listed in the cutting guides, using color choices for whichever angel you are making.

2. Next, make the two-triangle squares, using a speed method. Take the two fabric pieces as described in steps 3 to 8, and trace the number of $2^7/_8$" squares you are told to make onto the wrong side of one of the fabric pieces. Draw a diagonal line through each square. Then, pin both pieces of fabric together with right sides facing and stitch $^1/_4$" away from both sides of the diagonal lines (see figure 5–3A). After stitching, cut apart the squares along the marked square lines. Cut each square along the diagonal line also (see figure 5–3B). Press each resulting unit open to form a 2-triangle square (figure 5–3C).

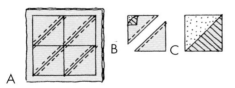

5–3. Making two-triangle squares. A. Marking and stitching. B. Cutting. C. The finished unit (in this case, an A square).

3. A squares: Take a 7" x 17" rectangle of red [pink] print fabric and another of white print [off-white print] fabric. Referring to step 2, draw ten $2^7/_8$" x $2^7/_8$" squares on the wrong side of one of the pieces of fabric. Draw diagonal lines through the squares. With right sides together, pin the two pieces of fabric and stitch $^1/_4$" away from the line along both sides of the diagonal. Cut apart the units and press each open. You will have twenty A squares, but only need eighteen. Set aside.

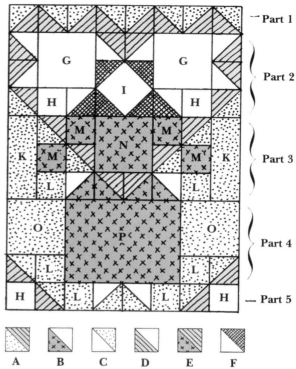

5–1. Construction diagram for the Christmas Angel quilt center.

5–2. Construction diagram for the Country Angel quilt center.

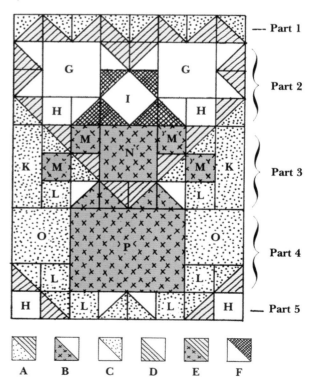

4. B squares: Take a 3½" square of green print [blue print] fabric and of flesh-colored fabric. Mark a 2⅞" square on the wrong side of one of the squares. Mark its diagonal line, and stitch ¼" away from the line along each side of the diagonal line. Cut the square on the ruled diagonal. Press open the two B squares and set aside.

5. C squares: Take two 3½" squares of the white print [off-white print] fabric and the flesh-colored fabric. As in step 4, stitch and cut two two-triangle squares. Press open the C squares and set aside.

6. D squares: Take a 3½" x 10½" piece of off-white solid fabric [same for both angels] and one of red [pink] fabric. Mark three squares, add their diagonal lines, and stitch. Cut 2⅞" two-triangle squares as you did in the previous steps. Press open the six D squares and set aside.

7. E squares: From the 3½" square of green print [blue print] and the one of red [pink] print, make two E squares the same way you made the B squares in step 4. Press open the two E squares and set aside.

8. F squares: From the 3½" square of gold print [light brown print] and one of off-white solid [same for both angels] mark, stitch, and cut as you did for the E squares. Press open the two F squares and set aside.

9. Stack the squares in individual piles.

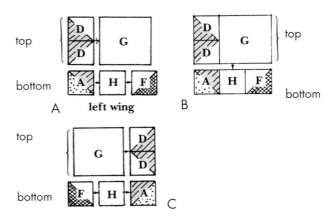

5–5. The wings. A. Making the left wing. B. Assembling the top and bottom of the left wing. C. Assembling the right wing.

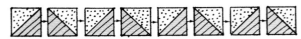

5–4. Assembling Part 1.

Assembling the Quilt Center Parts
See figures 5–1 or 5–2 for reference.

10. To make Part 1 of the block, stitch eight A squares together as shown in figure 5–4. Press and set aside.

11. Part 2 has three sections, a left wing section, a right wing section, and a head section (see figure 5–8). From the off-white solid fabric pieces [same for both angels] take two 4½" G squares and two 2½" H squares. Using four D squares, two A squares, and two F squares, plus the G and H squares, we will assemble one left wing section and one right wing section. For the bottom of the left wing, stitch an A square, an off-white H square, and an F square together as shown (5–5A, bottom). For the top of the left wing, stitch two D squares together and then stitch them to a G square as shown (5–5A, top). Last, join the left wings top and bottom (figure 5–5B). The right wing is made in the same order (see 5-5C). Set the wings aside after pressing them.

12. Take the flesh-colored 3½" I square [same for both angels] and two gold [light brown] 2⅞" squares. Cut each of the gold [light brown] squares in half on the diagonal to form two triangles for a total of four J triangles. Stitch one J triangle to each side of the I square to make the angel's head section, as shown in figure 5–6. Press and set aside.

5–6. Assembling the head.

13. Stitch two D squares together as shown in figure 5–7A and then stitch them to the head as shown (5–7B).

14. To assemble Part 2 of the angel, stitch one wing section to each side of the head unit, as shown in figure 5–8.

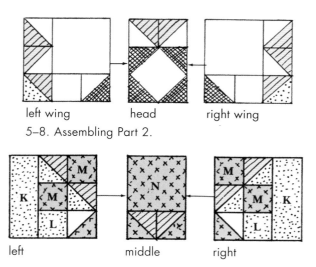

left wing   head   right wing

5–8. Assembling Part 2.

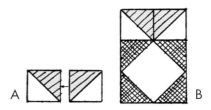

A ← → B

5–7. A. Stitch the D squares together.
B. Stitch the D squares to the head.

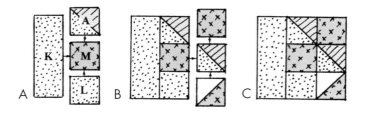

left   middle   right

5–9. The components of Part 3.

15. Part 3 of the angel is made in three sections, as shown in figure 5–9. First make the left section. From the white print fabric [off-white print fabric], take one 2½" x 6 ½" K strip and one 2½" L square. From the green print [blue print] fabric, take two 2½" M squares. Stitch together an A, M, and L square as shown in figure 5–10a, and then attach a K strip as shown (5–10A). Add another row of an M, A, and a B square stitched as shown in figure 5–10B, to make the completed left side of Part 3 (figure 5–10C). To make the right side of Part 3, stitch together an M, A, and B square in a row, as shown in figure 5–11A. Then stitch an A, M, and L square together in a row. Join both rows to a K strip to make the completed right side of Part 3 (figure 5–11B). Set it aside.

16. To make the middle of Part 3, stitch two E squares together as shown in figure 5–12, and stitch this to an N square as shown. Press.

17. Stitch the left, middle, and right sides of Part 3 together as shown in figure 5–9 and press. This completes Part 3. Set it aside.

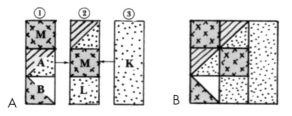

A   B

5–10. A and B. Piecing the left side of Part 3. C. The finished left side of Part 3.

5–11. A. Assembling the right side of Part 3.
B. The finished right side of Part 3.

18. To make Part 4, from the white print fabric [off-white print fabric] take two 4½" O squares and two 2½" L squares. Stitch one of each of these squares along with an A square as shown in figure 5–13A and B, to make a left side and a right side of Part 4. Press.

19. To complete Part 4, take the green [blue] 6½" x 8½" P rectangle. Stitch the left and right sides of Part 4 to the short sides of the green [blue] rectangle as shown in figure 5–14. Press it and set it aside.

20. To assemble Part 5, take two off-white solid [the same for both angels] 2½" H squares. From the white [off-white] print fabric take two 2½" L squares. Referring to figure 5–15, assemble these squares along with two A squares and two C squares, and stitch them together to make Part 5, as shown. Press.

21. Stitch Parts 1 through 5 together in order to form the quilt center (see figures 5–1 or 5–2 for reference) and press.

22. Referring to figure 5–16, take the two green [blue] 2½" x 22½" borders and stitch these to the long sides of the quilt center. Press. Take the two green [blue] 2½" x 20½" strips and stitch one to the top and one to the bottom of the quilt center. Press the seam allowances towards the green [blue] strips.

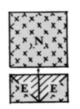

5–12. Making the center of Part 3.

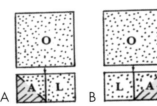

A

B

5–13. A. The left side of part 4.
B. The right side of Part 4.

5–14. Stitch one side unit to each short side of the P rectangle to form Part 4.

5–15. Stitch the squares together to form Part 5 of the quilt center.

Country Angel

23. From the white print [off-white print] fabric, take four 2½" L squares for the corner units. From the red [pink] fabric take the two 2½" x 26½" outer border strips and stitch one of these to each long side of the quilt center. Take two red [pink] 2½" x 20½" border strips; stitch one of the white print [off-white print] corner L squares to each short end of the two red [pink] strips. Stitch a strip that has the squares attached to the top of the quilt center and stitch one to the bottom of the quilt center (figure 5–16). Press.

24. Transfer the face markings (figure 5–17) to the angel's head (the I square) with water-soluble pencil.

25. Using two strands of the six-strand floss in your needle and following the face markings, embroider the mouth with the red floss using stem stitch. Embroider the eye lashes with the brown floss. Embroider the nose with the tan floss. (If you want to embroider the eyes instead of using buttons for eyes, do so at this point with black floss.)

Note: If the quilt is for a baby or a small child, use thread instead of buttons for eyes.

26. Tape the quilt backing, wrong side up, to your work surface, center the batting over it, and center the quilt top, right side up, over the batting. Hand baste or pin baste the layers together to prepare them for quilting. Hand quilt or machine quilt the project, as you wish.

27. Baste around all four sides of the quilt very close to the raw edges of the quilt top. Trim away the excess batting and backing that extends beyond the edges of the quilt top. Bind the quilt with the double-fold quilt binding.

28. Stitch the buttons to the eye area to complete the quilt, or use black embroidery thread to embroider the eyes.

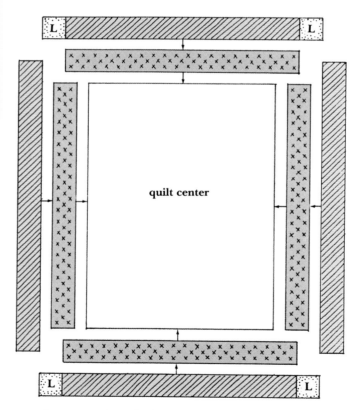

5–16. Attaching the borders (Christmas Angel). For the Country Angel, the inner border is blue print; the outer border is pink print.

5–17. Embroidery diagram for the angel's features, full–size.

Spring-on-the-Square Quilt and Pillows

A large scale floral pattern adds lively interest to the large squares in these projects, while the teal border is reminiscent of a cross-stitched design. Two colorful pillows carry the motif. You can make the quilt in just a few hours, because it is so simple. Finished size of quilt: 33" x 33". Finished size of each pillow: 14" x 14".

MATERIALS FOR ALL PROJECTS

¾ yard large scale floral print fabric

1¼ yards off-white fabric

¾ yard teal blue print fabric

35" x 35" piece of low-loft batting for the quilt

Two 15" x 15" pieces of quilt batting (one for each pillow)

35" x 35" piece of fabric for the quilt backing

Two 15" x 15" pieces of muslin (one for each pillow)

Two 15" x 15" pieces of backing fabric (one for each pillow)

4 yards of piping (2 yards of piping for each pillow)

4 yards of double-fold quilt binding (folded width, ½"; unfolded width, 2")

All-purpose threads to match the fabrics

DIRECTIONS

Construction is done with right sides of fabric facing and seam allowances of ¼", which are included in all the given measurements. The quilt center is made of six block rows and five sashing rows (see figure 6–1).

QUILT CUTTING GUIDE

Quantity	Size	Use
Large floral print fabric:		
Three	3½" x 44"	floral block rows
Six	3½" x 3½"	row ends
Four	1½" x 1½"	corner
Off-white fabric:		
Five	½" x 44"	quilt
Three	3½" x 44"	quilt
Eight	1½" x 3½"	quilt
Two	2½" x 23½"	inner border
Two	2½" x 27½"	inner border
Four	1½" x 1½"	corners
Two	1½" x 31½"	outer border
Two	1½" x 33½"	outer border
Teal print fabric:		
Three	1½" x 44"	quilt
Seven	1½" x 1½"	quilt
Two	3½" x 44"	border

first pieced border   outer border   second pieced border

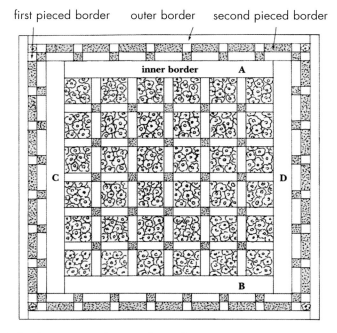

inner border

6–1. Construction diagram for quilt.

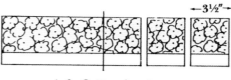

6–2. Cutting A units.

row end

6–3. Making a floral block row. Five A units plus a row end.

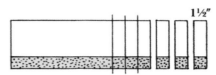

1½"

6–4. Cutting B units.

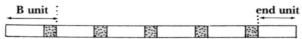

B unit

end unit

6–5. A horizontal sashing strip, made from five B units plus an off-white end unit.

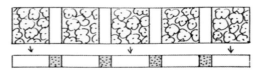

6–6. Stitching a horizontal sashing strip to a floral block row.

THE QUILT

Making the Block Rows

1. Cut out all the pieces needed for your project (either just the quilt pieces or the quilt and pillow pieces, if you prefer to cut them all at once).

2. Stitch a floral print 3½" x 44" strip on its long side to 1½" x 44" off-white fabric strip. Press. Make two more two-strip units the same way. Take each two-strip unit and cut across it to make 3½"-wide A units (figure 6–2). You will need thirty A units for the quilt. Set them aside.

3. Referring to figure 6–3, stitch together five A units, adding a 3½" floral square at the right of the last A unit, to make a floral row. Make a total of six of these rows. Set them aside.

Making the Horizontal Sashing Rows

4. Stitch one off-white 3½" x 44" strip to a teal 1½" x 44" strip on a long side. Make two more two-strip units the same way. Press. Take a two-strip unit and cut across both strips to make nineteen 1½"-wide B units (see figure 6–4). Cut nineteen 1½"-wide B units from the second two-strip unit. Cut eighteen B units from the third two-strip unit. You will have a total of fifty-six B units.

5. Stitch together five B units on their short sides, as shown in figure 6–5; at the end of this add a 1½" x 3½" off-white strip. This completes one horizontal sashing row. Make a total of five horizontal sashing rows.

6. To assemble the quilt center, attach a floral row to a horizontal sashing row as shown in figure 6–6. Continue adding floral block strips, alternating with sashing strips, to complete the quilt center (a total of six floral block strips and five horizontal sashing strips; see figure 6–1, the construction diagram, for reference). Press.

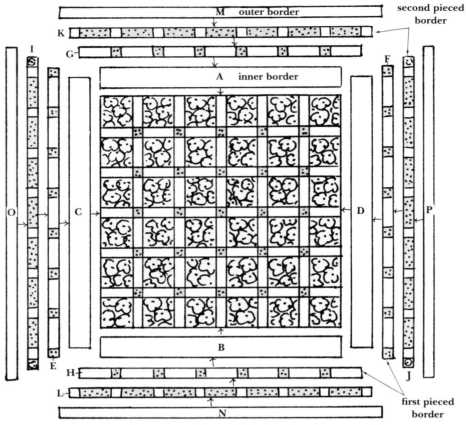

6–7. Diagram showing attachment of the borders, from A to M.

Making the First Pieced Border

Refer to figure 6–7 for attachment of all borders (steps 7 through 13).

7. Stitch one off-white border strip (2½" x 23½") to the top of the quilt center and the second to the bottom of the quilt center (A and B in figure 6–7). Stitch your 2½" x 27" off-white border strips to the sides of your quilt center for the side inner border strips C and D in figure 6–7. Press.

8. To make the first pieced border strip, make a row by stitching together six B units as shown in figure 6–8, along with one off-white 1½" x 3½" strip. Press. Make another first pieced border strip the same way. Stitch these strips to the top and bottom of the quilt center and press (see figure 6–1 for reference). Set the unit aside.

9. Stitch together seven B units, adding a 1½" teal end square at the end, as shown in figure 6–9, to make the top first pieced border (G in figure 6–7). Stitch another seven B units and teal square together to make the bottom first pieced border (H in 6–7). Stitch them to the top and bottom of the quilt center. Press. Set the unit aside.

Making the Second Pieced Border

10. Stitch a 1½" x 44" off-white strip on its long side to the long side of a 3½" x 44" teal strip. Make another two-strip unit the same way. Press. Cut across the two-strip units to make twenty-eight 1½"-wide C units (see figure 6–10).

6-8. An E or F first pieced border strip, made of six B units plus an end unit.

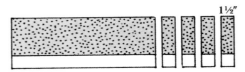

6-9. G or H first pieced border strips. Seven B units plus a teal square end unit.

1½"

6-10. Cutting the C units.

C unit

6-11. An I or J second pieced border strip. Seven C units plus a white square end unit.

C unit

6-12. K or L second pieced border strip. Seven C units, a floral square on the left, and white and floral squares on the right.

11. Stitch together seven C units along with one off-white 1½" square, as shown in figure 6–11. Press. Make another strip the same way. These will become second pieced border strips (I and J in figure 6–7). Stitch them to the right and left sides of the quilt center unit made in step 9. Press. Set it aside.

12. Stitch seven C units together, adding a 1½" off-white square to the teal end. Press. Stitch one of the 1½" floral squares to each end of the strip you just made (see figure 6–12). Make another strip the same way and press both. These will be the K and L border strips (see figure 6–7). Stitch them to the top and bottom of the quilt center unit made in step 11. Press.

Outer border

13. Take two 1½" x 31½" off-white strips for the outer border (border strips M and N in figure 6–7). Stitch them to the top and bottom of the quilt center unit you made in step 12. Take two 1½" x 33½" off-white strips and stitch them to the remaining two sides of the quilt center unit (border strips O and P in figure 6–7). Press. The finished quilt will look like figure 6–1.

Basting, Quilting, and Binding

14. Tape the 35" x 35" backing fabric, right side down, to your work surface. Center the batting over the backing fabric, and center the quilt top, right-side up, over the batting. Hand baste or pin baste the layers together. See Chapter 8—How to Quilt, pages 434 to 445. Machine quilt or hand quilt the project, as you desire.

15. After quilting, baste around the raw edges of the quilt top, about ½" in from the raw edge. Trim away any excess batting and backing fabric that extend beyond the edge of the quilt top. Bind the quilt to complete it.

FOUR-BLOCK PILLOW CUTTING GUIDE

Quantity	Size	Use
Large floral print fabric:		
Four	3½" x 3½"	blocks
Off-white fabric:		
Eight	1½" x 3½"	sashing
Two	1½" x 7½"	border
Two	1½" x 9½"	border
Teal print fabric:		
One	1½" x 1½"	center square
Two	3" x 9½"	border
Two	3" x 14½"	border

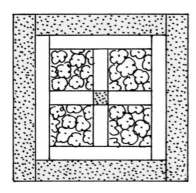

6–13. Construction diagram of the four-block pillow.

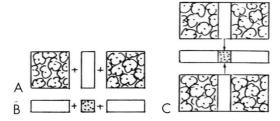

6–14. Four-block pillow construction. A. Joining two blocks to an off-white strip to make a row. B. Joining two off-white strips to a teal square to make a sashing strip. C. The two-block rows stitched to the sashing strip.

THE FOUR-BLOCK PILLOW

1. Cut four 3½" squares of floral fabric, one 1½" square of teal fabric, and four 1½" x 3½" strips of off-white fabric, if you have not already done so. Stitch a floral square to either side of a strip of off-white fabric on its 3½" sides (figure 16–14A) to make a block row. Make another block row the same way. Set them aside.

2. Make a central sashing strip by sewing two off-white strips (1½" x 3½") to either side of a teal square (figure 6–14B). Press.

3. Stitch a block row to the top of the sashing strip and one to the bottom of the sashing strip to make the pillow center, as shown in figure 6–14C.

4. From the off-white fabric, cut two 1½" x 7½" strips if you haven't already sone so, and stitch them to two opposite sides of the pillow center (A and B in figure 6–15). Cut two strips 1½" x 9½" from the off-white fabric, if you haven't already done so, and stitch them to the remaining two sides of the pillow center (they are C and D in 6–15) to complete the inner border.

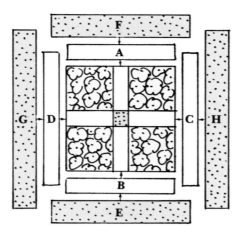

6–15. Adding the inner and outer borders, four-block pillow.

ONE-BLOCK PILLOW CUTTING GUIDE

Quantity	Size	Use
Large floral print fabric:		
One	6½" x 6½"	center block
Two	2½" x 10½"	outer border sides
Three	2½" x 14½"	outer border top and bottom
Off-white fabric:		
Four	1½" x 6½"	inner border
Two	1½" x 8½"	middle border sides
Two	1½" x 10½"	middle border top and bottom
Teal print fabric:		
Four	1½" x 1½"	corner pieces

5. From the teal fabric, cut two 3" x 9½" strips, if you have not already done so, and stitch them to the top and bottom of the quilt center (E and F in figure 6–15). Cut two 3" x 14½" teal strips and stitch them to the remaining sides (G and H in figure 16–15). Press. The finished pillow top looks like 6–13.

6. Tape a 15" x 15" muslin square to your work surface and center the batting over it. Center the pillow top over the batting square, right side up, and baste the three layers together. Quilt the pillow top as desired. Then baste about ¼" in from the raw edges of the pillow top all around and trim away any excess batting and muslin that extend beyond the pillow top. Baste the piping around the edges of the pillow top, with the raw edges facing out (see general directions for piping instructions).

7. Take the backing fabric and stitch the backing fabric to the pillow top, right sides facing, along all sides, leaving a 10" opening along one edge for turning. Clip the corners of the seam allowances for ease of turning and turn the pillow covering right-side out. Insert the pillow form and hand-stitch the turning opening closed to finish the first pillow.

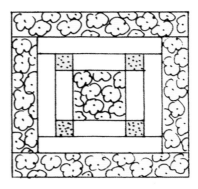

6–16. Construction diagram of the one-block pillow.

THE ONE-BLOCK PILLOW

1. If you haven't already cut these when you cut your quilt pieces, cut the following: Floral fabric: one 6½" square, two 2½" x 10½" strips, and two 2½" x 14½" strips. Off-white fabric: four 1½" x 6½" strips, two 1½" x 8½" strips, and two 1½" x 10½" strips. Teal: four 1½" squares.

2. Stitch a 1½" x 6½" off-white strip to the left side of the floral square and one to the right side (figure 6–17A). Set it aside.

3. Stitch a 1½" x 6½" off-white strip between two teal squares to make a top inner border for the center square (figure 6–17B). Repeat for the bottom border, and stitch the borders in place on the unit made in step 2 (figure 6–17C). Press.

4. For the middle border, take the two 1½" x 8½" off-white strips and stitch them to opposite sides of the pillow center unit made in step 3. Take the two 1½" x 10½" off-white strips and stitch them to the remaining two sides to complete the inner border (figure 6–17D). Press.

5. For the outer border, take the two 2½" x 10½" floral strips and stitch them to the opposite sides of the pillow center (see figure 6–17E). Press. Take the two 2½" x 14½" floral strips and stitch them to the remaining two sides of the pillow center. Press. This completes the pillow top.

6. Quilt and finish the pillow by the same procedure you used for the 4-block pillow (see steps 6 and 7 of the 4-block pillow instructions).

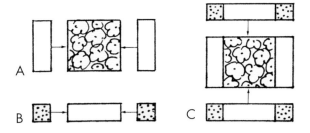

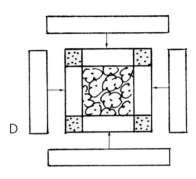

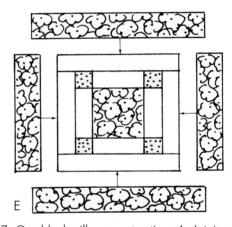

6–17. One-block pillow construction. A. Joining two off-white inner border strips to a floral block. B. Joining two teal squares to an off-white strip. C. Attaching the top and bottom inner borders. D. Attaching the second border strips. E. Attaching the third (floral) border strips.

Desert Nights Lap Quilt and Pillow

The generous size of this lap quilt makes it a perfect snuggler. Deep, rich colors give the feel of a desert night. If you would prefer a desert day, substitute pastels for the dark colors and eliminate the moon area, perhaps appliquéing a bright sun in its place. Finished size of the quilt: 50" x 54". Finished size of the pillow: 14" x 14".

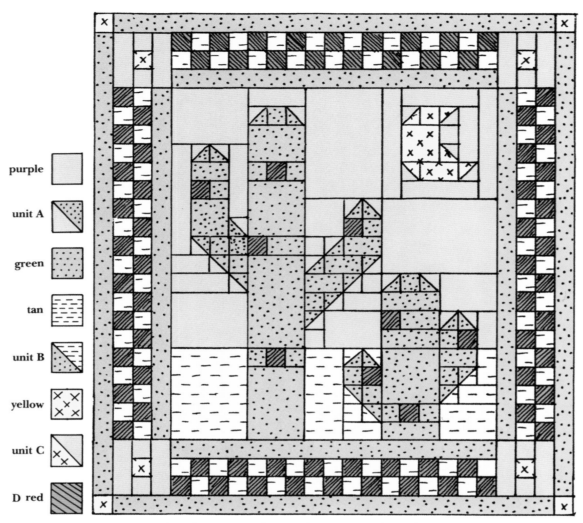

purple

unit A

green

tan

unit B

yellow

unit C

D red

7–1. Construction diagram for Desert Nights quilt.

MATERIALS

1½ yards deep purple fabric

1½ yards green fabric

1 yard tan fabric

¼ yard red fabric

½ yard mustard yellow fabric

54" x 58" piece of fabric for the backing

54" x 58" piece of batting

All-purpose threads to match the fabrics

6 yards of double-fold quilt binding (½" folded width; 2" unfolded width); tan in the model)

14" square pillow form

14 1½" x 14½" piece of batting

14½" x 14½" piece of muslin

2 yards of piping for the pillow

QUILT CUTTING GUIDE

Quantity	Use	Size

Green fabric:

Quantity	Use	Size
Eighteen	G squares	2½" x 2½"
Seven	E rectangles	2½" x 4½"
One	F square	4½" x 4½"
Two	Q squares	6½" x 6½"
One	N rectangle	4½" x 6½"
One	O rectangle	6½" x 10½"
Two	DD rectangles	2½" x 6½"
One	for purple-green two-triangle squares	7" x 16"
One	for tan-green triangle squares	4" x 7"
Two	inner border strips	2½" x 34½"
Two	inner border strips	2½" x 38½"
Two	outer border strips	2½" x 46½"
Two	outer border strips	2½" x 50½"

Purple fabric:

Quantity	Use	Size
Two	R rectangles	8½" x 12½"
Two	H rectangles	6½" x 8½"
Two	S rectangles	4½" x 6½"
Two	I strips	2½" x 12½"
Eleven	K rectangles	2½" x 6½"
Three	Y rectangles	2½" x 8½"
Three	L rectangles	2½" x 4½"
Twelve	U squares	2½" x 2½"
One	for purple-yellow two-triangle squares	4" x 7"
One	for purple-green two-triangle squares	16" x 7"

Red fabric:

Quantity	Use	Size
Five	to make borders	2½" x 44"
Nine	D squares	2½" x 2½"

Yellow fabric:

Quantity	Use	Size
One	rectangle	4" x 7"
One	BB square	4½" x 4½"
Nine	AA squares	2½" x 2½"
One	CC rectangle	2½" x 4½"

Tan fabric:

Quantity	Use	Size
Five	for borders	2½" x 44"
One	M rectangle	8½" x 1½"
One	V rectangle	4½" x 10½"
One	for green-tan two-triangle squares	4" x 7"

DIRECTIONS

All construction is done with right sides of fabric facing and seam allowances of ¼", which are included in the given measurements. For the quilt, to speed things along, do your cutting first, either with a rotary cutter or scissors. The construction diagram is given in figure 7–1. Figure 7–5 shows the pieces that make up the quilt center. As you cut the pieces, pin those of the same size and color together and tag them with a piece of tape or label so you can find them easily when it comes to construction.

QUILT

1. See the cutting charts for the green, purple, red, and gold fabrics, and cut out and label your fabric pieces.

2. Next, we'll make some two-triangle green-purple A squares by a speed method. On the wrong side of the 16" x 7" green fabric rectangle, mark ten 2⅞" squares. Draw a diagonal line through each square. Take the 16" x 7" purple rectangle and place the two pieces of fabric together, right sides facing. Stitch ¼" from each side of the diagonal lines you drew (figure 7–2A). Cut apart the squares along the marked square lines through both layers of fabric. Then cut each square along the marked diagonal line (figure 7–2B). Press each unit open to make a two-triangle A square as shown (figure 7–2C), for a total of twenty Unit A squares. Set them aside.

3. Take the green 4" x 7" rectangle and the tan rectangle the same size. Using the same speed method as in Step 2, mark three 2⅞" squares on the wrong side of the tan fabric, mark diagonals, sew the lines, and cut out and press the six two-triangle squares (figure 7–3). Each is a Unit B. Set them aside.

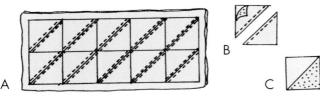

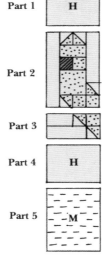

Part 1 H

Part 2

Part 3

Part 4 H

Part 5 M

7–2. Making Unit A (purple-green) two-triangle squares. A. Marking and sewing. B. Cutting the units apart on the ruled lines through both layers. C. The finished Unit A.

7–3. Making Unit B (green–tan) two–triangle squares. A. Marking and sewing. B. The finished unit.

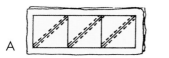

7–4. Making Unit C (purple-gold) two-triangle squares. A. Marking and sewing. B. The finished unit.

7–6. Diagram of Section 1 of the quilt center, showing the parts.

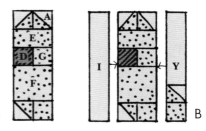

7–7. Part 2 of section one. A. The center unit. B. The center plus side units.

7–8. Making Part 3 of Section 1.

4. Repeat step 3 again, but using the 4" x 7" rectangle of yellow fabric and one of purple to make six yellow-purple two-triangle squares (Unit C); see figure 7–4. Set them aside.

Piecing the Quilt Center

The quilt center will be pieced in four sections (see figure 7–5). Each section is made up of parts (see figures 7–6, 7–13, 7–14, and 7–20).

Section 1 of the quilt center

Look at figure 7–6 to see how the parts are assembled to make Section 1. There are two purple H rectangles, a tan M rectangle, and two assembled parts (Part 2 and Part 3). First make the assembled parts.

5. To make Part 2, stitch two of the A units (purple-green, two-triangle squares) together with the green fabric meeting at the center as shown at the top of figure 7–7A. Stitch a 2½" x 4½" E rectangle just below the joined A units. Stitch a red

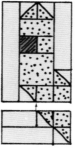

7–9. Joining Part 2 and Part 3 of Section 1.

7–10. Making an A–G–A unit for Part 1 of Section 2.

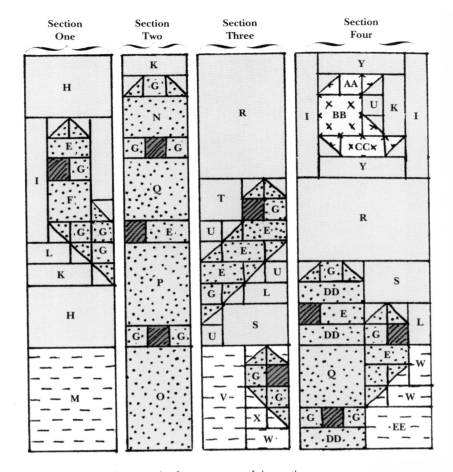

| Section One | Section Two | Section Three | Section Four |

7–5. Diagram showing the four sections of the quilt center.

2½" D square to a green 2½" G square and stitch the D+G squares just below the E strip (see 7–7A). Stitch the green 4½" F square on next, just below the D+G squares. Press.

6. Stitch the purple 12½" I strip to the left of the center unit made in step 5, as shown in 7–7B. Set it aside. Stitch an A unit and a green 2½" G square to the end of the purple 8½" Y strip and stitch the pieced strip thus formed to the right side of the center unit as shown in 7–7B. Press.

7. To make Part 3, stitch a purple 4½" L rectangle, an A unit, and a green 2½" G square together as shown in figure 7–8A (top row). Set it aside. Stitch an A unit to the end of a purple 6½" K rectangle as shown in 7–8A, bottom. Press. Stitch these two units

together as shown in figure 7–8B. This becomes Part 3 for section one. Join it to Part 2 as shown in 7–9.

8. To assemble section 1, pin together the units shown in figure 7–6: two H rectangles of purple fabric, a tan M rectangle, and the Part 2+3 unit you just completed. Set it aside.

Section 2 of the quilt center

9. Referring to figure 7–10, stitch together two A units (purple-green, two-triangle squares) and a green 2½" G square. Press.

10. Pin the A-G-A unit made in step 9 between a purple K strip and a green 4½" x 6½" N rectangle, as shown in figure 7–11, and stitch them together. This is Part 1 of Section 2. Press. Set it aside.

11. Stitch one of the red 2½" D squares between two green 2½" G squares (see figure 7–12, top). Make another three-square unit the same way. Set them aside for Part 2 and Part 6 of section 2. Stitch one D square to a green E 2½" x 4½" rectangle (see 7–12, bottom). Press. Set it aside for Part 4 of Section 2.

7–11. The finished Part 1 of Section 2.

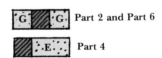

7–12. Three more units for section 2. Top. Part 2 and Part 6. Bottom. Part 4.

12. To assemble Section 2, take the green Q, O, and P rectangles and part 1, 2, 4, and 6 you just made, and pin and stitch them together as shown in figure 7–13. Press. Set Section 2 aside.

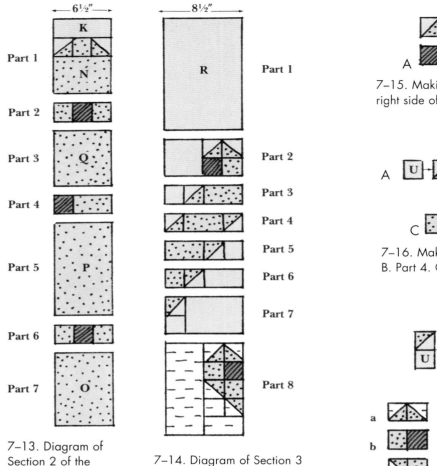

7–13. Diagram of Section 2 of the quilt center, showing the parts.

7–14. Diagram of Section 3 of the quilt center, showing the parts.

A

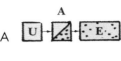
B

7–15. Making Part 2 of Section 3. A. Making the right side of Part 2. B. The finished Part 2.

A  B

C D

7–16. Making some parts of Section 3. A. Part 3. B. Part 4. C. Part 5. D. Part 6.

 P7–17. Making part 7 of Section 3.

a
b
c
d
e

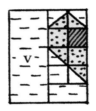

7–18. Right side of Part 8, Section 3.

7–19. Completed Part 8 of Section 3.

Section 3 of the quilt center

Look at figure 7–14 to see how Section 3 is made. It is composed of eight parts, and seven of them have to be assembled from smaller pieces before they are stitched together.

13. First make Part 2. Stitch two A units together with the green sides meeting at the center (figure 7–15A, top). Set it aside. Stitch a 2½" red D square to a green G square the same size (figure 7–15A, bottom). Referring to 7–15A, join the A–A unit to the D–G unit. Stitch the purple 4½" T square to the left side of the unit you just made (figure 7–15B). Press. Set it aside as Part 2.

14. Stitch one purple 2½" U square to an A unit and a green 2½" x 4½" E rectangle as shown in figure 7–16A. Press. Set it aside as Part 3. Stitch one A unit to each side of a green 2½" x 4½" E rectangle as shown in figure 7–16B. Press. Set it aside as Part 4. Stitch a 2½" x 4½" green E strip on one side of an A unit and a purple 2½" U square to the other side as shown in 7–16C. Press. Set it aside as Part 5. Stitch a green 2½" G square to one side of an A unit and stitch a 2½" x 4½" purple L rectangle to the other side as shown in figure 7–16D. Press. Set it aside as Part 6.

15. Stitch an A unit to a 2½" purple U square (see figure 7–17, left). Stitch this unit to a 4½" x 6½" purple S rectangle as shown in figure 7–17. Press. Set it aside as Part 7.

16. To make Part 8, look at figure 7–18. Work from top to bottom to sew the right half first. Stitch two B units together (figure 7–18A); a B unit is a two-triangle square of green and tan. Set it aside. Stitch a green 2½" G square to a red D square the same size (figure 7–18B). Set it aside. Stitch one B unit to a green 2½" G square as shown in figure 7–18C. Set the unit aside. Stitch one tan 2½" square to a B unit as shown in 7–18D. Lay out the parts from figure 7–18 A through D you just made as shown in the figure and pin them together. Then stitch them together. Stitch a 2½" x 4½" tan W strip at the bottom (figure 7–18E). This completes the right half of Part 8. Stitch a 4½" x 10½" tan V rectangle to the left side of Part 8; the complete Part 8 is shown in figure 7–19. Press. Set it aside.

17. Assemble Section 3: Lay out all of the parts from 1 through 8, which you made in steps 13 through 16, along with an 8½" x 12½" purple R rectangle, as shown in figure 7–14. Pin the pieces together, check the layout, and stitch them together. Press. Set Section 3 aside.

Section 4 of the quilt center

Section 4 (see figure 7–20) is made in several parts. First we'll make the top part, the moon block.

Moon Block

18. To start the moon block, stitch a C unit (a purple-yellow two-triangle square) to each side of a 2½" yellow AA square as shown in figure 7–21. Press. Set it aside as Part 1 of the moon block.

19. Stitch a C unit to a 2½" purple U square as shown in figure 7–22A. Stitch the CU unit to the 4½" yellow BB square as shown in figure 7–22B. Press. Set it aside as Part 2 of the moon block.

20. Stitch one C unit to a 2½" x 4½" yellow CC rectangle as shown in figure 7–23. Press. It is Part 3 of the moon block.

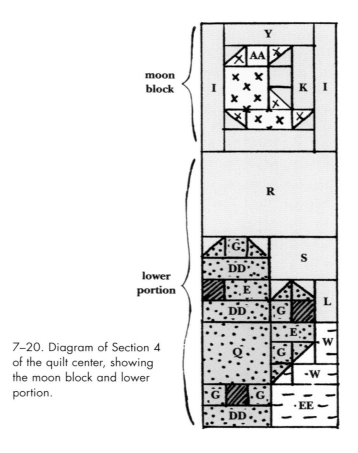

7–20. Diagram of Section 4 of the quilt center, showing the moon block and lower portion.

7–21. Making Part 1 of the center of the moon block. Stitch two C units to a yellow AA square.

7–22. Making Part 2 of the center of the moon block. A. Stitch a U square to a C unit. B. Stitch a BB square to the UC unit.

7–23. Making Part 3 of the center of the moon block. Stitch a C unit to a CC rectangle.

21. Lay out, pin, and stitch together Parts 1 through 3 as shown in figure 7–24A. Set it aside. Stitch a C unit to the end of a 2½" x 6½" purple K rectangle, as shown in figure 7–24B. Press. This is Part 4 of the moon block; stitch it to the right of the unit shown in figure 7–24A. The result (figure 7–24C) is the center of the moon block. Press.

22. Stitch one of the 2½" x 8½" purple Y strips to the top and one to the bottom edge of the moon block center, as shown in figure 7–25. Press. Stitch a 2½" x 12½" purple I strip to either side of the moon block (see figure 7–25). Press.

23. Stitch a 12½" x 8½" purple R rectangle on a long side just below the moon block (figure 7–26). This completes the upper portion of Section 4. Press it and set it aside.

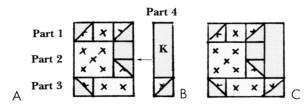

7–24. A. The joined parts 1 through 3 of the moon block. B. Adding Part 4 of the center of the moon block. C. The finished center of the moon block.

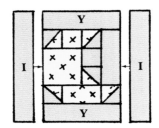

7–25. Attaching the I rectangles to the moon block; the Y rectangles are already attached.

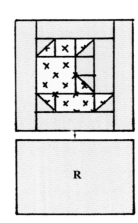

7–26. The upper part of Section 4.

Lower unit of section 4

The lower unit of Section 4 (see figure 7–5 for reference) is made in two parts: left and right (see figure 7–27). First make the left part.

24. Stitch an A unit to each side of a 2½" green G square (figure 7–28A). Press. Set it aside as Part 1 of the left side. Stitch one red D square to one green 2½" x 4½" E strip (figure 7–28B). Set it aside as Part 3 of the left side. Stitch one red D square between two green 2½" G squares (figure 7–28C). Set it aside as Part 6 of left side.

25. Lay out, pin, and stitch together the three assembled units (Parts 1, 3, and 6) made in step 24 along with the three 2½" x 6½" green DD strips and the 6½" green Q square (figure 7–29.) Press. This is the left side of the lower unit of Section 4.

26. For the right part of the lower unit of Section 4, look at figure 7–30. Part 1 is a purple rectangle, 4½" x 6½" (S). To make Part 2, stitch together two A units, one red D square and one 2½" green G square as shown in figure 7–31. Press Part 2 and set aside.

27. To make Part 4, stitch one unit B to one 2½" green G square as shown in figure 7–32. Press and set aside.

28. To make Part 5, stitch a ½" x 4½" tan W rectangle to a purple L rectangle of the same size, as shown in figure 7–33.

29. Referring to figure 7–33, left, stitch together Parts 2, 3, 4, and 5, as shown (Part 3 is a 2½" x 4½" green rectangle, E).

30. To make Part 6 of the lower right unit, stitch the remaining B unit to the remaining 2½" x 4½" tan W strip as shown in figure 7–34. Press.

31. Stitch Part 6 to the bottom of the unit made in step 29. Press. Stitch the tan 4½" x 6½" EE rectangle to the bottom of the unit you just made, as Part 7, referring to the figure 7–30. Stitch the purple 4½" x 6½" S rectangle to the top of the unit. Press. This completes the right part of the lower unit of Section 4.

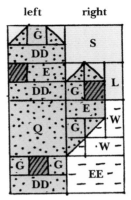

left right

7–27. The lower unit of Section 4, showing left and right parts.

A  B C

7–28. Making the lower unit of Section 4, left side. A. Part 1. B. Part 3. C. Part 6.

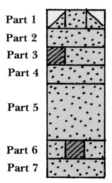

Part 1
Part 2
Part 3
Part 4
Part 5
Part 6
Part 7

7–29. Diagram of the left part of the lower unit of Section 4, showing parts.

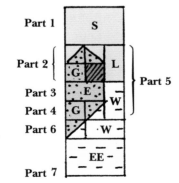

Part 1 S
Part 2 L
Part 3 E
Part 4 W
Part 5
Part 6 ·W·
Part 7 EE

7–30. Diagram of the right part of the lower unit of section 4, showing parts.

7–31. Part 2 of the right part of the lower unit of Section 4.

7–32. Part 4 of the right part of the lower unit of Section 4.

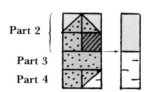

Part 2
Part 3
Part 4
Part 5

7–33. Part 5 is sewn to the assembled Parts 2, 3, and 4.

7–34. W strip is sewn to a B unit to make Part 6 of the right part of the lower unit of Section 4.

32. Stitch the right part of the lower unit of Section 4 to the left part of the lower unit, which you completed in step 25 (see figure 7–35). This completes the lower portion of Section 4.

33. Referring to figure 7–20, stitch the upper portion (completed in step 23) and lower portion of Section 4 together to complete it. Press.

34. Referring to figure 7–5, stitch Sections 1 through 4 together to make the quilt center. Press.

Corner Units and Borders

NOTE: See figure 7–40 for all border attachment instructions.

35. To make the corner units for the border, you will need four yellow 2½" AA squares, eight 2½" purple U squares, and eight 2½" x 6½" purple K strips, which you probably already cut. Using one yellow AA square, two purple U squares and two purple K strips, assemble a corner unit as shown in figure 7–36. Press. Make four of these corner units and set them aside.

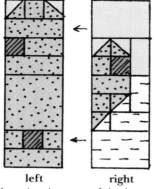

7–35. The left and right parts of the lower unit of Section 4 are sewn together.

left   right

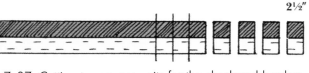

2½"

7–37. Cutting two-square units for the checkered borders.

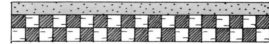

7–38. A checkered border unit made of nineteen red-tan two-square units.

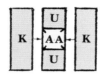

7–36. A corner unit for the quilt.

7–39. A green inner border strip, sewn to a checkered border of nineteen units.

36. Stitch together one red and one tan strip, both 2½" x 44", along one long edge. Repeat with the remaining 2½" x 44" red and tan strips to make five two-strip units. Cut across the joined strips to make 2½" wide units as shown in figure 7–37. You need seventy-two of these units for the quilt. Cut six extra for the pillow, if you will make the pillow, and set them aside.

37. Making a checkerboard pattern, stitch together nineteen of the two-square red-tan units you just cut together to form a row as shown in figure 7–38. Make another nineteen-unit row the same way. Stitch one of the green 2½" x 38½" inner border strips cut earlier to one side of each of these checkered strips (see figure 7–39) to make a side border unit. Stitch one of these side border units to the left side of the quilt center and one to the right side, with the green strip joining the quilt center (see figure 7–40). Press.

38. Stitch together seventeen red-tan two-square units as shown in figure 7–41 to make a border unit for the top of the quilt center. Make another the same way for the bottom of the quilt center.

Stitch a green 2½" x 34½" inner border strip to one side of each of these two border units (figure 7–42).

39. Stitch one of your corner units (made in step 35) to each short end of the two border units you made in step 38 (figure 7–42). Stitch one border unit + corner unit to the top of the quilt center with the green strip edge touching the quilt center (figure 7–40). Stitch the second border unit + corner unit to the bottom of the quilt center. Press.

40. Stitch a 2½" x 50½" green outer border strip to the left side of the quilt center. Stitch another one the same size to the right side of the quilt center. Take four 2½" yellow squares, and stitch one to each short end of the two remaining green outer border strips (2½" x 46"). Stitch one of these border units to the top of the quilt center and one to the bottom of the quilt center (figure 7–40). Press. This completes the quilt top.

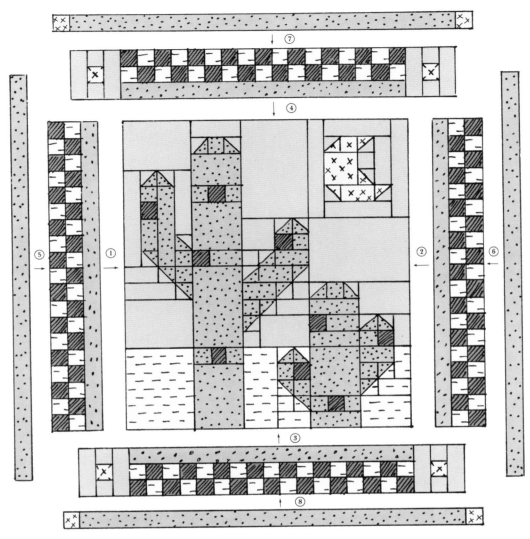

7–40. Border attachment to quilt. Circled numerals indicate order.

Basting, Binding, and Quilting

41. Tape the 54" x 58" backing fabric wrong side up on your work surface and center the batting over it. Center the quilt top, right side up, over the batting. Hand-baste or pin-baste the layers together. Machine quilt it as desired. (See Chapter 8— How to Quilt, pages 434 to 445.)

42. Baste all around the quilt top, about ¼" from the raw edge, and trim away the excess batting and backing that extends beyond the quilt top. Bind the quilt with the bias binding to complete it.

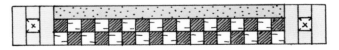

7–41. A checkered border unit made of seventeen red-tan two-square units.

7–42. A seventeen-unit checkered border with corner units and green border strip added.

PILLOW CUTTING GUIDE

Quantity	Use	Size
Green fabric:		
Two	strips	2½" x 10½"
Two	strips	2½" x 14½"
Purple fabric:		
Two	K rectangles	2½" x 6½"
Two	U squares	2½" x 2½"
Red fabric:		
Two	D squares	2½" x 2½"
Yellow fabric:		
One	AA square	2½" x 2½"
Tan fabric:		
Two	squares	2½" x 2½"

PILLOW

1. To make the matching pillow (figure 7–43), make a corner unit as for the quilt (see figure 7–36). Set aside.

2. Take the six extra red-tan two-square units cut in step 36 of the quilt project, and two 2½" red squares and two more 2½" tan squares. Join a two-square unit to a red square as shown in 7–44A, and attach it to the top of the corner unit (see 7–45). Make another three-square unit the same way and attach it to the bottom of the corner unit. Make a five-square unit for the left side of the corner unit and another for the right side (see figure 7–44B). Attach them to the sides of the corner unit as shown in figure 7–45.

3. Take the two 2½" x 10½" green fabric strips and the two 2½" x 14½" strips. Attach a 10½" strip to the top and one to the bottom of the unit you pieced in step 2. Attach the 14½" green strips to the sides (figure 7–45).

4. Lay out the muslin, with the batting centered over it and the pillow top, face up, centered over the batting and quilt the pillow top as desired. Baste the piping around the edges of the pillow top, with the raw edges facing out.

5. Cut a 14½" square of any of the leftover fabrics to make the backing for the pillow. Baste the backing to the pillow front, right sides facing, and stitch closed along all four sides, leaving a 10" turning opening along one side. Clip the corners of the seam allowances and turn the pillow covering right side out. Press. Insert the pillow form and hand stitch the turning opening closed.

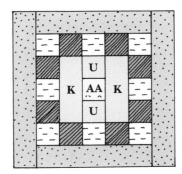

7-43. Pillow construction diagram.

7-44. Pillow inner borders. A. For top and bottom. B. For side borders.

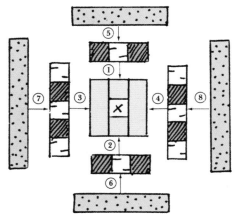

7-45. Attaching pillow borders. Numbers indicate order of piecing.

Ocean Breeze Lap Quilt and Pillow Set

This quilt may look difficult, but it is quite easy to construct. Using a rotary cutter to speed cut the triangles simplifies the work. There are twelve 10" x 10" blocks in the quilt. Finished size of the quilt: 42" x 52". Finished size of the pillow: 14" x 14".

dark
green

gray-
green

blue

white
print

solid
white

8–1. Construction diagram for the quilt.

MATERIALS FOR QUILT AND PILLOW

2 yards white print fabric

1¼ yards dark blue print or dark blue
    solid-color fabric

¾ yard solid-white fabric

23" x 36" piece of dark green fabric

23" x 36" piece of gray green fabric

44" x 54" piece of traditional-weight quilt batting
    for the quilt

44" x 54" piece of backing fabric for the quilt

15" x 15" piece of muslin for pillow

15" x 15" piece of batting for pillow

15" x 15" piece of fabric for the pillow backing

14" square pillow form

2 yards of piping for the pillow

Thread to match the fabrics

6 yards of double-fold quilt binding, dark green in
    the model. (Folded width, ½"; unfolded width, 2".)

CUTTING GUIDE

Quantity	Size	Use
Dark blue print fabric:		
Seven	2¼" x 44"	for triangles
Two	2½" x 34½"*	inner border
Two	2½" x 40½"*	inner border
Two	2½" x 10½"	pillow border
Two	2½" x 14½"	pillow border
Solid white fabric:		
Seven	2¼" x 44"	for triangles
White print fabric:*		
Two	½" x 44½"*	outer borders
Two	4½" x 42½"*	outer borders
Two	23" x 36"	for triangles

*Cut the white and dark blue border strips first.

DIRECTIONS

Construction is done with right sides of fabric facing and seam allowances of ¼", which are included in the measurements given. See fabric cutting guides and cut the pieces you need first.

QUILT

Overview. The construction diagram of the quilt is shown in figure 8–1. There are two kinds of blocks. See block diagrams shown in figure 8–2. Each block is made of four quarters, which in turn has two halves, a two-triangle half and a half made of two strips. First make the two-strip halves.

1. Take the seven solid white fabric strips, each 44" x 2½", and the seven of the same size cut from the dark blue fabric. Stitch one solid white strip to one dark blue strip along one long side. Press and set aside. Repeat to make seven two-strip units.

2. Referring to figure 8–3, cut 45-90-45-degree triangles from each two-strip unit. The long side of the triangles are 7¾", as shown. You will have fifty-four two-strip triangles. Those with dark blue tops, we'll call these S triangles. Those with solid white tops; we'll call these R triangles. You need twenty-four S triangles and twenty-four R triangles

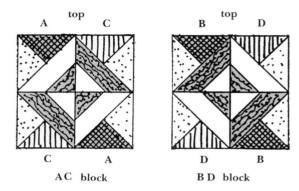

8–2. Block construction diagrams for the quilt, showing the two blocks, the AC block and the BD block.

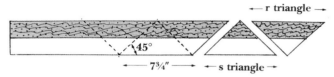

8–3. Cut the two-strip unit into right triangles as shown; their longest side is 7¾ units; the small angles are 45 degrees.

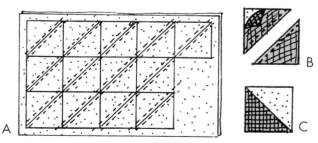

8–4. Making two-triangle squares. A. Marking the squares and stitching lines (dashed lines) for two-tringle squares. B. Cutting the squares apart. C. The pressed two-triangle square.

for the quilt. For the pillow, cut two S and two R triangles.

3. To make the two-triangle corners of the blocks by a speed-triangle method, take the two 23" x 36" white print rectangles. On the wrong side of each mark thirteen 6⅜" squares as shown in figure 8–4A. Mark a diagonal line through each square. Take the 23" x 36" dark green and gray-green rectangles and place one green rectangle against each marked white print rectangle, right sides together. Stitch ¼" from each side of the diagonal lines (figure 8–4A). Cut the squares apart along the marked lines and cut along the diagonals through both layers of fabric (figure 8–4B). Press each unit open to form a two-triangle square (figure 8–4C). You will have fifty-two of these two-triangle squares: twenty-six dark green + white print and twenty-six gray-green + white print. (This includes enough for the pillow.)

4. Referring to figure 8–5A, cut each dark green + white print two-triangle square in half diagonally, perpendicular to the line of stitching, to make two pieced triangles. You will get a total of fifty-two dark green + white print triangles. Look closely at 8–5A. You only want to keep the h dark green + white print triangles, Separate out all the reverse k

triangles and put them away for another project. The h triangles have dark green on the right (see 8–5A). You need twenty-four of them for the quilt, and two for the pillow.

5. Referring to 8–5B, cut each gray-green + white print square in half diagonally, perpendicular to the line of stitching, to make two pieced regimens, for a total of fifty-six gray-green + white print triangles. Look closely at 8–5B. You only want to keep the m gray-green + white print triangles. The m triangles have light green on the left side. You need twenty-four for the quilt and two for the pillow. Separate out all the reverse p triangles and put them away for another project.

6. Now assemble the four quarters that make up each block in the quilt. There are four different kinds of quarters: A, B, C, and D (see figure 8–6). For the quilt blocks you will need to make:
Fourteen A quarters
Ten B quarters
Fourteen C quarters
Ten D quarters

7. Quarter A: Stitch an h triangle (from step 4) to an s triangle from step 2, as shown in figure 8–6. Repeat to make a total of fourteen A quarters. Set aside.

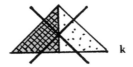   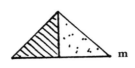

8–5A. Cut each dark green-white print two-triangle square diagonally into halves; put away or discard the k halves (green on the left) and keep the h halves (green on the right).

8–5B. Cut each gray-green + white print two-triangle square diagonally into halves; put away or discard the p halves (gray-green on the right) and keep the m halves (gray-green on left).

8. Quarter B: Stitch an h triangle to an r triangle (from step 2). Repeat to make a total of ten B quarters. Set aside.

9. Quarter C: Stitch an m triangle (from step 5) to an r triangle. Repeat to make a total of fourteen C quarters. Set aside.

10. Quarter D: Stitch an m triangle to an s triangle. Repeat to make a total of ten D quarters. Now proceed to the blocks from the quarters.

11. The AC blocks: Study the AC block in figure 8–2. Take two A quarters and two C quarters, position them as shown in 8–2 to make an AC block, pin them together, and stitch them together. Make a total of seven AC blocks the same way. Press them and set them aside.

12. The BD blocks: Look at the BD block in figure 8–2. You need to make five BD blocks for the quilt, and one for the pillow. Take two B quarters and two D quarters and position them as shown in 8–2 to make a BD block. Pin and stitch them together. Make a total of five BD blocks the same way. Press and set aside.

13. You are ready to assemble the blocks for the quilt center. You will make four rows of three blocks each. See figure 8–7 for guidance in positioning the blocks. Be sure to note how the top of the block is turned in the row. Pin the blocks together for row 1, check it with the construction diagram (figure 8–1), and stitch the blocks together. Tag the row with masking tape and set it aside. Repeat the same procedure for rows 2 through 4.

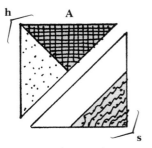

An A quarter = h triangle + s triangle.

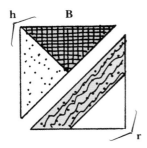

B quarter = h triangle + r triangle.

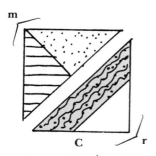

C quarter = m triangle + r triangle.

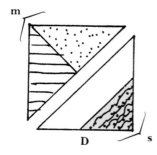

D quarter = m triangle + s triangle.

8–6. Assembly diagrams showing the four kinds of quarters that are used to make blocks.

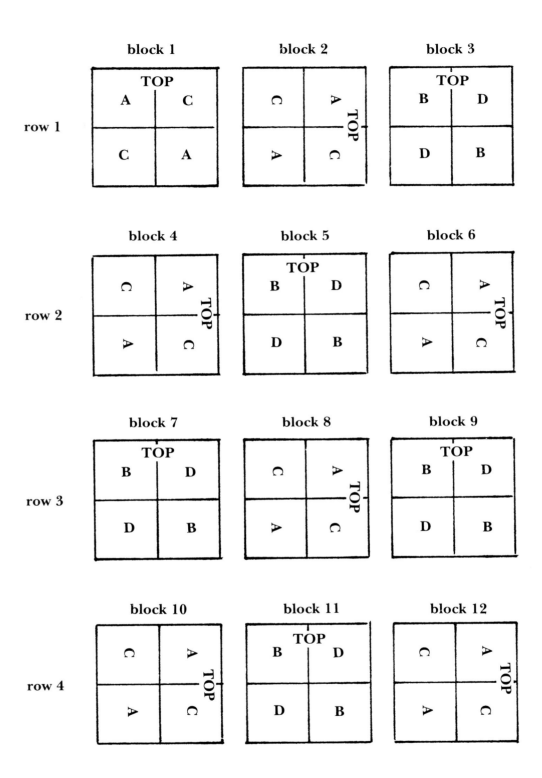

8–7. Block layout for center of quilt. Note orientation of tops of blocks.

14. Once the blocks are sewn into rows, pin the rows together, matching seams and checking their positioning with figure 8–1. Stitch row 1 to row 2, and so on until you have completed the quilt center.

15. Take two 34½" dark blue inner border strips. Stitch one to the left and one to the right of the quilt center; see figure 8–1 for reference. Press. Take two 40" dark blue border strips. Stitch one strip to the top and one to the bottom of the quilt center.

16. Take two 42½" white print outer border strips. Stitch one to the left and one to the right of the unit you made in step 15. Take two 44½" white print border strips. Stitch one print border strip to the top and one to the bottom of the unit. Press. This completes your quilt top.

17. Basting, Quilting, and Binding. Tape the quilt backing to your work surface, wrong side up, and center the batting over it. Center the quilt top right-side up over the batting. Hand baste or pin baste the layers together. Refer to Chapter 8— How to Quilt, pages 434 to 445.

18. After quilting, baste all around the quilt top, about ¼" in from the raw edges of the quilt top, and trim away any excess batting and backing fabric that extend beyond the quilt top. Bind the quilt to complete it.

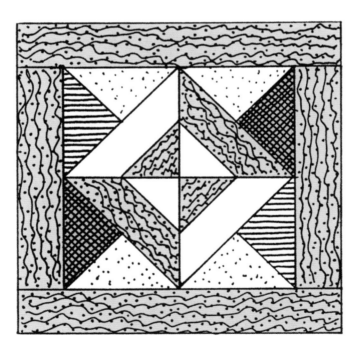

8–8. The pillow top.

PILLOW

1. For the pillow, make one block as you did for the quilt.

2. Take the two dark blue fabric 2½" x 10½" strips and two 2½" x 14½" strips. Stitch the 10½" long strips to two opposite sides of the block, referring to figure 8–8. Then stitch the 14½" strips to the remaining two sides.

3. Tape the muslin square to your work surface, center the batting square over it and the pillow top face up over that. Quilt the pillow as desired.

4. Baste about ¼" in from the raw edges of the pillow top all around, and trim away the excess batting and backing that extends beyond the pillow top. Baste the piping around the edges of the pillow top, with edges out, and stitch the backing to the pillow top, with its right side facing the right side of the pillow top, along all four sides, leaving a 10" opening for turning. Clip the corners of the seam allowance and turn the pillow covering right side out. Insert the pillow form and hand stitch the turning opening closed to complete the pillow.

A quilt composed of the "Dawn Flower" foundation-pieced blocks.
Directions for block construction can be found on page 354.

CHAPTER 7
Foundation-pieced Quilt Blocks

by Mary Jo Hiney

The "Frog King" waits for dragonflies under the stars, as fashioned with
foundation-pieced quilt blocks designed and made by Mary Jo Hiney.

The technique of foundation piecing is a quick and easy way to make beautiful, complex-looking quilt blocks without the time associated with traditional piecing.

Foundation piecing is sewing fabric pieces to a foundation, such as paper or fabric, following a numerical sequence. Lines are drawn on the wrong side of the foundation. Fabric is placed on the unmarked (right) side of the foundation with right side up and sewn on the marked (wrong) side. This technique allows the quilter to piece even the smallest pieces more quickly and accurately, since all sewing follows drawn lines.

Provided for each quilt block in this section are a full-color photograph of the actual block, its size, level of difficulty, full-sized pattern pieces for tracing onto your foundation, a full-color unit placement diagram of the assembled block, and a black-and-white seam line diagram of the assembled block. Many of these blocks are made of separate units. The colored diagram indicates how each unit is placed in the block. The black-and-white diagram indicates seams.

When reading the seam line diagram, blue lines indicate a seam and magenta dots indicate where units must be matched together. When there are two or more of one unit in a block, only one seam is indicated with blue lines.

MATERIALS & TOOLS

Size and quantity of materials will depend on project and size desired. If planning a quilt, please refer to "Planning a Quilt" for dimensions.

Materials

- Batting
- Binding: bias, quilt
- Fabrics: colors of choice, cotton, for backing, foundation, and binding; colors of choice, cotton scraps, for foundation piecing
- Interfacing: lightweight, nonwoven, or tear away, for foundation
- Thread: coordinating color, cotton

Tools

- Fabric glue stick
- Iron and ironing board
- Needles: quilting, sewing
- Paper: computer, copy, newsprint, notebook, or tracing, for foundation; tracing
- Pen or pencil for marking and transferring
- Pins: quilt, safety
- Quilting frame
- Rotary cutter and cutting board
- Ruler: Quilter's, small and large
- Scissors: craft, fabric
- Sewing machine
- Spray bottle

FABRIC

Cotton fabric is recommended for all projects in this section. Pieces will stay in place easily after finger-pressing. Some quilt blocks shown in this book are made with silks and velvets for added beauty. Keep in mind these fabrics are more difficult to work with.

Finger-pressing will not stay in place with these fabrics or others, such as polyester cotton. They will need to be pinned, glued, or iron-pressed in place after each step. If planning a quilt, please refer to "Planning a Quilt" for dimensions.

If planning to make a washable project, test fabric to make certain it is colorfast and preshrunk. Do not trust labels. For the puckered look of an antique quilt, use fabrics with various shrinkage differences and do not preshrink.

If this is not the desired look, wash and dry all fabrics before beginning. Fabrics that continue to shrink after washing and drying several times should not be used for quilt block projects.

To test for color fastness and shrinkage:
1. Cut a precise 2" x 6" strip of each fabric, using fabric scissors.
2. Place each fabric strip separately into a clean bowl of extremely hot water, or hold each fabric strip under hot running water. If unsure fabric is colorfast, place wet strip on a dry paper towel, and watch for bleeding on the paper towel.
3. If fabric strip bleeds a great deal, wash all of that fabric until excess dye washes out. Fabrics that continue to bleed, after washing several times, should not be used for quilt block projects.
4. To test for shrinkage, iron each saturated strip dry, using a hot iron.
5. When fabric strip is completely dry, measure and compare it to original measurements.

CUTTING THE FABRIC

For foundation piecing, pieces do not have to be cut perfectly. Use strips, rectangles, squares, or any odd-shaped scrap material. Make certain fabric is at least ³⁄₈" larger on all sides than the area it is to cover. As triangle shapes are more difficult to piece, use generous-sized fabric pieces and position pieces carefully on the foundation. Some fabric is wasted using foundation piecing, but the time saved is well worth it.

FOUNDATION MATERIAL

Decide what type of foundation to use for piecing the blocks—lightweight interfacing, fabric, paper, or tear-away interfacing. For fabric, choose a light-colored, lightweight fabric that can be seen through for tracing. Batiste, muslin, and broadcloth work well and will give extra stability to the blocks. For paper, choose one that can be seen through, such as tracing paper, copy paper, newsprint, or computer paper. For greatest speed and least bulk, use the lightest-weight nonwoven interfacing for foundation. Use a light touch when preparing the foundation.

NOTE: Keep in mind that using a fabric foundation will add another layer to quilt through. Paper tears away after sewing is completed. For tear-away interfacing, choose a type that can be removed easily.

MIRROR IMAGE

Foundation quilting will create a mirror image of the pattern. If an exact replica of the pattern is desired, reverse the pattern on the foundation, following the method for mirrored image units below. The patterns shown are a mirror image of the photograph shown. This has been designed so each set of patterns and instructions will result in an exact image of the photograph shown.

Many of the quilt blocks in "Foundation-Pieced Quilt Blocks" have left and right mirrored units. Only one pattern is given. Trace two unit patterns, but make one unit pattern on the wrong side. This is just one advantage to using a see-through foundation. If a see-through foundation is not used, make a copy of the pattern. Flip the paper over and hold up to a light source and trace onto foundation.

NOTE: Mirrored units are represented on colored unit placement diagrams with (m). For example: A(m).

PREPARING THE FOUNDATION

Tracing the Block

1. Trace pattern onto foundation material, using a ruler and a fine-point permanent marking pen or a #2 pencil. Include all numbers.

2. Draw ¼" seam allowance around outside edges.

3. Cut foundation ½" from seam allowance of the block or unit.

4. Repeat for number of blocks needed for project.

TIP: If desiring a block to look exactly like the pattern, reverse pattern before tracing onto paper, then trace onto foundation material.

Transferring the Block

Another method of pattern transfer is to transfer pattern onto foundation material, using a transfer tool. Include all numbers.

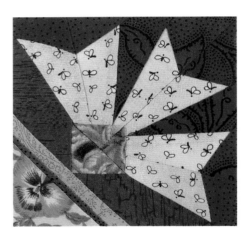

STEP-BY-STEP INSTRUCTIONS FOR FOUNDATION PIECING

NOTE: Instructional photos show assembly of Flower Bouquet quilt block found on page 364.

1. Transfer pattern onto foundation, as shown in figure 7–1, using a #2 pencil or a fine-point permanent marking pen; write all numbers on foundation. Mark for a mirror image, if applicable.

7–1.
Use a #2 pencil or a fine-point permanent marking pen to transfer pattern to foundation.

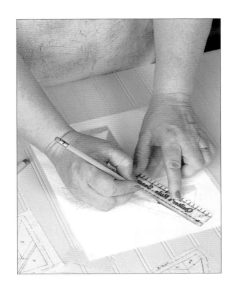

7–2.
Place fabric piece 2 on fabric piece 1, right sides together. Pin, glue, or hold in place.

7–3.
Stitch fabric piece 2 to fabric piece 1 along line between shapes 1 and 2. Repeat with unit A(m), stitching on unmarked side of foundation. Begin and end two or three stitches beyond line.

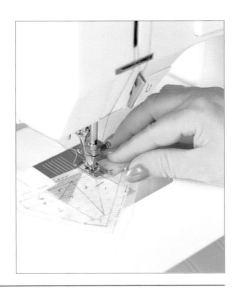

2. Cut fabric pieces for block. Make a chart as an aid to note fabrics, number placements, cut sizes, and quantities needed for each fabric.

3. Turn over foundation with unmarked side up. Place fabric piece 1, right side up, on shape 1. If foundation is not sheer, hold foundation up to a light source to make certain that fabric overlaps at least ¼" on all sides of shape 1. Pin, glue, or hold in place.

4. Make certain that fabric piece 2 overlaps at least ¼" on all sides of shape 2. Place fabric piece 2 on fabric piece 1, right sides together, as shown in figure 7–2 on facing page. Duplicate steps for mirror image unit A(m) while making unit A. Be certain fabric is placed on correct side to make mirror image.

5. Turn over foundation, with marked side up. Sew along line between shapes 1 and 2, with marked side of foundation up, using a very small stitch. (This is helpful if paper has been used as the foundation.) Begin and end two or three stitches beyond line, as shown in figure 7–3. Trim excess fabric ⅛" to ¼" past seam line.

6. Turn over foundation, with unmarked side up. Open fabric piece 2 and finger-press seam. Pin or glue in place, if necessary.

7. Make certain that fabric piece 3 overlaps at least ¼" on all sides of shape 3. Place fabric piece 3 on fabric piece 1, with right sides together. Pin, glue, or hold in place.

8. Turn over foundation, with marked side up. Sew along line between shapes 1 and 3. Begin and end sewing two or three stitches beyond line. Trim excess fabric ⅛" to ¼" from seam line, being careful to not cut into foundation material when trimming, as shown in figure 7–4.

9. Turn over foundation, with unmarked side up. Open fabric piece 3, finger-press seam. Pin or glue in place, if necessary. Continue sewing and trimming fabric pieces in numerical order through piece 5.

7–4.
Trim excess fabric ⅛" to ¼" from seam line. Fabric may be trimmed prior to stitching.

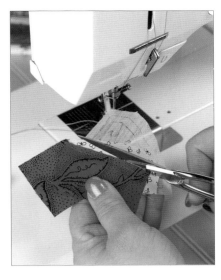

7–5.
To preseam, first trim the seam area. Next, trim the pieces to shape that must be preseamed.

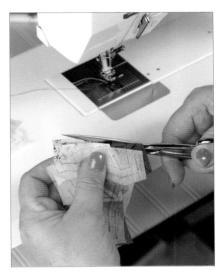

7–6.
Third, seam the trimmed pieces. Last, stitch preseamed piece in place on foundation.

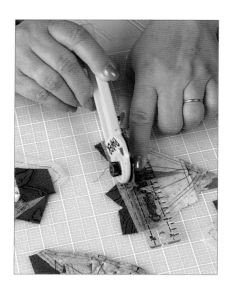

7–7.
After stitching in between the seam allowance, trim away excess fabric, using a rotary cutter.

7–8.
Stitch units together, matching at dots for assembly, following individual block instructions. Clip angled seams, if necessary.

10. Some blocks require preseamed pieces. This is designated by a mark (") on the patterns at the seam. To preseam, first trim fabric pieces 4–5 that are already on the foundation ¼" past seam line. With marked side of foundation face up, place foundation piece 6, wrong side up, on shape 6, extending piece ¼" over 4–5 seam line. Trim piece at preseam ¼" past seam line. Set piece 6 aside. Place fabric piece 6a, wrong side up, on shape 6a and trim at the preseam in the same manner, as shown in figure 7–5. Stitch trimmed pieces together, taking a ¼" seam and press seam open. Stitch fabric piece 6–6a to fabric pieces 4–5, right sides together,

matching preseam to seam between 4–5, as shown in figure 7–6. It will be necessary to pin the preseamed piece in place where the seams must match. Before stitching, fold pinned piece open, checking placement. Alter seam line of 6–6a if necessary.

11. Press the unit when all fabric pieces are stitched to foundation. Stitch in between seam allowance around all edges. Use a ruler to trim unit even at the ¼" seam allowance markings, as shown in figure 7–7.

12. Pin unit A to unit A(m), right sides together, matching at dots. Stitch, taking a ¼" seam. Press seam open. Blocks having angled seams may need to be clipped prior to stitching. Clip unit B to inner seam where it angles upward. Pin and stitch unit B to assembled unit A–A(m), right sides together, with a ¼" seam, as shown in figure 7–8. Press seam open.

BACKING & BATTING

Backing

Use cotton fabric for quilt backing. If hand sewing your quilt, avoid bed sheets for backing. They are difficult to quilt through. When making a bed-sized quilt, the fabric may need to be pieced to fit the quilt top.

Batting

Batting is traditionally used as the middle layer of a quilt or sometimes in clothing and doll making. There are numerous types of batting available. Bonded cotton batting gives a flat, natural appearance and will require a great deal of quilting to secure layers, with quilting lines less than 1" apart. Felt may be substituted and renders the same appearance as bonded cotton.

Polyester batting gives a puffy appearance and is a good choice for machine quilting. Thick batting is recommended for tied quilts.

TIP: Remove batting from the package a day before using. Open it out to full size. This will help the batting lie flat.

ASSEMBLY

Planning a Quilt

Determine the quilt size desired, using the following guidelines:

Bed Type	Mattress Measurements
Crib	27" x 51"
Twin	39" x 75"
Double	54" x 75"
Queen	60" x 80"
King	76" x 80"

A small wall quilt can be any size, and easily completed in a short time.

Add the drop (part of the quilt hanging over edge of the mattress) and tuck (part tucking under the pillows) to the mattress measurements.

Example: If desiring the quilt to hang 12" over the edge of the mattress with a 12" tuck, add 24" to the length and width of the mattress size.

Example: For a twin-size quilt, made with 7" x 7" blocks and a finished size of 6" x 99", use 60 blocks. Sew six blocks across and 10 rows down, with 2" sashing in between blocks and rows, and around outer edge. Finish quilt with a 3½" border.

Sizing Quilt Blocks

1. Lay out the quilt blocks in design order on your work surface. Measure each block vertically and horizontally and chart the measurements. Once sewn, the individual quilt blocks will not be square. Some edges will shrink and some will grow. Use your chart to find the smallest block measurement that must be used as the basis for trimming each block. Be certain to determine which block edge measurements must be identical.

Example: For the Frog King quilt assembly on page 324, frog blocks must be square. Vertical measurement of

each small star and wide star block must be the same. The horizontal measurement of each wide star block must be the same as vertical measurement of frog and dragon fly blocks.

2. Trim quilt blocks so they are trued up (square) and equally sized in relationship to each other, using a quilter's ruler, rotary cutter, and cutting board with grid lines. Leave a ¼" seam allowance around all edges.

Sashing & Borders

Sashing is done by sewing fabric around quilt blocks, in order to set them apart from each other. Sashing can be sewn either to vertical or horizontal edges first. An inner border sets the assembled quilt apart from the outer border or binding.

1. Measure vertical or horizontal edges of quilt block. Cut sashing according to quantity and width desired. By cutting sashing identical in size, it will be easy to keep the quilt square.

2. Sew blocks and sashing together in rows. Press seams.

3. Sew rows of blocks and sashing together.

4. Measure the vertical or horizontal edges of an assembled quilt top. Cut outer sashing or border strips to quantity and width desired.

5. Sew outer sashing or border strips to long sides of quilt. Press seams toward border.

6. If additional borders are needed, repeat steps 4 and 5.

7. Remove foundation from squares, if applicable.

TIP: For easier paper removal, dampen foundation paper, using a spray bottle of water.

Quilt Layers

Layer quilt with backing, batting, and quilt top. Place fabric for quilt back onto work surface, wrong side up. Stretch and secure fabric to work surface, using masking tape or pins. See Chapter 8—How to Quilt, pages 434 to 445 for further instructions.

Frog King

Just one example of many quilt possibilities.

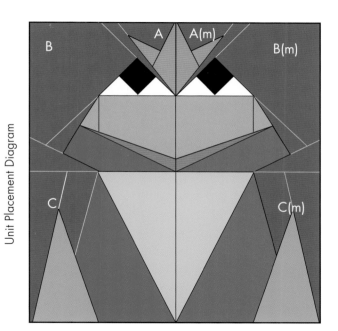

FROG KING

6" block (moderate)

1. Make one each of units A, B, and C. Make one mirror image each of units A, B, and C.

2. Sew units A, B, and C together in alphabetical order, matching at dots for assembly. Repeat for mirror image units A(m), B(m), C(m).

3. Sew unit A–B–C to mirror image unit A(m)–B(m)–C(m), matching at dots for assembly.

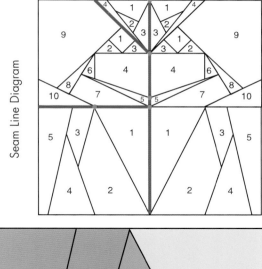

Frog King Unit Pattern B   Unit Pattern   A

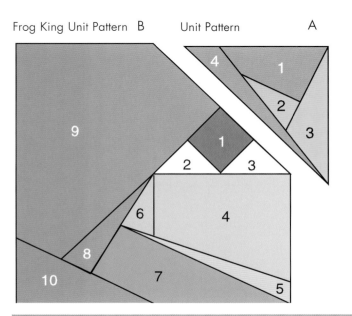

C

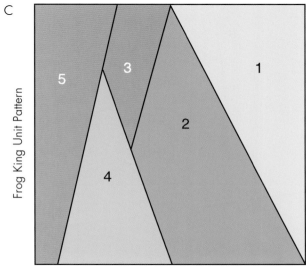

Frog King Unit Pattern

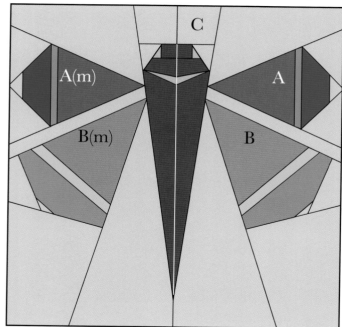

DRAGONFLY

6" block (moderate)

1. Make one each of units A, B, and C. Make one mirror image each of units A, B, and C.

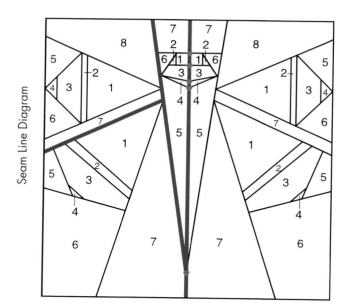

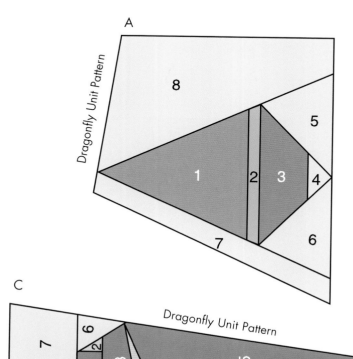

2. Sew units A, B, and C together in alphabetical order, matching at dots for assembly. Repeat for mirror image units A(m), B(m), C(m).

3. Sew unit A–B–C to mirror image unit A(m)–B(m)–C(m), matching at dots for assembly.

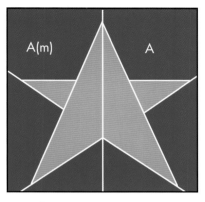

Unit Placement Diagram

Seam Line Diagram

SMALL STAR

2" block (easy)

1. Make one unit A. Make one mirror image of unit A.

2. Sew unit A to mirror image unit A(m), matching at dots for assembly.

A

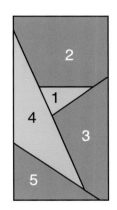

Small Star Unit Pattern

Dragonfly Unit Pattern

B

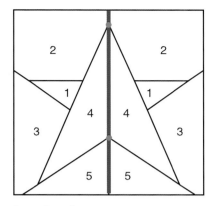

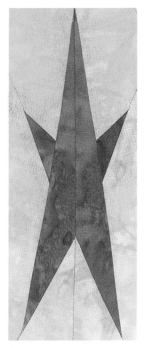

Narrow Star

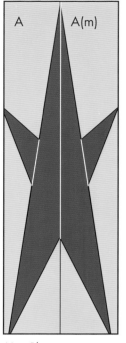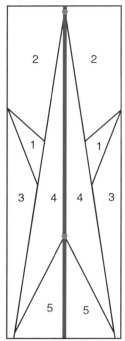

Unit Placement
Diagram

Seam Line Diagram

NARROW AND WIDE STARS

2" x 6" blocks (easy)

NOTE: Instructions apply to two separate blocks.

1. Make one unit A. Make one mirror image of unit A.

2. Sew unit A to mirror image unit A(m), matching at dots for assembly.

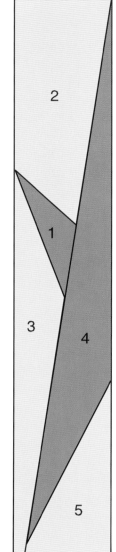

Narrow Star Unit Pattern

Wide Star

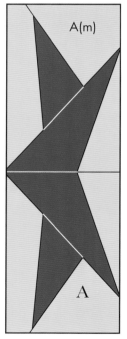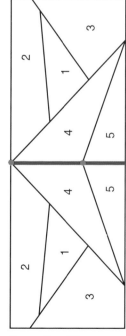

Unit Placement
Diagram

Seam Line Diagram

Wide Star Unit Pattern

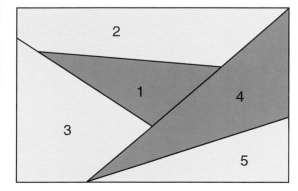

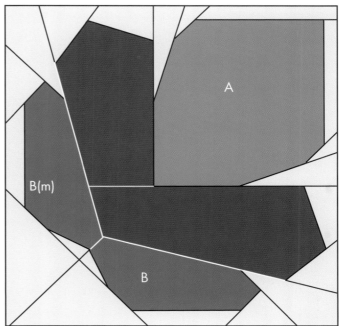

Unit Placement Diagram

IVY

4″ block (moderate)

Pieces 8 and 8a, and 9 and 9a are preseamed before sewing to unit A. See preseam instructions on page 321.

1. Make one each of units A and B. Make one mirror image of unit B.

2. Sew unit B to mirror image unit B(m), matching at dots for assembly. End seam at dot.

3. Sew unit A to unit B–B(m), matching at dot for assembly.

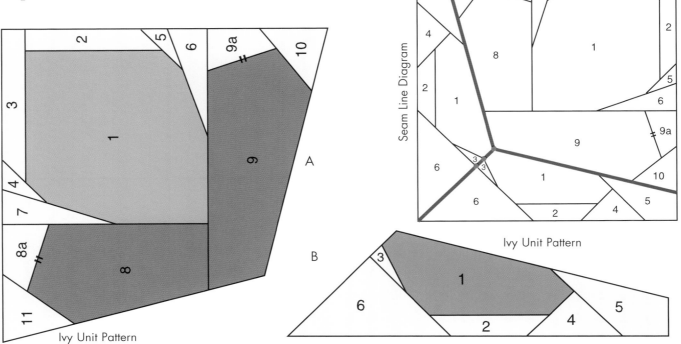

Ivy Unit Pattern

Seam Line Diagram

Ivy Unit Pattern

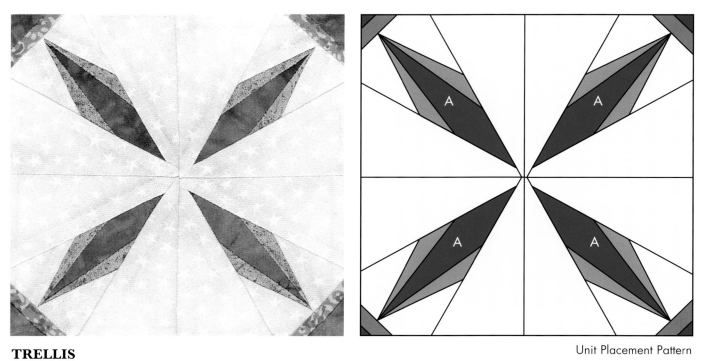

Unit Placement Pattern

TRELLIS

4″ block (moderate)

NOTE: This block may be made as an 8″ block by joining four blocks.

1. Make four of unit A.

Seam Line Diagram

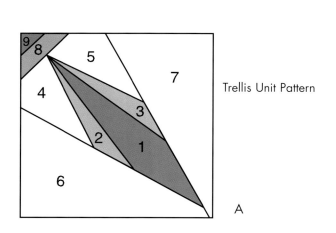

Trellis Unit Pattern

A

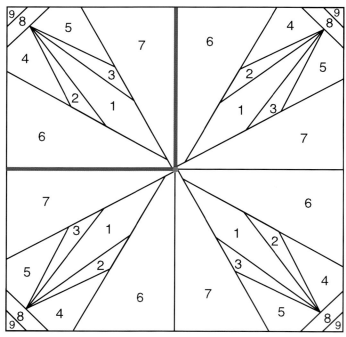

Terra-cotta Terrace

Use this grouping or experiment on your own.

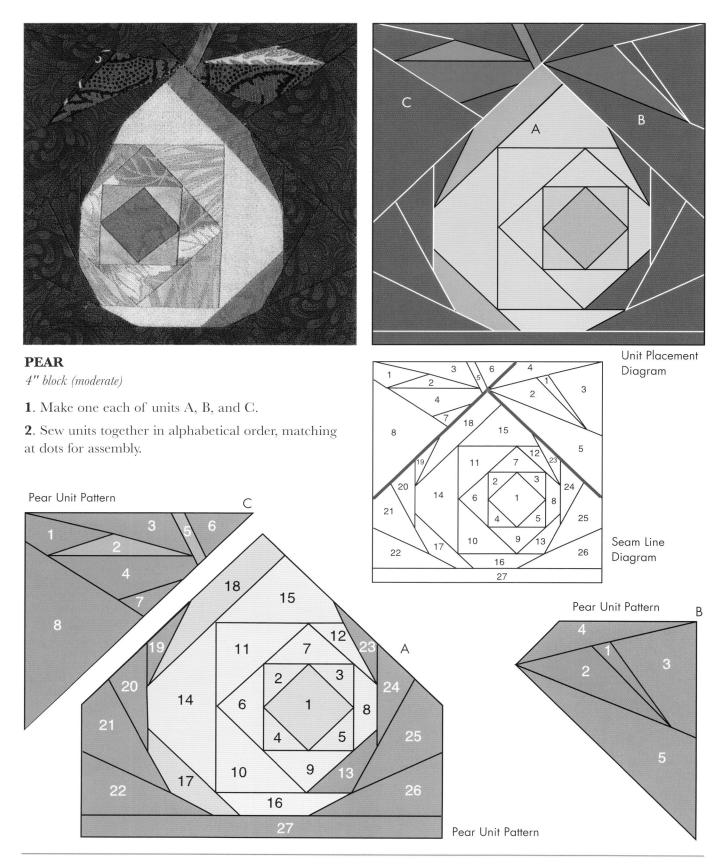

PEAR

4" block (moderate)

1. Make one each of units A, B, and C.

2. Sew units together in alphabetical order, matching at dots for assembly.

Pear Unit Pattern

Unit Placement Diagram

Seam Line Diagram

Pear Unit Pattern

Pear Unit Pattern

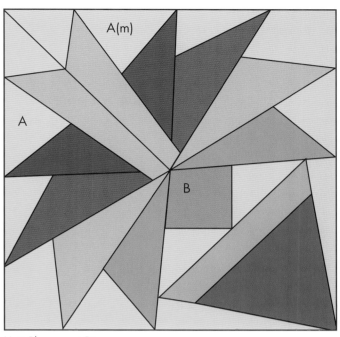

Unit Placement Diagram

CHRYSANTHEMUM

4" block (moderate)

Note: This block may be made as an 8" block by joining four blocks.

1. Make one each of units A and B. Make one mirror image of unit A.

2. Sew unit A to mirror image unit A(m), matching at dots for assembly.

3. Clip unit B to seam line at dot. Sew unit B to unit A–A(m), matching at dot assembly.

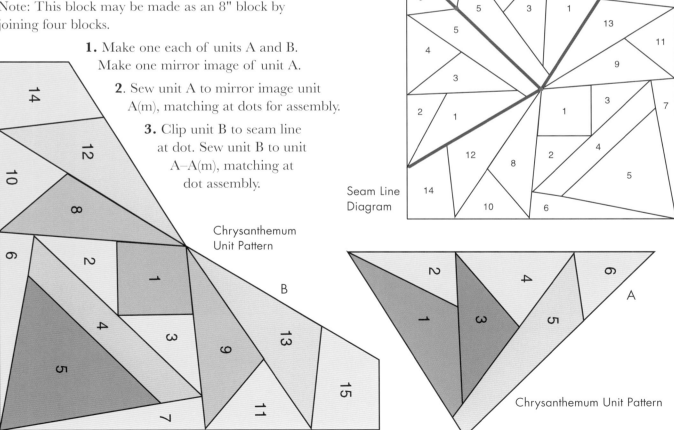

Seam Line Diagram

Chrysanthemum Unit Pattern

Chrysanthemum Unit Pattern

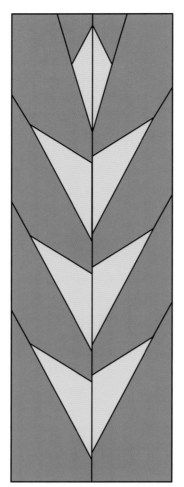

Unit Placement Diagram

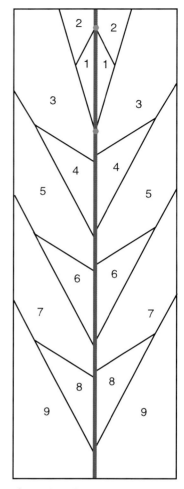

Seam Line Diagram

FLOWER SPRAY

2″ x 6″ block (moderate)

NOTE: Unit B is offset from unit A.

1. Make one each of units A and B.

2. Sew unit A to unit B, matching at dots for assembly.

Flower Spray Unit Pattern

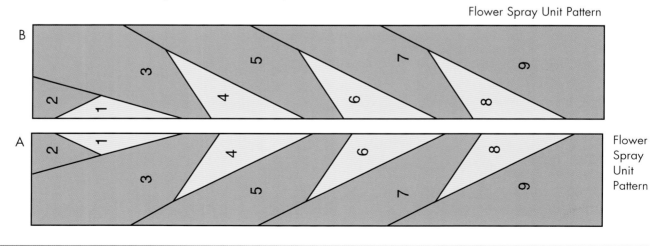

Flower Spray Unit Pattern

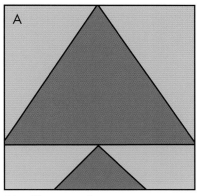

Unit Placement Diagram

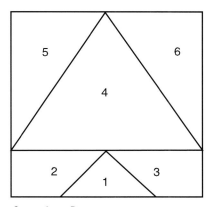

Seam Line Diagram

LITTLE TREE

2" block (easy)

NOTE: This block may be made as a 4" block by joining four blocks.

1. Make one unit A.

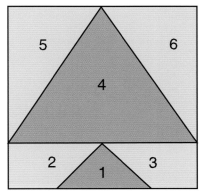

A

Little Tree Unit Pattern

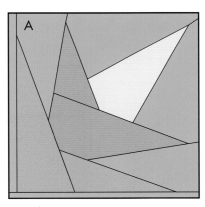

Unit Placement Diagram

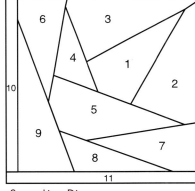

Seam Line Diagram

FERN

2" block (easy)

NOTE: This block may be made as a 4" block by joining four blocks.

1. Make one unit A.

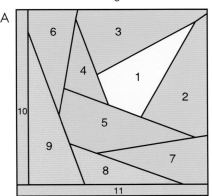

A

Fern Unit Pattern

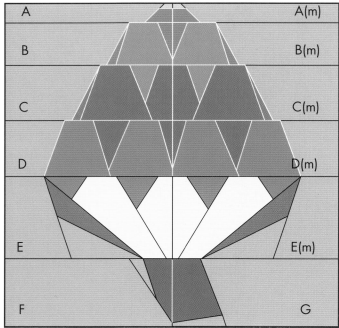

Unit Placement Diagram

ARTICHOKE

6″ block (difficult)

1. Make one each of units A, B, C, D, E, F, and G. Make one mirror image each of units A, B, C, D, and E.

2. Sew each unit to its mirror image, matching at dots for assembly.

3. Sew unit F to unit G, matching at dots for assembly.

4. Sew all units together in alphabetical order, matching at dots for assembly.

Artichoke Unit Pattern

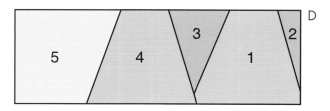

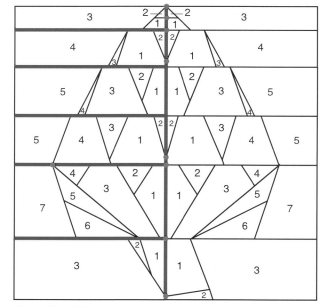

Seam Line Diagram

Artichoke Unit Pattern

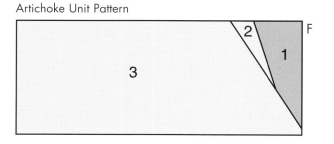

Artichoke Unit Pattern

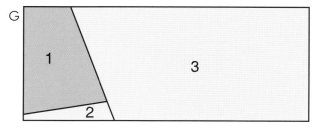

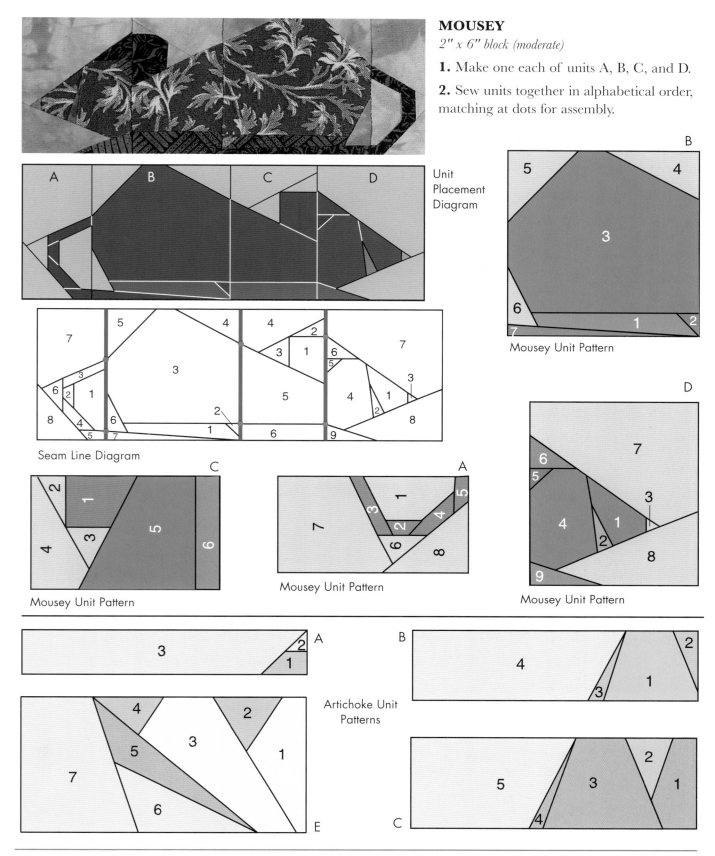

MOUSEY

2" x 6" block (moderate)

1. Make one each of units A, B, C, and D.

2. Sew units together in alphabetical order, matching at dots for assembly.

Unit Placement Diagram

Seam Line Diagram

B

Mousey Unit Pattern

C

Mousey Unit Pattern

A

Mousey Unit Pattern

D

Mousey Unit Pattern

Artichoke Unit Patterns

Taste of the Orient

Feel free to vary block placement and color themes.

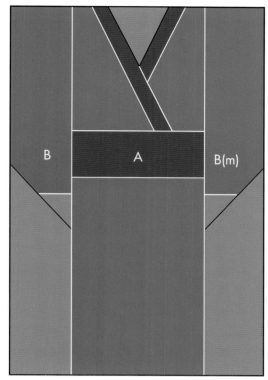

Unit
Placement
Diagram

KIMONO

4" x 6" block (easy)

1. Make one each of units A and B. Make one mirror image of unit B.

2. Sew unit B and mirror image unit B(m) to each side of unit A.

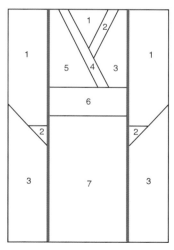

Seam Line
Diagram

Kimono Unit
Pattern

B

Kimono Unit Pattern

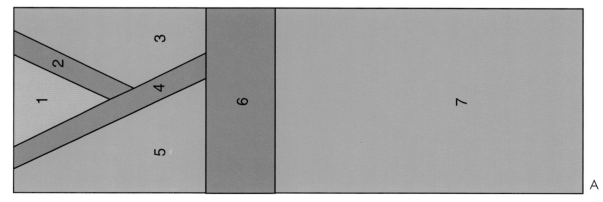

A

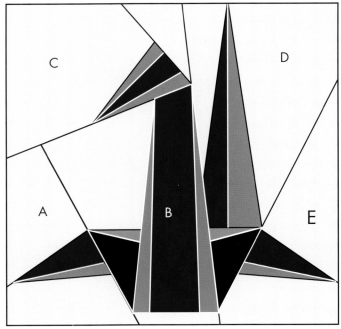

Unit Placement Diagram

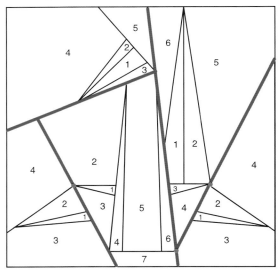

Seam Line Diagram

Left and below: Crane Unit Patterns

CRANE

4″ block (moderate)

1. Make one each of units A, B, C, D, and E.

2. Sew units A, B, and C in alphabetical order, matching at dots for assembly.

3. Sew unit D to unit E, matching at dots for assembly.

4. Sew unit A–B–C to unit D–E, matching at dots for assembly.

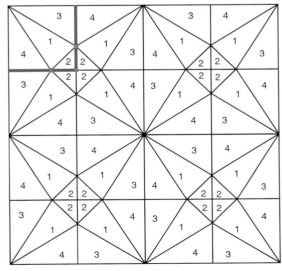

Sapphire Star Unit Placement Diagram

Sapphire Star Unit Pattern   A

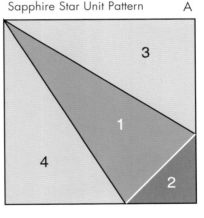

SAPPHIRE STAR

8" block (easy)

1. Make 16 of unit A.

2. Sew four units A together for a 4" block, matching at dots for assembly. Repeat for four 4" blocks.

3. Sew four 4" blocks together, matching at dots for assembly.

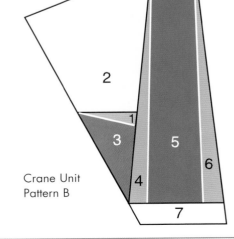

Crane Unit
Pattern B

Seam Line Diagram

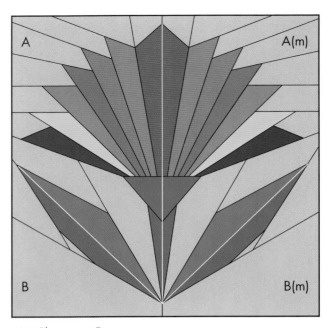

Unit Placement Diagram

CELESTIAL LOTUS

6" block (moderate)

Pieces 13 and 13a are preseamed before sewing to unit A. See preseam instructions on page 321.

1. Make one each of units A and B. Make one mirror image each of units A and B.

2. Clip unit B to seam line at corner dot. Sew unit A to unit B, matching at dots for assembly. Repeat for mirror image units A(m) and B(m).

3. Sew unit A–B to mirror image unit A(m)–B(m), matching at dots for assembly.

Seam Line Diagram

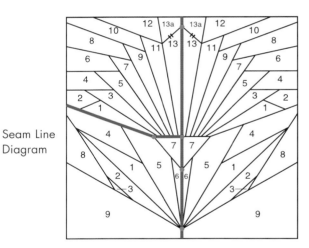

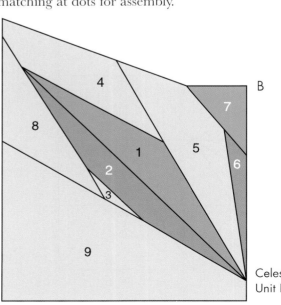

Celestial Lotus Unit Pattern

Celestial Lotus Unit Pattern

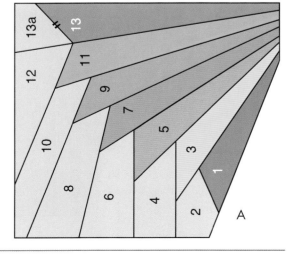

Out of Africa

Color and texture can have as much impact as the images you use.

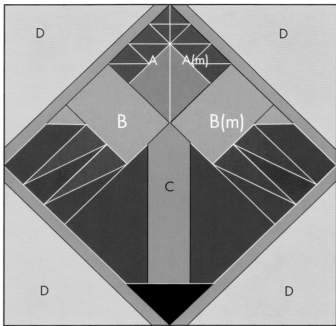

Unit Placement Diagram

A

6
5
4
3
2
1
7

Tree of
Life Unit
Pattern

TREE OF LIFE

6″ block (moderate)

1. Make one each of units A, B, and C. Make four of unit D. Make one mirror image each of units A and B.

2. Sew unit A to mirror image unit A(m), matching at dots for assembly.

3. Sew unit B to unit A–A(m).

4. Sew mirror image unit B(m) to unit C.

5. Sew unit A–A(m)–B to unit B(m)–C, matching at dots for assembly.

6. Sew each unit D to an outer, diagonal edge of unit A–A(m)–B–B(m)–C.

Tree of Life Unit Pattern

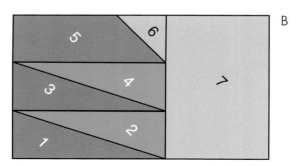

B

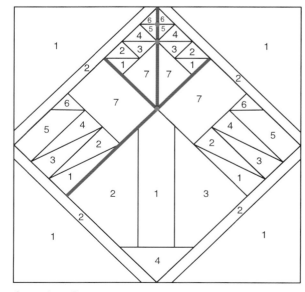

Seam Line Diagram

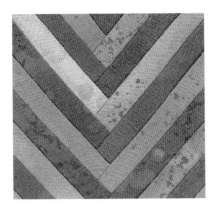

Unit Placement Diagram

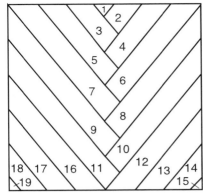

Seam Line Diagram

HERRINGBONE

2" block (easy)

1. Make one unit A.

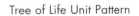

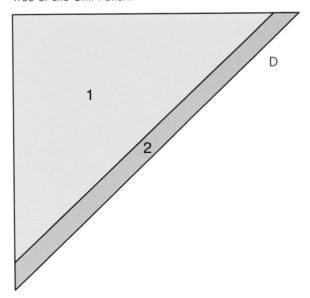

Herringbone Unit Pattern

Tree of Life Unit Pattern

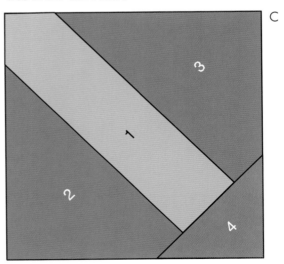

Tree of Life Unit Pattern

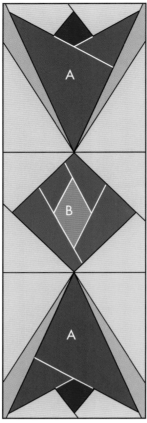

Unit Placement Diagram

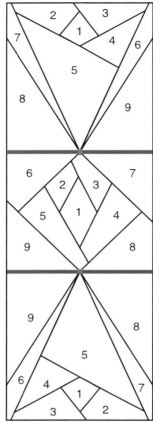

Seam Line Diagram

FLOWER ORNAMENT

2" x 6" block (moderate)

1. Make two of unit A. Make one unit B.

2. Sew one unit A to top and one to bottom of unit B, matching at dots for assembly.

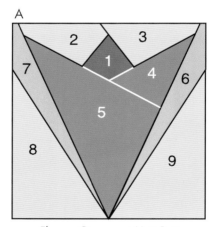

A

Flower Ornament Unit Pattern

B

Flower Ornament Unit Pattern

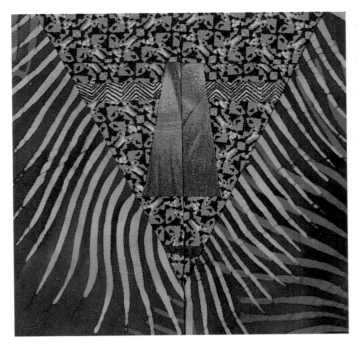

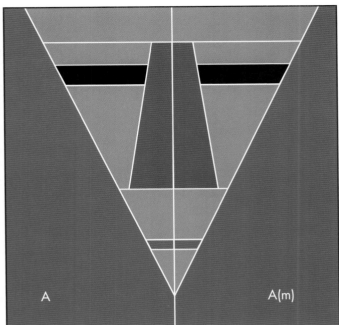

Unit Placement Diagram

LION

4″ block (easy)

1. Make one unit A. Make one mirror image of unit A.

2. Sew unit A to mirror image unit A(m), matching at dots for assembly.

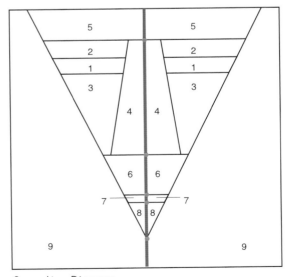

Seam Line Diagram

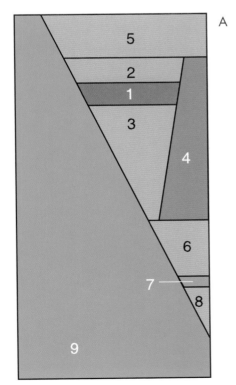

Lion Unit Pattern

Unit Placement Diagram

SUNRISE

4" block (easy)

1. Make one unit A.

Sunrise Unit Pattern

A

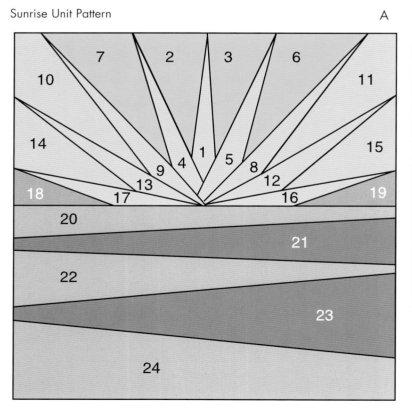

Seam Line Diagram

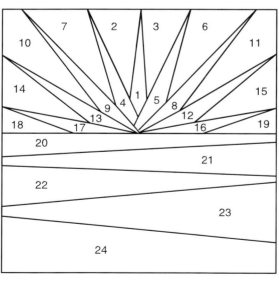

Sugar and Spice

A charming theme for a young girl.

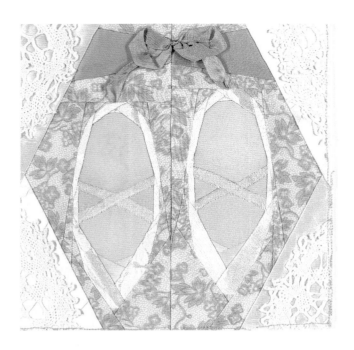

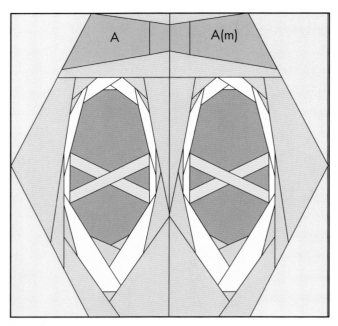

Unit Placement Diagram

Ballet Shoes Unit Pattern

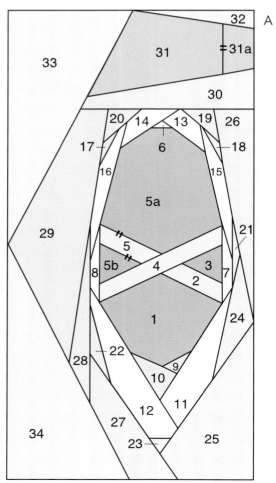

BALLET SHOES

6″ block (difficult)

NOTE: Pieces 5, 5a, and 5b, and 31 and 31a are preseamed before sewing to unit A and mirror image unit A(m). See preseam instructions on page 321.

1. Make one unit A. Make one mirror image of unit A.

2. Sew unit A to unit A(m), matching at dots for assembly.

3. Embellish with ribbons to make ties and lace in corners.

Seam Line Diagram

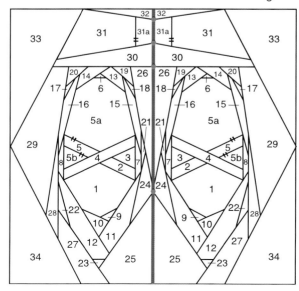

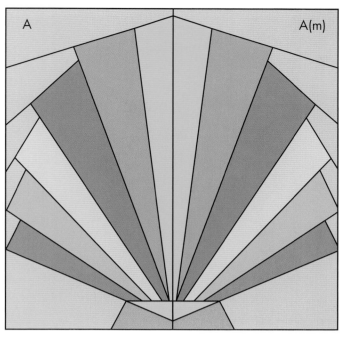

Unit Placement Diagram

SCALLOP

4" block (moderate)

NOTE: Pieces 13 and 13a are preseamed before sewing to unit A and mirror image of unit A. See preseam instructions on page 000.

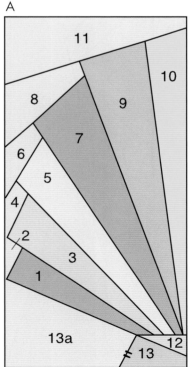

A

Scallop Unit Pattern

1. Make one unit A. Make one mirror image of unit A.

2. Sew unit A to mirror image unit A(m), matching at dots for assembly.

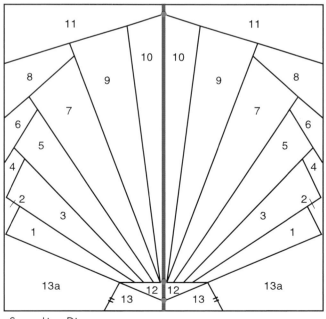

Seam Line Diagram

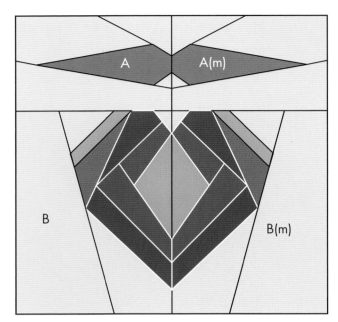

Unit Placement Diagram

HEART LOCKET

4" block (moderate)

1. Make one each of units A and B. Make one mirror image each of units A and B.

2. Sew each unit to its mirror image, matching at dots for assembly.

3. Sew unit A–A(m) to unit B–B(m), matching at dots for assembly.

Seam Line Diagram

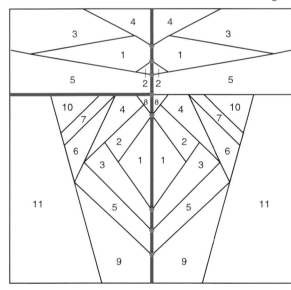

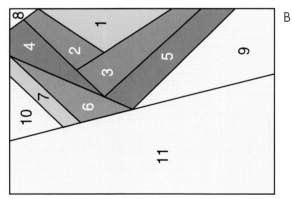

Heart Locket Unit Patterns

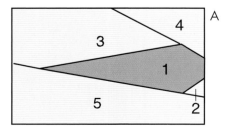

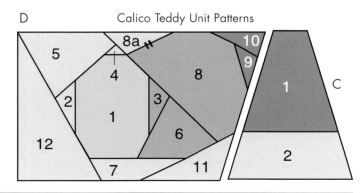

Calico Teddy Unit Patterns

Unit Placement Diagram

CALICO TEDDY

6" block (moderate)

NOTE: Pieces 8 and 8a, and 11 and 11a are preseamed before sewing to unit A and mirror image unit A(m). Pieces 8 and 8a are preseamed before sewing to unit D and mirror image unit D(m). See preseam instructions on page 321.

1. Make one each of units A, B, C, and D. Make one mirror image each of units A, B, and D.

2. Sew unit A to its mirror image, matching at dots for assembly. Repeat for unit B. End unit B seam at top center dot.

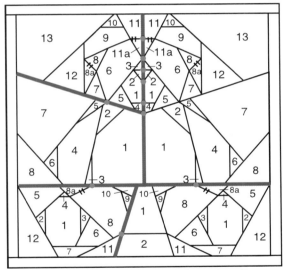

Seam Line Diagram

Calico Teddy Unit Patterns

A   B

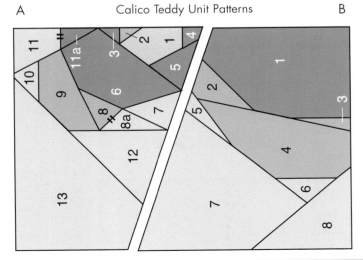

3. Sew unit A–A(m) to unit B–B(m), matching at dots for assembly.

4. Sew unit D to side of unit C, matching at dots for assembly. Repeat for mirror image unit D(m).

5. Sew unit A–A(m)–B–B(m) to unit D–C–D(m), matching at dots for assembly.

6. Sew 1/2" border to block.

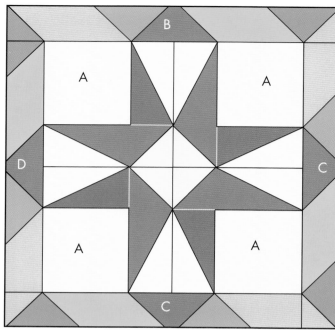

Unit Placement Diagram

DAWN FLOWER

6" block (difficult)

1. Make four each of unit A, alternating colors as shown. Make one each of units B and D. Make two of unit C, alternating colors as shown.

2. Sew four units A together, matching at dots for assembly.

3. Beginning with unit B and following in alphabetical order, sew units B, C, and D to outer edges of assembled unit A, matching dots for assembly.

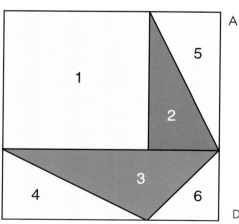

Dawn Flower Unit Patterns

Seam Line Diagram

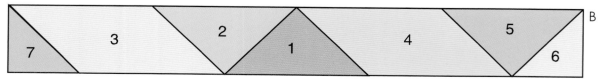

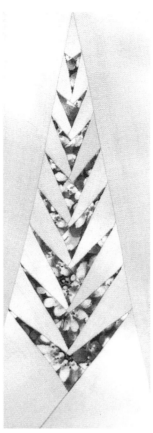

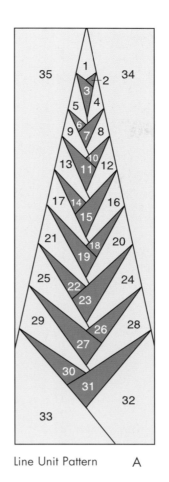

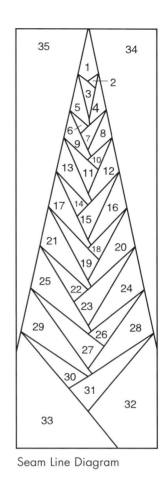

Unit Placement Diagram

Line Unit Pattern   A

Seam Line Diagram

LUPINE

2" x 6" block (moderate)

1. Make one unit A.

Dawn Flower Unit Patterns

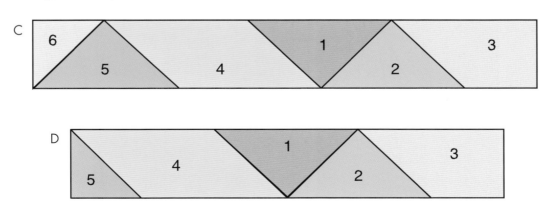

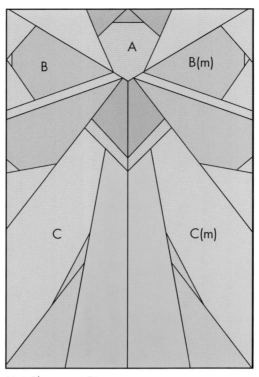

Unit Placement Diagram

FLOWER FAIRY

4″ x 6″ block (moderate)

1. Make one each of units A, B, and C. Make one mirror image each of units B and C.

2. Sew unit B to unit C. Repeat for mirror image units B(m) and C(m).

3. Sew unit B–C to mirror image unit B(m)–C(m), matching at dots for assembly. End seam at center top dot.

4. Sew unit A to unit B–C–B(m)–C(m), matching at dots for assembly.

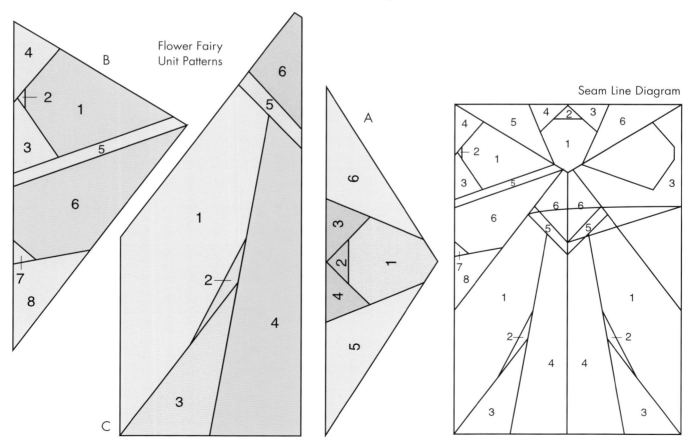

Flower Fairy
Unit Patterns

Seam Line Diagram

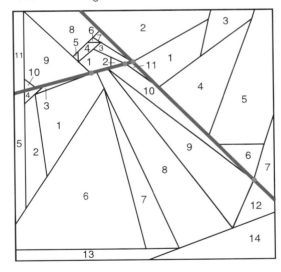

Unit Placement Diagram

ANGEL

4" block (moderate)

1. Make one each of units A, B, and C.

2. Sew unit A to unit B, matching at dots for assembly.

3. Sew unit C to unit A–B, matching at dots for assembly.

Seam Line Diagram

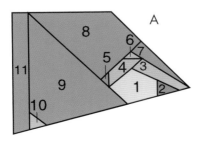

Angel Unit Patterns

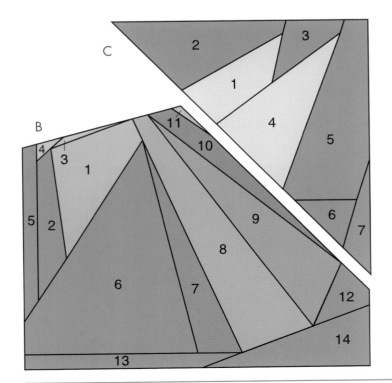

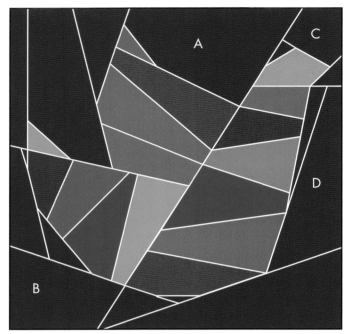

Unit Placement Diagram

DOVE

4" block (moderate)

1. Make one each of units A, B, C, and D.

2. Sew unit A to unit B.

3. Sew unit C to unit D, matching at dots for assembly.

4. Sew unit A–B to unit C–D, matching at dots for assembly.

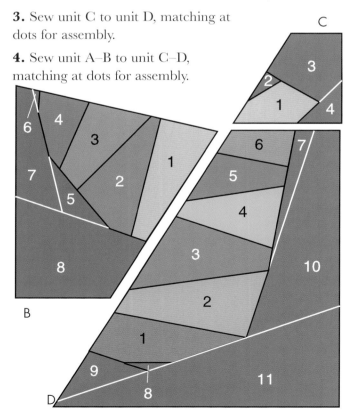

Seam Line Diagram

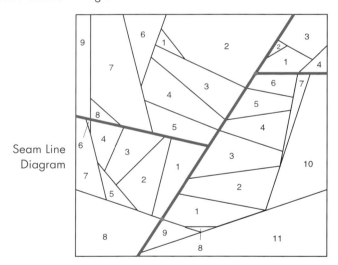

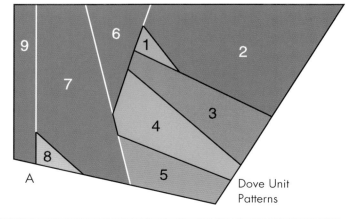

Dove Unit Patterns

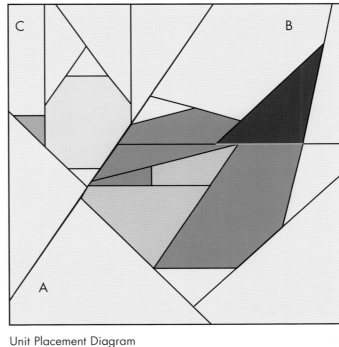

BLUEBIRD

4" block (moderate)

NOTE: Pieces 7 and 7a are preseamed before sewing to unit C. See preseam instructions on page 321.

1. Make one each of units A, B, and C.

2. Sew units together in alphabetical order, matching at dots for assembly.

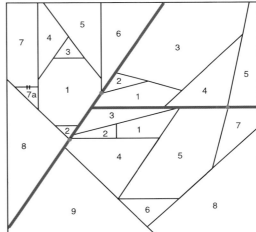

Seam Line Diagram

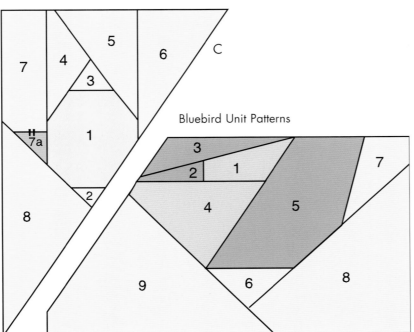

Bluebird Unit Patterns

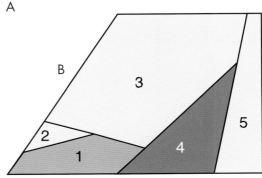

Calico Country

A critter theme is always popular.

ROOSTER

4" block (moderate)

NOTE: Pieces 6 and 6a are preseamed before sewing to unit F.
See preseam instructions on page 321.

1. Make one each of units A, B, C, D, E, F, and G.

2. Sew units A, B, C, D, and E together in alphabetical order, matching at dots for assembly.

3. Sew unit F to unit G, matching at dots for assembly.

4. Sew unit A–B–C–D–E to unit F–G, matching at dots for assembly.

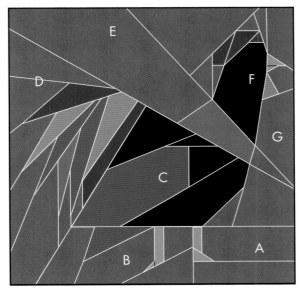

Unit Placement Diagram

Seam Line Diagram

Rooster Unit Patterns

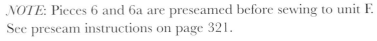

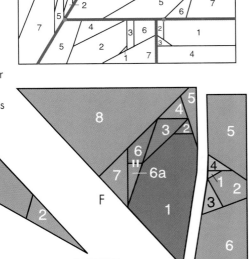

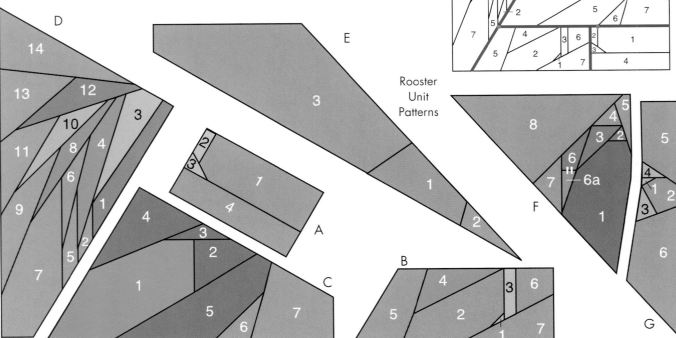

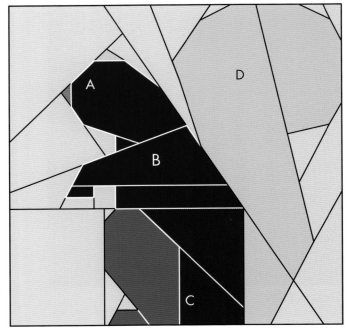

Unit Placement
Diagram

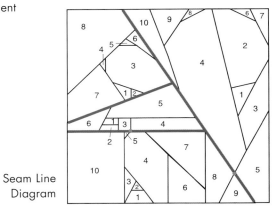

Seam Line
Diagram

C

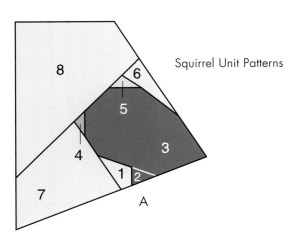

Squirrel Unit Patterns

SQUIRREL

4" block (moderate)

1. Make one each of units A, B, C, and D.

2. Sew all units together in alphabetical order, matching at dots for assembly.

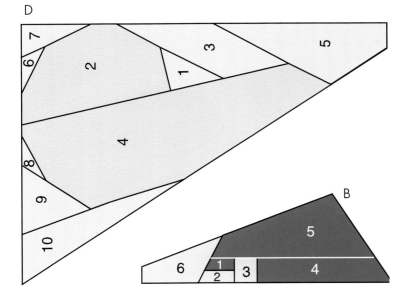

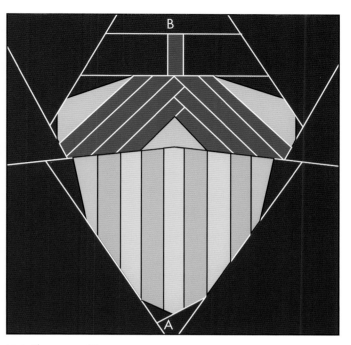

Unit Placement Diagram

ACORN

4" block (moderate)

NOTE: Pieces 16, 16a, and 16b are preseamed before sewing to unit B. See preseam instructions on page 321.

1. Make one each of units A and B.

2. Clip unit B to seam line at center dot.

3. Sew unit A to unit B, matching at dots for assembly.

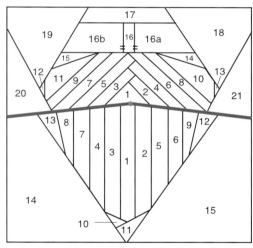

Seam Line Diagram

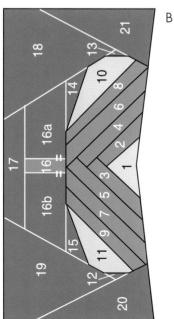

B

Acorn Unit Patterns

A

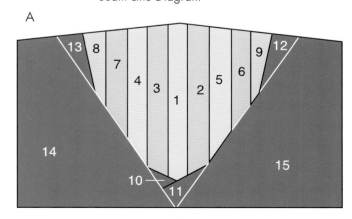

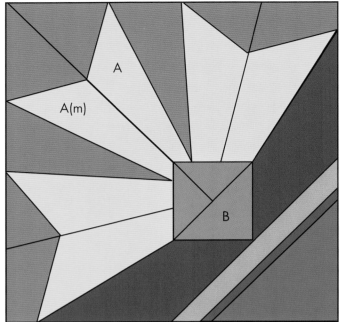

Unit Placement Diagram

FLOWER BOUQUET

4" block (moderate)

NOTE: Pieces 6 and 6a are preseamed before sewing to each unit A and mirror image unit A(m). See preseam instructions on page 321.

1. Make one each of units A and B. Make one mirror image of unit A.

2. Sew unit A to mirror image unit A(m), matching at dots for assembly.

3. Clip unit B to seam line at center dots. Sew unit B to unit A-A(m), matching at dots for assembly.

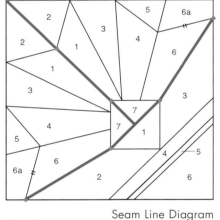

Seam Line Diagram

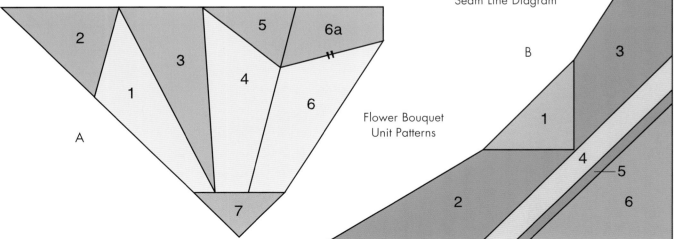

Flower Bouquet
Unit Patterns

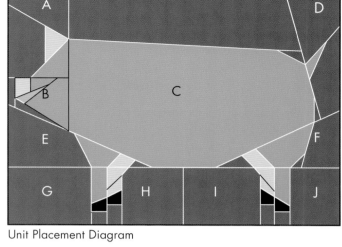

Unit Placement Diagram

PIG

4" x 6" block (moderate)

1. Make one each of units A, B, C, D, E, F, G, H, I, and J.

2. Sew unit A to unit B.

3. Sew unit C to unit D.

4. Sew unit A–B to unit C–D.

5. Sew unit E and unit F to unit A–B–C–D.

6. Sew units G, H, I, and J together in alphabetical order.

7. Sew unit A–B–C–D–E–F to unit G–H–I–J.

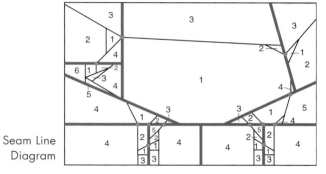

Seam Line Diagram

Pig Unit Patterns (continued on next page)

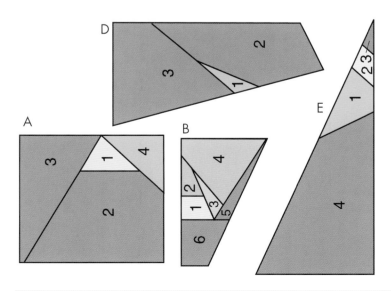

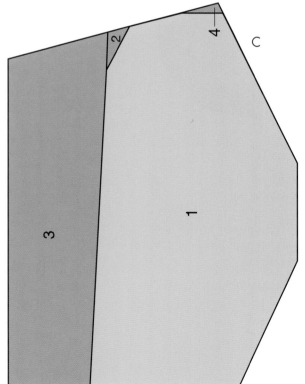

Pig Unit Patterns (continued from previous page)

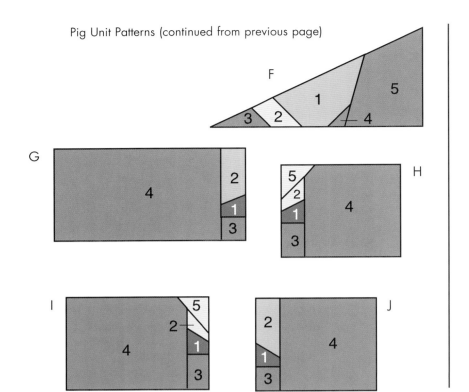

Zebra Toy Unit Pattern

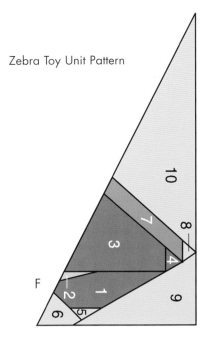

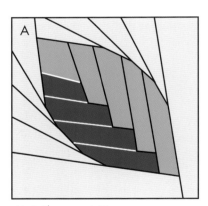

Unit Placement Diagram

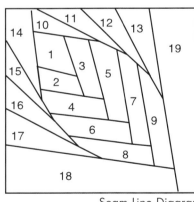

Seam Line Diagram

LEAF

2" block (easy)

NOTE: This block may be made as a 4" block by joining four blocks.

1. Make one unit A.

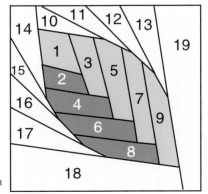

Leaf Unit Pattern

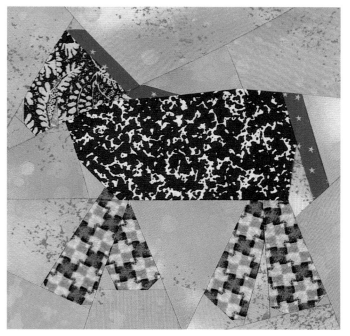

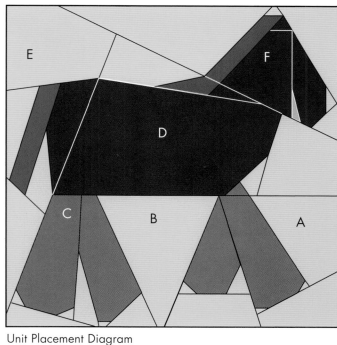

Unit Placement Diagram

ZEBRA TOY

4" block (moderate)

NOTE: Pieces 4 and 4a are preseamed before sewing to unit C.
Pieces 5 and 5a are preseamed before sewing to unit D. See
preseam instructions on page 321.

1. Make one each of units A, B, C, D, E, and F.

2. Sew all units in alphabetical order, matching at dots for assembly.

Seam Line Diagram

Zebra Toy Unit Patterns

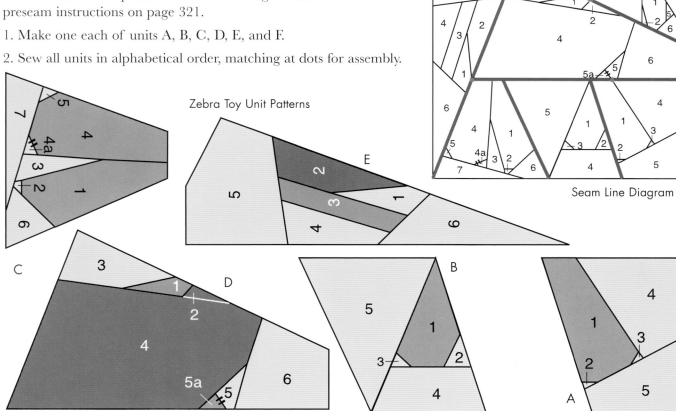

Traditional

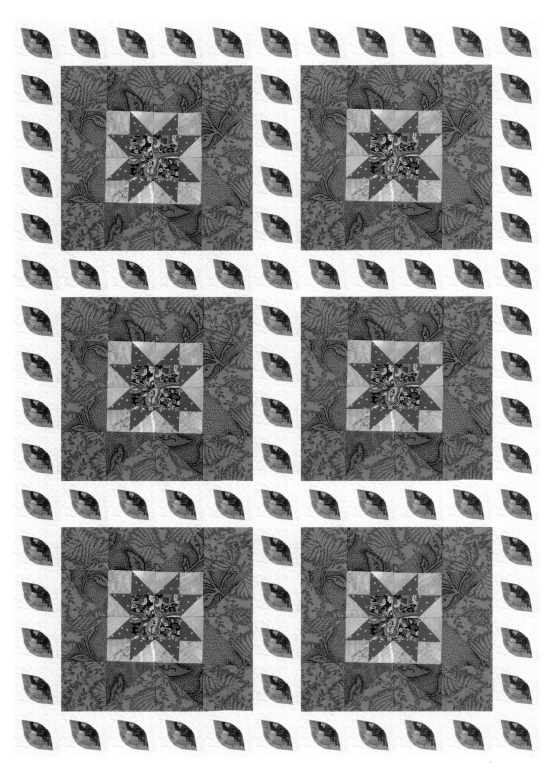

Achieve a classic-looking quilt with foundation piecing.

STARS AND SQUARES

8" block (moderate)

1. Make four of unit A. Make four mirror images of unit A.

2. Sew each unit A to a mirror image unit A(m), matching at dots for assembly.

3. Sew four units A–A(m) together, matching at dots for assembly.

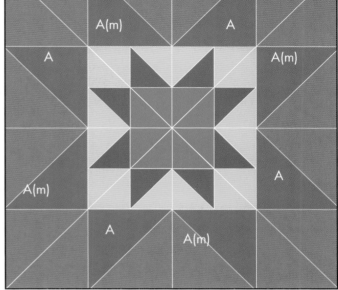

Unit Placement Diagram

Seam Line Diagram

Stars and Stripes Unit Pattern

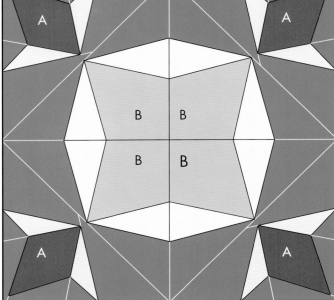

Unit Placement Diagram

EVENING FLOWER

6" block (moderate)

NOTE: Pieces 4 and 4a, and 5 and 5a are preseamed before sewing to each unit A. See preseam instructions on page 321.

1. Make four each of units A and B.

2. Sew each unit A to a unit B.

3. Sew four units A–B together, matching at dots for assembly.

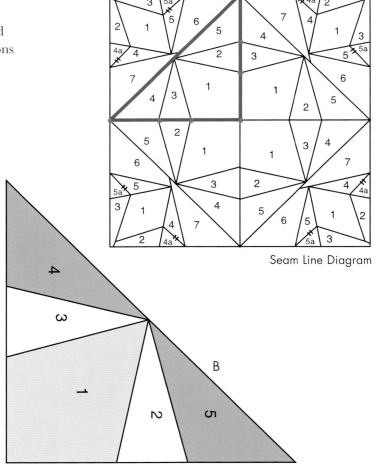

Seam Line Diagram

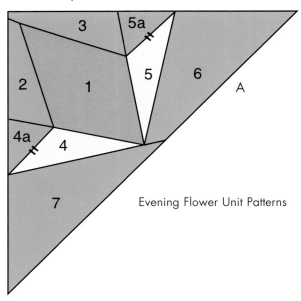

Evening Flower Unit Patterns

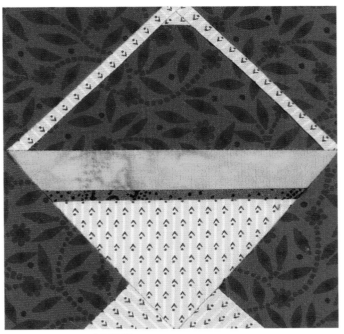

FLOWER BASKET

4" block (easy)

NOTE: Pieces 4 and 4a, and 5 and 5a are preseamed before sewing to unit B. See preseam instructions on page 321.

1. Make one each of units A and B.

2. Sew unit A to unit B, matching at dots for assembly.

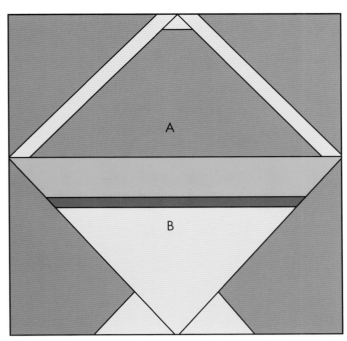

Unit Placement Diagram

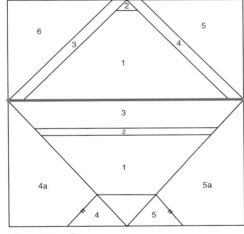

Seam Line Diagram

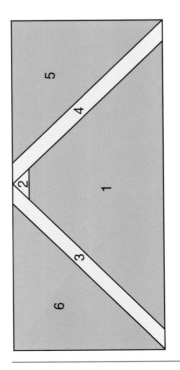

Flower Basket
Unit Patterns

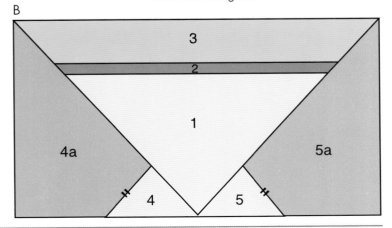

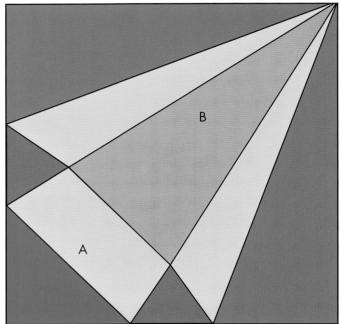

ARROWHEAD

4" block (easy)

NOTE: This block may be made as an 8" block by joining four blocks.

1. Make one each of units A and B.

2. Clip unit B to seam line at inside dots.

3. Sew unit A to unit B, matching at dots for assembly.

Unit
Placement
Diagram

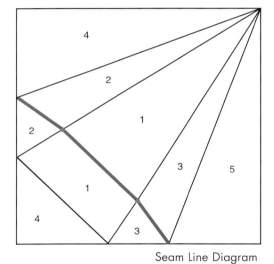

Seam Line Diagram

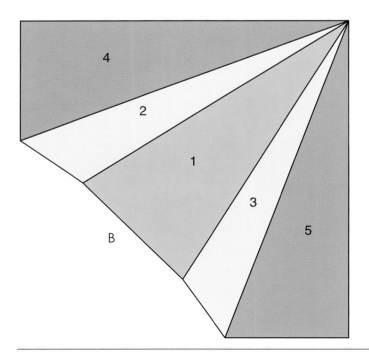

Arrowhead
Unit Patterns

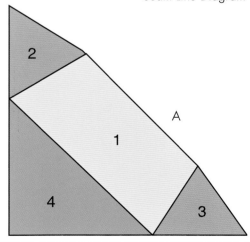

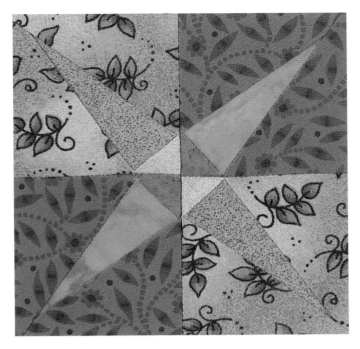

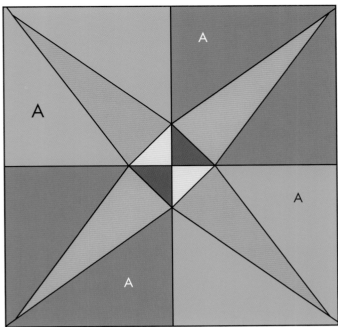

Unit Placement Diagram

DIAGONAL CANOES

4" block (easy)

NOTE: This block may be made as an 8" block by joining four blocks.

1. Make four of unit A, alternating colors as shown.

2. Sew four units A together, matching at dots for assembly.

Diagonal Canoes Unit Pattern

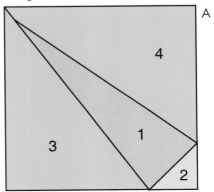

Seam Line Diagram

Art Quilts

From the Dairy Barn Cultural Arts Center Competition

Overlay 4 *(Award of Excellence)*
54" by 54". Made of hand-dyed and commercial cottons, with screen printing, machine piecing,
and machine quilting. "*Overlay 4* contrasts the rigidity of the grid and the controlled value gradation of the
background with the playful unpredictability of irregular strip piecing." —Ruth Garrison, artist, Tempe, Arizona

Persiennes

45" by 63". (Persiennes means Venetian shutters in French.) Made of silk and cotton fabrics and machine pieced using the paper piecing method. Machine quilted. "I am fascinated by geometric lines, light, colors, and fabrics. Silk is my favorite fabric, as it shines and lives at the same time.... The quilt reminds me of the times in my childhood when I enjoyed the light coming through my room's shutters." —Odile Texier, artist, Saint-Aunes, France

J. C. Raulston Arboretum

57" by 57". Made of cotton fabric, each piece cut using individually designed plastic templates specially positioned
to make use of patterns in the cloth. Machine pieced and hand quilted. "A rainy June walk in the arboretum . . . [to]
a huge wicker dome entwined by red flowering vines and lorded over by raucous birds. Under your feet is
a tiled floor depicting trees with interlaced limbs." —Ann Harwell, artist, Wendell, North Carolina

Miyabi

76" by 76". Made of Japanese kimono silk, embroidered, hand and machine pieced, hand and machine quilted.
"This is [made from] my parents' kimonos from about 70 years ago, which could have otherwise been thrown away.
This work allowed my thoughts to fly back to the times when artisans carefully created those kimonos, thus reminding me
of a sense of duty to pass a piece of history on to the next generation." —Harue Konishi, artist, Tokyo, Japan

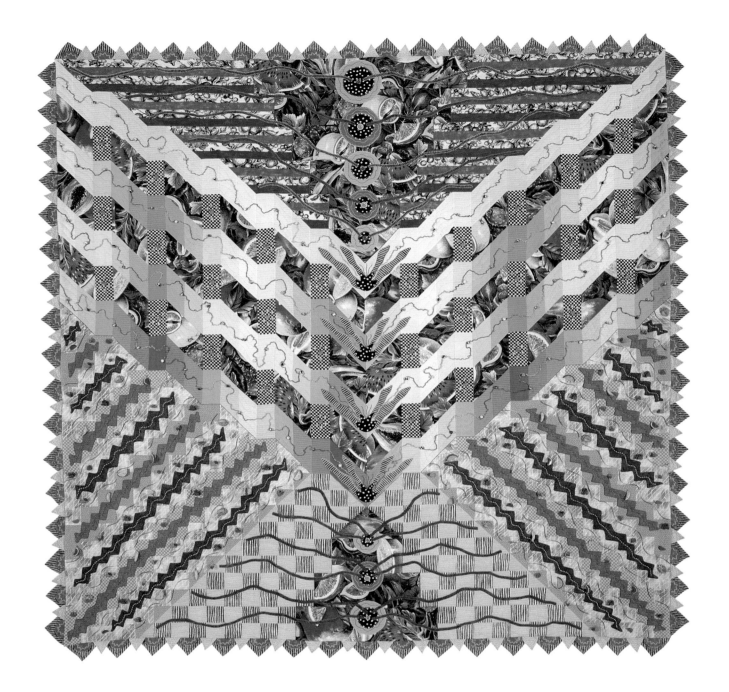

Tutti Frutti

72" by 72". Made of various materials, including cotton fabric, embroidery floss, buttons, beads, chenille fiber, and perle cotton. Machine pieced, hand quilted, hand appliquéd, and hand embroidered. "...The rich cornucopia of life choices the world offers us. Though there may be many twists and turns in this 'mixed salad,' if you really want to, you can find a way to accomplish anything...reach out, pick one, take a bite, seize the day!" —Jill Pace, artist, Glendale, Arizona.

Je t'aime
63" by 60". Made of fabric, beads, buttons, paint, clothing, gloves, gold leaf, color pencil, china markers, pastels, and playing cards. Machine pieced, hand appliquéd with beads, embellished and monoprinted. "I started intuitively putting images together from materials I had collected and received as gifts. I made a monoprint from the blouse and rickrack glove, using the originals as plates.... Suddenly I realized the quilt was just a big old nine-patch about romantic love." —Jane Burch Cochran, artist, Rabbit Hash, Kentucky

Wisteria

88" by 88". Made from cottons and blends, machine pieced, hand appliquéd (look closely to see all the petals and leaves), and hand quilted. "In Japan, the wisteria are now in full bloom every spring. The purple flowers and fresh, verdurous leaves are beautiful swaying in the wind. This quilt is one picture of scenery in Japan." —Kuniko Saka, artist, Tokyo, Japan

Breaking Ground

56" by 56". Made of hand-dyed cottons and commercial fabrics, machine pieced and machine quilted. Notice the diamond in a square and subtle blocks. "After a devastating fire destroyed my next-door neighbors' house, I looked out of my studio window at an ash-covered lot for 18 months. Finally, work began to rebuild the house. I started the quilt *Breaking Ground* the day the construction equipment moved onto the lot and started moving ground for the house foundation." —Janet Steadman, artist, Clinton, Washington

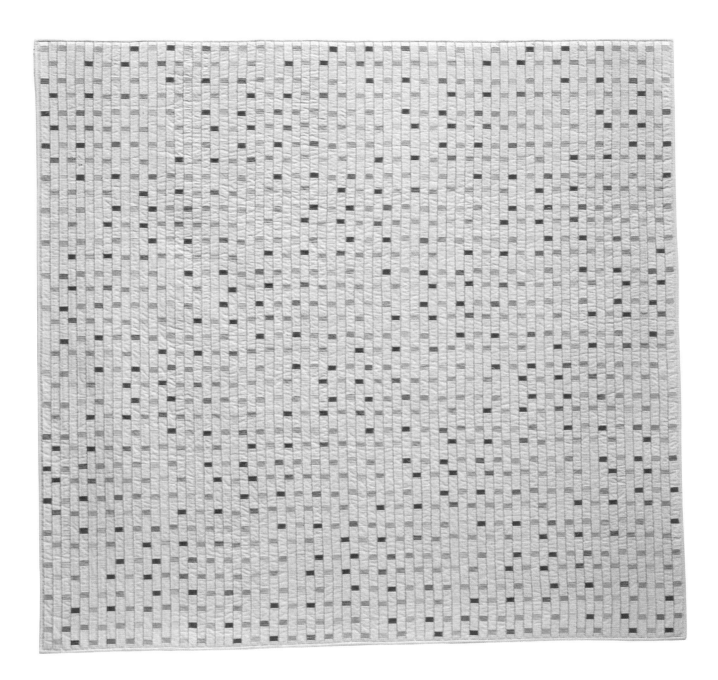

Ikat Quilt / Rhythm II

79" by 78". Owned in a private collection. Made of hand-dyed cotton, machine pieced and machine quilted.
"This is an attempt to transform one old textile technique (ikat weaving) into another (piecing and quilting). I enjoy the contrast between a rigid concept and the floating pattern of the 11 rainbow colors." —Inge Hueber, artist, Köln, Germany

Tumbling Reds

60" by 60". Photographed by David Caras. Made from 100 percent cotton, hand dyed by Heidi Stoll-Weber (see page 387). Machine strip pieced and machine strip quilted in the quilt-as-you-go technique. "I express myself with fabric [in] images that would be next to impossible to create with paint, but can quite easily be accomplished using the techniques natural to cloth, such as cutting apart and reconnecting with thread." —Judith Larzelere, artist, Belmont, Massachusetts.

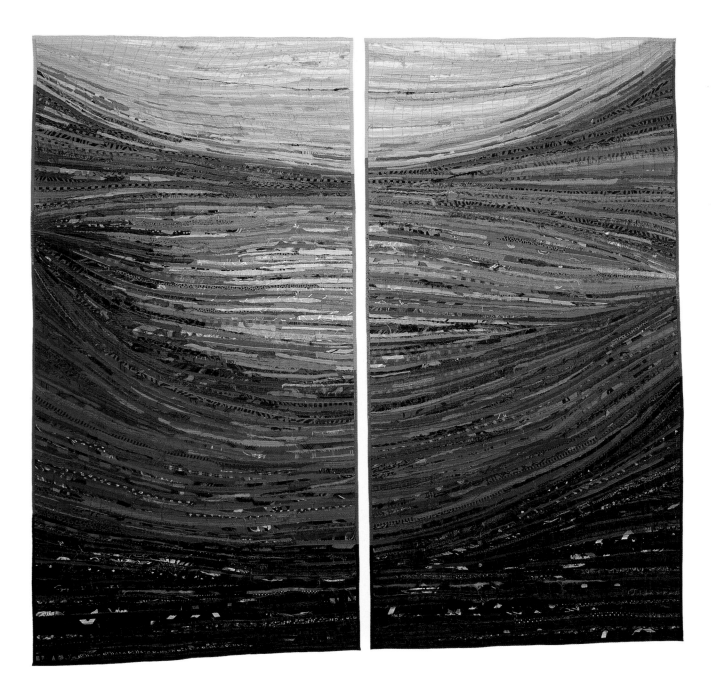

Mothers/Daughters #6...Lines of Communication

78" by 78". Made of cotton blends, torn fabrics, layered and machine stitched to cotton batting, and machine quilted. "Family relationships are fragile at times of stress and emotional upheaval. The bond between mother and daughter is stretched to the fracture point. To help preserve a special and loving relationship, the lines of communication, though tenuous, need to be kept open." —Judy Hooworth, artist, New South Wales, Australia

After the Gold Rush *(Rookie Award, sponsored by Studio Art Quilts Associates)*
26" by 21". Inspired by a photograph by Ray Atkeson, courtesy of the Ray Atkeson Image Archive.
Made from silk crepe de chine, hand painted using acid dyes, water-based resist, salt, and alcohol techniques.
Machine quilted with monofilament and rayon threads. "I have tried to beautify an unnatural landscape through a play of color
and texture on silk. The landscape is I–5 . . . crossing the California Aqueduct, the man-made river [that] irrigates farm fields
in what once was a desert. This is the second mining of California . . ." —Linda Gass, artist, Los Altos, California

Relief *(Juror's Award of Merit)*
74" by 52". Owned by Dan and Donna Wilder. Made of hand-dyed cotton from the artist's dye studio,
machine pieced and machine quilted. "Like all my work, this quilt is a study in color and light. I start laying out most
of my composition on a flannel-covered wall and keep adding details while I'm piecing. The whole process is
very satisfying: it's like painting with hand-dyed fabrics." —Heide Stoll-Weber, artist, Frankfurt, Germany

A Sunny Day in April *(Juror's Award of Merit)*

83" by 62". Made from hand-dyed and commercial cottons, machine appliquéd and machine quilted.
"Because my husband and I bought our first house in the winter, we were unaware of the wonderful gardens planted
by the previous owners. Spring was full of surprises, as hundreds of green shoots popped their heads through
the snow. The profusion of tulips, combined with the happiness I was feeling in my new home, gave me a
wonderful new enthusiasm for my work." —Emily Parson, artist, St. Charles, Illinois

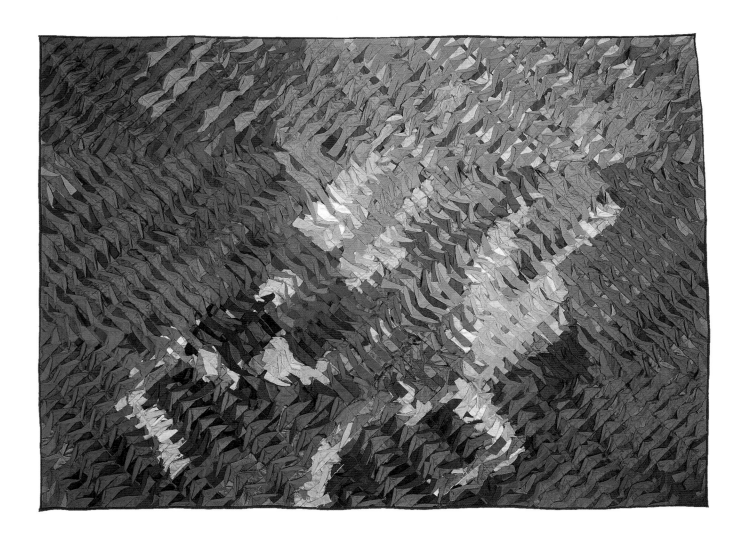

Swimmers

80" by 60". Made from silk and cotton duck fabrics, reverse appliquéd, layered, stitched, cut, restitched, and cut again. "The representation of two underwater swimmers in a pool is partially obscured—but also revealed—by my reverse appliqué method....I use an iridescent silk that is reflective, like water. The surface texture is a broken-up wave pattern such as you might see in a pool [and] perspective is accomplished by a subtle foreshortening of the torsos and elongation of the arms. Light/shadow and figure/ground relationships create the illusion of depth." —Tim Harding, artist, Stillwater, Minnesota

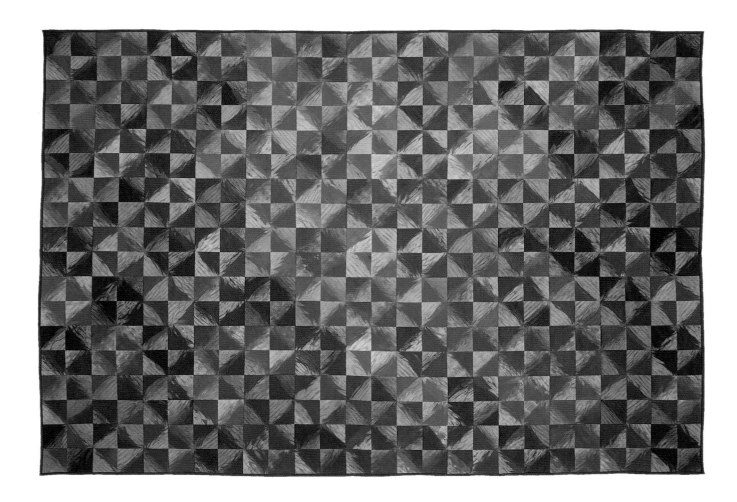

Grandmothers' Influence

88" by 62". Made of 100 percent cotton fabric Shibori dyed in Procion dyes with multiple immersions. Machine pieced and quilted. "This quilt is in honor of our grandmothers, who, in their respective ways, taught us the beginnings of our art. Debra's grandmother taught her to sew four-patch quilts as a child, while Michael's grandmother taught him jewelry making and gem cutting at an early age. We thank them both for their vision." Debra Lunn and Michael Mrowka, artists, Lancaster, Ohio

Yon and Beyond

51" by 48". Made of hand-dyed and commercial fabrics, machine pieced and hand quilted. Note that the motif is repeated in the quilting of the irregular rectangle patches. "On a spring trip to South Africa I traveled about 4,000 miles by car, and the beautiful directional arrows on the pavement were the inspiration for this motif. The colors of Northern Arizona inspired the colors." —Marla Hattabaugh, artist, Scottsdale, Arizona

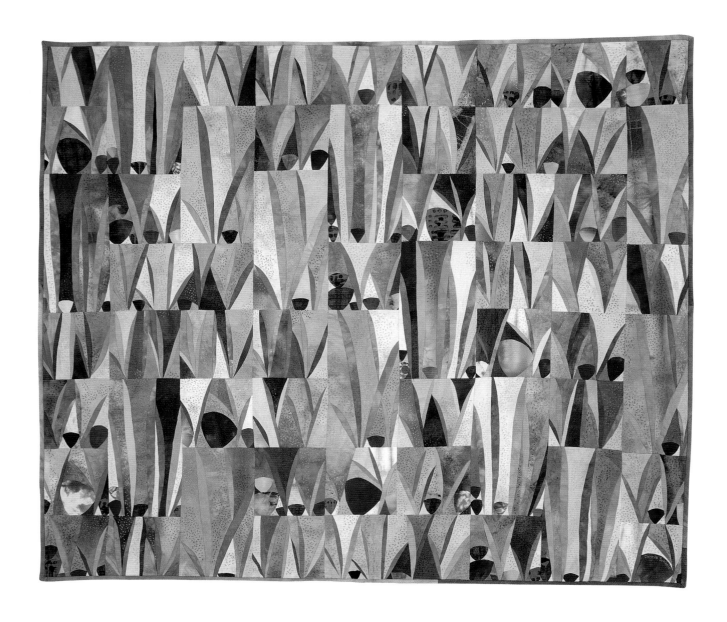

In the Shallows *(Domini McCarthy Award)*
53" by 46". Made using hand-dyed cottons. Machine pieced and hand quilted. Note the irregular blocks and the painstaking, pointillist stipple quilting among the leaves. "After doing a number of River Rocks quilts, I did a few quilts of foliage and grasses. This quilt is an integration of the two, and is reminiscent of the northern Wisconsin lake country that is very important to me." —Connie Scheele, artist, Houston, Texas

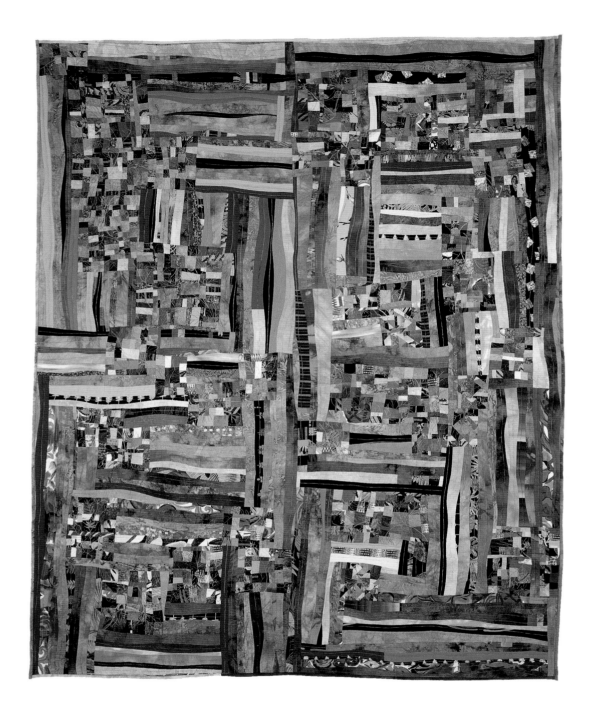

In the Smoky Mountains

71" by 90". Made from cotton fabric and batting, machine pieced and quilted. Note that the piecing is reminiscent of Log Cabin construction. "This quilt was inspired by a trip through the Smoky Mountains and the beautiful diffused colors of those mountains. The quilting design was taken from the shrubs and trees growing in the area." —Jutta Farringer, artist, Constantia Cape, South Africa

Requiem for an Ashtree
40" by 40". Made of cottons (many Marimekko fabric scraps), machine pieced and machine quilted. "The battle of wills between the bold Marimekko fabrics from the '60s and my idea of a quilt was fought on my design wall while a beloved old ash tree was taken down after a slow death over a number of years." —Sylvia H. Einstein, artist, Belmont, Massachusetts

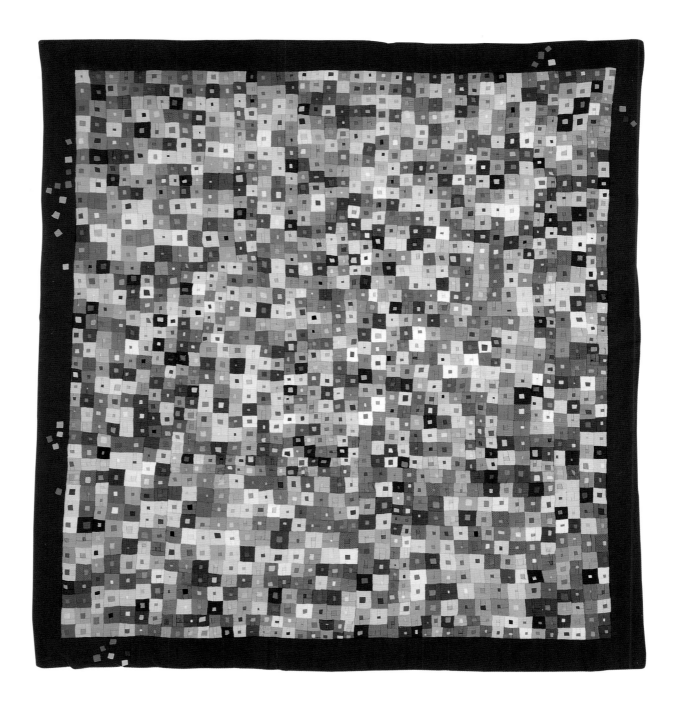

Colours in Disorder
35" by 38". Made from commercial fabrics including cotton, blends, silk, and wool. Pieced and appliquéd by hand, machine and hand quilted. Note how the tiny blocks have a classic quilt construction, but the end result is completely and joyfully unconventional. "Colours have always been very important for me, and patchwork is a good way to play with them. I try to express my feelings and ideas with colours and simple forms." —Beatrice Lanter, artist, Niederlenz, Switzerland

PART III

The Essentials of Quilting

CHAPTER 8

How to Quilt

With material by Cheryl Fall, Bettina Havig, Karol Kavaya, Maggie Malone, Fran Roen, Linda Seward, and Vicki Skemp

Jenny's Flowers, designed by Jennifer and Libby Woodruff, pieced and quilted
by the Community Quilters of Madison County, NC

Tools & Supplies

The tools needed for quiltmaking are relatively simple. If you have done any sewing you probably have most of them already. At the simplest level, beautiful quilts have been made using only a needle, thread, and scissors, old garments or feed sacks cut up for fabric and old blankets used for batting.

Once you're hooked, you may be interested in taking advantage of the tools and supplies developed specifically for quilters. Acquiring some of these nifty little gadgets can make the whole process faster or easier. Here are the tools you will need for virtually any project—those marked with an asterisk are essential.

TOOLS

Cutting Tools

- **Craft, or X-acto knife.** This is a handy tool for cutting out, for cutting card stock templates and quilting stencils.
- **Rotary Cutter.** A sharp circular blade with a handle; some blades are protected by a cover, which moves up when you press down, exposing the blade. Not necessary, but a rotary cutter is a huge time saver for cutting. You will also need a gridded cutting mat, preferably "self-healing," and a specially marked plastic ruler. Do not attempt to cut with a rotary blade if you do not have a rotary cutting mat. When choosing a rotary cutter, pick the one that feels the most comfortable in your hand. Replacement blades can be purchased when yours gets dull—if the rotary cutter skips along the fabric as you cut, it is probably nicked, and you need a new blade. *Always* cut away from you, and keep out of the reach of children.
- **Scissors.*** A really good, sharp pair of scissors is essential. Tag them FABRIC ONLY and use an older pair of scissors for cutting paper or plastic and/or cardboard. (You will dull the edges of your fabric scissors if

you use them on paper. Use an old pair for making templates.) The nonquilters in your house may try to use your fabric scissors for cutting paper or whatever. Foil them in this by putting out alternate scissors for them, and keep your fabric scissors tucked away when you're not using them for cutting fabric. Your scissors should not cause you any discomfort when you cut. If they do, you may need to have them sharpened and the joint oiled. You may want to use small scissors or snips for cutting thread.

Measuring Tools

It is important to be precise when you are measuring and cutting fabric for the piecing used in quilting. In patchwork and piecing, accuracy is important because a seemingly insignificant error repeated many times can lead to a big mess!

- **Cardboard.** The most common material used for templates. Writing tablet backs, empty soap cartons, shirt cardboard, etc. are all readily available cardboards to recycle as template material. They are easy to cut

After just a bit of practice, the rotary cutter can be a very efficient way to cut fabric for quilts.

with a mat knife. Cardboard's major drawback is that it wears down quickly, so you should make several templates to complete the marking of one quilt. Back them with sandpaper to prevent slipping on the fabric.

- **Drafting compass.** Useful tool for making accurate circle patterns.
- **Plastic or Lucite sheets.** For templates, this eliminates the wear problem, and is useful when you want to cut the same pattern many times. Sheets are usually available in packages of two. Coffee-can or margarine tub lids are of a good sturdy plastic for smaller pieces and styrene plastic trays can also be easily cut into templates. Back with sandpaper to prevent slipping.
- **Plastic rotary cutting rulers.** There are a wide variety of rulers available for use with rotary cutters and mats. All are made of clear plastic with measurement and sometimes angle markings. For the most versatile ruler, use the 6" x 24" size. For cutting squares and triangles, triangular and square rotary cutting rulers are also available. To keep your ruler from slipping as you cut, you can secure sandpaper squares or dots on the wrong side of the ruler. If you hit the side of a metal ruler with a rotary cutter, you may damage the blade, which is why a plastic ruler is preferable.
- **Precut Plastic Strips.** These are available commercially in widths of 1" to 3½" and a length of 24". You could make your own from Plexiglas (acrylic plastic), long enough to fit across the entire width of fabric, but you must be sure that they are absolutely accurate. A few small squares of sandpaper glued to one side will help prevent slippage. Use these strips to guide you when marking directly on the fabric, or with your rotary cutter.
- **Quilting stencils.** Used for marking quilting stitch designs and patterns onto fabric.
- **Ready-made templates.** There is a wide assortment of templates in both metal and plastic for many traditional patterns. The metal ones are the cutout type, allowing you to mark both the seam line and cutting line. For the more unusual designs, you will need to make your own templates.

- **Ruler.*** Any type of ruler can be used as long as it is perfectly straight and accurate. The plastic transparent rulers, in either 12" or 18" lengths are preferred by many quilters because the markings on the rulers allow you to make perfect squares and angles, but you may find that another tool, such as a carpenter's square or right triangle, may also be used. The gridded cutting mat for a rotary cutter is also an excellent measuring tool.
- **Tape measure.*** No needleworker should be without at least one of these.

Marking Tools

There are many options available for marking and transferring quilting patterns or motifs onto fabric, and there are advantages and disadvantages to each method. You will probably develop a preference for one tool over the course of time.

- **Carpenter's chalk.** This is usually blue in color and can be used for straight-line designs across the quilt top. The chalk can also be used with perforated patterns and templates. Test it on your fabric to make sure it will wash out.
- **Dressmaker's carbon paper.** Use this with a tracing wheel for relatively simple designs. For marking more intricate patterns through the carbon paper, use the point of a knitting needle or a stylus. Caution: If

A few of the items you may need for quilting.

Clockwise from top: pattern template, masking tape, marker, thread, thimble, finger guard, scissors.

using the red or dark-blue carbon, it may take several washings to remove all traces of the markings. Test first!

- **Dressmaker's pencils.*** These are nice to have on hand for marking dark fabrics. They can be hard to sharpen as they tend to crumble easily.

- **Masking tape.*** Use for marking straight guidelines. Apply masking tape only after the quilt is on the frame. Do not leave masking tape on the quilt overnight, since the tape can leave a sticky residue that is hard to remove. Buy new masking tape to use for quilting—an old roll is far more likely to leave residue.

- **Pencils.*** For marking pieces for cutting, a soft, dark lead pencil or a fine-line ballpoint pen can be used. For seam lines, use a hard lead pencil since it won't smudge as easily. Be sure the pencil is sharp at all times.

- **Powdered dressmaker's chalk.** There are several marking devices that use powdered chalk. One has a tiny wheel that distributes chalk as it is rolled. Other are a bit more difficult to use, but are worth a try.

- **Quilter's tape.** On some delicate projects, you may want to get this ¼" tape, which is available from your quilting supplier.

- **Vanishing markers.** These contain purple ink that vanishes within 24 hours, sometimes sooner. Not suitable for marking your quilt ahead of time. There is some doubt among quilters as to its long-term safety for the fabric.

- **Water-soluble markers.** There are some made just for quilters. They provide good clear lines that don't rub off and they vanish when dabbed with cold water. Some authorities warn that the ink may deteriorate the fabric over a long period of time, and some have found that the ink is difficult to remove entirely. Test and wash a scrap of your fabric first.

Pressing Tools

Pressing is essential at many steps of construction to produce crisp edges or creases.

NOTE: There is a difference between ironing, the back and forth smoothing used on yardage, and pressing, the lifting up and pressing down of the iron that is used to press seams and to remove wrinkles without stretching the fabric or patchwork. You will iron your fabric before beginning a project; thereafter, you will press your work when required.

- **Iron.*** Next to your needle or sewing machine, your iron is the most important tool for achieving outstanding results. Instead of jumping up and down to run to the ironing board, bring the iron to you so that you are not tempted to skip this important step.

- **Ironing board.** If you have an adjustable ironing board, set it at a convenient height and place it right by your chair. If you do not, or if you have one that is not adjustable, pull a small table close to your chair and cover it with a doubled bath towel. Plug in your iron and you're all set.

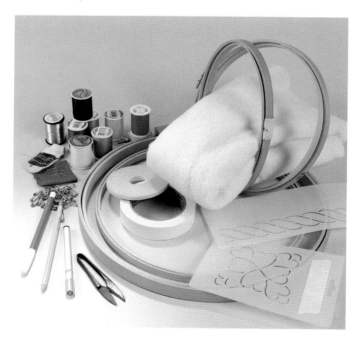

Quilting tools and supplies—including batting, stencils, tape, marking tools, needles, and thread—surround these hoops.

SEWING MACHINE THREAD TENSION

Always keep your sewing machine in good working condition—especially if you plan to do any machine appliqué. Your sewing machine needs to be cleaned and serviced periodically. Regularly oil your machine and remove the debris that can clog the feed dogs or jam the machine. A noisy machine is a machine in need of oil.

Referring to your owner's manual, adjust the thread tension properly. for satisfactory results, tension *must* be evenly balanced. Adjust as follows:

1. Hold the bobbin case in your hand and slide the bobbin into it, threading the bobbin as if it were in the machine. Then let go of the case while holding onto end of the bobbin thread. If the case slides down to the floor, leaving you with a 4-foot tail of thread, your tension is too loose.

2. If the case does not move, gently shake the thread and watch the bobbin case: if it doesn't go anywhere, your tension is much too tight. If it slips ever so slightly, you have nearly perfect tension.

3. Replace the bobbin case and bobbin in the machine. Thread the sewing machine with the same weight of thread used in the bobbin, but in a different color. Test-sew a length of straight stitch on a doubled scrap of fabric and look at the resulting stitch. If the top thread has been pulled to the bottom side of the folded fabric, your upper tension is too loose.

4. Adjust the upper tension and test again until the stitch becomes balanced. If you have tried these steps, and the tension is still not balanced, have your machine professionally serviced.

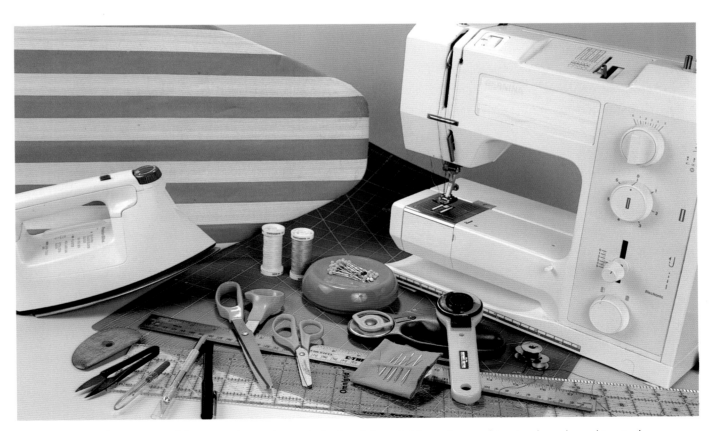

You are likely to have many of these supplies at home, including (left to right): an iron and ironing board, marking tools, measuring and cutting implements, and sewing machine and notions.

Stretching Tools

- **Quilting frame.** Frames are available at quilting stores. It is easy to build one, or one can be improvised with two long, 2" x 2" rails, four ladder-back chairs, and four C-clamps. Many quilters today user a frame apparatus made from square or rectangular PVC pipe.

- **Quilting hoop.** A more substantial cousin of an embroidery hoop—they allow you to keep your work properly stretched and the layers tight while you are working, to facilitate good quilting. A 14" or 18" quilting hoop is recommended. Keeping some flex in the top allows you to rock your needle.

Stitching Tools

- **Betweens, or quilting needles.** A very short needle used to produce the tiny stitches for quilting. There is a range of betweens—the higher the number, the shorter the needle. A number 12 would be challenging for a beginner, so you may find it easier to start with a needle in the 5 to 10 range, then, as your skill grows, switch to a smaller needle.

- **Embroidery needles.** These needles have large eyes to accommodate several strands of embroidery floss at once. You will need these for any embroidery using cotton floss, silk twist, or fine yarn.

- **Pincushion.** Magnetic ones are terrific, or small ones with elastic that fit on your wrist.

- **Safety pins.** Medium-sized safety pins can be used as a substitute for hand basting.

- **Sewing Machine.** You do not need a fancy, multi-stitch wonder. The simplest machine is all that is required. In fact, many of the projects could be sewn entirely by hand, if you so desired, but the instructions assume that you are using a sewing machine.

- **Sharps.** These all-purpose needles are used in general sewing and for appliqué. Sharps are used in many projects, so have some on hand.

- **Straight Pins.** You need not always pin when working, but when you do, the pins with brightly colored, round heads are easier to see and handle.

- **Thimbles.** Most quilters use a thimble on the middle or index finger of their quilting hand. There are various kinds of thimbles (metal, leather, and plastic, for example) and you should experiment to find what is comfortable for you.

SUPPLIES

You should be able to find these supplies at your local craft, fabric, or quilting shop.

- **Batting.** There are many different types of batting. Some battings require closer quilting than others do; again, check your package for these requirements. The batting may require prewashing, according to the instructions on the package. Prepackaged batting is available in the following sizes: craft, 36" x 45"; crib, 45" x 60"; twin, 72" x 90"; full, 81" x 96"; queen, 90" x 108"; and king, 120" x 120".

- **Beeswax.** Run all-cotton thread through this to keep your thread from tangling and knotting while hand sewing.

- **Bias tape.** Prepackaged bias tape comes in a variety of widths, folds, and colors, and it can be used to bind the edges of some projects. See the individual project instructions for specific information regarding bias tape.

- **Embroidery thread or floss.** Pearl cotton, or 6-strand 100 percent cotton embroidery floss is used for hand embroidery, whichever is noted in the individual project. Special threads, such as rayon or metallic thread, may also be used for embroidery or machine appliqué. Again, see the individual project instructions for any specific information regarding threads.

- **Fabric.** Most traditional quilters choose to sew all-cotton fabric, because it feels soft and ages gracefully. Prewash in hot water, dry, and iron before cutting. (Be careful with imported fabrics, because the colors may bleed. Reds and blues seem especially prone to this.) If creating a piece that will not be washed, like a wall hanging, you will not need to be as concerned with the fabric's colorfast properties.

- **Freezer paper.** When you are tracing pattern templates, freezer paper works quite well for this application.
- **Fusible webbing.** Used to bond appliqués to the background fabric of the quilt top prior to machine appliqué. (Not needed for hand appliqué.) When a project calls for fusible webbing, choose a paper-backed, non-woven webbing that becomes sticky on both sides when it is pressed with an iron. (Read the instructions from the manufacturer to see how hot to make your iron.) Fusible webbing goes by various brand names, and it may be sold by the yard or in prepackaged units at fabric stores. Most webbing sold by the yard is 18" wide. Choose a lightweight webbing (it is difficult to quilt through heavy webbing).
- **Graph paper.** Good for enlarging patterns and mapping out blocks when planning your project. You can fill in squares with colored pencils to try alternate color and design combinations for your blocks. Assign a measurement to each square to help you figure how much yardage you will need to buy.
- **Quilting Thread.*** Used for the stitching of quilting designs, it is specifically designed for hand quilting and comes in a wide variety of colors. You can match the fabric on which you are quilting, or go for a contrast. Metallic quilting thread produces a striking effect, but should not be used in a project that will be laundered often.
- **Seam ripper.** It is better to rip than to have a crooked quilt. Nobody is a perfect stitcher all the time, so have several of these handy—it means that you care enough about what you're doing to do it properly. They tend to get dull after repeated use. Replace them as necessary.
- **Sewing Thread.*** All-purpose thread (cotton-wrapped polyester) for piecing and quilting has a better range of colors to choose from, and is stronger. You may also use 100 percent cotton thread. Run the thread through beeswax so it doesn't tangle easily.
- **Stabilizer.** A layer of lightweight paper or non-woven fabric placed under your base fabric to give extra body, stability, and maneuverability while you do machine appliqué. The stabilizer should be cut slightly larger than the base fabric. Stabilizer is sold in fabric stores, by the yard or prepackaged. Get the tear-away kind, so it can be torn off when you are through machine-stitching your appliqué. You may also use scratch paper such as tracing paper for stabilizer. Pin a piece of stabilizer to the wrong side of the base fabric at the corners.
- **Tracing paper.*** Useful for tracing templates and patterns to transfer to your quilt top.
- **Unbleached Muslin.** This economical, 100 percent cotton fabric is useful as the foundation for strip-pieced, foundation pieced, and crazy quilt projects. It is available in many weights and widths.

Planning a Project

THEME

As you begin to plan your project, it will help things come together more enjoyably if you have a theme. Use your imagination to make the process and the product meaningful to you and the recipient. A theme may be suggested by the project itself—is this a quilt for a new baby? Is it to be a wedding present? Or perhaps you are working on something for a certain room in your own home. You may be looking for a specific color scheme or design. Sometimes there are more than one theme—for instance, color and motif: pink flowers; or design and contrast: plain and patterned circles. Because the choice of blocks, colors and patterns is entirely up to you, your creation will be different from anyone else's. Also, because of the vast range of choices, you need not ever make the same project twice.

Color, theme, and design ideas may come from nature, art, magazines, catalogs, quilting books, or you may want to choose something to match a décor or a personality. You can also refer to the color wheel to help guide your choices. Anyone can achieve a pleasing effect by using analogous colors (colors next to each other on the color wheel, such as violet and blue, red and orange, etc.). A bold look will result from the use of complementary colors (colors opposite each other on the color wheel, such as violet and yellow, or reddish orange and bluish green, etc.).

Experiment with blocking out your pattern ideas and color combinations with colored pencils or markers on large-grid graph paper, where you can plan out quilting blocks and color them in various combinations until you find one that is pleasing. This method will also help you when you get to the stage of figuring measurements.

CHOOSING FABRIC

When you have selected a project and a theme and/or color scheme, the next step is to choose your fabrics. The favorite fabric of most quilters is 100 percent cotton. Cotton is very easy to work with and it will not slide as you stitch, as a blend or a polyester can. Its smooth, soft finish allows the needle to glide easily through the fabric during both the piecing and quilting processes. Cotton is also very forgiving if you happen to make a mistake. Cotton feels good to the touch, wears well, washes well, and ages softly. You can find many 100 percent cottons in both prints and solids that are designed especially for quilters.

Blends may also be used, but make sure they have a higher percentage of cotton than of the other fibers. Fabric availability is subject to fashion trends. Right now, natural fabrics are in good supply, but next year cotton may be hard to come by. Cotton is subject to fading and shrinking, and color and print selections may be limited. Blends have a tendency to slip and slide, or to fray when washing.

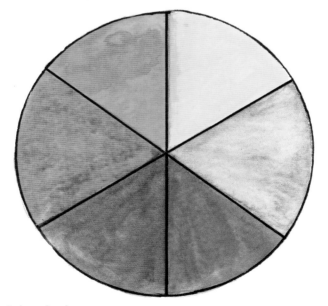

Color wheel.

Another thing to consider in choosing cotton blends over cotton is durability. The cotton blends haven't been around long enough to compare to a hundred-year-old cotton quilt, but keep in mind that most antique quilts that have survived to the present were "best quilts" that

You will choose from a wide variety of fabrics and supplies for your quilting projects.

were taken out to honor special guests, then either packed away or placed in a dark, unused bedroom, safe from use and fading. They were not subjected to frequent washing in harsh chemicals. The cotton/polyester blends can be an excellent choice for quilting. They are always available, come in a wide range of colors and prints, do not fade or shrink, and are almost as easy as cotton to sew. This is your most important supply, so choose it wisely and have fun while you are doing it.

Denim and fine-wale corduroy are good choices for children's quilts. These fabrics can take all the abuse a child will give, and stand up well to the frequent washings necessary. Corduroy used as a backing has the added advantage of providing traction—it will not slip off a bed as readily. These fabrics are also good choices for a masculine quilt, giving a rugged texture that many

men like. Because of their heavier hand these fabrics might be less easy to hand-quilt, but are good candidates for machine quilting.

T-shirts have even made their way into quilting. With all the designs being printed on them, they can make a really fun quilt top. One might even say that using T-shirts in a quilt is today's answer to the use of feed sacks in a bygone era. It carries on the tradition of recycling what is readily available. Because of the stretch in T-shirt material, however, it is necessary to back the fabric with very lightweight iron-on interfacing.

Scraps of new fabrics from other sewing projects can also be used to advantage. A word of warning should be given, however, about using worn clothing for quilt making. Do not include worn or threadbare sections of garments in your quilt. Only use those areas that are still strong and look almost new. Worn pieces of cloth will wear out more quickly than newer pieces, so that your quilt will not last as long as it should, and you will be faced with having to patch it. After all the hours you spend making your quilt, you don't want it to look worn and tired within a year or two.

Use with Care—Specialty Fabrics
Some quilters have occasionally used beautiful imported fabrics for wall hangings. It has been found that these fabrics, particularly batiks, madras, and wood-block prints, are not always colorfast and will bleed. The blue and red dyes seem especially prone to this. Use these specialty fabrics only on pieces that will never be washed. It is heartbreaking to have a piece of work you've spent many hours on ruined when it is washed and the colors run.

Exceptions to the Rule
There are some exceptions to the cotton mandate. One is the crazy quilt—the traditional crazy quilt uses an assortment of different fabrics, such as velvet, velveteen, silks, satins, and sometimes wool. They are suitable for a

very special quilt that won't see a lot of hard wear, since the real thing is easily damaged and must be dry-cleaned. We do now have the advantage of modern imitation velvets, silks and satins made from synthetics, many of which are washable, that can give the appearance and texture of those luscious fabrics without the necessity of special care.

Wool is a lovely fabric, available in a wide range of colors and weights. The heavier wools would be excellent candidates for a tied quilt, while the lighter-weight wools can be machine-quilted, or even hand-quilted. Be mindful that, unless you choose only the new washable wool fabrics, special cleaning methods will need to be used.

Another exception is the art quilt, made only for display, which may incorporate non-washable or specially treated fabrics in order to achieve a specific look not obtainable with cotton.

WHAT SIZE QUILT?

The starting point in determining the size of your finished quilt is the mattress size. This is especially important when making a medallion type of quilt or some of the appliqué designs. For that type of design you want the focal point of the quilt to be properly centered on the mattress with the borders falling from the sides. For an all-over patchwork design, with a binding or narrow border, the design allows for more give or take. The only time exact measurements are critical is when the design must fit the mattress top exactly.

Another thing to consider is whether you want the quilt to cover the pillows. A general allowance is 18", but there is so much difference in the size of pillows that you should probably measure to be sure. To measure, make up the bed with a bedspread that fits the way you like it. Hold the end of a tape measure under the pillow, as far back as the tuck of the spread. Bring the tape out and up over to the back of the pillows. Add this figure to the length of the quilt. You do not need the pillow allowance if the quilt will just be used as a cover or hanging, rather than as a spread.

It is always best to have measurements of the bed on which the quilt will be laid. If the mattress is old and suffers from middle-age spread, or if it is one of the newer, extra deep mattresses, it can make a difference in the effect the quilt will have on the bed. There could be several inches difference between the standard size and the mattress for which the quilt is intended.

For the overhang at the bottom and sides, measure the depth from the surface of the mattress to the point where you want the overhang to reach. If you have a bed with sideboards you may want the quilt to reach only to the bottom of the boards, so measure to that point. If you want it to reach the floor, measure to the floor. For the sides, double this measurement and add it to the measurement of the width of your mattress.

DOING THE MATH

Once you've decided how large you want the quilt, it's time to determine what size block you will use. Remember, it is absolutely crucial to figure the seam allowances into the calculations. If you plan that ten

As a general guideline, mattress sizes* are as follows:

California King	72" x 84"
King	76" x 80"
Queen	60" x 80"
Double	53" x 74.5" (approx. 75")
Twin	38" x 75"
Cot	30" x 75"
Crib	27" x 52"

* U.S. mattress sizes are given here.

blocks whose cut pieces total 8" across will make a quilt of 80" across, it can be devastating to discover when the top is sewed that it measures only 75" across. Unless you remember to figure at least ¼" extra for every edge that will be seamed, your calculations will be off.

It is easiest if you can be somewhat flexible when it comes to the size, because too often the block size won't come out evenly to your measurements. If your desired

As an example, if your overhang measurement is 12", add 24" to the width. Add 12" to the length.) In this instance, your finished quilt would measure:

	Width	Length
Mattress size, double bed	54"	75"
Allowance to cover pillows		18"
Overhang on each side	24"	
Overhang at foot		12"
Total	78"	105"

size of quilt is 78" wide by 105" long, as above, your first adjustment might be to make it 104" or 106" long.

As you can see, the only block size that comes out with the side borders of equal width to the top and bottom borders, is the 14" block. If you decide to use a 12" block, you can either increase the side borders to equal 10" or decrease the top and bottom border to total 5", or choose some middle width for both, such as 7". You could also use an intermediate block size (e.g., 12½") by enlarging or reducing your patterns a bit, or adding more space around the block pattern.

Setting the quilt with sashing strips is another very popular method of getting the quilt size you want. In fact, in the above examples, it would be easier to set the 18" block this way, rather than try to adjust the borders to allow for an 11" difference in the combined border widths of the two side borders vs. the combined width of the top and bottom borders.

The following chart shows an example of the calculations and adjustments needed when using sashing. In this example, the quilt size is 77" x 106", and border and sashing strips are of equal width to each other. The sashing strips in the second table could be increased to 5" or 6" in width, depending on the block size, or you could add an outer border if the quilt is still too small after making these adjustments.

VARIOUS BLOCK AND BORDER* COMBINATIONS FOR A QUILT

Approximately 78" x 106"

Block Size	Blocks Across	Blocks Down	Total Blocks Needed
8"	9 blocks = 72" + 6" border	12 blocks = 96" + 10" border	108
9"	8 blocks = 72" + 6" border	11 blocks = 99" + 7" border	88
10"	7 blocks = 70" + 7" border	10 blocks = 100" + 6" border	70
12"	6 blocks = 72" + 6" border	8 blocks = 96" + 10" border	48
14"	5 blocks = 70" + 8" border	7 blocks = 98" + 8" border	35
15"	5 blocks = 75" + 3" border	7 blocks = 105" + 1" border	35
15"	4 blocks = 60" + 18" border	6 blocks = 90" + 16" border	24
16"	4 blocks = 64" + 14" border	6 blocks = 96" + 10" border	24
18"	4 blocks = 72" + 6" border	5 blocks = 90" + 16" border	20

* The border allowance includes the width of both borders (two side borders or a top and a bottom border) to total 78" x 106".

Blocks Set on the Diagonal

To determine the size of blocks when set on the diagonal, you must multiply by 1.42. This figure is then divided into the desired size to determine how many blocks are needed. The chart on the next page shows the width of the block on the diagonal and how many blocks you need to make a quilt 82" x 107" (rounded to nearest quarter inch).

All this may seem like a lot of unnecessary math, but a familiarity with it will be helpful to you. Once you have made a few quilts you will have a general idea of the sizes that work for you. As mentioned earlier, the only time exact measurements are critical is when the design must fit the mattress top exactly.

ESTIMATING YARDAGE

Now that you have determined the quilt size and how many blocks are needed, you are ready to estimate how much fabric is needed. We will use a simple nine-patch block of five dark and four light squares as an example.

VARIOUS BLOCK AND SASHING STRIP* COMBINATIONS FOR A QUILT

Approximately 77" x 106"

Block Size	Blocks Across	Blocks Down	Total Blocks Needed
8"	Eight blocks = 72" Nine 2" strips = 18"	Ten blocks = 80" Eleven 2" strips = 22"	Eighty Finished size: 82" x 102"
9"	Seven blocks = 63" Eight 2" strips = 16"	Ten blocks = 90" Eleven 1½" strips = 16½"	Seventy Finished size: 79" x 106½"
10"	Six blocks = 60" Seven 3" strips = 21"	Eight blocks = 80" Nine 3" strips = 27"	Forty-eight Finished size: 81" x 107"
12"	Five blocks = 60" Six 3" strips = 18"	Seven blocks = 84" Eight 3" strips = 24"	Thirty-five Finished size: 78" x 108"
14"	Four blocks = 56" Five 3" strips = 18"	Six blocks = 84" Seven 3" strips = 21"	Twenty-four Finished size: 71" x 105"
15"	Four blocks = 60" Five 3" strips = 15"	Five blocks = 75" Six 3" strips = 18"	Twenty Finished size: 75" x 105"
If the lattice strips are made 4" wide:	Five 4" strips = 20"	Six 4" strips = 24"	Finished size: 80" x 99"
16"	Four blocks = 64" Five 4" strips = 20"	Five blocks = 80" Six 4" strips = 24"	Twenty Finished size: 84" x 104"
18"	Three blocks = 54" Four 4" strips = 16"	Five blocks = 90" Six 4" strips = 24"	Fifteen Finished size: 70" x 114"

* Border is assumed to be same as sashing here.

Diagonal Block Measures:	Number of Blocks for Width:	Number of Blocks for Length
8" block = 11.36" or 11½"	7 = 80½"	9 = 103½"
9" block = 12.78" or 12¾"	6 = 76½"	8 = 102"
10" block = 14.2" or 14"	5 = 70"	7 = 98"
11" block = 15.62" or 15½"	5 = 77½"	6 = 93"
12" block = 17.04" or 17"	4 = 68"	6 = 102"
13" block = 18.46" or 18½"	4 = 74"	5 = 92½"
14" block = 19.88" or 20"	4 = 80"	5 = 100"
15" block = 21.3" or 21¼"	3 = 63¾"	5 = 106¼"
16" block = 22.72" or 22¾"	3 = 68¼"	4 = 91"
17" block = 24.14" or 24"	3 = 72"	4 = 96"
18" block = 25.56" or 25½"	3 = 76½"	4 = 102"

1. Total number of units per block for each color.

5 dark squares   4 light squares

2. Multiply by total number of blocks.

(9" block; finished size 81" x 99"; 99 blocks)

5 x 99 = 495 dark squares

4 x 99 = 396 white squares

3. Add seam allowance and measure each unit, both length and depth.

3" squares + ¼" seam allowance on all sides = 3½" square

4. Find the width on the accompanying chart. Go to the column titled Number of Units Across and find how many 4" squares can be cut across the width of the fabric. In this case, 11.

5. Find the length under Number of Units Down. Since this is a square we again look for 4". Nine pieces can be cut down the fabric length.

6. Multiply the number of units obtained in width by the number of units obtained length to determine how many can be cut from 1 yard of fabric.

11 x 9 = 99

7. Divide the total number of units needed by the number of units per yard to obtain total yardage required.

495 divided by 99 = 5 yards dark

396 divided by 99 = 4 yards white

A WORD TO THE WISE

Bolts of 100 percent cotton fabric that are marked 45" wide may, in fact, actually measure narrower. It is not uncommon to find that they are 44" or even less in width. Make sure you check, and allow for this discrepancy. Figure that 100 percent cotton may shrink, and also that you will lose between ½" and 1" in width when you remove the selvages and rectify the grain of the fabric. It is always wisest to buy a little more fabric than your measurements would indicate. What you have left over can be used another time in a scrap quilt or small project!

CHOOSING A BACKING

The choice of backing material is almost as broad as that for the top. You can pick up one of the fabrics used in the top for the backing, or find a color that sets off or contrasts with the top.

Using a busy print for backing will mask any unevenness of stitches if you are a beginning quilter. If you are surer of your stitches, a solid backing in a color that contrasts with the top allows the quilt to be displayed on either side. If you plan on showcasing some decorative quilting patterns, a deep, solid color will set them off to very good advantage.

Unit Size	Numbers of Units Across (45" fabric)	Number of Units Down (36" fabric)
1"	45	36
1½"	30	24
2"	22	18
2½"	18	14
3"	15	12
3½"	12	10
4"	11	9
4½"	10	8
5"	9	7
5½"	8	6
6"	7	6
6½"	6	5
7"	6	5

A nice, cozy backing for a quilt can be fine-wale corduroy or cotton flannel. The soft cuddly warmth and non-slip properties make either a good choice for a child's quilt, or one that will get lots of use on a bed. Flannel sheets are readily available, so you may not even have to seam the pieces together. Do not pay a lot for a flannel sheet just to back a quilt, however. Since they are a seasonal item, wait for the spring closeouts to stock up. They can probably be found at your local discount store for a very reasonable price.

Figuring Yardage for Backing

For a small quilt that is 30" wide or less, a single length of standard 45-inch-wide fabric will be ample. A larger or wider quilt will require piecing the back (see Prepare the Backing, on page 431) or using wider fabric that is especially intended for quilt backing. Since the selection of colors and prints in the wider fabrics is quite limited, you may want to piece the back in order to achieve the look you desire.

If your quilt is 70" wide or less, multiply the length of the quilt by two. Now add 1 yard to allow for the extra 5" per side and fabric for a sleeve for hanging the quilt. Note: If you choose not to have a sleeve, ¾ yard extra will be adequate.

If your quilt is more than 70" wide, you will need three lengths of material. For example, if your quilt is 76" x 90", you will require 300" or approximately 9 yards of fabric plus ¼ yard for your sleeve.

PREPARING FABRIC

IMPORTANT! Once you have assembled all your fabrics, and even before the all-important step of prewashing them—unless you are working with velvets, woolens, silks, or other special materials, or you know that the quilt will never be washed—test a swatch of each fabric to see if it bleeds or "crocks" (loses its dye into the wash water). Test-wash each swatch in hot water and detergent. Replace any fabrics that aren't colorfast, as the dye may spoil your completed project when it is laundered later on. Most fabric stores will allow you to cut a small swatch off the bolt, so you can perform this test even before making any investment in yardage.

If there is any evidence that the fabric is not colorfast (the colors will bleed), wash the fabric again or soak it in a solution of three parts cold water and one part white vinegar. Rinse the fabric and spread it on white toweling while wet. If there is still evidence of color bleeding, discard the fabric and select another. It is far better to make this effort in the beginning than to experience the horror of washing a finished project only to find that it has been ruined by colors bleeding.

Exception to the Rule

There are quilters who prefer the new look and feel of unwashed cotton fabric for its crispness and body. Those working with detailed appliqué often find that unwashed cotton is easier to use. In this case, it might be wise to test a swatch just to make sure it is colorfast. For an art quilt, or any quilt that will never be washed, it is fine to skip this step.

Prewashing & Straightening

If you are using cotton or cotton-blend fabric, you must prewash and iron all your selections before beginning a project. Prewashing removes any sizing or starchy finishes that are added to the fabric by the manufacturers. It makes the fabric easier to handle, will take care of any shrinkage, and also assures you that the dye in your fabrics won't run later.

Before putting new fabrics in the washing machine, clip ¼" into the selvages (finished edges) at 2" intervals to accommodate shrinkage. Wash fabrics of a similar color in the very hottest water. To wash scraps, place similar colors in a net bag before putting in the machine—this will eliminate much of the inevitable fraying that occurs.

Some quilters prefer to hang the fabrics to dry, as tangling in a clothes dryer can twist the fabrics off-grain. If this is not practicable, tumble them in a hot dryer, but do not cram the dryer. Make sure to remove the fabrics immediately after the machine stops. If possible, iron the fabrics while they are slightly damp. The dampness makes it easier to remove all the wrinkles and rectify the grain of the fabric.

Check the Grain

Be sure your fabrics are on grain after they are washed. The crosswise and lengthwise threads of the fabric should be exactly perpendicular to each other. If they aren't perpendicular grasp the four corners of the fabric and pull diagonally from opposite corners simultaneously to straighten the grain (this is better done with two pairs of hands). Repeat this pulling alternately from opposite corners until the threads are perpendicular to one another.

If you cut rectangular pieces when the fabric is off grain, the pieces are more likely to stretch out of shape while you work with them, because the bias is stretchier than the straight grain of the fabric. (However, for appliqués, it is not necessary to use the straight grain.)

Prepare the fabrics for cutting as follows: Accurately cut off the selvages (side edges) to avoid any temptation of using them—those little printed words or white bands won't look good on your quilt top, and selvages tend to pucker with washing, which can ruin the look of your quilt.

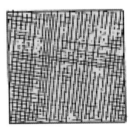

Off-grain fabric.

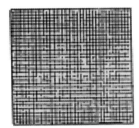

On-grain fabric.

Measuring and Cutting

Measure an even distance from each edge (selvages are usually ¼" but can be as wide as ½"). Draw a cutting line with a pencil and ruler. Cut away the edges along the pencil line (a rotary cutter works well for this). Next, using a right triangle and a ruler, draw a line across the end of the fabric that is exactly perpendicular to the cut selvage edge (figure 8–1). Cut away any excess fabric beyond this line. You are now ready to make your templates, mark your fabric and cut out your pieces.

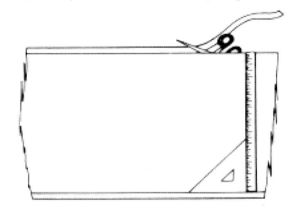

8–1. Cutting away the selvages.

Because accuracy is essential in quilting, make sure you are measuring and cutting a precise square, rectangle, or strip. You can choose several ways to measure and cut exact shapes: ruler and right triangle, quilter's graph paper, carpenter's square, or rotary cutting mat and ruler (even if you don't use the rotary cutter). Then, use shears or the rotary cutter (see below) to carefully cut your pieces.

ROTARY CUTTING

The beauty of rotary cutting is its precision and speed. Using it for straight-edge shapes—strips, squares, rectangles, and triangles—will halve the amount of time you spend on a project. While the initial expense may seem high, the accuracy you'll achieve and the savings in time will more than make up for it. You will need a rotary cutter with a large wheel, a cutting board designed for a rotary cutter, and a thick plastic ruler with marked grid or cutting lines. They can be found in any well-stocked quilting shop. The cutting board can also be found in most art supply shops; ask for the "self-healing" type.

Four to six layers of fabric can be cut at one time, depending on the fabric weight. Beginners should work with four layers. You will learn to recognize the sound and feel when the blade cuts through all the layers. *Always cut away from you!* If you notice that your blade is skipping threads, it is time to buy a new one. As with scissors, do not use your rotary blade on paper, as it will dull the blade. Use your *old* rotary blade for cutting paper. Mark it: PAPER with an indelible pen, and remember to change back to the sharper blade when cutting fabric.

Taking fabric that you have prewashed and trimmed as just explained, fold it in half with the

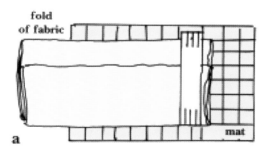

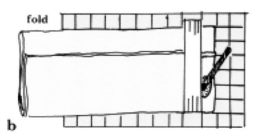

8–2. a: Evening up the jagged raw edge. b: Cutting strips.

trimmed selvage edges together, so that the fold is directly along the grain of the fabric (the warp, or lengthwise grain, in this case). The whole width (selvage to selvage) of your fabric should fit on the rotary cutting mat. If it does not, fold it again on the lengthwise grain.

Align the end of the fabric with a horizontal grid on your rotary cutting mat to make sure the end is perpendicular to the fold. If not, put the short end of the plastic ruler on the fold of the fabric, lined up with a vertical grid on the mat just a bit in from the fabric's raw edge. Press down firmly on the ruler with one hand. Take the rotary cutter in your other hand and place the blade against the edge of the ruler, just in front of the fold nearest you. Press down on the blade and, keeping it against the ruler, roll it away from you until you feel it go through all the layers of fabric and reach the opposite fold, trimming off any unevenness of the fabric (figure 8–2a).

When you have a straight edge, you can proceed to cut strips in needed widths, as your project requires. Use the grid on the mat and/or the grid on the ruler to measure. To cut a strip, measure off the desired width of the strip on your mat. Move your ruler that amount away from the trimmed end of the fabric (see figure 8–2b). Cut as you did for trimming the edge.

Remember to add ½" for seam allowances. For example, if your project requires 1" strips, your strip will need to be 1½" to accommodate the ¼" seam allowances at each edge. Position the ruler on the fabric so that where you will cut is 1½" away from the end of the fabric (figure 8–3). Run the blade of your rotary cutter along the edge of the ruler to cut the strip. To cut squares, trim one edge of the strip to remove the folds. Turn the strip and measure 1½" inches away from the cut end; cut along this measurement and you'll have four perfect squares. If you measure correctly and cut firmly, your squares will be extremely accurate without having to use a template. Save any leftover strips in a bag for a future scrap projects.

MAKING TEMPLATES & CUTTING PIECES

Using tracing paper and a pencil, or acetate and permanent marker, trace the templates for the designs you have chosen. Mark each tracing with the name of the design and the letter, or number, of the template. Glue the tracing to medium-weight cardboard or plastic and allow the glue to dry. Cut out each template using an X-acto knife or other cutting blade. For straight lines, use a straight metal edge to guide the knife.

8–3. Using a rotary to speed-cut strips and squares.

Unless otherwise noted, the edge of the template is the sewing line; therefore, a ¼" seam allowance must be added when marking the templates on the fabric. The best way to do this is by drawing a ¼" seam allowance on the wrong side of the fabric along the lengthwise and crosswise cut edges (figure 8–4a). You can then place the edge of your template on the marked line. Trace around the edge of your template. Use a ruler to mark a ¼" seam allowance around each of the remaining edges before marking the next template. Continue to mark all your templates on the wrong side of the fabric in this way.

To avoid waste and conserve fabric, mark your pieces so that they can be cut along a mutual edge (figures 8–4b and 8–4c). As a rule, the longest edge of any template should be placed on the straight (lengthwise) grain of the fabric. All edges of squares and rectangles should be on the straight grain.

Follow the list given with each design for the number of pieces to be cut and how to cut them. Symmetrical pieces do not need to be flipped over or "reversed," but many of the designs are made up of asymmetrical pieces, thus their mirror image or reverse side is needed to complete a pattern. This need to reverse is always indicated with each list. When a design is asymmetrical and you are not instructed to reverse the template, it means the template has already been reversed for you. Where the list indicates a number of pieces are "reversed," turn your template over to the opposite (wrong) side and mark the necessary number of pieces on the fabric. You can check your work by studying the assembly diagram of your block.

After you have marked your pieces, carefully cut them out along the cutting lines. Accuracy—in both marking and cutting—is essential to the successful completion of each project. If you are cutting out all of your pieces at once, carefully gather and keep the pieces for each project in a separate, labeled envelope or plastic bag to avoid confusion when sewing time arrives.

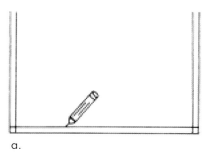

a.

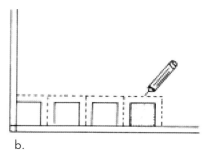

b.

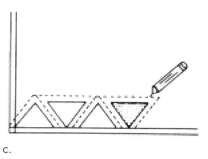

c.

8–4. Tracing around templates and allowing the ¼" seam allowance.

Piecing Patchwork

You have arrived at the construction stage. Most projects involve piecing, also called patchwork—stitching square-to-square, triangle-to-triangle, and so on—to create the design. Just as with cutting, accuracy is extremely important in all piecing. With a variation of as little as ⅛", seams or corners will not match. This is especially important when working on a small project where you may immediately notice any mistake.

It is assumed you will use a sewing machine to sew the pieces or patches for each project, although it is perfectly acceptable (though much slower) to do the piecing by hand. Most of the designs in this book are accompanied by complete piecing instructions and assembled in sub-units (squares, triangles, strips) that are then joined to complete the design.

After cutting all the necessary pieces, stitch them together, right sides facing each other while you stitch. Use a neutral-colored thread to piece your quilt, unless there is too much contrast in the fabrics to use a neutral. In that case, choose a thread that is one shade darker than the lightest fabric in the quilt.

PRESSING TO PERFECTION

Get into the habit of always pressing your seam allowances after stitching. *Remember!* Pressing is different from ironing. Pressing is applying pressure straight down on the fabric, lifting the iron, then reapplying pressure on the next spot. Do not move the iron back and forth as in ironing. Always press with a dry iron—both steam and/or ironing back and forth can stretch and distort the pieces. You need to keep their proper shape for accurate piecing.

For best results, first set the seam: press along the line of stitching you've made before opening out the joined pieces. Next, open out the pieces so that the seam allowance is folded toward the darker fabric and press again, setting the seam allowance into position (figure 8–5a).

To save time, try to set aside groups of units to be pressed—this way you won't feel as if you're constantly bouncing from the machine to the ironing board! Also, don't use an iron with an automatic shutoff feature if you plan on sewing for any length of time—you'll be constantly re-starting the thing!

When pressing joined pieces with intersecting seam lines, press each set of seam allowances in opposite directions (figure 8–5b). This reduces the bulk you will be quilting through later.

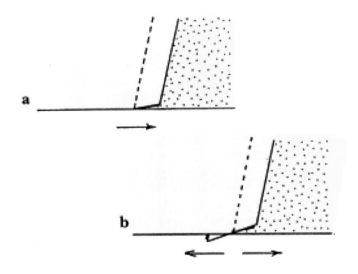

8-5. Pressing seam allowances. a: Press single seam allowances toward the darker fabric. b: Press intersecting seam allowances in opposite directions.

MACHINE PIECING

Important! If your sewing experience has been confined to standard garment making and you are accustomed to using ⅝" seam allowances, be aware that quilt piecing routinely uses ¼" seams. Unless you are directed otherwise in the individual project instructions, practically all the construction in this book is done assuming a ¼" seam allowance (figure 8–6a). If you are unsure of stitching an exact seam allowance when machine piecing, measure ¼" from the right side of the needle and place a small piece of masking tape so its right edge falls at the ¼" mark on your sewing machine. Use this tape as your stitching guide.

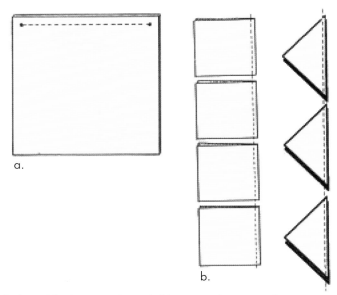

8–6. a: Machine piecing, stitching two pieces together.
b: Chain piecing multiple units to save time.

CHAIN PIECING

To save time, chain piece when possible. Align all the pairs of pieces to be joined with their right sides facing, and feed them through the machine one pair at a time, butting but not overlapping the units. Continue to stitch the units without cutting the thread between them (figure 8–6b). When you have sewn all the units, clip the connection stitching between the units to separate them. This method can be used for joining triangles, squares, or any other units that repeat.

STRIP PIECING

Another method of piecing that is a great time-saver is strip piecing. This is best used for obtaining repeating sections of small diamonds, squares, or strips. Two or more long strips of the width specified in the pattern are seamed together along their long edges and pressed.

From these striped pieces are cut strips depending on your pattern—straight across for squares or rectangles (figures 8–12 and 8–13), diagonally for diamond shaped pieces (figure 8–14), or using arch-shaped templates for curved strips (as for Double Wedding Ring in Chapter 1—Best-loved Classics, page 17). Strip piecing is most successfully done with the aid of a rotary cutter, but may also be used with scissors, although you will need to mark off the strips for cutting with scissors. If you use a rotary cutter, mat, and ruler, marking will not be necessary.

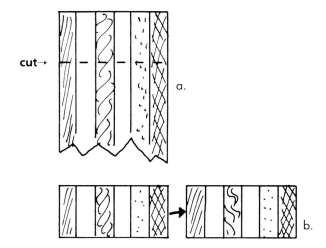

8–7. a: Strip-piecing ready to be cut into units.
b: Joining two strip units.

SPEEDY TRIANGLE SQUARES

There are a number of methods of "mass producing" triangle squares (squares consisting of two right-angle triangles seamed together on their long edge). The following three methods are all for speed construction of finished triangle squares that will measure 4" on each side, not counting the seam allowances. Adjust measurements up or down for your pattern, always remembering to allow an extra inch that will be taken up in seam allowances for each square.

Method 1. Cut two equal-size rectangles, (31" x 16" for this example) from the two fabrics you want to use in the triangle squares.

Using a ruler, mark a grid of 5" squares on the wrong side of the lighter fabric, five across and three down. Next, mark exact diagonals through all the squares (see figure 8–8) as solid lines, and sewing guidelines on either side of that line as dotted or broken lines.

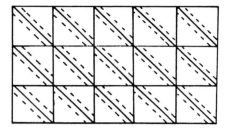

8–8. Diagram for speed piecing triangle squares (Method 1). Dashed lines are sewing guidelines, solid lines are cutting lines.

With right sides together, align all edges of the marked rectangle with the second rectangle and pin together, ready to sew. Line up the fabric on your sewing machine so that the needle is exactly on a sewing guideline, and sew following the broken lines. *Make sure that you pick up the needle and skip over each triangle point. Do not sew through them!*

Be careful to keep the fabric flat and do not pull or stretch it off-grain as you sew, or your triangles will become distorted. When you have finished the first line, lift the presser foot, rotate the material 180-degrees, and continue back in the same way along the sewing guideline on the other side.

When you have sewn along all the sewing guidelines, clip your thread and cut (with scissors or rotary cutter) along all solid lines. You will have 15 completed triangle squares.

Method 2. Cut two bias strips, ($3\frac{1}{2}$" wide for this example) from the two fabrics you want in your triangle squares. With the right sides of the fabric strips facing, seam both long sides leaving $\frac{1}{4}$" seam allowances, taking care not to stretch the bias.

Cut a $4\frac{7}{8}$" x $4\frac{7}{8}$" square template, mark its diagonal and cut along that line, making two triangle shaped

templates. Place the long edge of a template flush with the raw edges of one of the seamed edges of your strips and trace around it. Flip the triangle over so its long side is flush with the opposite raw edge and trace another triangle (see figure 8–9a). Cut out the triangles through both thicknesses, open out and press the seams.

Method 3. Cut two bias strips, ($3\frac{1}{2}$" wide for this example) from the two fabrics you want in your triangle squares. With the right sides of the fabric strips facing, and a $\frac{1}{4}$" seam allowance, seam along just one long side of the strips. Be careful of the bias edge as you sew, so that it does not stretch and ripple. Open and press the seam allowance toward the darker fabric.

Cut a $4\frac{1}{2}$" x $4\frac{1}{2}$" square template, mark its diagonal, and use the diagonal mark to align the template with the seam (figure 8–9b). Trace around it and cut out the squares.

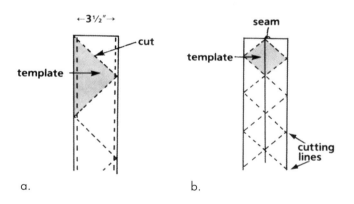

8–9. a: Cutting triangle squares (Method 2). b: Cutting triangle squares (Method 3).

SPEEDY QUARTER-SQUARE TRIANGLES

A quarter-square triangle is one-quarter of a square. When you piece four quarter-square triangles together on their bias edges, you have a four-triangle square (figure 8–10c). Using any of the three methods for triangle squares described above, you can cut the resulting triangle squares into two quarter-triangle pieces. (See figures 8–10a, 8–10b, and 8–10c.)

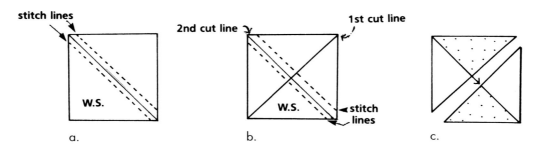

stitch lines

2nd cut line

1st cut line

W.S.

a.

W.S.

stitch
lines

b.

c.

8–10. a: A square unit cut out of a Method 1 grid for triangle squares, wrong side of fabric shown. b: Marking the first cut line for four-triangle squares, wrong side of fabric shown. c: Joining two pieced triangles to form a four-triangle square.

FOUNDATION PIECING

In foundation piecing, the fabric pieces—as well as being sewn to one another—are sewn directly onto a muslin base. Foundation piecing can be done in crazy quilt-style piecing, log cabin-style piecing, and marked foundation piecing.

Crazy quilt-style piecing uses randomly shaped scraps; either with straight edged pieces, or with curved pieces, although curved shapes are harder. You begin by placing the first scrap right side up at one edge of your muslin foundation. Place a second scrap right side down on top of the first, aligning the two edges that you want to stitch together (figure 8–11). Sew along that edge, leaving a ¼" seam allowance, then open the pieces right sides out and press. Add the third scrap, right side down

onto the right side of the previously stitched scraps, aligning one edge as before. Stitch and press. Your object is to cover the entire muslin foundation, and it's okay if your scraps extend beyond the edges of the foundation muslin. When the foundation is covered, you will trim the scraps along the edge and staystitch all around the piece for stability (see figure 8–12).

Log Cabin strip piecing is similar to the method above, but you begin with a square placed in the middle area of your foundation piece (figure 8–13). You sew a strip to one side of the square, then continue adding strips, building outward around the square, not unlike building a log cabin—hence the name. Press after each piece is added.

Marked foundation piecing differs from the first two methods of foundation piecing in that your foundation

8–11. Placing the first two pieces in a crazy quilt construction.

8–12: Trimming the edges after completing a crazy quilt unit.

8–13. A modern adaptation of Log Cabin piecing. This project is also marked with tape for quilting.

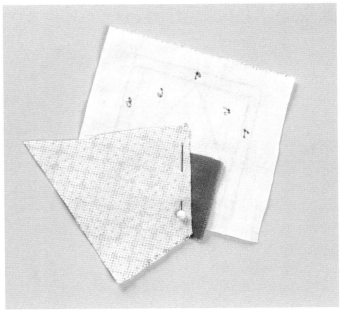

8–14. Pinning the first two pieces on a marked foundation prior to sewing.

muslin is marked with a pattern of lines along which you sew to create a specific image. The marked foundation also has numbers that tell you the order of stitching (figure 8–14). Sewing is done with the fabric pinned to the unmarked side and the marked side of the muslin facing you. You sew on the guidelines marked, on the muslin (figure 8–15). Press after sewing each seam.

In all foundation piecing, the fabrics applied to the muslin will not be secured around the outer edges. The project will be easier to work with in subsequent steps if you staystitch the edges; hand or machine baste ⅛" from the raw edge to stabilize the edges.

The individual projects that use these methods will provide specific instructions on the application of these techniques. See Chapter 3—Foundation-pieced Quilt Blocks, page 317, for more detailed instruction and patterns for foundation piecing.

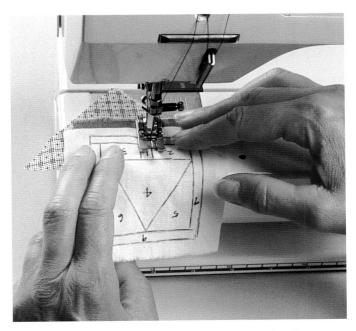

8–15. The marked foundation is on top as a guide when stitching pieces.

Assembling the Top

CHECK MEASUREMENTS

When you have all your quilt squares completed, go over them one last time. If you have been checking measurements at every stage, the blocks should be the right dimensions. If any of the block sides vary by more than ¼" you should remake that block. If it varies by ⅛" up to ¼" this is remediable, but tag the block with a safety pin for special treatment when you are sewing the rows together.

If the block is too big, trim the edges carefully if you can do so without affecting the pattern. Some patterns will suffer; if, for instance, points of triangles are cropped. In that case, you should take apart and reassemble the block, trying to adjust the measurement.

If the block is too small by no more than ¼", use a ⅛" seam allowance when joining that block to its neighbors. If it is too small by more than ¼", consider using

Use a ⅛" seam allowance when joining a slightly smaller block to a standard-size block.

a narrow sashing around that block to build up the circumference. It works best if the sashing fabric is the same as the predominant color or the background color of the quilt.

LAYOUT

Lay the blocks out on a bed, a clean or protected floor, or any flat surface large enough to accommodate the full size of the quilt. Arrange them into the pattern you want. Now is a great time to try different colors for sashing, borders, backing, and binding.

After you have decided on the quilt's layout, stack each row of blocks in the correct order, left to right, with the leftmost block on top. Pin a label with the row's number on each stack of blocks. This will help you keep your place in case your sewing is interrupted.

Sew the blocks together one row at a time, using ¼" seam allowances. If you had some blocks marked with pins because the seam allowance was too small, now is the time to make the correction to a ⅛" seam allowance for those blocks. Leave the labels on the left-hand block of each row to avoid getting the rows mixed up.

Press all seams on the top row to the left, the next row to the right, and so on, alternating all the way down. Now sew these long strips together, matching up your seams between blocks as shown in figure 8–16, pinning along the way. Press the long seams that join the rows all the same way—up or down, it doesn't matter.

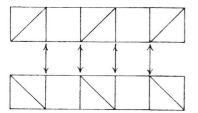

8–16. Match the seams between blocks.

If you have chosen to use sashing in your quilt, assemble the top in the same manner, always being careful to match seams with those on the other side of the sashing, eyeballing as best you can. (See figure 8–17.)

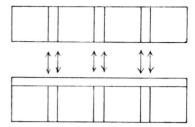

8–17. Match the seams of the sashing.

CLIPPING CURVES AND CORNERS

This terribly important step is often overlooked when making a project, and it results in curved areas that will not lie flat or corners that are rounded when you want them to be square. Clipping the curves of the seam allowances of a rounded project (figure 8–18) will give you a nice, flat curved edge, and it will also eliminate the bulk of the seam allowance in a project. This neatens its appearance and makes it easier to quilt as well. You certainly wouldn't want an oval placemat that curls towards your place setting, or one with bulky edges. Clipping the corners off the seam allowances of a rectangular project (figure 8–19) reduces the bulk at the corners, allowing the corners to lie flat and have a nicely pointed appearance. Always clip close to but not through the stitching lines.

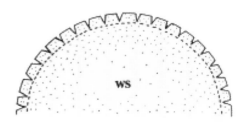

8–18. Clipping curves.

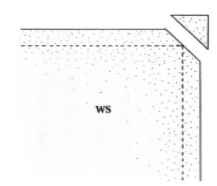

8–19. Clipping corners.

EXTRA DESIGN FEATURES

You can use special techniques to enhance or finish a project.

How to Inset

Sometimes, pieces of a design must be inset into one another. While this procedure is slightly tricky at first, it is possible to get perfect corners every time by using the following method:

1. A triangular or square piece is inset into two other pieces that are sewn together to form an angle (figure 8–20a). When sewing together the pieces that form the angle, end your stitching ¼" away from the edge (see dot in diagram 8–20a).

2. Pin the piece to be inset along one edge of the angle (figure 8–20b) and stitch from the seam to the outer edge (in the direction of the arrow).

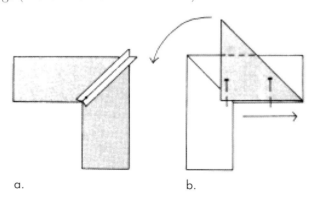

a.   b.

8–20.

3. Folding the excess fabric out of the way, pin the unsewn edges together and stitch from the central point to the outer edge (figure 8–20c).

4. Open out the fabrics and carefully steam-press (figure 8–20d). If you notice any puckers at the corner, you can usually eliminate them by removing a stitch from one of the seams just sewn.

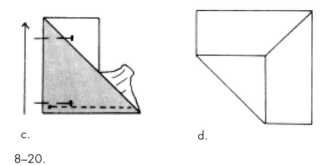

c.

d.

8–20.

Embroidery

Embroidery is a beautiful embellishment for many quilted items. It is crucial for traditional crazy quilts, which actually have only embroidery and no real quilting.

Use any standard 6-strand cotton embroidery floss (thread). Separate a piece of floss into individual strands, and use the number of strands indicated in the project instructions. This will take the twist out of the floss and allow your stitches to lie flat.

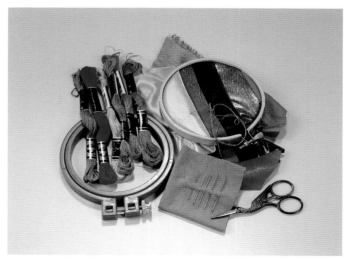

Embroidery tools and supplies.

If embroidery lines are given on a design, transfer the lines to the right side of your fabric using a hard lead pencil and graphite paper; or you can draw the design freehand on the fabric with a pencil.

Stretch the area to be embroidered in an embroidery hoop to hold the fabric taut; reposition the hoop as necessary while you are working. If the fabric sags in the hoop, pull it taut again. Embroider the design following the individual directions and stitch details (figure 8–21).

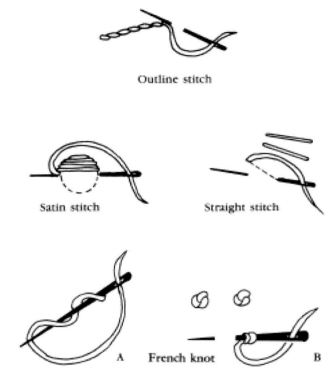

Outline stitch

Satin stitch

Straight stitch

A   French knot   B

8–21.

Each time you begin embroidering, leave extra thread dangling on the back of the fabric and embroider over it as you work to secure, holding the thread flat against the fabric with your free hand. Do not make knots. To end a strand or begin a new one, weave the floss under the stitches on the back. From time to time, allow the needle and floss to hang straight down to unwind; this will prevent the floss from kinking or twisting while you embroider.

How to Appliqué

"Appliqué" means to apply to a larger surface or, in this technique, to apply one piece of fabric over another. To appliqué a piece of fabric onto a background fabric, begin by pinning or basting the appliqué piece to the background fabric. With the blindstitch and no pre-pressing., you simply turn under the raw edges of the pieces as you appliqué. You could mark a fine pencil line to turn on, but it is generally just as easy to gauge a ⅛" to ¼" margin and turn under.

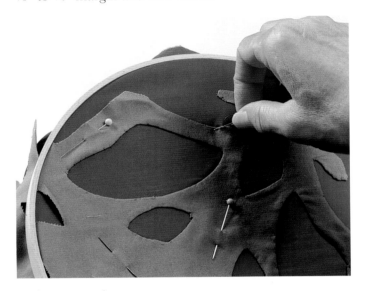

Stitching an appliqué.

Thread your needle and make a small knot in one end of the thread. Bring your needle up through the folded edge of the piece you are appliquéing so the knot is hidden in the fold. Insert your needle into the background fabric, just under the fold of the appliqué, next to where the needle came out of the piece. Pull the needle up through the background fabric and catch the edge of the fold about ⅛" away. Continue around the whole piece using a blindstitch. Hide your finishing knot on the back.

Please see Chapter 3—Appliqué Quilt Patterns, pages 131 to 155, for more detailed instructions.

Ruffle

Cut the fabric strip to the required size, piecing the strip, if necessary, for additional length. With right sides together, stitch the short ends to each other (figure 8–22a), forming a continuous circle of fabric. Fold the fabric in half lengthwise with wrong sides together and press; machine-baste ¼" away from the raw edges all around (figure 8–22b). Gently pull the basting stitches, gathering the ruffle to approximately fit the edges of the

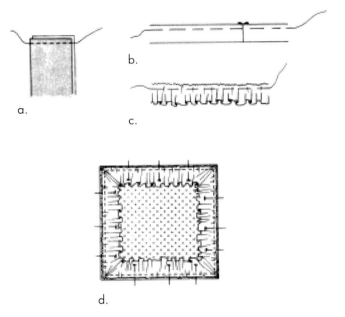

8–22.

project (figure 3–22c). With raw edges even, pin the ruffle to the right side of the project, adjusting the gathers evenly to fit; allow extra gathers to make a pleat at each of the corners (figure 8–22d). Stitch the ruffle securely to the project.

Lace

With raw edges even, pin the lace to the right side of the project; allow extra gathers or make a pleat or two at each of the corners, as with a ruffle (figure 8–22d). Overlap the beginning and end of the lace by about ¼"; then stitch the lace securely to the project.

Piping

Cut the fabric strip to the required size, piecing the strip, if necessary, for additional length. Place the piping cord on the middle of the wrong side of the fabric; then fold the fabric in half lengthwise, enclosing the piping cord. Using a zipper foot on the sewing machine, stitch close to the cord (figure 8–23a). Trim the seam allowance to ¼".

To apply piping, lay the piping against the edge of your fabric, having the raw edges of the piping against the raw edge of the fabric and baste in place using a ¼" seam allowance.

To pipe a rectangular shape, when you get near the corner, stop stitching ¼" from the edge. Make a small clip in the seam allowance of the piping, but do not cut through to the area containing the cord itself (figure 8–23b). Continue basting the trim along the next edge, until you come around to the beginning. Overlap the beginning of the piping by 1". Remove 1" of stitching from the end of the piping, push back the excess fabric, and trim away only the cord so that the beginning and end of the cord are flush (figure 8–23c). Now straighten out the excess fabric and finger press the raw edge ½" to the wrong side (inside) by running your finger over the fold a few times. Slip the beginning of the piping inside the end so that the excess fabric covers all raw edges (figure 8–23d); pin or baste in place.

To pipe a curved edge, clip into the seam allowance of the trim in the same way as above, every ½" or so to make the trim lie flat. Be careful not to cut past the seam allowance and into the piping itself.

The piping will be permanently sewn in when you stitch on the layer (whether backing, border or binding, in the case of a quilt).

Loops & Ties

Many of the projects in this book are meant to be hung or attached to something in some way. Loops and ties can be made quickly and easily in a fabric that matches the binding.

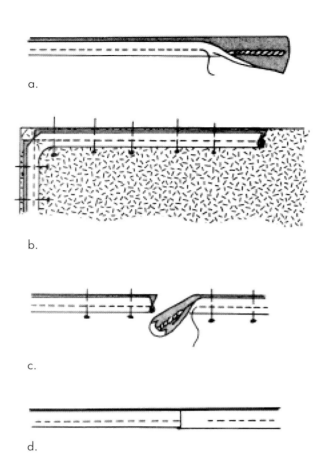

a.

b.

c.

d.

8–23.

Cut your chosen fabric to the size indicated for your project. Press the strip in half lengthwise, wrong sides together. Open the strip and press each of the long raw edges exactly to the pressed central fold, again with the wrong sides together. Fold and press each of the short ends ¼" to the wrong side; then press the strip in half again, sandwiching all raw edges inside; topstitch the folded edges together. Attach the loops or ties to the project following the individual instructions.

Using A Tube Turner

A tube turner can be used to turn a loop, tie or strap inside out. There are two types of tube turners. The standard American style has a hook with a catch at the end as illustrated in figures 8–24a and 8–24b; the British version has an eye at the end.

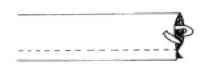

a.

b.

8–24.

Stitch a strip of fabric together lengthwise with wrong sides facing, forming a tube. Insert the tube turner into the tube, gathering the strip onto the tube turner as necessary. Hook the end of the tube turner through the edge of the fabric, and work the catch so it holds the fabric securely in the hook (figure 8–24a); or sew the eye of the tube turner to the edge of the fabric using the thread ends of the seam allowances. Ease the fabric back over the tube turner, working it along section by section. Pull until the strip turns right-side out (figure 8–24b).

BORDERS

A Note On Borders: After you have sewn the patchwork top together, if your quilt design incorporates borders, it is time to add them. Solid, non-pieced borders are an easy way to add size to your quilt and provide a nice background for fancy quilting.

Before you cut borders, measure your quilt. Suppose you planned it to be 72" x 94", but you measure the four sides, and find that each opposing side is slightly different. Do not cut your borders to these different lengths. Find the average of each pair. For example, if one side is 73" and the opposite is 71", cut your two borders to 72". The quilts in this book call for ¼" seam allowances, but unless you are an absolutely perfect stitcher, your work will no doubt vary. Normally, seam allowances tend to be a bit more than ¼".

Note: Get a patchwork or piecing foot. They are available for just about all machines and have a perfect ¼" side on the foot, for accurate piecing. They rarely are included in the machine's supplies, so check with your local sewing machine dealer to purchase one for your model. If you do not have one, mark a guide for the ¼" seam allowance on the machine bed by placing a piece of masking tape so its edge is exactly ¼" from the needle.

Here is a hint for equalizing the borders. For the sides, measure down the center of the quilt and cut the border strips to this measurement. Forget the sides of the quilt, as they are each a different length and you need a common measurement. To apply the borders and square-up the quilt, stitch the borders so that the longer length of fabric is against the feed dogs—be it the border strip or the quilt. For example, if the left side of the quilt top is a bit longer than the strip, place the quilt top right side up against the feed dogs and the border strip on top, wrong-side up. The action of the feed dogs will help ease the extra fabric on the quilt top to fit the border strip. If the border strip is longer than the side of the quilt top, place the border strip face up against the feed dogs and the quilt on top, wrong-side up. Repeat the same steps, if necessary, for the upper and lower borders.

Press and Check the Top
After the top is sewn together, press it carefully and completely. This will be your last chance to do so. Take this time to look for forgotten pins. Check all your seams for any gaps, and repair them. Find the center of each of the four sides of your quilt, and mark each center with a safety pin at the edge of the quilt. This will help you align the top with the backing when it is time to put your three layers together.

Marking the Quilting Pattern

A quilting pattern is the design you will follow with quilting stitches on your project. It is not a piece of paper on which a pattern is printed. The word motif is sometimes used to describe a quilting pattern, as well.

8–25. A quilting pattern or motif.

There are varying opinions about marking the quilt with the quilting pattern at this stage. Some projects need to be marked before sandwiching and basting, some after. The tool that you choose will be a factor—for example, a disappearing pen will disappear, so if you use that type of marker, you can't mark too far in advance of the actual quilting. If you will be doing only outline or in-the-ditch quilting, you will not need to mark the quilt. Similarly, if you are using only straight lines in your quilting, these can be marked as you go with masking tape.

If you will be using a stencil to execute smaller designs block by block, you may want to wait to mark the quilt when it is on the frame. Since some quilting markers tend to wear off as the quilt is handled, the markings often need to be redone while quilting. For this reason, some quilters always wait until it is on the frame to mark the quilt.

It's certainly easier to mark your design before it goes on the frame. It provides the advantage of marking a single layer of fabric on a hard surface. If you have chosen an allover quilting pattern that you cannot mark with masking tape then you will need to mark the quilt now.

If your plan is to mark all the designs before basting, it is a great help to have the use of a lightbox, light table, or other light source. Use only marking pencils that you have tested, that you are sure can be removed easily or will brush away as you quilt. Nothing mars the look of a finished quilt like visible guidelines remaining on the quilt.

MARKING TOOLS

Most quilting and fabric stores carry a wide range of marking pens or pencils for quilters. When choosing a marker; bear in mind the color of the fabric you will be marking.

- Blue, water-soluble, felt-tip markers provide good clear lines that don't rub off and they vanish when dabbed with cold water. Since some authorities warn that the ink may deteriorate the fabric over a long period of time, it may be best to leave the ink on your quilt as short a time as possible. Some have found that the ink is difficult to remove entirely.

- Purple vanishing markers contain ink that vanishes within 24 hours, sometimes much sooner. This is not suitable for marking your quilt ahead of time. Like all felt markers, it dries up sooner than you think it should, and there is still some doubt among many quilters as to its long-term safety for the fabric.

- Quilt-marking pencils can be used to mark the quilt on or off the frame. They tend to wear off with handling. Most, but not all, are easy to remove completely when quilting is done. They are vexing to sharpen, since they have a tendency to crumble. Unlike felt-tip markers, they do not dry up.

- Hard-lead pencils (#3 or #4) make a thin clear line that can be mostly hidden with close quilting stitches. Their lines are hard to see and follow on dark or busy fabrics. They can be used to mark the top before it is layered with the batting and backing—however, *do not* use a #2 graphite pencil!
- For dark fabrics, choose a pencil with white, silver, or yellow lead or a washable marker. There is a silver marking pencil specially designed for marking fabric, which is widely available and is easy to wash out.
- Masking Tape is great to use for straight guidelines. Apply masking tape to the quilt only after the quilt is on the frame, and *never* leave masking tape on the quilt overnight, since the tape can leave a sticky residue that is hard to remove. Mark a small section, quilt, and then move the tape for each successive section. Buy *new* masking tape to use for quilting—the old roll lurking in the toolbox or kitchen drawer is far more likely to leave dreaded residue.
- White tailor's chalk pencil would work for small sections at a time once the quilt in on the frame or in a hoop. The lines tend to rub off.
- Several marking tools that use powdered chalk also are available. One has a tiny wheel that distributes chalk as it is rolled, which is very handy for marking large areas for "filler" (background) quilting. Other marking devices that use powdered chalk are a bit more difficult to use, but are worth a try.
- You might try a yellow pencil made for marking blueprints, available at art supply stores.
- If all else fails, try a narrow sliver of mild soap, just like great-grandmother did—and the Amish still do.

Always use water-soluble pens or pencils for marking fabrics. There are quilters who even use fine ballpoint pens to mark their quilts. Whatever you select, be sure to test it on a swatch of fabric before marking your quilt top. Mark a few lines on a scrap of the fabrics you are using in the quilt, and wash the scrap as you would the finished quilt. If the markings do not come out after one washing, try a different marking tool.

PLAN THE PATTERN FIRST

Many of the quilting patterns in this book (see Chapter 10—Quilting Patterns, page 511) have units that can be put together to make interesting border and block arrangements. This gives you as many options as possible.

Some of the border designs also have a corner unit that fits into the corners of your project, allowing you to quilt corners smoothly, without interrupting the flow of the design (figure 8–26). Some of the motifs have open areas in the center. You can use one of these areas for signing and dating your quilt, or for personalizing it with the name of the recipient.

8–26. A border design with a corner unit.

It is important to measure and plot your pattern before you mark it on the quilt top. When marking a pattern on the quilt, it's easiest to start with the large areas. On the borders, for the sake of balance, start at the corners and work your way to the center of each side. Because every quilt varies, not all the border patterns given will space themselves perfectly along your borders. If you find that the border patterns will not meet perfectly at the center of a side, you can stretch or condense the final motif to fit, or plan a complementary pattern unit from the same pattern group. You may also use this spot for your initials or for personalizing the quilt in some other way.

The designs in Quilting Pattern Suites on page 531 are given in different sizes. This gives you flexibility, as you may have a quilt with plain squares that are 14" across, as well as pieced or appliquéd squares with smaller open areas that require some special quilting. Your quilt may have an inner border or block sashing

8–27. Tracing a pattern directly from a book.

that is 2" or 3" wide, and a large outer border that may be up to 12" wide. Choose an appropriate-size design to go in each area of the quilt you want to quilt, depending on the size of each area. The kind of batting you plan to use will also affect how far apart you can put the quilting lines.

TRANSFERRING THE QUILT PATTERN

Following are five methods of transferring a design to your quilt top. Please note that the first four need to be done before the layers of the quilt have been basted together. The fifth method should be done after the layers are basted. The complexity of the quilting in your design will partly determine how long your project will take to complete.

Method 1. If you need to transfer a quilting design onto a light-colored fabric, simply lay the quilt top face up over the pattern (either in the book or a photocopy) and trace the design directly onto the right side of the cloth (figure 8–27). This is perhaps the easiest method.

Method 2. Make a quilting stencil from template-weight plastic or lightweight cardboard. If your plastic is transparent or translucent, trace the quilting design directly onto it with a permanent pen. Cut quilting channels along the marked lines with a sharp knife or an electric stencil cutter. Leave "bridges" every inch or so, connecting the parts of the stencil to keep the template together (figure 8–28).

While many quilting patterns have been included in this book, you may find that it is simpler to purchase a

stencil in a similar design and mark from that. Manufactured stencils come in many styles. Visit your quilting supplier to see what is available. Before you go, however, be sure to measure the piece you will be quilting, so that you buy the right size stencil.

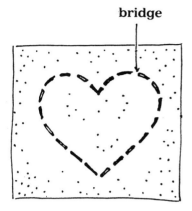

8–28. A heart stencil cut in plastic. "Bridges" hold the stencil together.

Method 3. Use a tracing wheel and dressmaker's carbon paper to transfer the designs. First, trace the pattern onto ordinary tracing paper. Align the design on the quilt front where you want it, and place the dressmaker's carbon under the paper with the colored side against the right side of quilt top. Using the tracing wheel, mark along the lines on the tracing paper to transfer the design.

Method 4. You can freehand the design onto the fabric, using one of the many motifs for inspiration. Place the fabric on a hard surface and draw the lines directly onto the quilt top. In general, designs with curved lines take longer to quilt than those with straight lines.

Method 5. Buy a few yards of a very lightweight stabilizer. Trace the quilting designs onto pieces of the stabilizer and pin or baste these to the already assembled quilt (all the layers are already basted together). Hand or machine-quilt directly through the stabilizer, and tear it away when you have finished quilting.

Making the Quilt "Sandwich"

PREPARE THE BACKING

If you have not already prepared the backing fabric—washed it, removed its selvages, and ironed it as directed on pages 412 to 415, do so now. Next, measure your finished quilt top. You need enough backing to extend 3" to 5" on each side of the top to accommodate the drawing up of the backing that happens when the layers are quilted together. If you are planning to have a self-bound edge, where you roll the backing edge forward and stitch it all around the quilt, make sure you allow enough extra to do this when the quilting is completed.

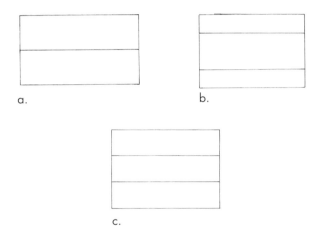

a. b.

c.

8–29. Three ways of piecing the backing.

Unless you are making a small quilt (less than 34" wide), or are using the extra-wide fabric made especially for quilt backing, you will have to piece your backing. The three most usual ways of doing this are:

1. Two equal lengths of fabric joined by a vertical center seam (figure 8–29a).

2. Three equal lengths of fabric consisting of one central panel, with strips of equal width on either side (figure 8–29b). To do this, make two equal lengths of fabric of the length you want your backing. Cut one of them vertically down the middle, then sew the resulting two strips to either side of the center panel. Though the center-panel method may seem like more trouble, it provides a better-looking reverse side to the quilt. Also, if this applies to you, quilt-show judges are said to prefer the center-panel method.

3. If your quilt is as wide as 120", you will need to sew together three panels of 45" to achieve this width (figure 8–29c).

Once you have sewn your backing together, press the seam(s) open, which will make for a little less bulk when quilting. Then press the entire piece. Find the centers of each side, and mark the edge there with a safety pin. This will help with alignment in the next step.

BATTING AND FILLERS

This is the material that goes between the top and the backing. In the past, every imaginable material has been used for this purpose, from corn husks to straw to raw cotton. Old blankets and worn quilts were often recycled as fillers for new quilts. Such quilts were usually tied rather than quilted.

Quilt batting is normally sold by the precut piece in a bag, or by the yard from a bolt. *Important:* When purchasing batting, always read the package carefully. Notice that the manufacturer gives recommendations on spaces between lines of quilting. If you plan to do a minimal amount of quilting, choose a batting with a wider spacing ratio. If not, your batting will shift when you wash the finished item and it could become a lumpy mess. Also, do not choose a high loft or "fat" batting for hand or machine quilting. They are meant for tied quilts and are very difficult to quilt through.

• **Cotton batting.** Until recent years, this was the only batting available. If you are trying to emulate the look of an antique quilt, this is the filler to use. It gives a flat appearance to the finished quilting. Cotton batting must be closely quilted. There should be no more than an inch between lines of quilting or it will bunch up and shift when washed.

- **Silk or wool batting.** Quilters who prefer pure, natural fibers may also want consider using these. Like cotton, they must be quilted at no more than $1\frac{1}{2}$" intervals to prevent lumps from forming when the project is washed. It may be best to dry-clean projects made with wool batting, however.

- **80 percent cotton/20 percent polyester batting.** This is a low loft blend well-liked for its ease of use. It is very easy to quilt and can be used without a backing. It comes pre-packaged in several sizes.

- **Fleece.** A very dense form of polyester batting, sold by the yard. Should be used for placemats and runners, as it gives the finished piece a bit more stiffness than regular batting would.

- **Bonded polyester batting.** Made of a polyester material that has been treated with a glaze to hold the fibers together, it is easy to work with since the layers of the batting will not shred or tear, giving a smooth, uniform surface. The finished quilt has a puffy look, and the quilting stitches stand out in sharp relief to the background. Since it will not shift, it can be quilted in lines up to 4" apart.

- **Unbonded batting.** This is also made of synthetic materials, but has not been treated with the glazing chemicals. It gives an even puffier look to the finished quilt than the bonded batting. Care must be taken in spreading the batting because it will shred or tear, causing thick and thin spots. This is easily fixed by pulling fibers from the thick spots or from the edges to fill in the thin spots. Once quilted, the batting will not shift, so that quilting can be done in lines up to 4" apart.

For small projects, it is best to use a thin batting to keep the puffiness in scale with the size of the finished design. A thicker batting can be used for larger projects, such as blankets and wall hangings or for designs that are quilted and then stuffed, such as pillows.

PREPARE THE BATTING

Read the manufacturer's instructions that come with the batting you have purchased. Some batting must be pre-washed. Follow the directions *exactly*. (They *mean it* when they say "don't agitate," as many quilters have found to their sorrow.)

If your batting doesn't need prewashing, take it out of the package and spread it flat on a bed. Smooth out the wrinkles and leave it for a few hours. This will relax the creases caused by the packaging so it will be easier to work with.

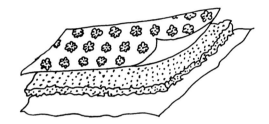

8–30. The layers of a quilt.

LAYERING

Spread the backing flat on the floor or on a protected table large enough to accommodate your entire quilt's size. Seams, if there are any in the backing, should be face up. When it is smoothed flat but not stretched, anchor the backing with pins or tape.

On a carpeted floor, you can place T-pins all around the edge of the backing. If you are working on a table-top, protect it with dressmaker's cutting boards—they are made of cardboard and will allow you to put pins in to anchor the work, or you may tape the backing to the work surface. Make sure the grain is straight and that all corners make 90-degree angles.

Next, gently spread the prepared batting, centering it on the quilt back. If you must piece the batting, butt the edges and baste them together with large cross-stitches.

Press the pieced top carefully—this will be the last time it will be ironed, so be thorough. Carefully trim away any uneven seams on the back, and any threads or raveled edges. Finally lay your quilt top down face-up and centered on the batting and backing. Align the safety pins you placed to mark the center of each edge. Check the grain in both directions, and be sure that all corners make right angles.

Cut the batting to the size given in the project instructions before basting. Batting dimensions given in the projects are usually several inches larger than the top. Anchor all three layers to avoid their slipping while you baste.

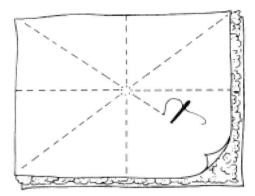

8-31. Basting the "sandwich."

BASTING

Beginning at the center of the quilt top, baste by hand through all three layers. Use a basting thread that contrasts in color to your quilt top and a long, fine needle (called a "sharp"). Take stitches that are very large, $\frac{1}{2}$" to 2" long which makes it easier to find and remove the basting stitches when you're finished.

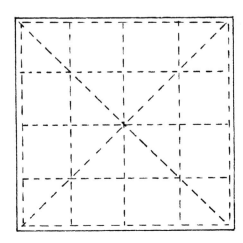

8-32. A standard basting pattern.

Run a line of basting stitches from the center to the top edge, smooth any wrinkles toward the edge as you baste. Occasionally check the back of the quilt to make sure there are no wrinkles. If there are, take out your stiches and baste again. Next, baste to the bottom edge, then to each side and corner. Each line of basting begins in the center of the quilt (figure 8–31).

In each quadrant, crisscross the space with horizontal and vertical lines of basting. For these lines of basting, begin at the center axis lines and space your basting lines not more than 9" or 10" apart.

Finally, run basting all around the outer edges of the quilt, holding all three layers together to prevent slipping and puckering (figure 8–32). These last basting stitches will remain in place even after you have completed the quilting and removed all the rest of the basting stitches. They help insure that the edges of the quilt are secure for the binding.

Basting with Safety Pins

For small quilts—baby quilts, and wall hangings—some quilters use medium-sized safety pins instead of basting stitches. Pin every 3" or 4" and try to avoid pinning near where you're going to have to stitch later on.

Safety pins are quicker to use and are easier to redo if you find a wrinkle. This is only recommended if you are sure to finish your quilting in a short time. Do not use them for larger quilts, for fear of damaging the quilt top. Pins will leave marks if left in over time, and basting will not.

Fold-Finishing

This is a type of type of "binding" that should be done before the project has been quilted. Trim the raw edges of the back even with the top; then fold the raw edges of both the top and back $\frac{1}{4}$" towards each other to conceal the raw edges inside the project. Slipstitch together invisibly and securely. To quilt, baste strips of muslin to the finished edge of the project so that it can be placed in a frame or hoop.

Quilting

HOOPS & FRAMES

With the top complete, the back and batting ready, and the three layers basted together, finally, it is time to quilt—as the Amish say: "It's not a quilt 'till it's quilted."

When working with a small piece of quilting, appliqué, or embroidery too small to use a hoop, you can sit at a table to support your work. Or, for maximum comfort, stretch out on the sofa with a firm pillow in your lap and spread out the piece on the pillow—just be sure not to sew your project to the pillow!

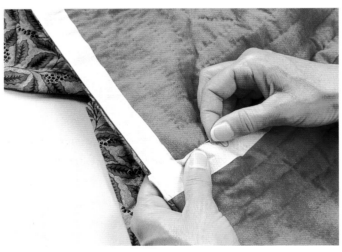

Completing a garment with echo quilting.

Larger projects work best when you place the piece in a quilting hoop or on a frame. If you are using a hoop, baste strips of fabric, 6" to 12" wide, to the edges of the project so that it can be held in the hoop when you are quilting the outer edges. It is also a good idea to add some additional basting (concentric squares) for extra safety, and never leave the hoop on your work when you are not actually quilting, as it could stretch or warp the fabric.

For instructions on building and using a quilting frame, see Chapter 4—Community Quilting, page 177.

Start from the center of the quilt and work outwards.

MARKING THE QUILT ON THE FRAME

Masking tape is great for marking straight lines on projects. Apply masking tape to the quilt only after the quilt is on the frame, to one area at a time. Do not mark the entire project at once in this way. It is best to mark a small section, quilt, and then move the tape for each successive section.

Masking tape can leave a sticky residue that is hard to remove, so never leave it on the quilt overnight. Buy new masking tape to use for quilting. An old roll is far more likely to leave residue than a nice fresh roll.

Many quilters and most Amish mark the designs in the quilting frame as the quilting progresses. This may be your choice also. If so, you need a template or stencil of the design. This is placed on top of the quilt and traced. You may develop your own quilting designs, using the suggestions and instructions in the section on designing motifs in Chapter 10—Quilting Patterns, page 511, or you may select from hundreds of commercially produced quilting stencils. We encourage you to try your hand at creating your own designs. They will better fit the spaces you have and will add your unique personal touch to the quilting.

This piece was marked with masking tape for the straight lines of quilting, and with a marking pen and stencil for the cable-patterned quilting.

HAND QUILTING

Good quilting is 90 percent practice, but the most important elements of successful quilting are:

- An even running stitch that passes through all three layers each time
- Starting knots that are buried in the batting layer
- Ending threads that are contained in the batting layer

Quilters are constantly experimenting to improve their stitch. You will find many different methods of reaching this goal.

EQUIPMENT

A thimble or some other protection for the pushing finger of your sewing hand is essential, and will be important to success. Quilting needles have a sharp eye that will quickly tenderize an unprotected finger.

Your opposite hand index or middle finger—the under-the-quilt finger—will serve as a fulcrum for the needle, and it will get pricked, poked, and sore. Eventually it will develop a good quilter's callous, but do not hesitate to try what some other quilters use to protect that finger: another thimble, a small piece of adhesive tape, or the cut off finger of an old kid glove might work for you, too.

Carefully consider what thread you will be using. Hand-quilting thread is a bit heavier than machine sewing thread, and is less likely to tangle. There are several brands of hand-quilting thread on the market, most of which are 100 percent cotton. If you plan on using just one color of thread for the entire quilt, choose a neutral color that harmonizes well with all the fabrics in the quilt. Or, if you prefer a bolder look, use a contrasting thread. There is no "right" or "wrong" color; it's all a matter of personal preference.

When sewing multi-colored projects where one of your fabrics is very light in color, a darker thread will stand out in the lighter sections on the finished piece, so light gray thread is a good choice—if only dark colors are being used in a multi-colored project, dark gray thread works well.

You'll need hand-quilting needles, called "betweens," that range from size 7 to 10. A rule to remember with needles: the higher the number, the smaller the needle, so choose accordingly. An 8 needle is a good size for most quilters.

8–33. Making the quilter's knot.

QUILTER'S KNOT

Thread your needle with a single length of quilting thread that measures slightly longer than the distance from your fingertips to your elbow (about 18"). Using a longer thread will slow you down, as it will knot and tangle, or fray from going in and out of the fabric too many times.

Hold the needle in your "active" hand (right hand if you are right-handed—otherwise, your left hand) and the long end of the thread in your opposite hand. Put the end of the thread against the needle and grasp it there with the "active" fingers. With the opposite hand, wrap the thread around the needle near the point three or four times (figure 8–33). Holding this wrapped thread against the needle with your "active" fingers, take the point of the needle in the opposite fingers and pull it all the way through the wrapped thread. You should have a tiny, tidy knot left at the end. Trim any tail.

Two Ways of Hiding the Knot

One way to hide your knot is to push the needle into the top of the quilt approximately ¼" from where you want to start quilting. Go into the batting, but not through the backing. Bring the needle back up to where the line of quilting is to begin. Pull gently until the knot rests on the surface of the quilt. Take one or more sharp tugs to pop the knot through the top and hide it in the batting (figure 8–34a). The closely worked quilting stitches will anchor that knot. If your knot pops all the way through, it's too small; if you can't get it into the batting, it's too large.

A second method is to put your needle, thread knotted on the end, into the quilt from below, pushing up at the spot where you want to begin quilting. As the needle comes out of the top of the quilt, take the needle in your sewing hand and pull the thread upward. Pinch the backing fabric directly under your needle, gently pulling the fabric down while pulling the needle and thread up. When your thread is mostly through the quilt, grasp it with your sewing hand near the quilt top and tug, pulling the knot up into the batting. It should make a satisfying popping noise. Again, too large or too small a knot won't work. Look or feel carefully on the quilt's underside to be sure the knot has indeed gone through the backing and does not show on the back.

THE QUILTING STITCH

After you have set your knot, begin by inserting the needle straight down. The quilting stitch is a simple running stitch—a straightforward stitch in and out through all three layers of the work. Hold the index finger of your left hand (for right-handed quilters) or right hand (for left-handed quilters) beneath the project just below the spot where you wish to make your stitches. Use this finger to feel whether the needle has penetrated all the layers and to turn it back upwards.

Try to achieve a smooth rhythm, rocking your needle to the back, and then returning it again to the surface one or two stitches at a time. Never pull the needle to the back of the quilt. When you are satisfied with the size and consistency of your stitches, try working three at a time, then four.

Counting on top, consider five or six stitches per inch a satisfactory beginning. Aim for consistency in the size of the stitches and the spaces between them. The more you quilt and strive for even stitches, the smaller your stitches will become—perhaps even as small as ten

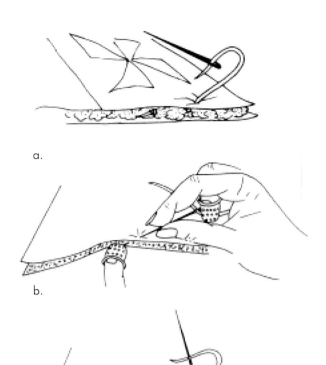

8–34. a: A knot pulled beneath the surface of the quilt top. b: Using thimbles to protect your fingers. c: A row of even quilting stitches.

or eleven stitches per inch, counting on top. But in the beginning, concentrate on making the stitches the same length on the top and on the back.

Figure 8–34b shows how to use the thimble to help push the needle through the fabric and how the finger beneath pushes up to compress the batting, making it easier to take several stitches at a time. Figure 8–34c is a cross-section diagram showing how the quilting stitches should look when done correctly.

Ending Your Quilting

When you have only 3" or 4" of thread left on your needle, secure your thread with a tiny backstitch at the end of the stitching line. After you have taken this backstitch, run the point of the needle under the top and come up about a half-needle length away. Pull the thread tight and snip close to the top of the quilt, being careful not to nick the fabric. Rethread your needle and continue.

8–35. Alternate ending stitch.

An alternative method, more complicated to explain than it is to do, is a good method if you are making a quilt you know will be used and washed (see figure 8–35). Make the last stitch a backstitch and pull your needle out at the far end of that stitch. Tuck the needle back in the center of that stitch, under the thread and into the batting. Using your lower hand to make sure the needle does not poke through the backing, push the needle back through the batting three stitches in the direction you came from. Come up at the end of that third stitch. Push the needle back in under the thread at that stitch's center and travel through the batting approximately 1". Bring the needle to the surface. Trim your thread end so it won't show, taking care not to snip the fabric.

Background or Filler Quilting

Allover patterns or fill designs consist of repeated straight or curved lines. Filler quilting is an excellent way to fill up large areas of a quilt. It can be very decorative, and also is fun to do. Several patterns for filling are given here: Clamshell (using a saucer or cardboard circle as a template, figure 8–37; cross-hatching (figure 8–66); diamond cross-hatching (figure 8–38); and diagonal lines (figure 8–39).

Study your quilt top when choosing the best fill design for your particular project, as it should complement the patchwork pattern, the fabric, and the other quilting motifs you have already used on your quilt. Always mark your background or filler patterns last. For straight lines—mark filler patterns on your quilt top

with a clear plastic ruler or masking tape. For curved lines—use a template or freehand. Make sure to measure and space your lines of filler pattern evenly.

- **Stippling.** Another free-motion technique. It starts at the edge of a seam or appliquéd piece and meanders through the area to be quilted. Space the stippling

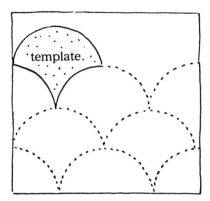

8–36. Clamshell fill.

8–37. Cross-hatching.

8–38. Diamond cross-hatching.

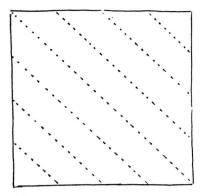

8–39. Diagonal lines.

8–41. Echo quilting.

8–40. Stipple quilting.

8–42. Echo quilting around an appliqué.

lines about ¼" to ½" apart. Try not to cross a previous line of quilting; you should not have intersecting lines. The finished results took similar to a jigsaw puzzle (figure 8–40).

- **Echo quilting.** A popular method of filler quilting. Work parallel lines of quilting to emphasize a portion of a design (figures 8–41 and 8–42). Lines can be ¼" to ½" apart, depending upon the size of the project. This is called "echo quilting" because the lines of stitching parallel or "echo" the shape of the piece you wish to accentuate.

- **Outline Quilting.** Work one row of quilting around the edge of a piece, either in the seam (called quilting "in-the-ditch") or just next to the seam as shown in the illustrations (figures 8–43, 8–44, and 8–45).

OTHER QUILTING METHODS

In addition to the traditional type of quilting just described, three other methods are often used to quilt: the tufting stitch, the quilt-as-you-go method, and machine quilting. Follow the instructions below for each method.

Tufting Stitch

The tufting stitch, or hand tying, can be used on the right or wrong side of a project, depending upon whether or not you wish the knot to show. Following along with the steps shown in figure 8–46, and using a length of quilting thread, make a backstitch through all three layers of the project (8–46a); the ends should be even (8–46b). Tie the ends in a simple knot (8–46c); tie another knot over the first (8–46d). Pull tight and trim the ends close to the knot (8–46e).

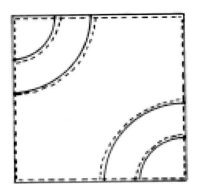

8-43. Outline quilting

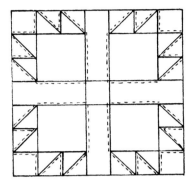

8-44. Outline quilting on a pieced block.

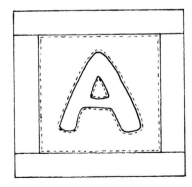

8-45. Outline quilting on an appliquéd block.

Quilt-As-You-Go Method

Use the quilt-as-you-go technique for simple patchwork designs. Piecing and quilting are done at the same time, using a sewing machine. This method considerably shortens the time needed to make a project, because when the sewing is done, the project is finished, except for binding. Follow the yardage requirements for the project you are making to cut the back and batting

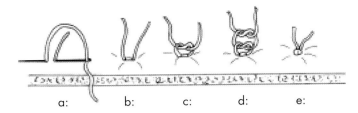

8-46. Tufting stitch. Also known as hand-tying.

pieces. The batting should be ¼" smaller than the backing at each edge.

Place the batting in the center of the wrong side of the backing piece. Baste in place—diagonally or horizontally and vertically—so that the threads will cross in the exact middle of the block. These lines will serve as guidelines for placement of the patchwork. Place the basted piece, batting side up, on a flat surface. Position the first patchwork piece, right side up, on the batting and baste in place all around the piece (figure 8–47).

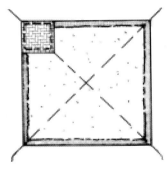

8-47.

Pin the second piece over the first with right sides together and raw edges even. Stitch together ¼" from the edge, making sure all the layers feed smoothly under the presser foot of the sewing machine (figure 8–48).

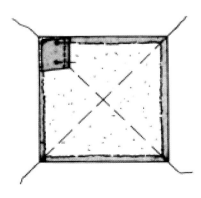

8-48.

Remove the pins and fold the second piece to the right side. Finger-press by running your finger over the seam a few times (figure 8–49). Do not be tempted to use an iron for pressing or you may be faced with melted batting!

Continue adding pieces, as directed, until the entire base is covered, finger-pressing after each new piece is added. Complete the project, following the individual instructions.

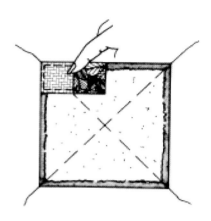

8–49.

MACHINE QUILTING

Machine Quilting Tips

To machine quilt, loosen the upper tension of the machine very slightly. Insert a size 14 needle in your machine. Use a good quality sewing machine needle, and replace it often. If your machine is skipping stitches or pulling fibers in the fabric, you definitely need a new needle. Keep a supply of sewing machine needles size 8 to 14 on hand.

Thread the top with a neutral color, all-purpose thread. Load the bobbin with thread to match the color of the backing fabric. Set the machine stitch length to between 8 and 14 stitches per inch, depending on how fine you want the stitch line to look.

For best results, use a quilting foot or walking foot if you have one. These feet push the top layers of the quilt through the machine at the same rate that the feed dogs under the throat plate push the bottom layer. When using a standard foot, the feed dogs tend to push the bottom layer of the quilt through faster than you can hand-push the top layers of the fabric. You will end up with unsightly puckers, because the bottom layer of fabric is pushed through the machine too quickly.

Also helpful are darning or embroidery feet. Darning and embroidery feet are meant for the free-motion styles of machine quilting, and for highly decorative quilting designs. Refer to the owner's manual of your sewing machine. Some machines need to have the feed dogs dropped down out of use when you use these feet; or else you may need to have the feed dogs covered by a metal plate so that they do not make contact with the fabric.

You will now have to do all maneuvering of the fabric through the machine by hand, but you will be able to make curves and swirls, instead of stitching in a straight line. Learn to use these feet, as the results are worth it. It takes some practice at first, but if you remember to stitch slowly, you will not lose control of your work. With your hands, spread the layers of your well-basted project under the machine foot to imitate the tension of a quilting frame. Always machine-quilt in the same direction across a project to prevent the layers from shifting.

Machine Quilting Techniques

When machine quilting, it is best to stitch-in-the-ditch along the main seamlines before beginning the decorative machine quilting in the spaces. This helps keep your quilt layers from shifting. To stitch-in-the-ditch, run a line of straight stitching along the seamline where two pieces of fabric meet (called the "ditch"). Machine quilt around the edges of any appliqué; echo quilt again ¼" from the seamlines and any appliqué edges.

If you have chosen batting that needs to be heavily quilted, quilt open areas with a filler stitch, such as cross-hatched lines, stipple quilting, or echo quilting. If your batting doesn't require such heavy quilting, you can space your quilting lines further apart.

Preparing the Quilt for the Machine

Roll the basted quilt in from both sides like a scroll, leaving a few feet unrolled at the center to work on, and secure the rolls with quilt clips. Fold the quilt back and forth on itself like an accordion and place the bulk of it in your lap. Start to machine quilt at the top of the center area, working down towards the part of the quilt nearest you.

When you complete the unrolled center area, unroll a bit more to the right and take up what you have just quilted on the left roll. Continue in this fashion until you have quilted the entire right roll of the "scroll." Rotate the quilt 180-degrees so that what used to be the (unquilted) left roll is now on the right. Proceed with quilting as before.

If you are quilting a diagonal pattern, roll the quilt in from the corners, instead of from end to end, and follow the above instructions.

Each time you begin and end a line of stitching, the thread ends must be finished off, which can be very time-consuming. For speedier machine quilting, adapt your designs so as to quilt in a continuous line (such as by turning, and/or doubling back) thus avoiding finishing off the threads too many times.

To finish off a line of machine quilting, leave fairly long (at least 6") thread ends when you snip the threads. Turn the project to the wrong side. Pull the under thread-end gently, drawing the top thread through to the back. Pull through gently. Knot the threads together. Insert both threads into a needle and run them though the backing and batting, bringing the needle out at least one inch away. Pull gently and clip away excess thread close to fabric so that the ends will pop back into the batting out of sight.

BINDING

The effect of this simple detail on a quilt's appearance is substantial. Try different effects by laying out alternatives before you make a final choice. You can also take the unbound quilt to the fabric store to audition different binding colors.

Self-Binding

After the quilting is done, you can bind the project. Self-binding is a quick and easy way to finish a quilted project. However, this technique is not always recommended when the back is made from the same fabric as the border, because self-binding can make the edges of the project seem to fade away, particularly if the colors of the project are very strong. Another caveat: some quilters have found that self-binding does not wear as well on a quilt that will see active use.

Finger-press the edges of the back ½" inward to the wrong side of the fabric to make a folded edge. Wrap the back towards the pieced top, covering the raw edges of the batting and top. Pin the folded edge to the top (figure 8–50). Slip-stitch the folded edge of the back invisibly to the top. Miter the corners or conceal the raw ends. Remove all pins when finished.

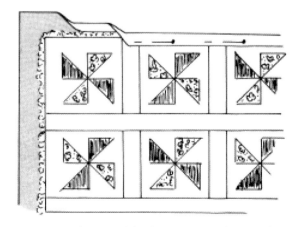

8–50. Pinning the turned backing in place for a self-binding.

Separate Straight Binding

A separate binding takes a bit more time to prepare than a self-binding, but it gives you the freedom to choose any contrasting color or pattern.

Measure and cut your chosen fabric to the length indicated for your project. For the circumference of a quilt, piecing will be necessary. Piece on a diagonal to avoid bulk at the join.

Press the strip in half lengthwise, wrong sides together. Open the strip and fold one long raw edge exactly to the pressed central fold. Press again with the wrong sides together; this folded edge will later be slip-stitched to the back of the project.

Pin the unpressed edge of the binding to the surface of the project, with right sides together and raw edges even. If you are binding a project with corners, allow extra fabric at each corner for mitering. For most other projects, about ¼" excess fabric should extend beyond each edge of the piece you are binding; this excess fabric is later folded and stitched under to conceal the raw edges.

Start stitching ¼" from the edge and stitch to the opposite corner. Wrap the pressed edge of the binding to the back over the raw edges of the project. Slip-stitch invisibly in place, folding the excess fabric under at each end to conceal the raw edges. Complete each strip of binding in turn before adding the next one.

How to Miter Corners

Fold the raw ends of adjacent border or binding strips back on themselves to form a 45-degree angle (figure 51a). Press. Pin and sew the edges together, matching the creases formed by the pressing. Check the right side to make sure that the corner is perfect, with no puckers. If there are puckers, you can usually correct them by removing one of the stitches. If the corner is perfect (figure 8–51b), trim away the excess seam allowance, leaving a ¼" seam allowance. Press carefully.

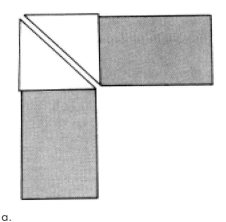

a.

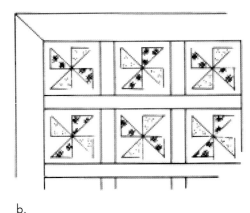

b.

8–51.

Custom Bias Binding

You can easily make your own bias binding, which is sometimes easier than trying to find a good match to your fabric. Fold a large square of cloth on the true bias, at a 45-degree angle to the straight grain. (With 45" wide fabric, you will need 1¼ yards to make a square. Bring the corners opposite each other on the diagonal to meet, as if folding a scarf into a triangle.)

The diagonal line is the true bias of the cloth. (figure 8–52a). Measuring parallel to the diagonal line, mark and cut strips of the desired width. All the strips must have 45-degree angles at the ends (figure 8–52a. Stitch the ends of the strips together (as shown in figure 8–52b) to make a long length of bias binding. Keep adding strips until you get the yardage of bias binding

you need, as indicated in the materials list of your project. Clip off the little tails of seam allowance after stitching the strips together (figure 8–52c) and press the seam allowances open.

To make the first fold of the tape, fold both sides of the strip so they meet at the center and press (figure 8–52d). Next, fold the strip down the centerline to make the center fold (figure 8–52e); this results in a double fold bias binding (figure 8–52f). The folded width will be ½" (¼ of the unfolded width).

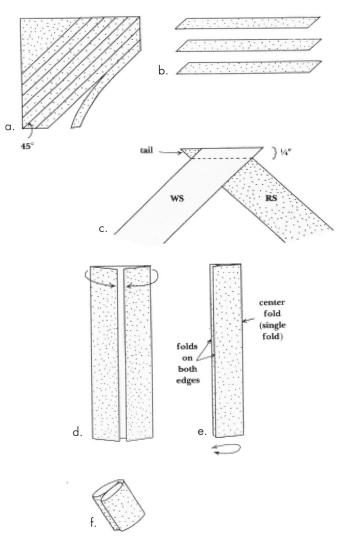

8–52. Making double-fold bias binding. a: Cutting strips at a 45-degree angle. b: The cut strips. c: Joining two strips. d: Folding the sides in to meet the center. e: Folding the strip in half so the two previous folds end up at the left. f: Cross-section of bias binding.

Packaged Bias Tape

There is no need to prewash packaged binding. Open the binding out, placing the outer fold to the top of the quilt with right sides together and raw edges aligned. You will want the narrower side to be on the top of your project. Sew along the fold line through all three layers of the quilt. This will stabilize the edge and prevent the batting from creeping away from the edge into the body of the quilt. Unless your quilt is very tiny, you will have to piece together several lengths of bias tape. You can sew these together beforehand or add them in as you work your way around the quilt's edge. You will need to allow 1" of tape for the overlap. As you come to each corner, sew the binding in a gentle curve.

Once the binding is sewn around the entire quilt, fold it over and down around the quilt's edge to the backing. When you turn the quilt over, you should be looking at the right side of the bias tape. Pin the binding to the backing at intervals, then blind stitch it to the quilt. Be sure that you only stitch through the backing and batting. Check the quilt top frequently for stitches that went all the way through. If they show, undo them. Deal with corners as neatly as possible, folding the tape and securing with tiny stitches to create the illusion of a mitered corner on the back.

Folding the tape and securing it with tiny stitches makes a neat corner.

Sew on the fold line of bias binding through all three layers.

The Clean Edge

Match all the edges of the fabric; the batting may be slightly larger. Smooth all the layers, making sure there are no lumps in the batting or wrinkle in the backing. Put the batting down first; then add the backing fabric, right side up; and lastly the top fabric, right side down, as shown in figure 8–53. Pin well around the edges. Stitch with a 1/4" seam allowance, leaving a gap at one end for turning the piece right side out. Trim the batting almost to the seam line, being careful not to cut your fabric. Trim the corners, being careful not to cut the stitches. Turn the piece right side out, and blindstitch the gap closed.

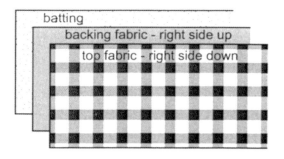

8–53: Sandwiching method for a clean edge.

Topstitching

Topstitching, done by hand or machine, is a finishing stitch. In most projects that use this technique, stitch ⅛" from an edge to create a crisp, tailored look.

Topstitching to finish a project.

TO HANG OR DISPLAY A QUILT

After your quilt is complete, follow the steps listed below if you wish to hang your quilt:

1. Determine which quilt edge will be at the top.

2. Cut a strip of fabric (usually the same fabric as your quilt back) 8" wide and of length equal to the top of your wall hanging minus one inch. (For example, if the top is 43", the strip would be 8" x 42".)

3. With right sides of fabric facing, fold the tube in half down its length and stitch the two long edges together, ¼" from the double raw edges (figure 8–54a). Turn the tube right-side out.

4. Turn in a hem of ¼" at the ends of the tube and secure them with stitching (figure 8–54b).

5. Press the tube so that one long side is plain and one long side has the seam line down the middle of it.

6. Attach the folded edge of the "tube" along the top of the quilt back, (figure 8–54c) using a hand stitch and strong thread.

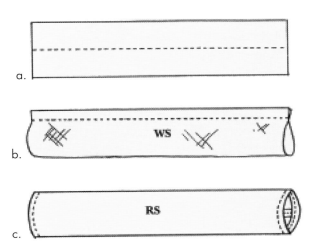

8–54. Making a tube for hanging a quilt.

7. A dowel, stick, curtain, rod, or branch can be inserted in the sleeve for hanging. Make sure it is slightly longer than the quilt top. Put the dowel or rod through the "tube" of material you attached on the quilt back. It will distribute the weight of the quilt evenly and allow your wall hanging to hang straight and flat.

8. If you wish, cut your dowel or rod 1½" longer than the quilt top and select a pair of decorative wooden knobs or heads that fit the dowel.

9. There are several ways to suspend the quilt.
  • Attach picture-frame eyelets to the dowel ends and insert fishline, picture wire, or other suitable support to the rod ends.
  • Make loops of wire or line around the dowel ends.
  • Rest the dowel on cup hooks or nails that are hammered into the wall at the level of the top edge of the quilt.
  • Suspend the rod from curtain rod holders
  • Use picture wire and S-hooks to hang the quilt from a moulding.

Attaching the Sleeve

According to several authorities, the best way to stitch a sleeve to the back of a quilt is to use large, rather loose cross-stitches. This type of stitching puts the least strain on the fabric and is, therefore, the best choice for a quilt that will hang indefinitely rather than occasionally, or for an antique quilt with fragile fabric. You now have attached the tube by both long sides, leaving the ends open.

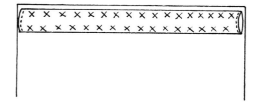

3–55. The hanging sleeve with cross-stitches.

Making a Hanging Strap

If you prefer to hang the project from a strap, cut a length of fabric 1½" wide to the length you need for the project. Fold the strip in half lengthwise with right sides facing and edges even. Stitch down the long edges and across one short edge, using a ¼" seam allowance. Turn to the right side using a tube turner (see figure 8–24 on page 427). Press carefully. Fold the raw edges at the open end ¼" inside and slip-stitch closed.

IDENTIFICATION PANEL

Your project will have greater personal and historic value if it is signed and dated. Embroider your name and the date on the front or back with embroidery floss or sign your name and date on the back with indelible ink. Make a panel large enough to hold all necessary information. Turn the edges of the panel under and hand-stitch the panel to the bottom of the back of the quilt. Again, don't let your stitches show on the top.

Use unbleached muslin or pastel cotton, prewashed and ironed, to make your panel. Write with indelible ink, using a fine-point pen intended for marking fabric, first testing the pen on the fabric to make sure it doesn't bleed. Information to include may be the name of the quilt, recipient(s), date of presentation, occasion for the quilt (wedding, birth, etc.), where it was made, name(s) of designer/organizer, and names of all participants.

CHAPTER 9
Quilt Templates

With material by Karol Kavaya, Maggie Malone, Vicki Skemp

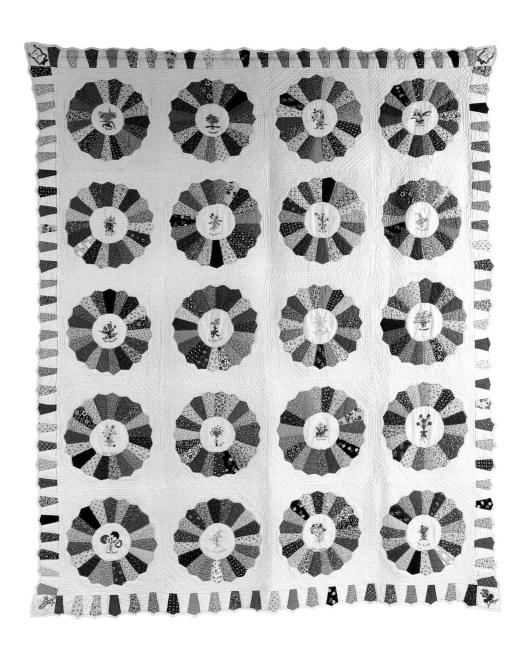

Rose and Tulip (pattern on page 452)

Pineapple (pattern on page 454)

Indiana Rose (pattern on page 455)

Laurel Leaves (pattern on page 456)

Clover (pattern on page 456)

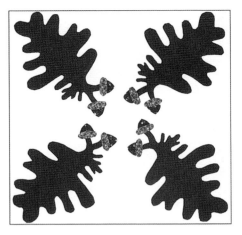

Oak Leaf and Acorns (pattern on page 457)

Cherry Tree (pattern on page 458)

Whirling Tulips (pattern on page 460)

Tulip Square (pattern on page 461)

Crossed Tulips (pattern on page 462)

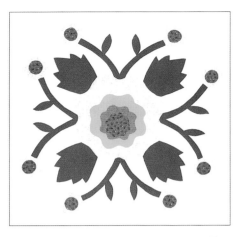

Harrison Rose (pattern on page 463)

Christmas Cactus (pattern on page 464)

Dresden Plate I (pattern on page 465)

Dresden Plate II (pattern on page 465)

Fancy Dresden Plate (pattern on page 465)

Sunbonnet Sue #1 (pattern on page 466)

Sunbonnet Sue #2 (pattern on page 467)

Overall Bill #1 (pattern on page 468)

Overall Bill #2 (pattern on page 469)

Appliqué Quilt Templates

Rose and Tulip
18" block

Cut one each of rose components.

Rose and Tulip, continued

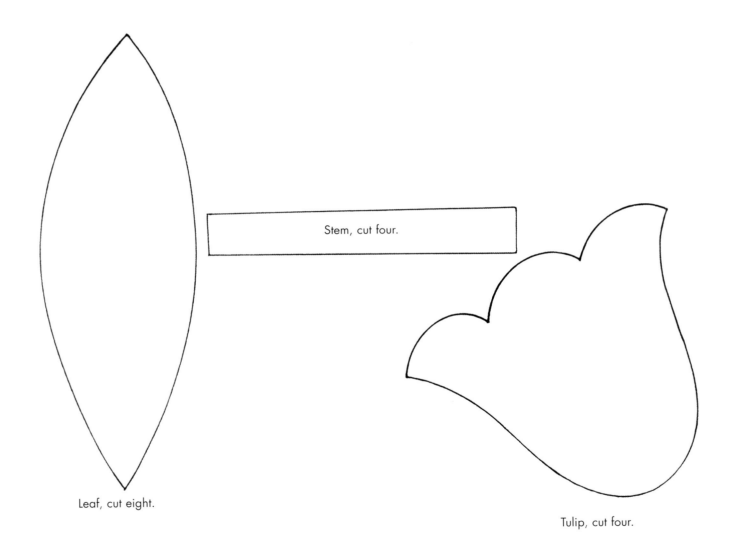

Leaf, cut eight.

Stem, cut four.

Tulip, cut four.

Pineapple
16" block

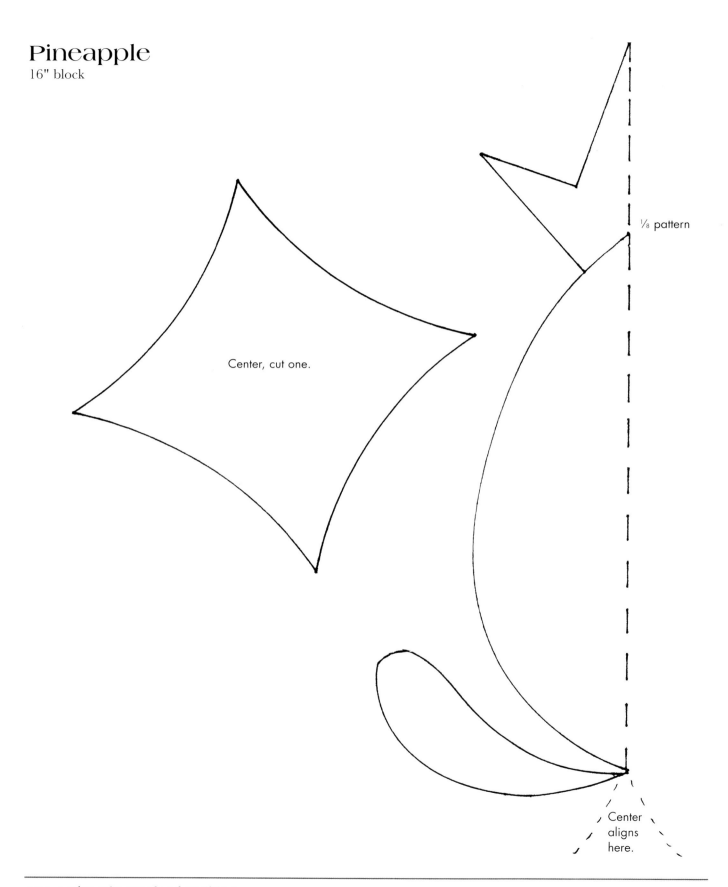

Center, cut one.

⅛ pattern

Center
aligns
here.

Indiana Rose

12" block

⅛ pattern

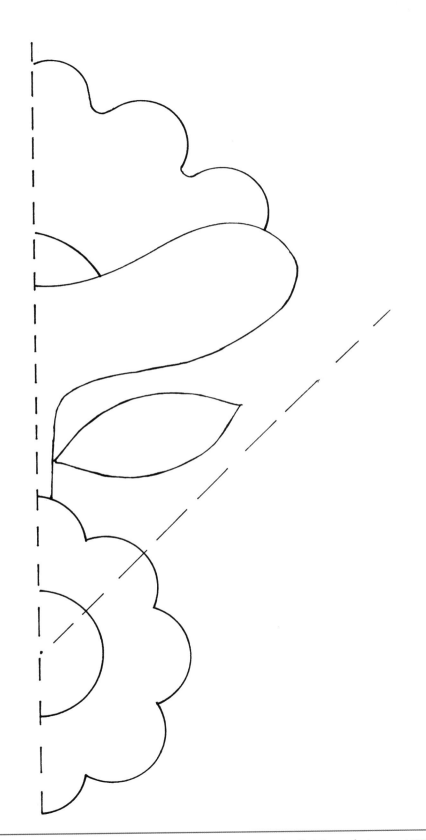

Laurel Leaves

18" block

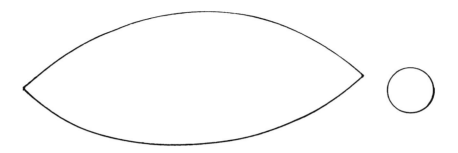

Cut two 1" x 13" strips for stems, final size of each, ½" x 12½".

Clover

12" block

Cut two 1" x 2¾" bias stems for side flowers; final size of each stem ½" x 2¼". Cut one 1" x 11½" center stem, final size ½" x 11".

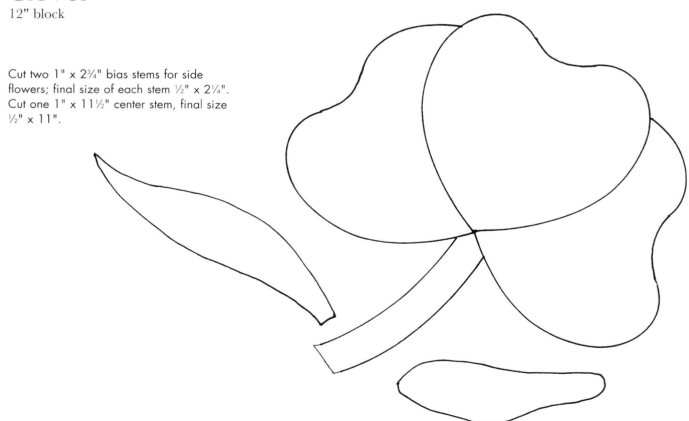

Oak Leaf and Acorns

18" block

Cut four.

Cherry Tree

15" block

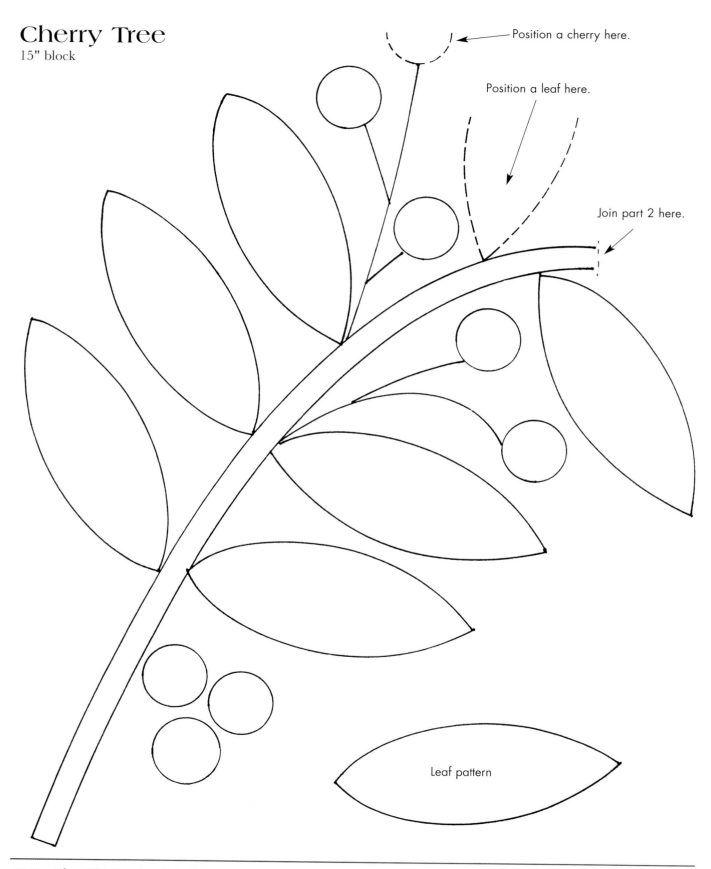

Position a cherry here.

Position a leaf here.

Join part 2 here.

Leaf pattern

Cherry Tree, continued

Join to part 1 here.

Cut enough pieces to make two branches. Position as shown on page 449.

Embroider stems for cherries.

Whirling Tulips

14" block

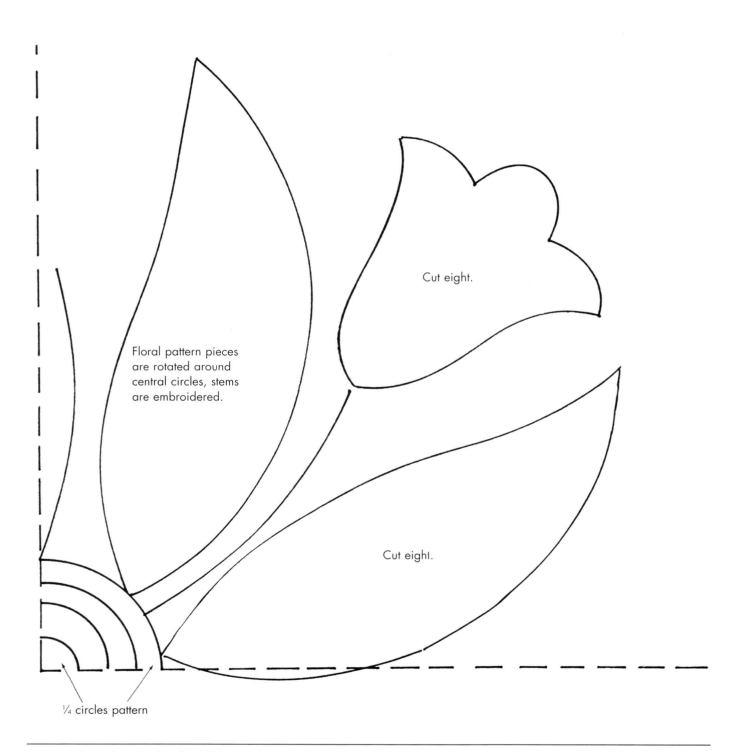

Floral pattern pieces
are rotated around
central circles, stems
are embroidered.

Cut eight.

Cut eight.

¼ circles pattern

Tulip Square
16" block
¼ pattern

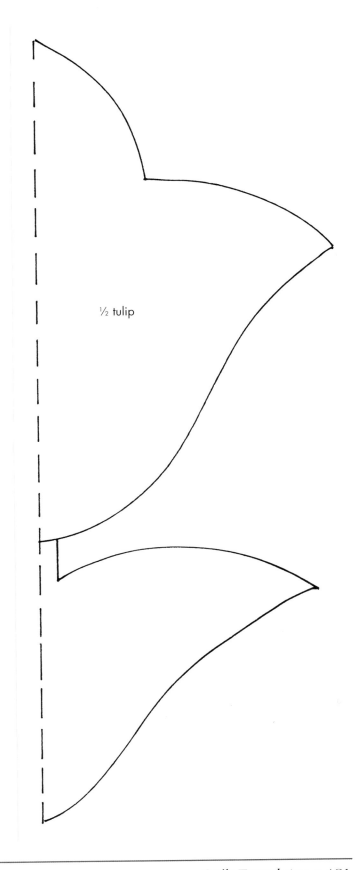

½ tulip

Crossed Tulips

15" block

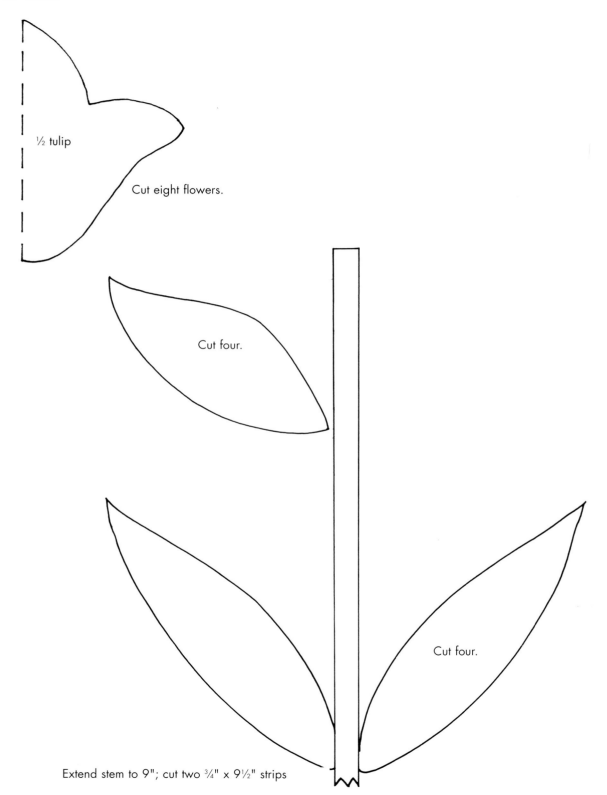

½ tulip

Cut eight flowers.

Cut four.

Cut four.

Extend stem to 9"; cut two ¾" x 9½" strips

Harrison Rose

18" block

¼ pattern

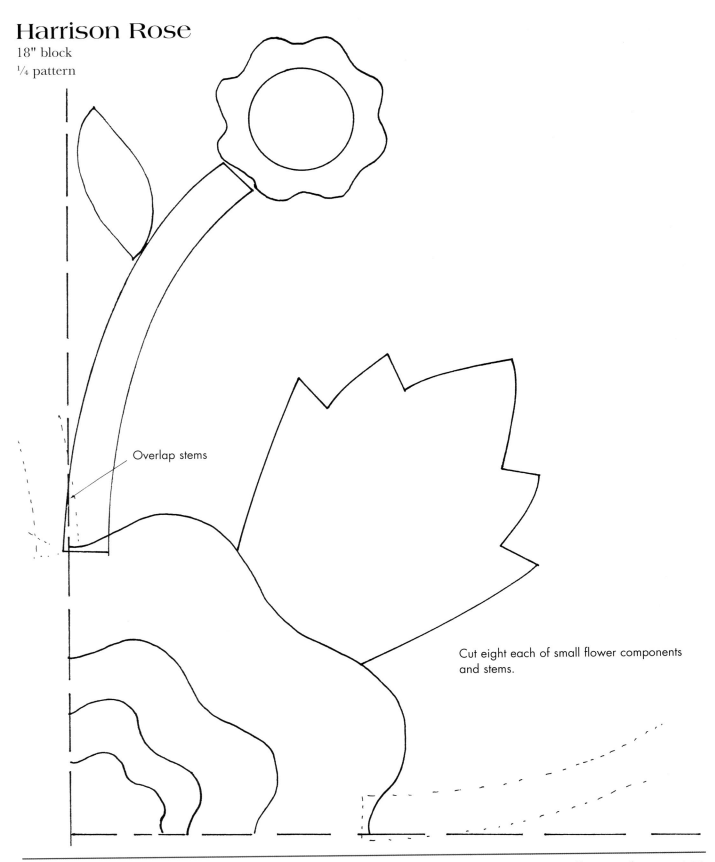

Overlap stems

Cut eight each of small flower components and stems.

Christmas Cactus

13" block pattern

$\frac{1}{8}$ pattern

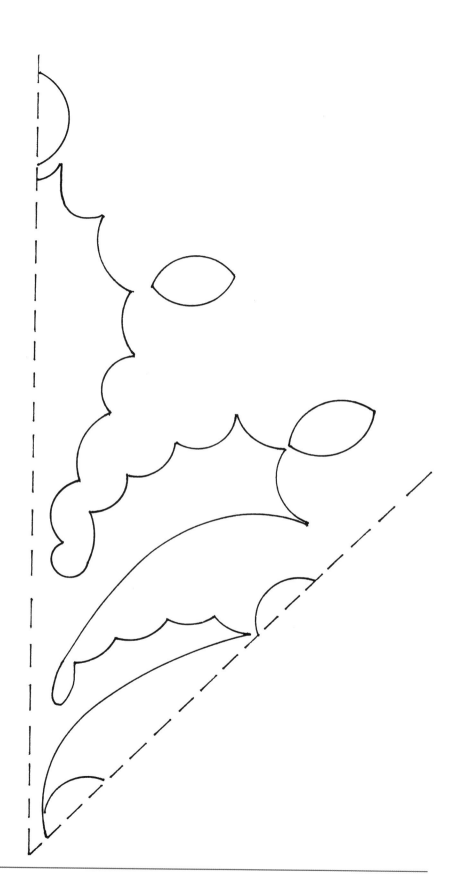

Dresden Plate

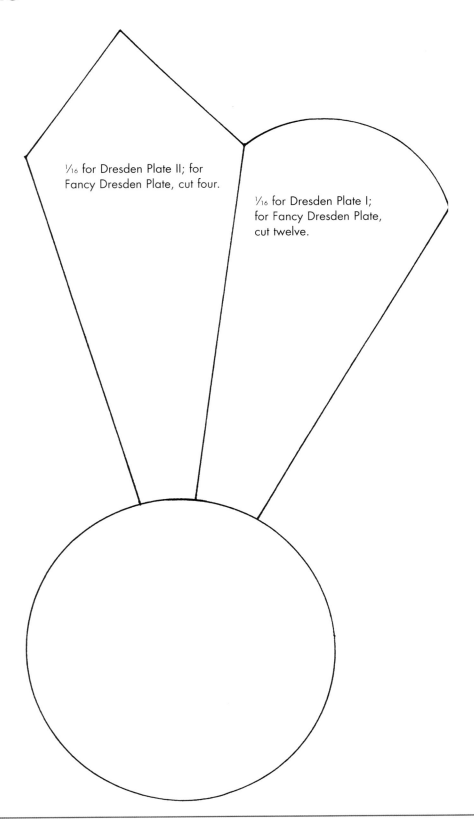

¹⁄₁₆ for Dresden Plate II; for Fancy Dresden Plate, cut four.

¹⁄₁₆ for Dresden Plate I; for Fancy Dresden Plate, cut twelve.

Sunbonnet Sue #1
8" block

Sunbonnet Sue #2
10" block

Photocopy patterns at 111% for 10" block.

Overall Bill #1

9" block

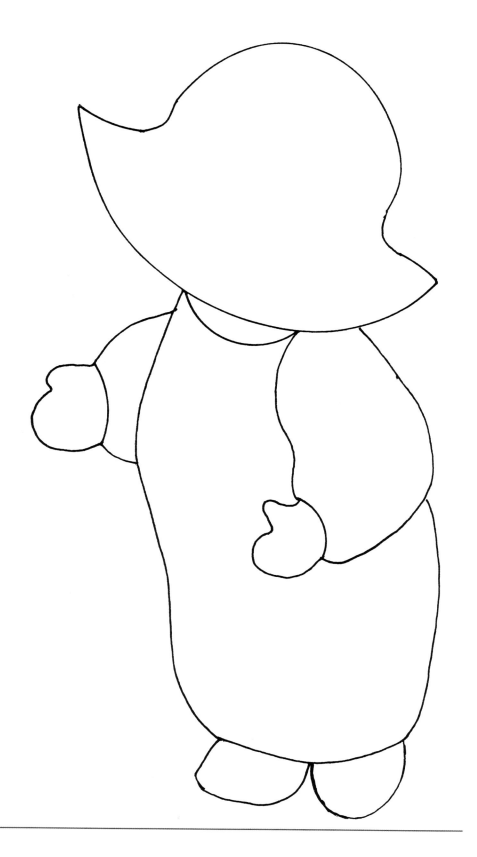

Overall Bill #2

10" block

Celestial Potpourri Bags, page 216

Silk Pillbox Hat, page 237

Delicates Travel Pouch, page 218

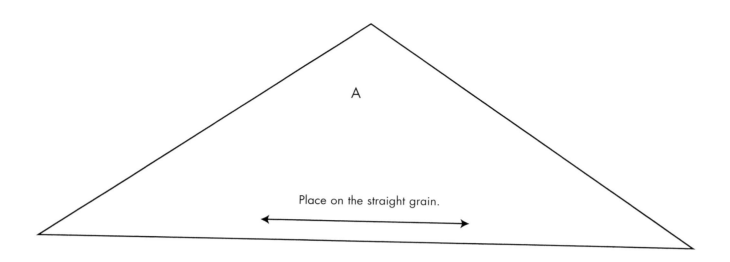

A

Place on the straight grain.

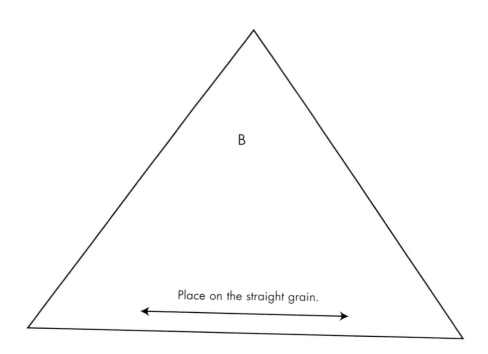

B

Place on the straight grain.

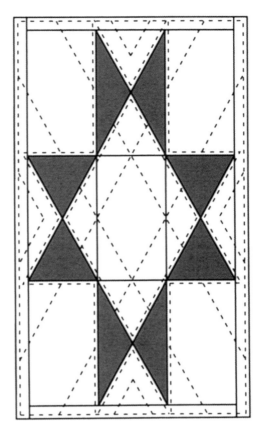

Evening Star Place Mat, page 231

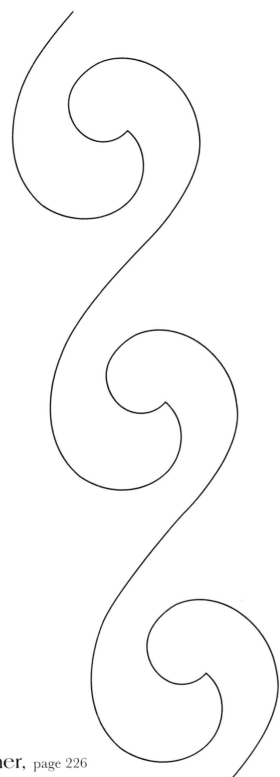

Tangy Table Runner, page 226

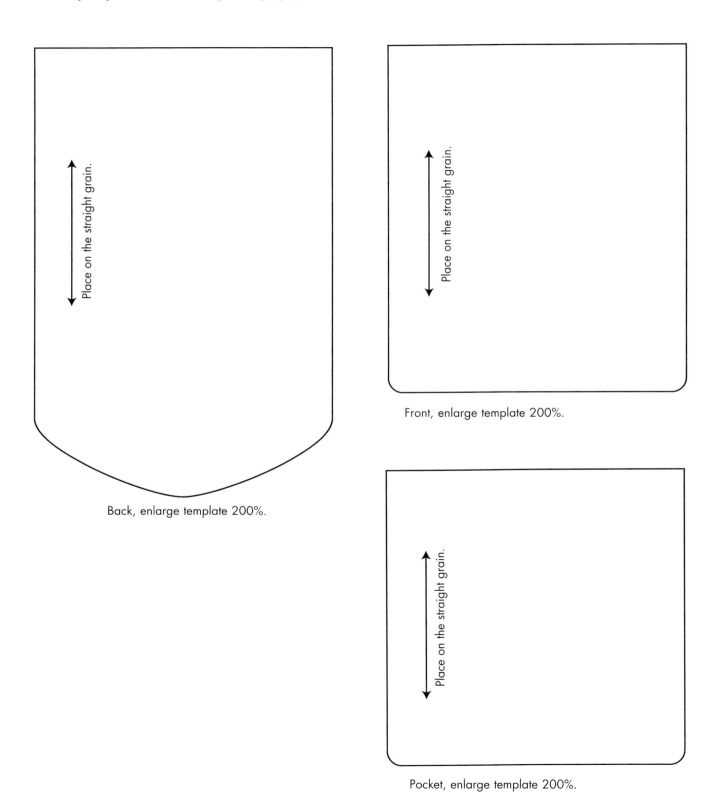

Place on the straight grain.

Place on the straight grain.

Back, enlarge template 200%.

Front, enlarge template 200%.

Place on the straight grain.

Pocket, enlarge template 200%.

Hawaiian Quilting Appliqué, page 241

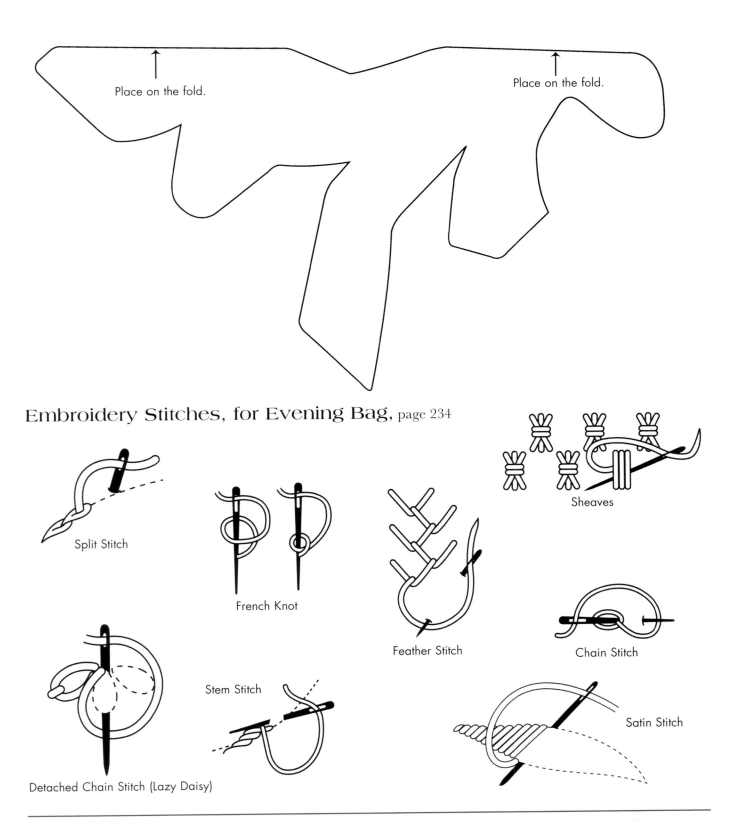

Place on the fold.

Place on the fold.

Embroidery Stitches, for Evening Bag, page 234

Split Stitch

French Knot

Feather Stitch

Sheaves

Chain Stitch

Detached Chain Stitch (Lazy Daisy)

Stem Stitch

Satin Stitch

Bear's Paw

Block size: 14"
Quilt size: 84" x 84"
No. of blocks: 36

Pieces per block		Per quilt
A	4 Print	144
B	4 Print	144
	1 Plain	36
C	16 Print	576
	16 Plain	576
D	4 Plain	144

FABRIC REQUIRED

4¾ yards Plain
¼ yard scrap fabric per block
   or a total of 6 yards

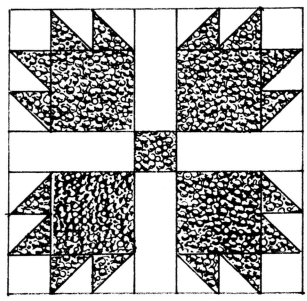

Bear's Paw Pattern

A

Add seam allowances.

Bear's Paw, continued

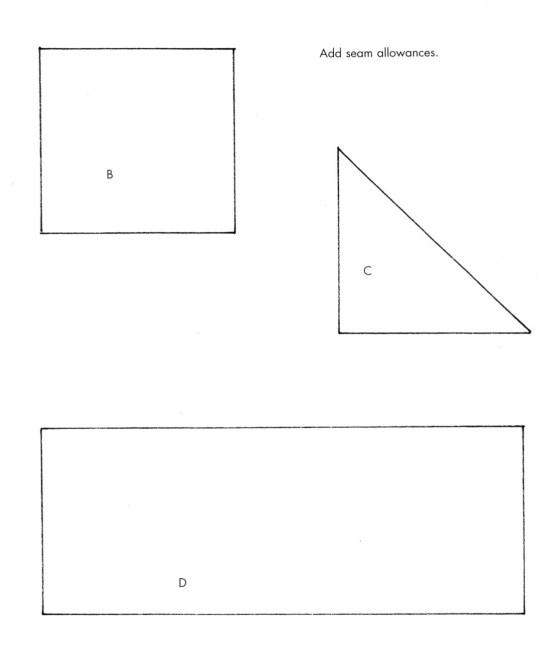

Add seam allowances.

B

C

D

Bird's Nest

Block size: 15"
Quilt size: 74" x 90"
No. of blocks: 30

Pieces per block		*Per quilt*
A	4 Dark	120
B	4 Dark	120
	12 White	360
C	12 White	360
D	9 Print	270
E	12 White	360

FABRIC REQUIRED
6½ yards white
1½ yards blue print
4 yards dark green

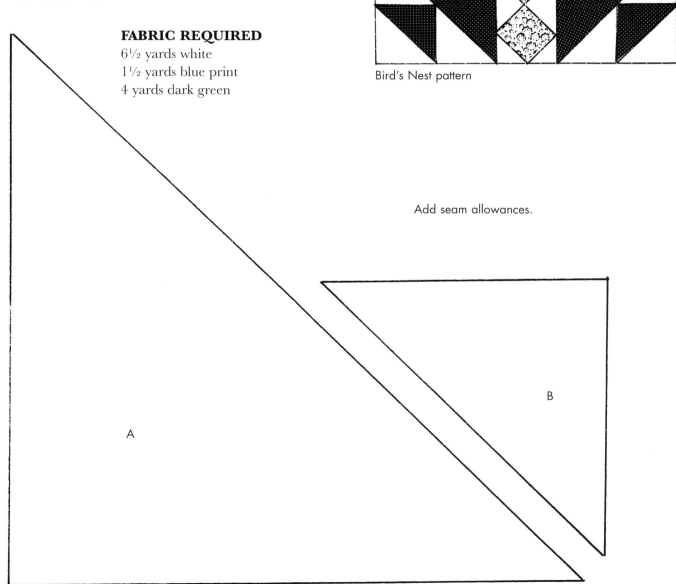

Bird's Nest pattern

Add seam allowances.

A

B

Bird's Nest, continued

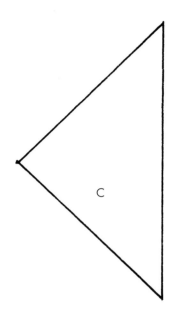

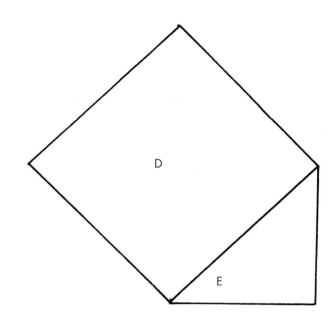

Add seam allowances.

Bow Tie

Block size: 8"
Quilt size: 80" x 88"
No. of blocks: 110

Pieces per block		Per quilt
A	2 White	220
	2 Print Scrap	220
B	1 Dark Scrap	110

FABRIC REQUIRED

3½ yards white
5" x 9" scrap per block
3" x 3" dark scrap per block

Bow Tie pattern

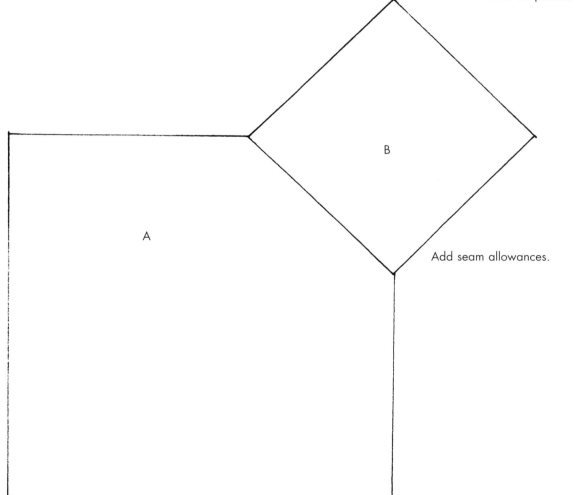

B

A

Add seam allowances.

Card Tricks

Block size: 12"
Quilt size: 84" x 84"
No. of blocks: 49

Pieces per block		Per quilt
A	4 White	196
	4 Print	196
	4 Plain	196
B	4 White	196
	4 Print	196
	4 Plain	196

FABRIC REQUIRED

4 yards white
This is usually made as a scrap quilt with different coordinating scraps for each block.

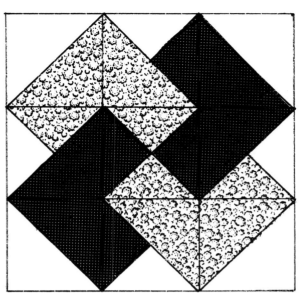

Card Tricks pattern

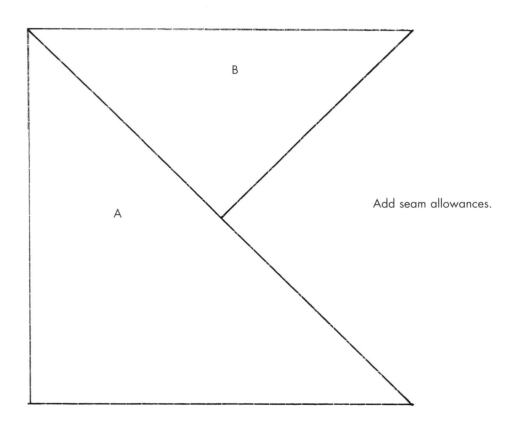

B

A

Add seam allowances.

Clay's Choice

Block size: 12"
Quilt size: 84" x 96"
No. of blocks: 56

Pieces per block		Per quilt
A	4 Print	224
	4 White	224
B	8 Dark	448
	4 White	224
	4 Print	224

FABRIC REQUIRED

4 yards print
3½ yards dark
4 yards white

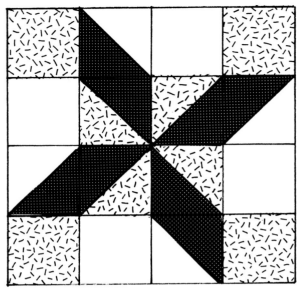

Clay's Choice pattern

The original pattern had a separate pattern for the dark center pieces. This is assembled from half-square triangles, which, if you use the chain-piecing method present in this book, you will find is much quicker even though you are dealing with more pieces. It also uses slightly less fabric.

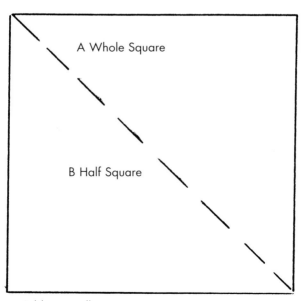

Add seam allowances.

Crazy Ann

Block size: 10"
Quilt size: 80" x 80"
No. of blocks: 64

Pieces per block		Per quilt
A	5 Dark	320
B	8 White	512
C	4 Print	256
D	4 Dark	256
	4 White	256

FABRIC REQUIRED

3¾ yards dark
5 yards white
3 yards print

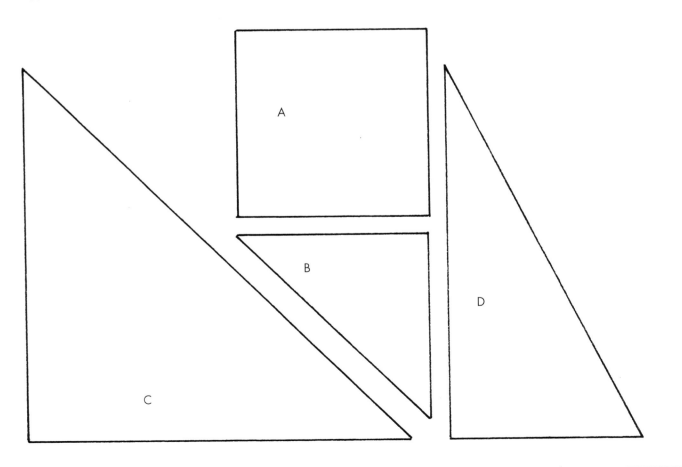

Crazy Ann pattern

Add seam allowances.

Double Pinwheel

Block size: 10"
Quilt size: 80" x 80"
No. of blocks: 64

Pieces per block		Per quilt
A	4 Print	256
B	4 Dark	256
	4 Plain	256

FABRIC REQUIRED

4¾ yards print
1⅔ yards dark
1⅔ yards plain

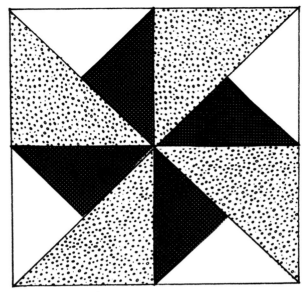

Double Pinwheel pattern

Add seam allowances.

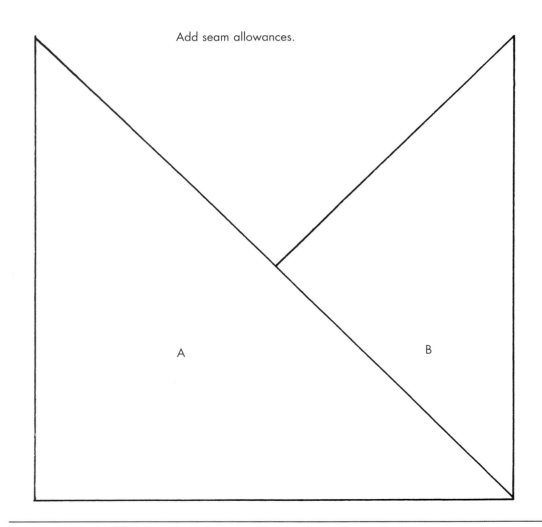

54-40 or Fight

Block size: 12"
Quilt size: 84" x 96"
No. of blocks: 56

Pieces per block		Per quilt
A	2 Dark	112
	10 White	560
	8 Print	448
B	8 Dark	448
C	4 White	224

FABRIC REQUIRED

4½ yards dark
2½ yards print
5½ yards white

54-40 or Fight pattern

Add seam allowances.

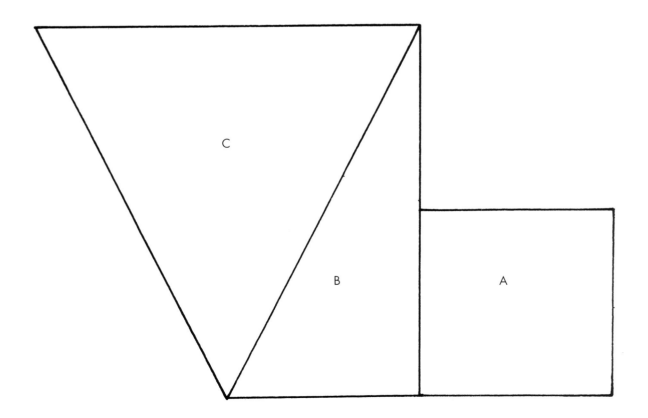

Handy Andy

Block size: 10"
Quilt size: 80" x 90"
No. of blocks: 72

Pieces per block		*Per quilt*
A	5 Plain	360
B	4 Print	288
	12 Plain	864
C	4 Print	288
D	8 Dark	576
	8 Plain	576

This could also be set with alternate plain blocks.

FABRIC REQUIRED
8¾ yards plain
4½ yards print
2⅓ yards dark

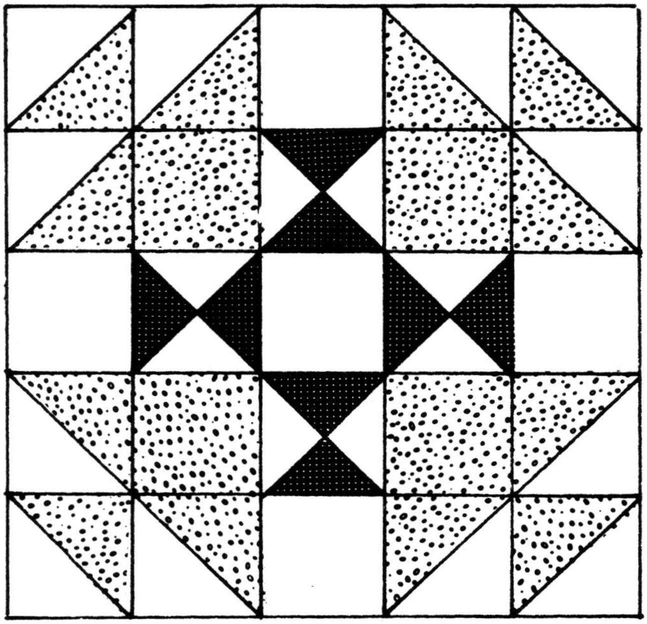

Handy Andy pattern

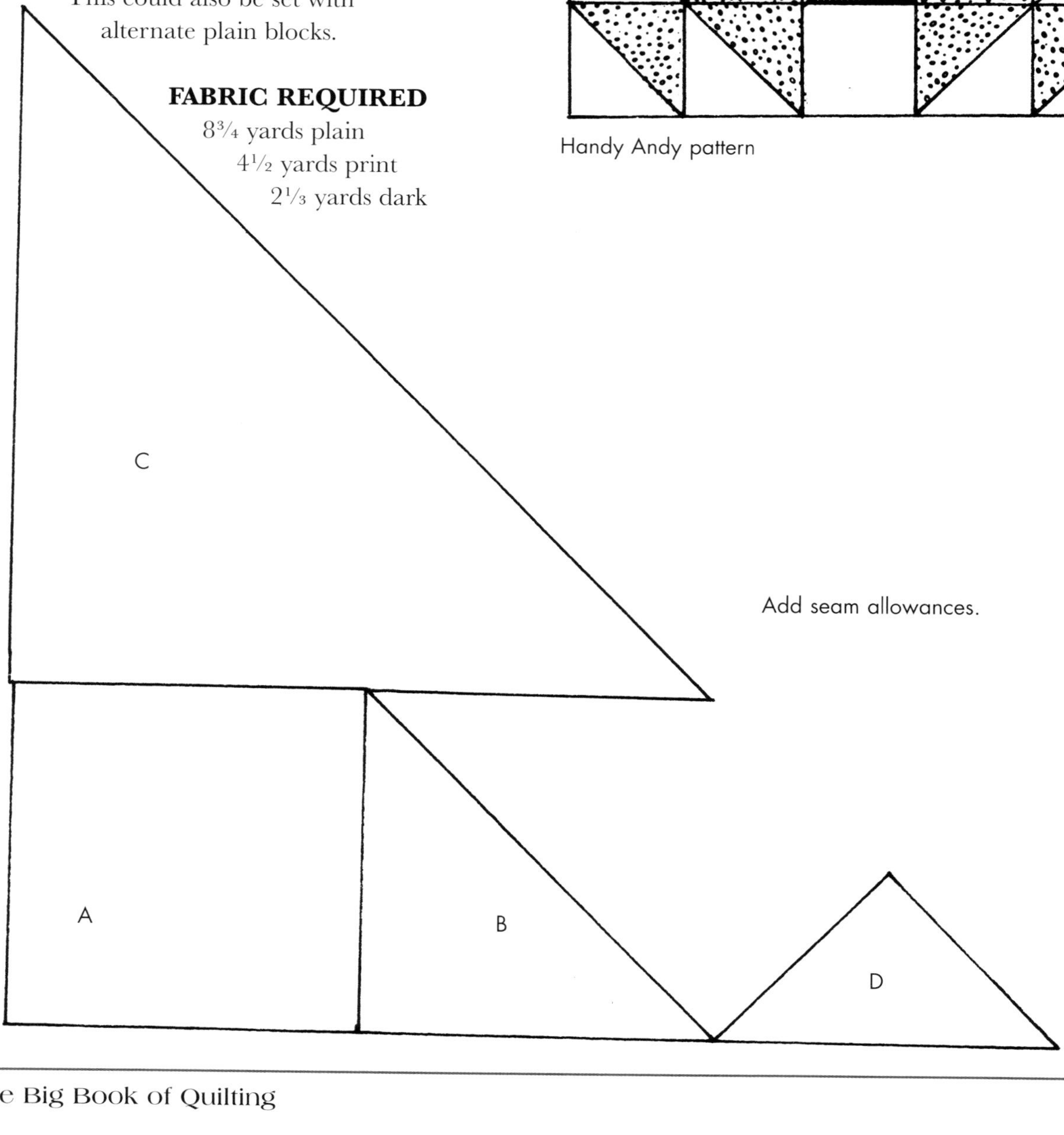

Add seam allowances.

C

A

B

D

Improved Four-patch

Block size: 8"
Quilt size: 80" x 80"
No. of blocks: 100

This quilt is made entirely from scraps. The scraps can be utilized in several different ways. You can use the diagram to place the various scraps; you can make each piece a different scrap, or you could make the outer triangles all the same color.

The quilt can be set solid, with lattice strips or alternate plain blocks.

Improved 4-Patch pattern

Add seam allowances.

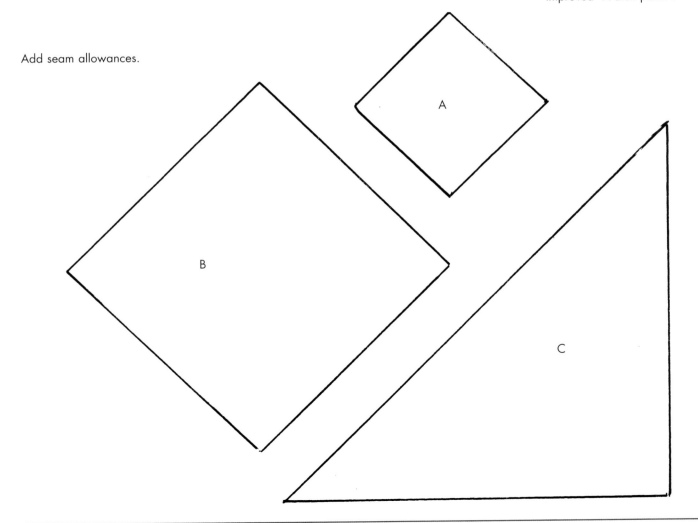

Indiana Puzzle

Block size: 12"
Quilt size: 84" x 84"
No. of blocks: 25 pieced
                  12 Plain
                  12 Print

	Pieces per block	*Per quilt*
A	Print	50
	2 Plain	50
B	2 Print	50
	2 Plain	50
C	2 Print	50
	2 Plain	50
D	2 Print	50
	2 Plain	50
E	2 Print	50
	2 Plain	
	12 Print 13" squares	
	12 Plain 13" squares	

FABRIC REQUIRED

5 yards print
7 yards plain

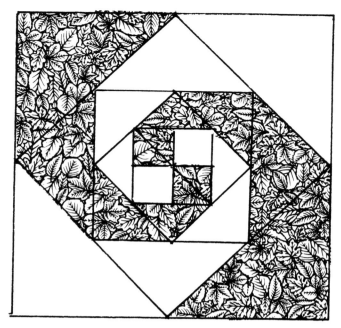

Indiana Puzzle pattern

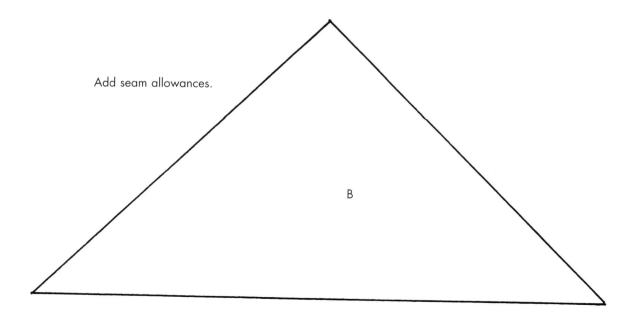

Add seam allowances.

B

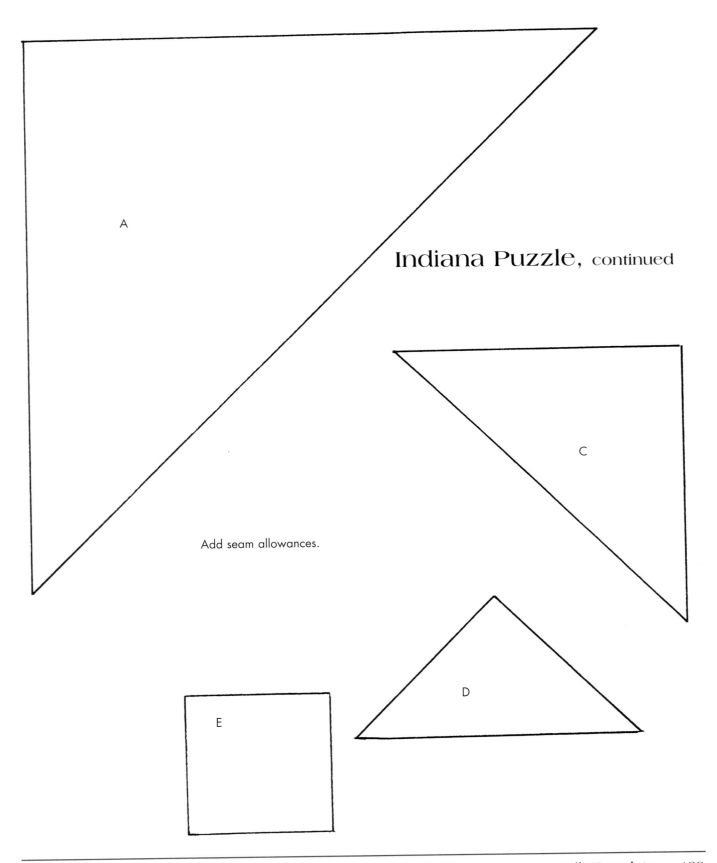

A

Indiana Puzzle, continued

C

Add seam allowances.

D

E

Tomahawk

Block size: 16"
Quilt size: 80" x 96"
No. of blocks: 30

Pieces per block		Per quilt
A	2 Dark	60
	2 Print	60
	2 Plain	60
B	24 Dark	720
	8 Print	240
	16 Plain	480
C	4 Plain	120
D	2 Plain	60
	1 Print	30
E	1 Plain	30
F	2 Plain	60
G	1 Plain	30

FABRIC REQUIRED

4¼ yards dark
2¼ yards print
8¼ yards plain

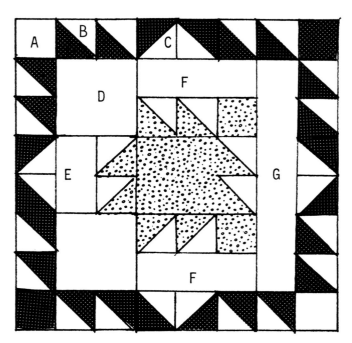

Tomahawk pattern

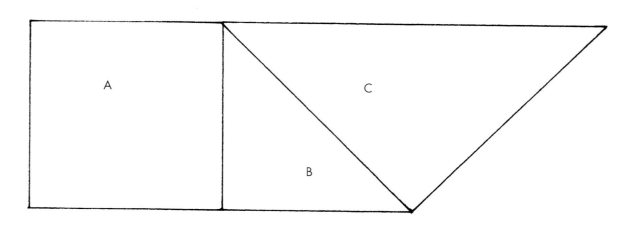

Add seam allowances.

Tomahawk, continued

Continue to solid line for F.

Cut at dash line for E.

For G, extend to measure 12".

D

Jack-in-the-Box

Block size: 10"
Quilt size: 76" x 86"
No. of blocks: 56
(28 pieced; 28 plain; 7 across by 8 down)

Pieces per block		Per quilt
A	1 White	28
B	4 Red Print	112
C	4 Red	112
D	4 Red	112
E	16 White	448

FABRIC REQUIRED

2½ yards red
6 yards white
3¼ yards red print

BORDER

3" red print strips

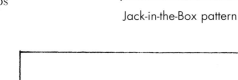

Jack-in-the-Box pattern

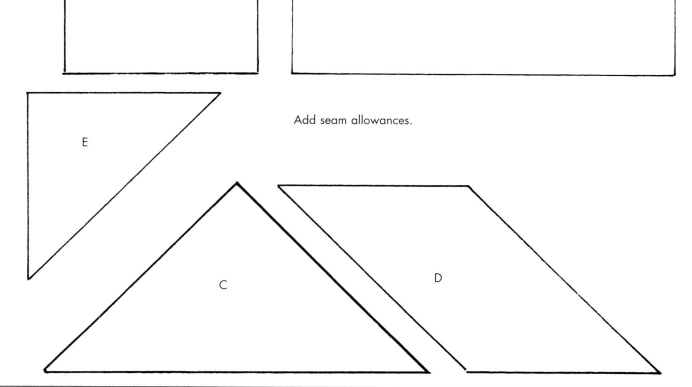

Add seam allowances.

Jacob's Ladder

Block size: 12"
Quilt size: 84" x 96"
No. of blocks: 56

Pieces per block		*Per quilt*
A	10 Dark	560
	10 White	560
B	4 Print	224
	4 White	224

FABRIC REQUIRED

3½ yards dark
2 yards print
5½ yards white

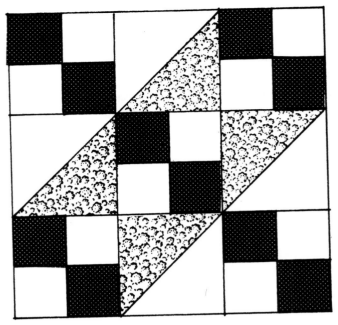

Jacob's Ladder pattern

Add seam allowances.

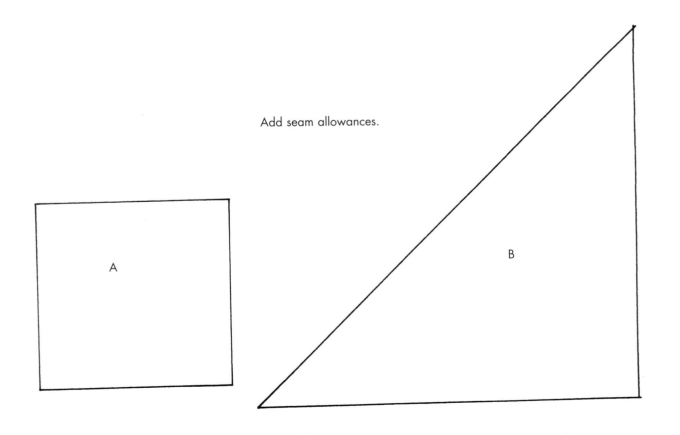

Kansas Troubles

Block size: 12"
Quilt size: 87" x 99"
No. of blocks: 56

Pieces per block		Per quilt
A	4 White	224
	4 Red	224
B	24 White	1344
	24 Red	1344
C	4 White	224

FABRIC REQUIRED

6 yards white
5 yards red

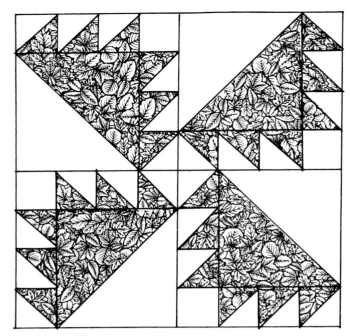

Kansas Troubles pattern

Add seam allowances.

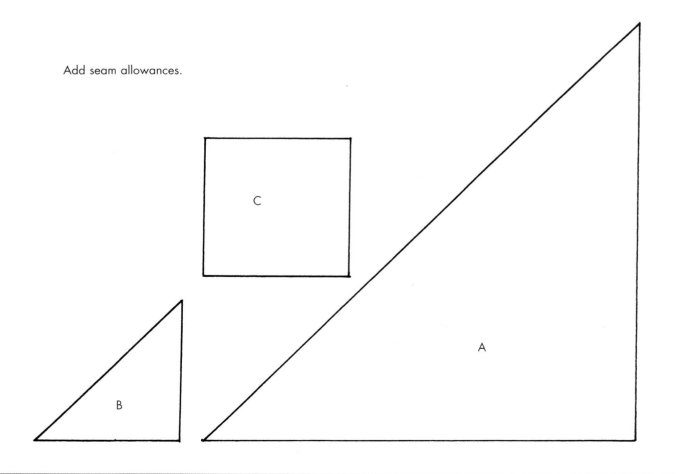

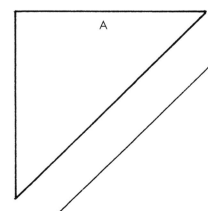

Lady of the Lake

Block size: 10"
Quilt size: 80" x 80"
No. of blocks: 64

Pieces per block		Per quilt
A	16 Print	1024
	16 Plain	1024
B	1 Print	64
	1 Plain	64

FABRIC REQUIRED

6¾ yards print
6¾ yards plain

Lady of the Lake pattern

Add seam allowances.

A

B

Milky Way

Block size: 12"
Quilt size: 84" x 84"

Pieces per quilt

A	Dark	242
	White	242
B	Print	220
	White	220
C	Print	50
	White	50

Add seam allowances

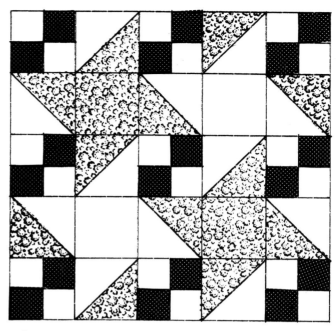

Milky Way pattern

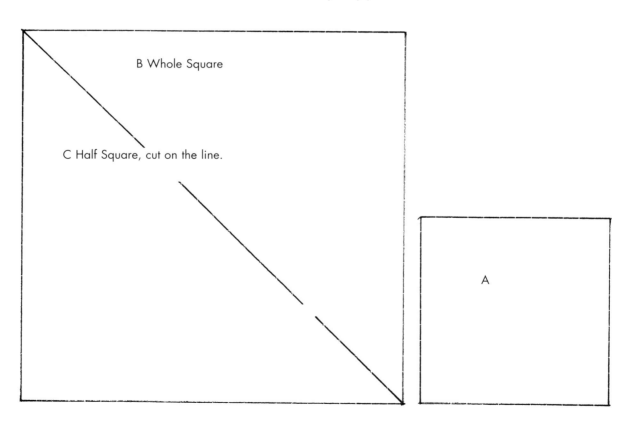

B Whole Square

C Half Square, cut on the line.

A

Ohio Star

Block size: 12"
Quilt size: 84" x 84"
No. of blocks: 49

Pieces per block		Per quilt
A	8 White	392
	8 Print	392
B	4 White	196
	1 Print	49

FABRIC REQUIRED

This is usually made as a scrap quilt with a different print for each block. If you prefer to use the same print throughout, you will need:

4 yards print
6½ yards white

Ohio Star pattern

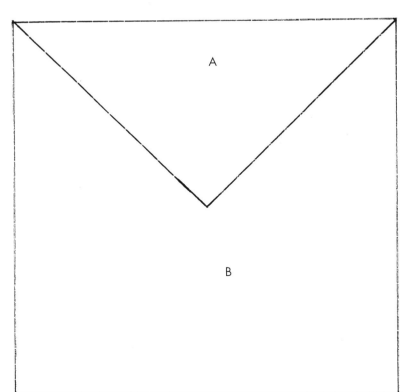

Add seam allowances.

Pine Tree

Block size: 20"
Quilt size: 85" x 85"
No. of blocks: 9

Pieces per block			Per quilt
A	3	White	27
B	42	Green Print	378
	36	White	324
C	3	White	27
D	2	Dark Green	18
E	2	Dark Green	18
F	2	White	18
G	1	Dark Green	9

Blocks are set on the diagonal
Four White 21" squares
Eight White Half-squares
Four White Quarter-squares

FABRIC REQUIRED

$6^2/_3$ yards white
2 yards green print
$1^1/_4$ yards dark green or brown

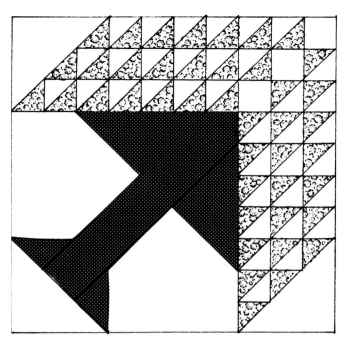

Pine Tree pattern

Add seam allowances.

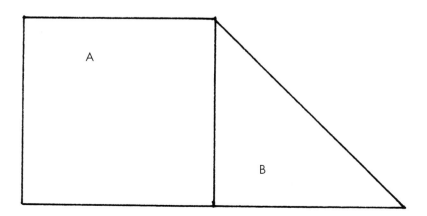

Pine Tree, continued

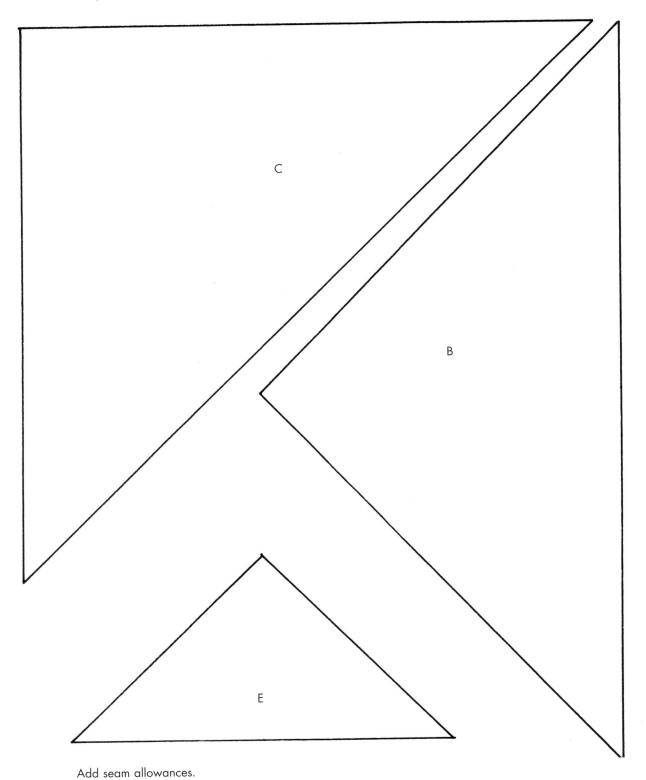

Add seam allowances.

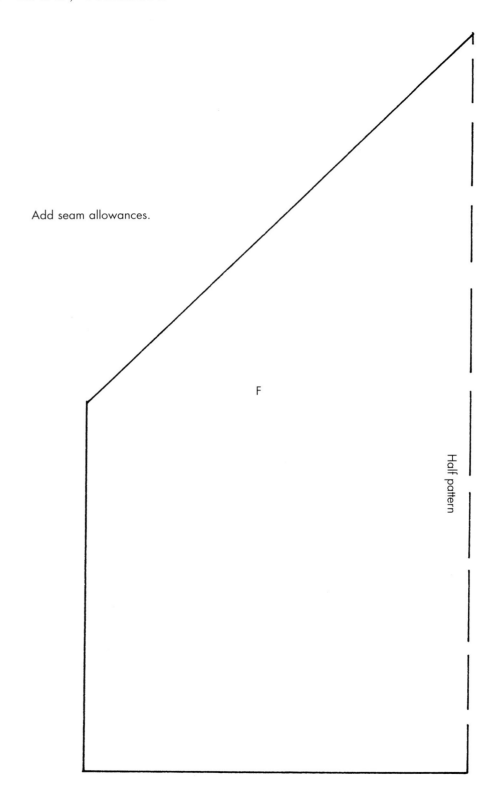

Add seam allowances.

F

Half pattern

Pine Tree, continued

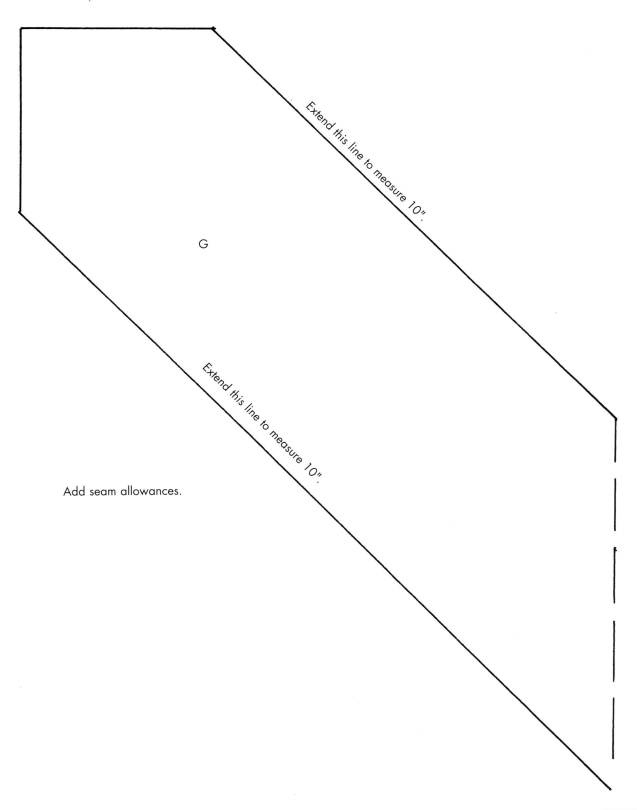

G

Extend this line to measure 10".

Extend this line to measure 10".

Add seam allowances.

Pinwheel Square Variation

Block size: 15"
Quilt size: 75" x 90"
No. of blocks: 30

Pieces per block		Per quilt
A	5 Print	150
B	4 Plain	120
C	4 Print	120
D	4 Print	120
	4 Plain	120
E	4 Plain	120

FABRIC REQUIRED
4¾ yards print
5 yards plain

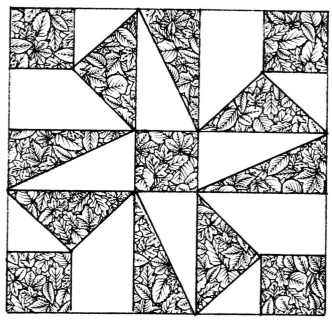

Pinwheel Square Variation pattern

For template E, use combined area of A and B.

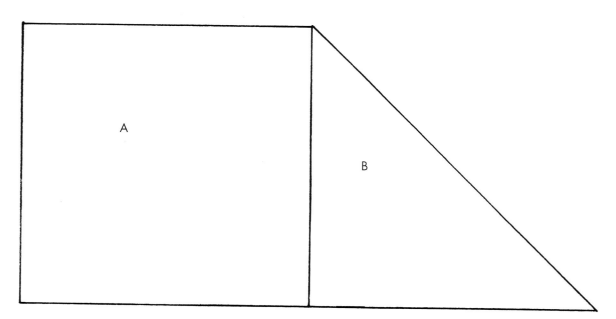

Add seam allowances.

Pinwheel Square Variation, continued

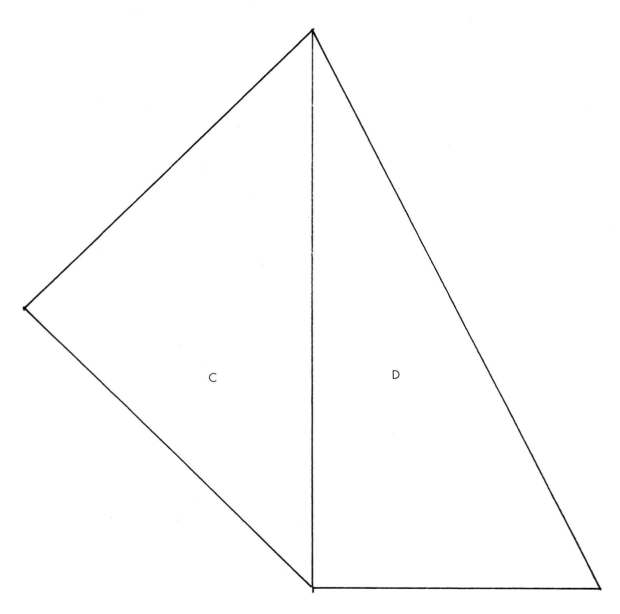

C

D

Add seam allowances.

Strawberry Basket

Block size: 12"
Quilt size: 85" x 85"
No. of blocks: 25 Pieced
25 Plain
Diagonal Set

Pieces per block		Per quilt
A	6 Dark	150
	9 White	225
B	6 Dark	150
C	2 Dark	50
	1 Dark Print	25
D	2 Light Print	50

FABRIC REQUIRED

5 yards white
2 yards dark
1½ yards light print
½ yard dark print

Strawberry Basket pattern

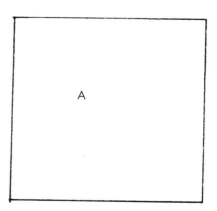

A

Add seam allowances.

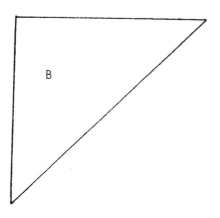

B

Strawberry Basket, continued

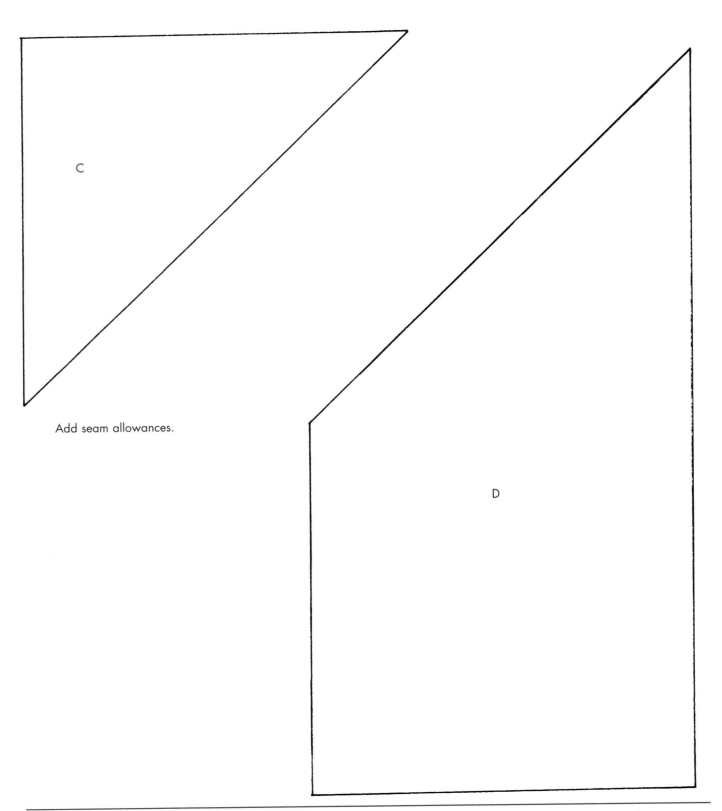

C

Add seam allowances.

D

Waste Not

Block size: 12"
Quilt size: 84" x 84"
No. of blocks: 49

Pieces per block		*Per quilt*
A	4 Print	196
B	4 Assorted Prints	196
C	4 White	196

FABRIC REQUIRED
$4\frac{1}{8}$ yards print
$4\frac{1}{2}$ yards white

Waste Not pattern

B is a scrap piece changing from block to block. A could also be treated as a scrap, if desired, changing from block to block, or you could use 4 prints within each block.

The diagram below shows a slight variation of this design which allows you to use even more scraps. Part A is cut as shown by the dash line on the pattern piece. When the prints are arranged as shown below, a secondary pinwheel pattern emerges. Scraps could also be used randomly.

Waste Not patterns combined

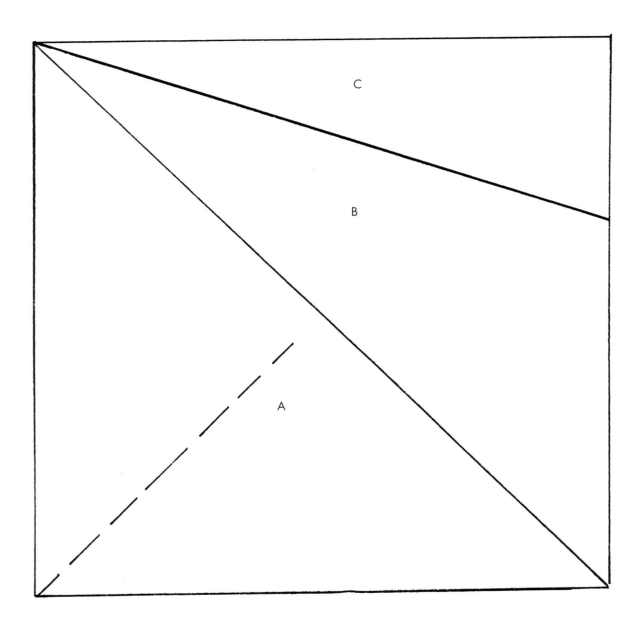

Add seam allowances.

World Without End

Block size: 16"
Quilt size: 80" x 96"
No. of blocks: 30

Pieces per block		Per quilt
A	8 Print	240
	8 Plain	240
B	8 Print	240
	8 Plain	240
C	2 Print	60
	2 Plain	60

FABRIC REQUIRED

5½ yards print
5½ yards plain

World Without End pattern

World Without End, continued

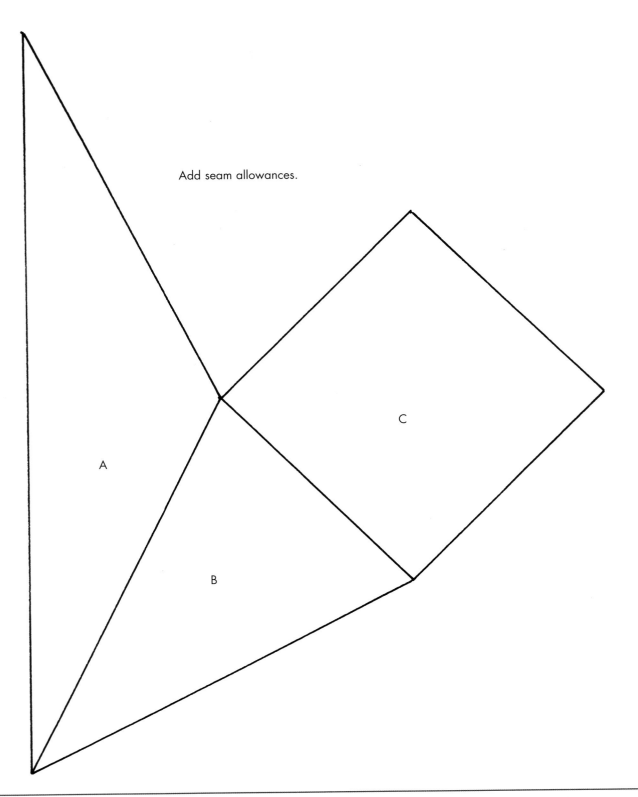

Add seam allowances.

A

B

C

Waterwheel

Block size: 12"
Quilt size: 84" x 84"
No. of blocks: 49

Pieces per block		*Per quilt*
A	4 Dark	196
	8 White	392
	4 Light Print	196
	2 Dark Print	98
B	2 Light Print	98
	2 Dark Print	98
	4 White	196

FABRIC REQUIRED

4 yards white
1 yard dark
2 yards light print
1¾ yards dark print

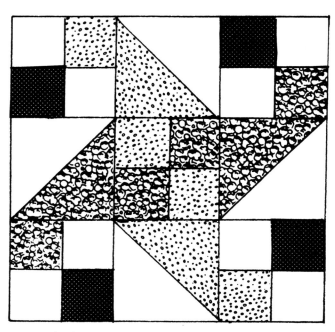

Waterwheel pattern

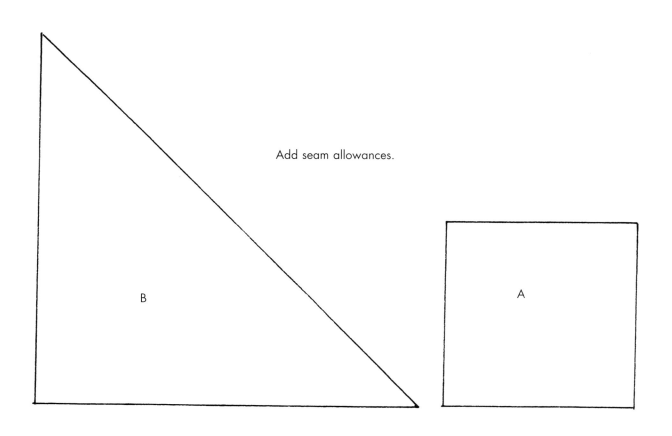

Add seam allowances.

B

A

CHAPTER 10

Quilting Patterns

With material by Fran Roen, Cheryl Fall, and Maggie Malone

Moorish Garden medallion motif. A quilting pattern appropriate for a central position or large open blocks, it is one of the Moorish Garden suite of patterns found in this chapter.

Lessons from the Amish

As you practice transferring designs, work on large sheets of newsprint, white shelf paper, or freezer paper. Map the areas for which you are designing and develop the design, making adjustments and changes as needed. For some people, the methods will become quite comfortable and natural; if you are one of them, you can then design directly on your quilt top. For many people, this may seem too daring. Paper first is a nice way to keep a reusable record of the motifs you design. It may fill the bill on some later quilt as well.

FEATHERING*

To do quilting designs based on feathering, start with a spine; the spine is the line defining the shape of the motif. It can be a straight line or closed or open line. You can also do feathering on a circle, an oval, a heart, or a twist. At first, however, work with a straight spine for practice.

Method 1: Feathering on a Straight Line
Start with a straight line, centered in the space you want your design to fill. You will be using a shape that is referred to as a feather. It is a slightly asymmetric teardrop shape (see figure Q1 on page 518. Feather Templates 1–4). On that feather you will find two little notches. The initial location of the notches is arbitrary, but they will

*See quilt templates section for specific motifs.

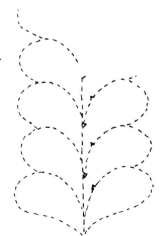

Tracing feathers on a central spine (reduced)

guide placement along the spine. Begin at the base of the straight line you drew and place the feathers so that the notch on the upper curve is on the spine, and trace around the feather shape. For the next feather, slide the feather template up so that the bottom notch on the second feather just hides the top of the first feather's curve and the top notch of the second curve remains along the spine. Outline the feather shape on your material beginning at the top of the previous feather, and follow it along the spine. Using the notches as guides, continue placing the feathers along the spine until you reach the topmost end of the spine line; the final frond is placed on top of the feather. Turn the template over and repeat the process on the other side of the line.

Method II: Feathering on an Open Curve
As with Method I, a spine is necessary to guide the feathering. Method II is used for an open curve (see figure Q5, right). Trace a feather template and cut it out (see figure Q1). Initial placement of the feather is arbitrary. When you have determined the angle and tilt of the selected feather template, mark or notch the feather where it touches the spine. Outline the feather shape on your material. As you slide the feather template along the spine, reposition the template each time to keep the notches on the spine. You will notice that the feathers will change in fullness (because they don't always overlap the same amount) as they flex around inside and outside curves of the spine.

Feathers on Curve-Shaped Corners

Since feathers make stunning border motifs, you will want to know how to feather the corners in a graceful manner. Begin by treating the corners and working out along the sides. To do that you need a line representing the imagined miter of the corner. Beginning at the miter line, draw a line curved to the configuration you want. You will do only half of the design and then it will be flipped over and the mirror image used to complete the corner (see template Q2). Begin at the miter line with either a frond or an oval shape. Then, using the feather as you did when you practiced on the straight spine, place feathers along the curve line, letting the base of the spine determine the position of the notches and tracing each new curve by starting from the preceding feather's back and going toward the spine. Be sure that you have completed a full design motif, one that can be repeated evenly along the border length. When marking the quilt, begin in the corner, tracing off your motif and approaching the center of the border. Any adjustments need to be made as you approach the center, as this is less likely to attract attention. On a serpentine, curved spine, you will be able to use the same size feathers on both sides of the curve.

Circles, Ovals and Hearts

For any close-curved design—for example, a circle—you will need two feather templates: a larger one for the outer curve, a smaller feather for the inner curve (see figure Q1). Mark your guidepoint at each quarter of the circle so you know when you are a quarter of the way around, halfway around, three quarters of the way around, or all the way around.

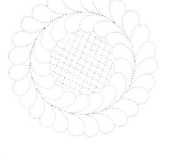

Using the larger feather, begin by tracing the motif at one of those quarter-circle indicators. Move evenly around the curve, making a placement adjustment at each quarter-mark to absorb feathers. For example, if you have four feathers in one quarter-circle, there should be four in each of the other quarters. This way you should be able to evenly distribute the feathers around the circle. On the inside of the curve, a smaller feather template is used, so that a similar number of feathers can be placed around the inside arc. Begin at a different quarter-circle mark than for the outside and place the feathers, distributing and adjusting the feather placement as before. You can draw additional concentric circles (or other curves) to guide the maximum outside feather size and the maximum inside size. Be sure that all the feathers flow in the same direction on the inside and outside arcs (see figure Q3).

Cable Designs

The single template needed for cable designs is either an oval with an interior oval cut away or a shallow S-curve. Using the oval template provided (Cable Template 1 of figure Q1), draw a guideline on a piece of tracing paper that will form the center of your cable design. It is important for the cable twist to gracefully turn corners. To ensure this, begin your design in the corner. Draw a line representing a corner miter line; place the cable template so that the long axis of the first oval is directly on the miter line (figure C1). Trace the inside curve and the outside curve of the template. To make the second oval, turn the cable template so that its point just touches the inside of the first oval drawn for the corner.

To complete the cable design along the tracing paper that turns the length of the sides of the work, continue to trace the inside and outside curves of the cable template, sliding the cable template along the guideline so the outer curve of the new oval just touches the lower edge of the inside curve of the previous oval and trace it in that position. Working from both corners toward the center, lay out the center of the cable motif, allowing for adjustments to be made

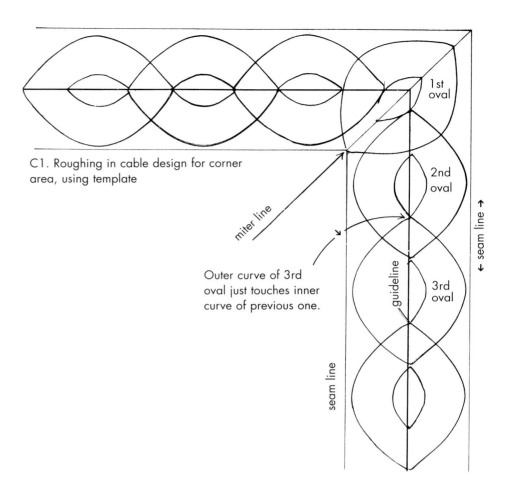

C1. Roughing in cable design for corner area, using template

miter line

Outer curve of 3rd oval just touches inner curve of previous one.

1st oval

2nd oval

3rd oval

← seam line →

guideline

seam line

at the center of each border. Make adjustments by simply lengthening or squeezing the last two or three oval shapes as they are placed into position.

Now that you have roughly drawn the cable design on your tracing paper, you need to determine which part is the upper and which part goes underneath in the cable. In order to provide the illusion of a twisting cable, one strand must always feed under the other (see figure C2 for an example). As you finalize your design, erase the outlines representing parts of the cable that pass under and connect the lines representing parts of the cable that pass over.

To create double or triple cables (see figure Q9) you must evenly space additional lines between the original cable boundaries. You might try using your seam gauge or your compass as a calipers. By guiding the

point of the compass along the already drawn cable boundary, and using a predetermined fixed spacing, you can mark a pencil line a fixed distance away from your first cable design, thereby creating your double or triple cable.

Pumpkin Seed Borders
The pumpkin seed border is a very popular narrow border fill for Amish quilts. It provides a simple, straight design to handle narrow inside borders or lattice strips. To create the pumpkin seed border with a simple template, you must decide the width of the border to be marked.

Cut a square from cardboard or plastic of a size such that the border width is the diagonal length of the square (figure P1).

Beginning with the border corner and working toward the center, place the square so that its corner points touch the outer edges of the border and the inner seam line of the border (figure P1). Keeping the square aligned with the diagonal perpendicular to the border, trace it end to end along the border. On your square template draw a line that represents the diagonal of the square and then draw two or three evenly spaced parallel guidelines on your template at regular intervals (P1).

These lines will give the placement of the echoed squares that fill the border (see Q10 for reference). To draw the fill lines, position your square template so that its sides are parallel to the triangular shapes that were formed as the template squares you drew earlier met end to end (figure P2). Slide the template toward the border seam until the first fill guideline on your template aligns with the border seam line. Trace the corner of the template so that the second guideline aligns on the border seam line; trace around the corner of the square template in its new position.

Repeat this process to fill each triangle space between the squares along the length of the border. When you have completed one side, begin the process of filling in the other side of the border. The pumpkin seed design actually takes its name from the cluster of four seed shapes in the design. Using the pattern provided (see Q10, pumpkin seed design), trace four pumpkin seeds meeting at the center point of each square. This quilting motif is rarely used on borders that are wider than 3". For an alternate treatment at the corners, begin so that the diagonal of the beginning square is in line with the seam joining the border to rest of the quilt.

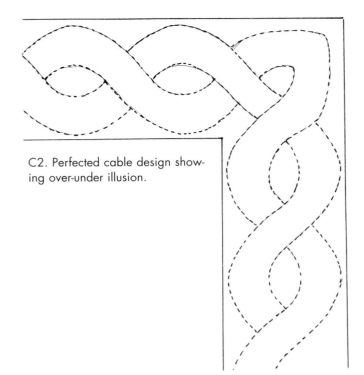

C2. Perfected cable design showing over-under illusion.

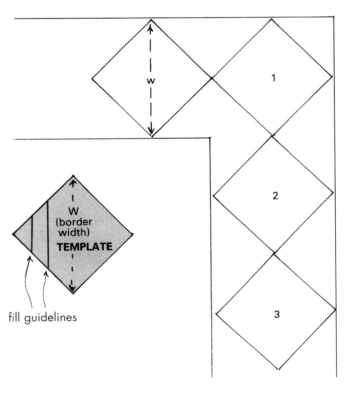

fill guidelines

P1. Pumpkin seed border. Cut a square template from cardboard or plastic whose diagonal measurement is equal to your border's width (w). Position and trace as shown, working from corner in.

Teacup or Tumbler Design

The teacup design is a simple, graceful, closed design used to fill narrow borders and bars. It uses a teacup or a juice tumbler as the basic template for the motif. The key to making this design a success is that you select a circular object that has a radius (the distance from the center to the curve of the circle) greater than the width of the border or bar to be filled. While the Amish do all of their marking directly on the quilt, you will probably want to develop a design on paper before moving to the quilt.

Position your circular template so that the outer curve lies a ¼" inside your seam (T1). Mark your template with a chalk line or pencil guildeline, to indicate where on the circle the opposite seam occurs. This will guide placement so that your curves remain uniform. Moving along one seam line, mark around the circle with your guideline lined up on the seam line (see figure T2). Move the template so that the new curve will begin at the end of the previous one; mark the curve, keeping the guideline lined up on the seam line. Continue marking along the entire length of the seam.

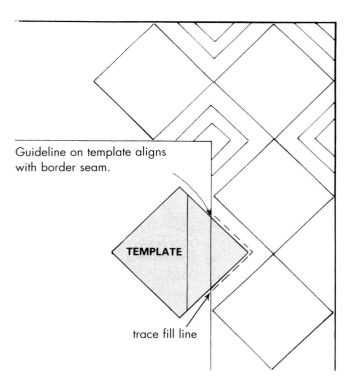

Guideline on template aligns with border seam.

TEMPLATE

trace fill line

P2. For pumpkin seed border fill of triangles, position guideline on seam line and trace edges of template to make pattern.

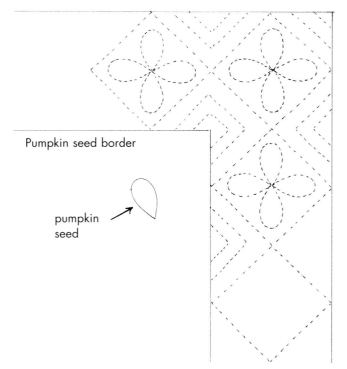

Pumpkin seed border

pumpkin seed

P3.

Next, place the guideline on the top inner seam line with the template curve touching the outer seam. Mark the arc from A to B (figure T3). Turn the template so that the guideline is on the right inner seam line and the edge of the template is exactly touching the outer top seam line. Mark the curve from A to D (figure T4). Smooth the finished corner curve from B to D. It will not be an arc of a perfect circle (T5). Continue drawing the rest of the curves to complete the border design. A sample appears in the Quilting Motif section (figure Q8).

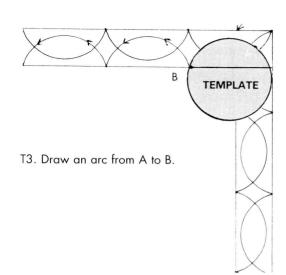

T3. Draw an arc from A to B.

T1. Teacup design. To mark the guideline on the template, place it so that its edge is ¼" in from the border seam line. Mark the guideline on the circle where the circle crosses the opposite border seam line.

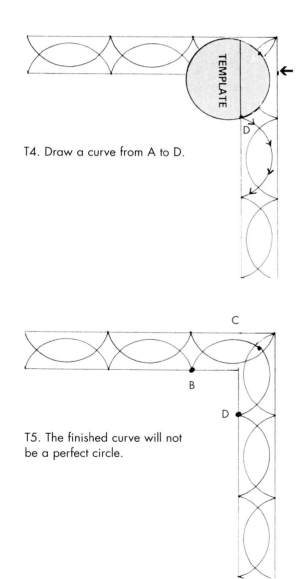

T4. Draw a curve from A to D.

T5. The finished curve will not be a perfect circle.

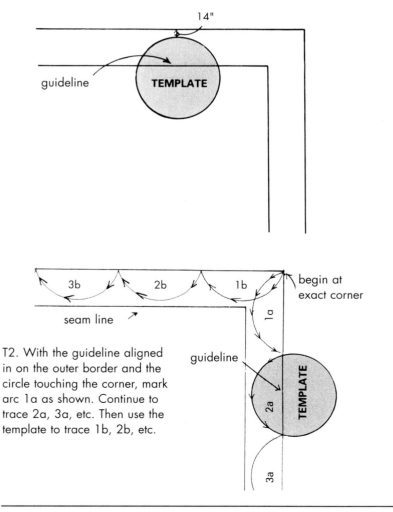

T2. With the guideline aligned in on the outer border and the circle touching the corner, mark arc 1a as shown. Continue to trace 2a, 3a, etc. Then use the template to trace 1b, 2b, etc.

Amish Quilting Motifs and Templates

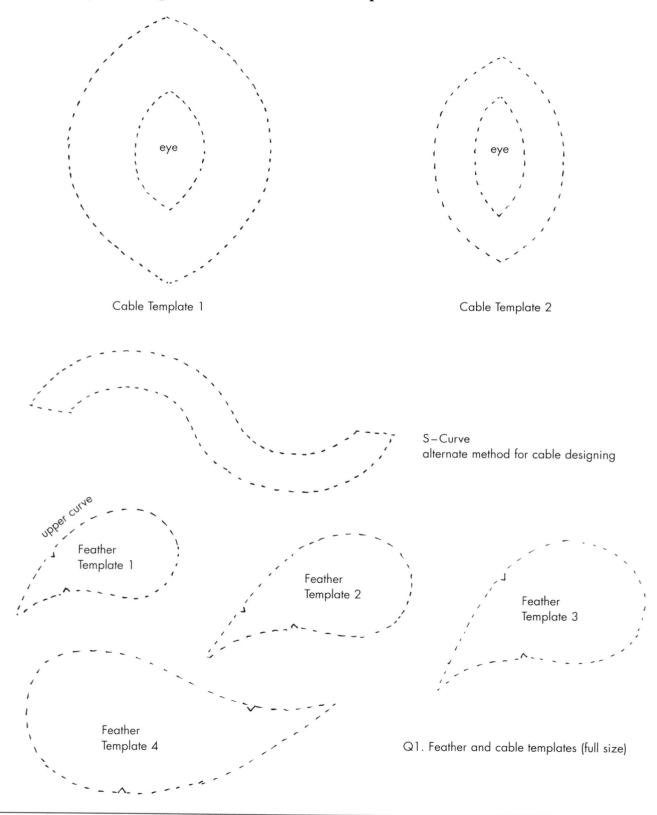

eye

Cable Template 1

eye

Cable Template 2

S–Curve
alternate method for cable designing

upper curve

Feather
Template 1

Feather
Template 2

Feather
Template 3

Feather
Template 4

Q1. Feather and cable templates (full size)

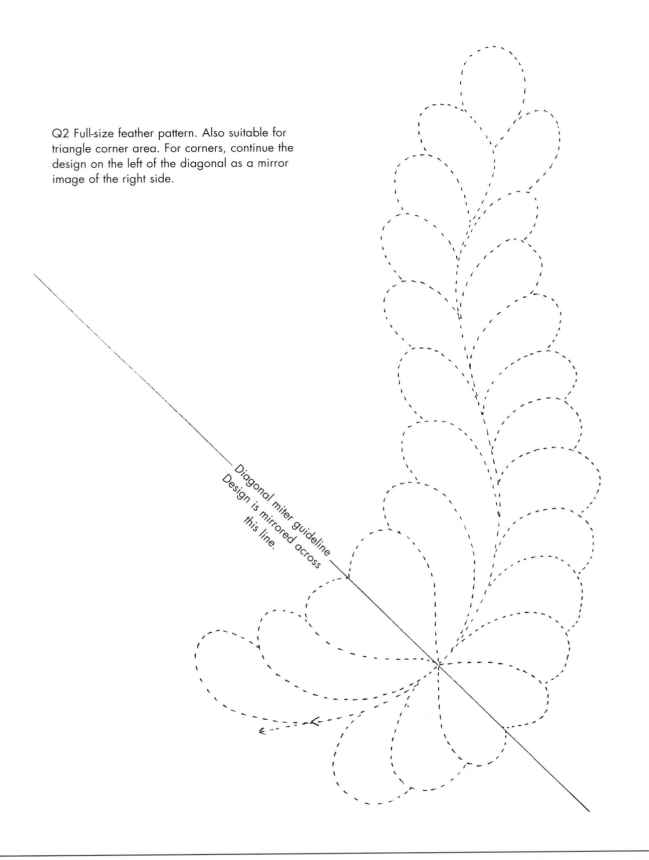

Q2 Full-size feather pattern. Also suitable for triangle corner area. For corners, continue the design on the left of the diagonal as a mirror image of the right side.

Diagonal miter guideline
Design is mirrored across this line.

Q3. Left: Feathered heart pattern, full size. Fits 3" to 4" square. Right: Feathered circle of wreath pattern, full size. Fits 3" to 4" square.

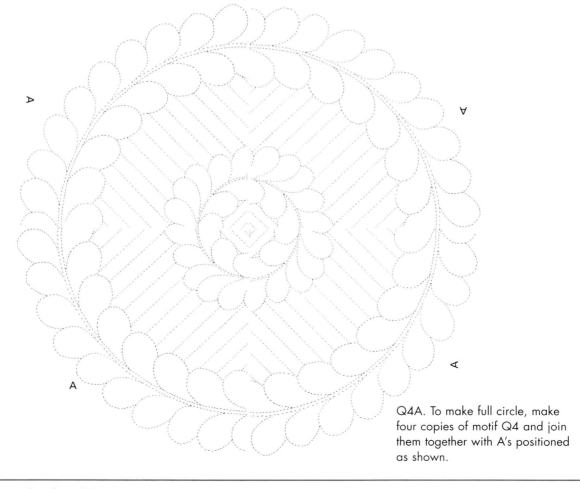

Q4A. To make full circle, make four copies of motif Q4 and join them together with A's positioned as shown.

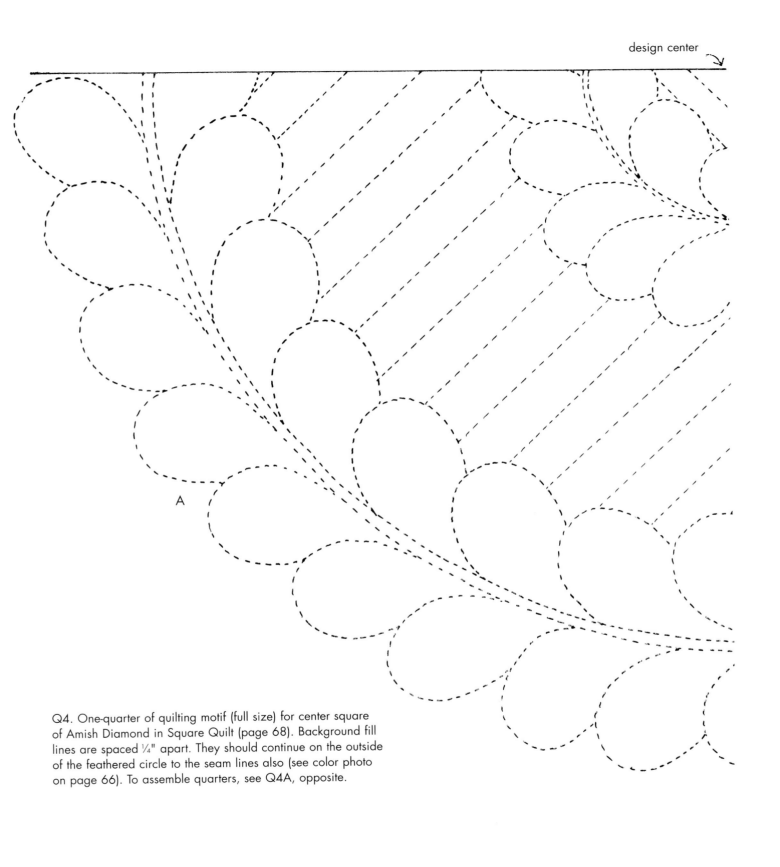

design center

A

Q4. One-quarter of quilting motif (full size) for center square of Amish Diamond in Square Quilt (page 68). Background fill lines are spaced ¼" apart. They should continue on the outside of the feathered circle to the seam lines also (see color photo on page 66). To assemble quarters, see Q4A, opposite.

Q5. Left: Full-size cable motif for 2½"- to 3"-wide strip or border space.

Right: Full-size feathered cable motif. (Feathers may be added to both sides of cable.)

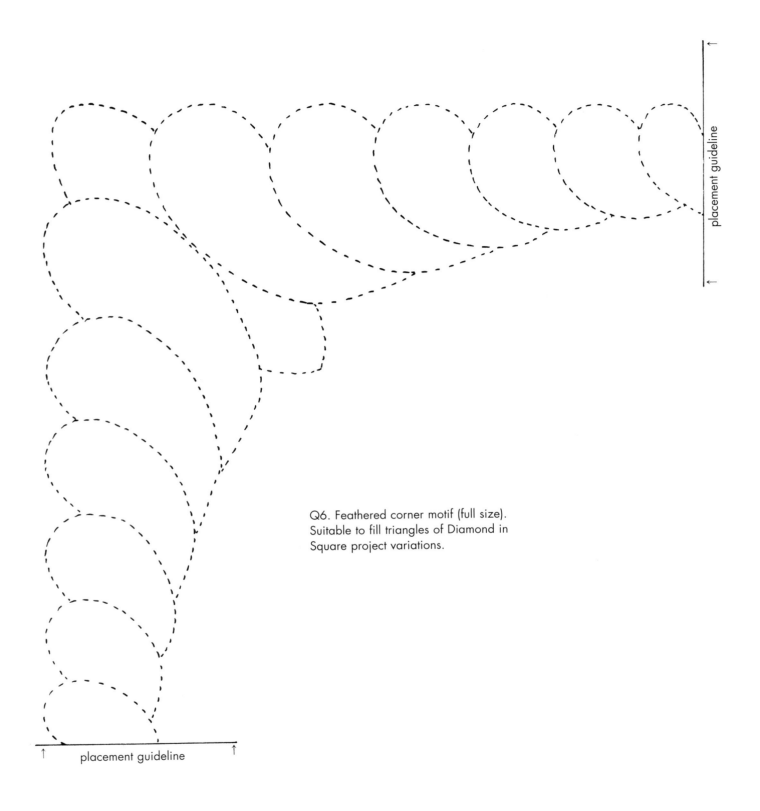

Q6. Feathered corner motif (full size).
Suitable to fill triangles of Diamond in
Square project variations.

placement guideline

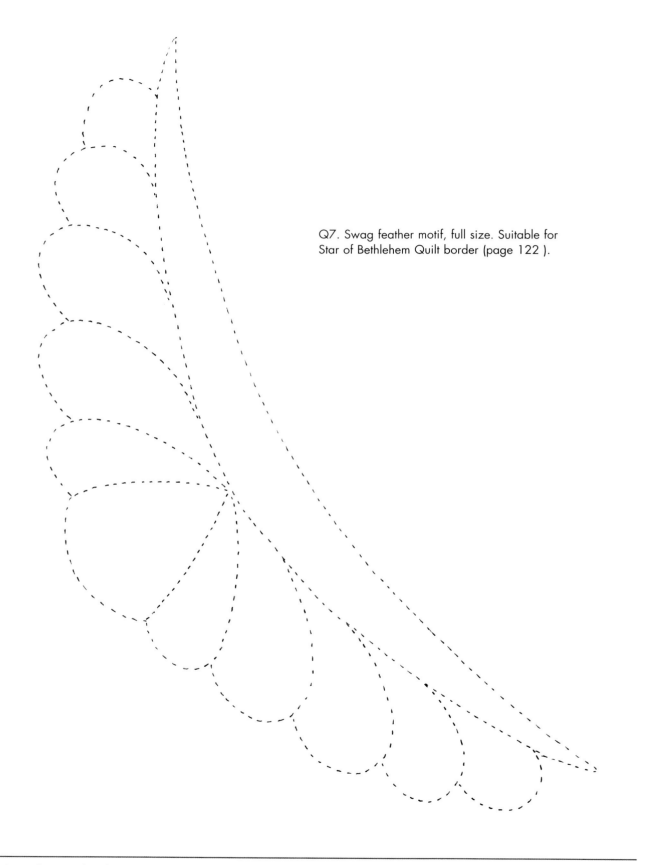

Q7. Swag feather motif, full size. Suitable for
Star of Bethlehem Quilt border (page 122).

Q8. Teacup motif for border, full size.

Q9. Double cable border design, full size. Suitable for pillow borders. The centerline may be deleted to produce a single cable design.

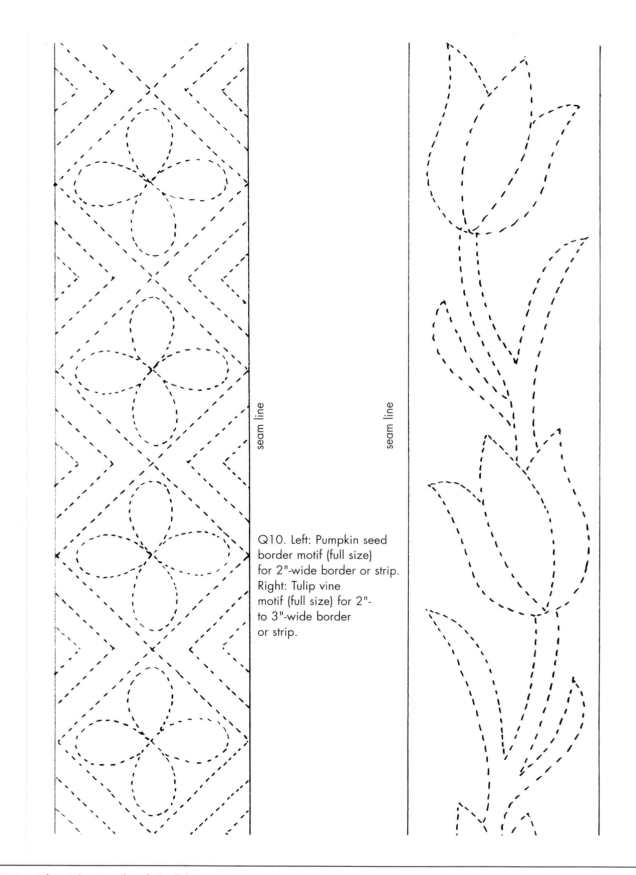

seam line

seam line

Q10. Left: Pumpkin seed border motif (full size) for 2"-wide border or strip. Right: Tulip vine motif (full size) for 2"- to 3"-wide border or strip.

Q11 Top: Arc, fan, or shell motif (full size). Bottom: Design that may be used for the setting squares of the Amish Ocean Waves Quilt (page 100).

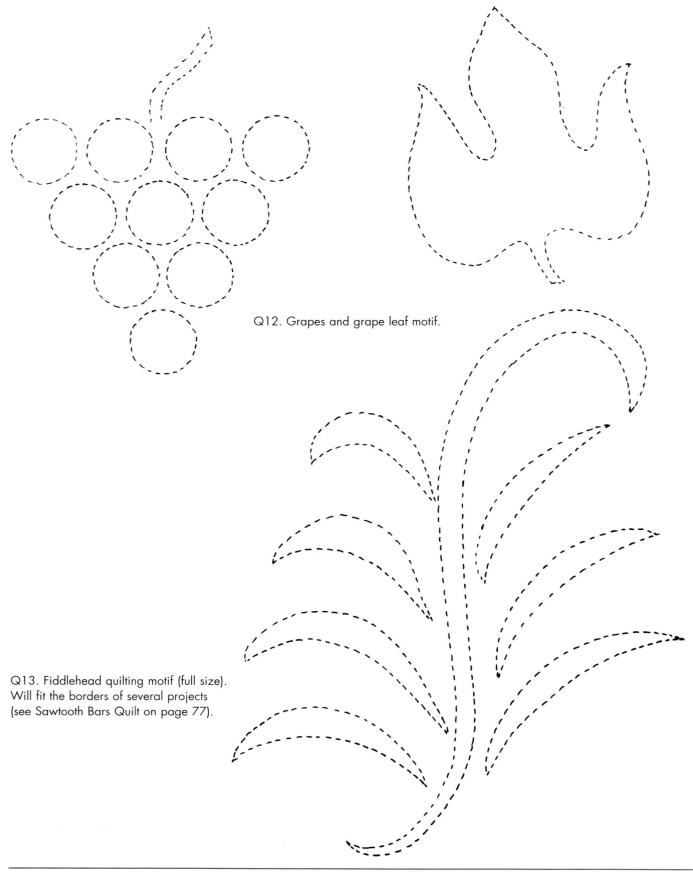

Q12. Grapes and grape leaf motif.

Q13. Fiddlehead quilting motif (full size). Will fit the borders of several projects (see Sawtooth Bars Quilt on page 77).

Q14. Full-size feathered quilting motif designed for
Double Irish Chain Quilt (page 73).

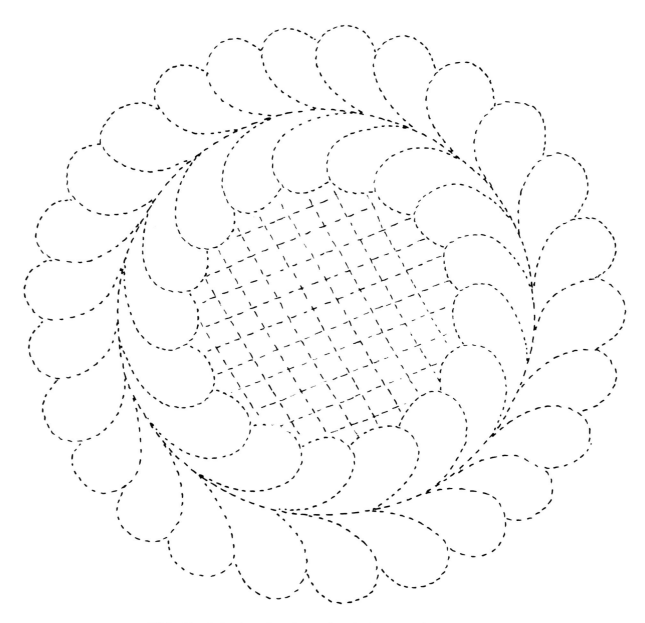

Q15. Classic feathered circle motif, with diameter of 6¼".
This is suitable for unpieced squares of about 8" size.
May be used on Whole Cloth Pillow center (page 93).

Quilting Pattern Suites

Moorish Garden

Block quilting pattern

Moorish Garden, continued

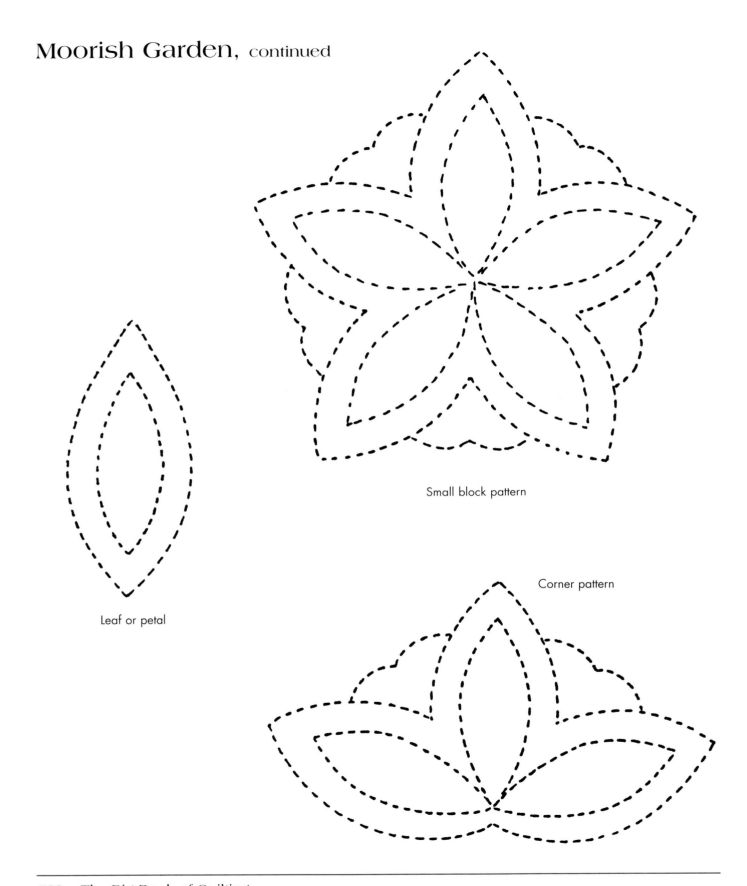

Small block pattern

Leaf or petal

Corner pattern

Moorish Garden,
continued

Border repeat

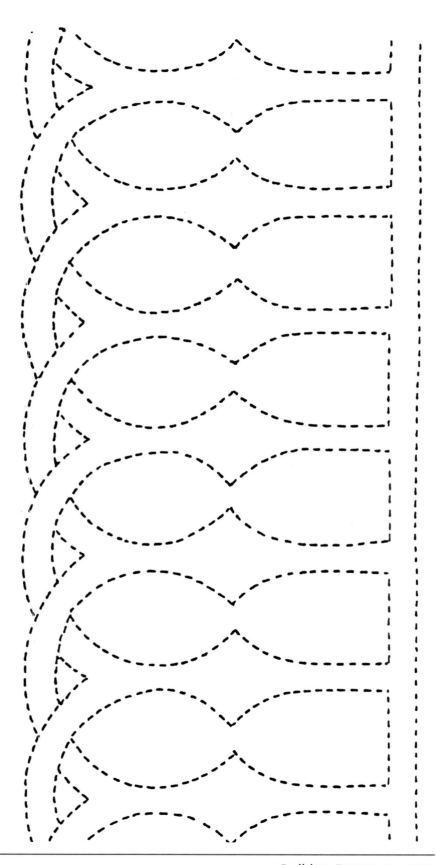

Moorish Garden, continued

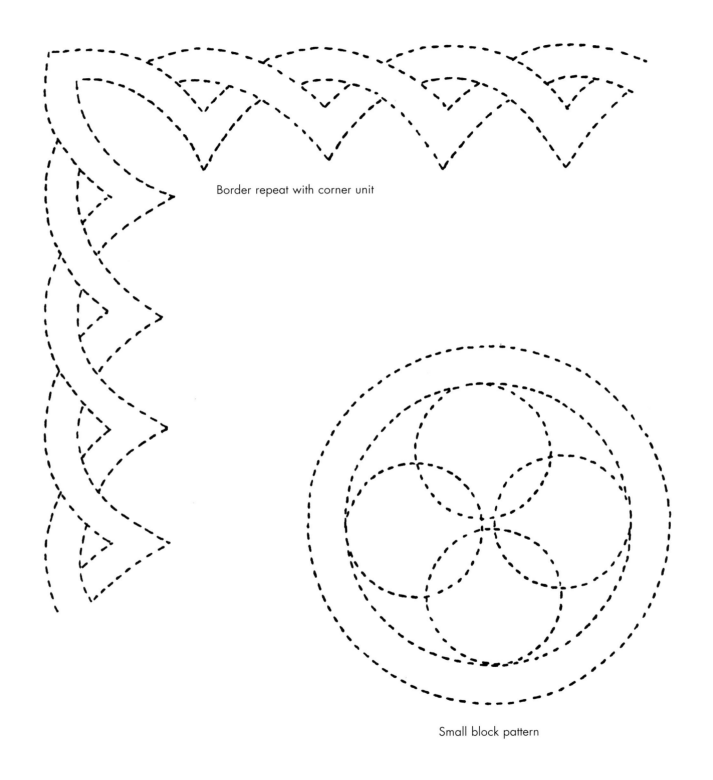

Border repeat with corner unit

Small block pattern

Moorish Garden,
continued

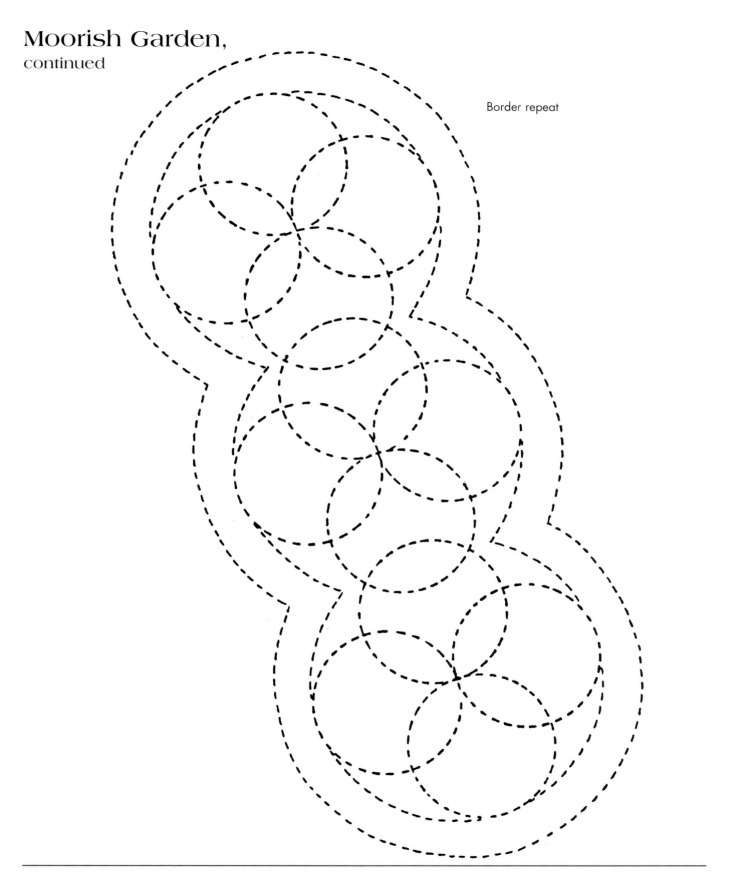

Border repeat

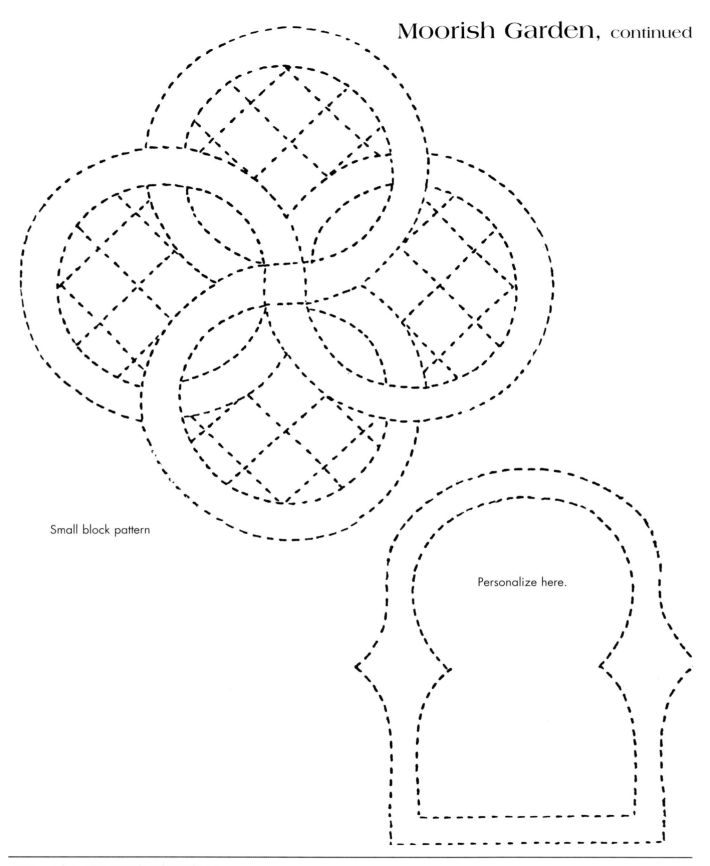

Small block pattern

Personalize here.

Moorish Garden, continued

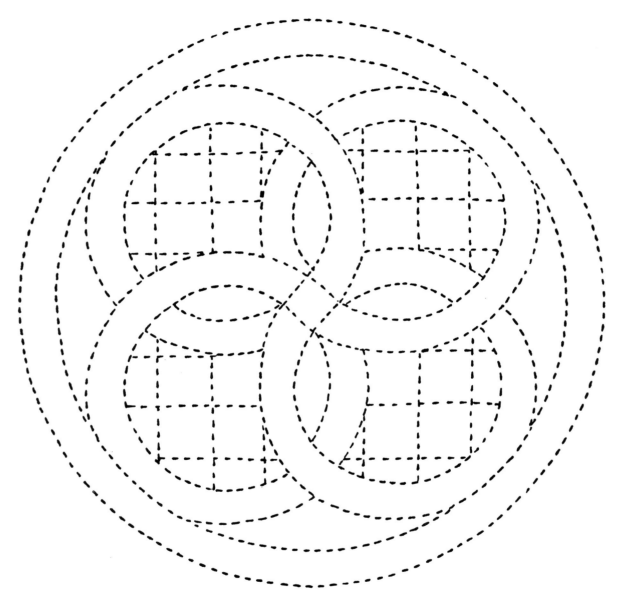

Block quilting pattern

Palace Gates

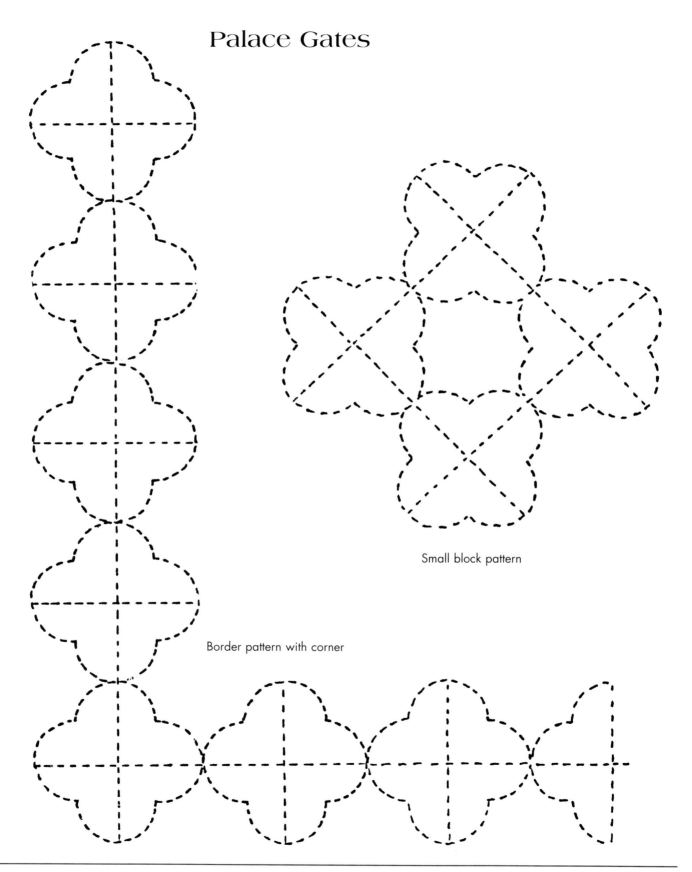

Small block pattern

Border pattern with corner

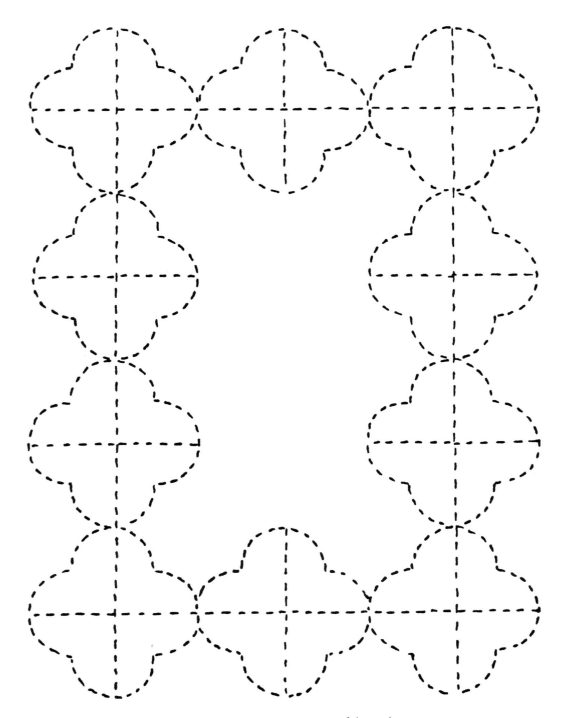

Pattern for a rectangular area of the quilt.
Personalize the center area if you wish.

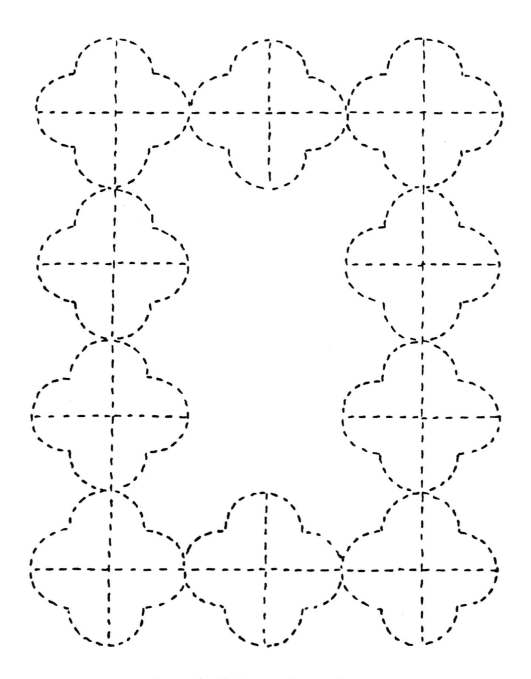

Rectangular block pattern for a smaller area

Palace Gates, continued

Block pattern. May be used as a diamond or a square.

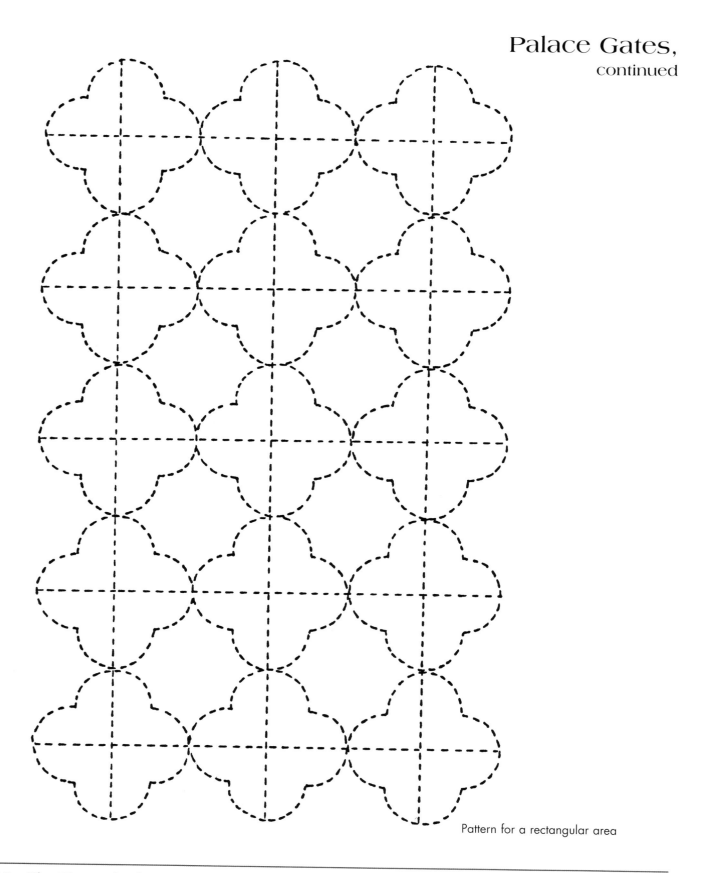

Pattern for a rectangular area

Palace Gates,
continued

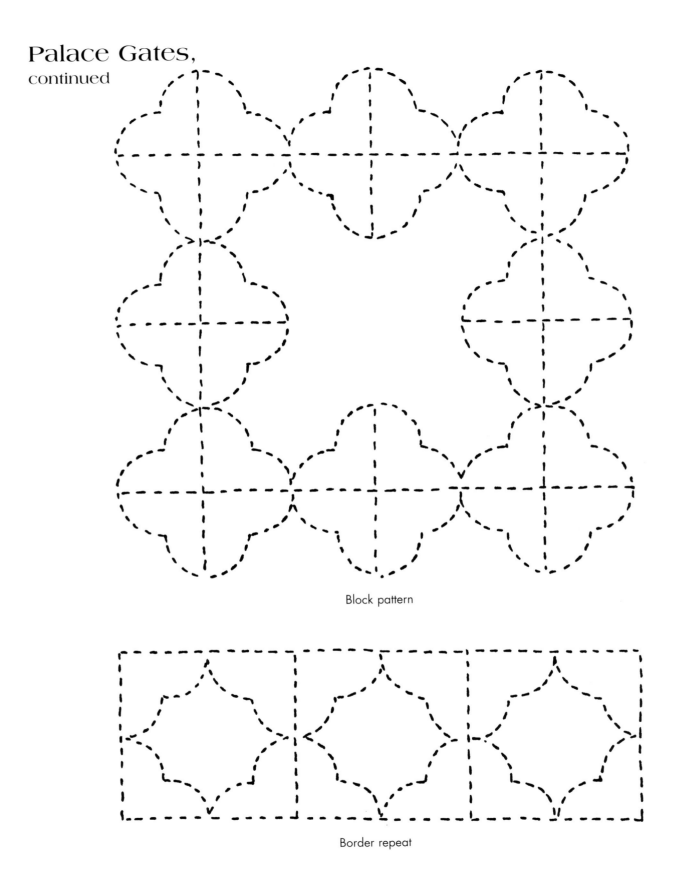

Block pattern

Border repeat

Winter Crocus

Smaller version of a block pattern

Winter Crocus, continued

Large pattern

Winter Crocus, continued

center line

Half of a large block pattern.
Use the mirror image for the
other side.

Small spray

Large spray

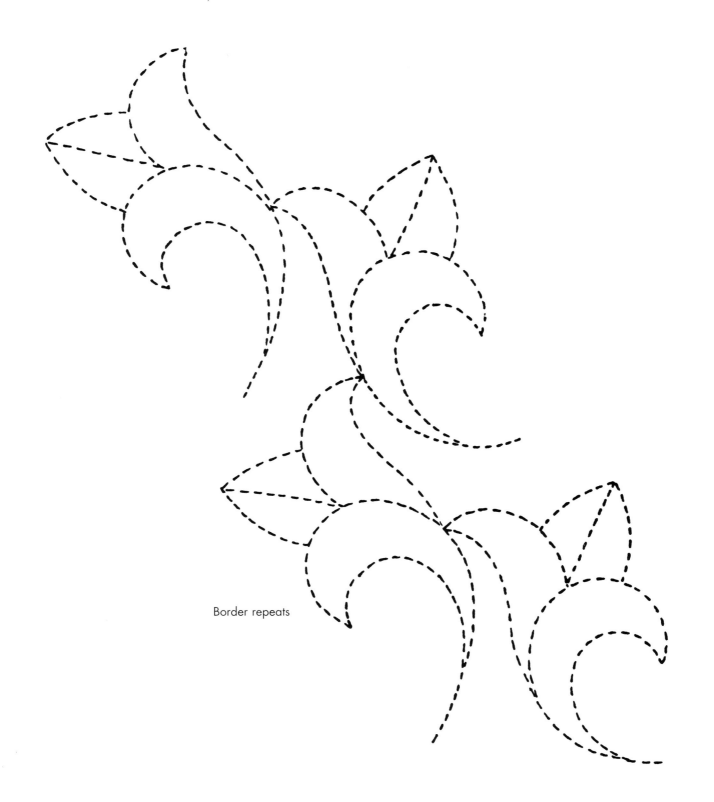

Border repeats

Winter Crocus, continued

Large and small block or border motifs

Winter Crocus,
continued

Border repeat

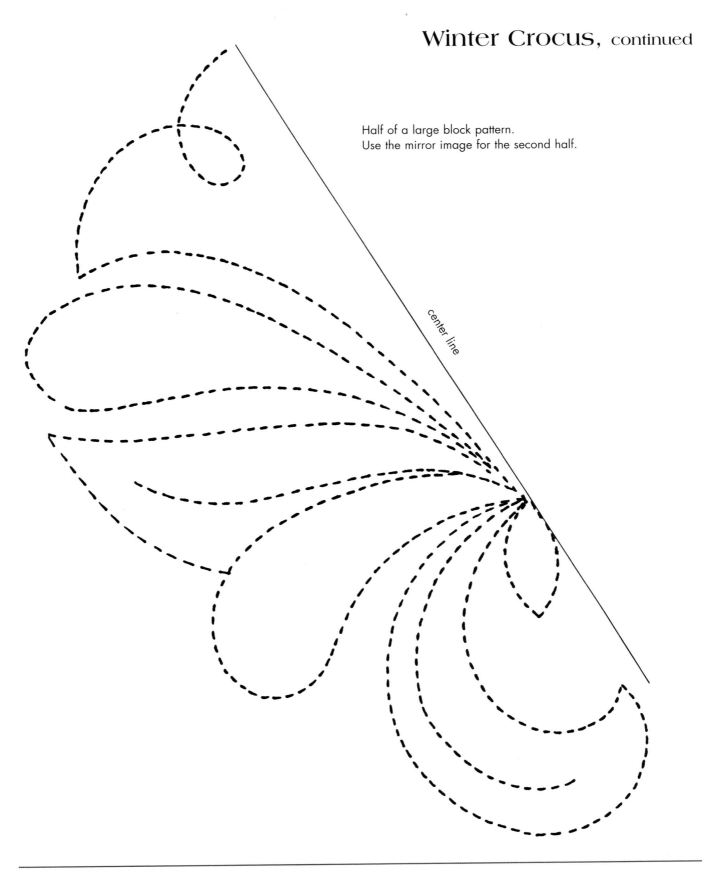

Half of a large block pattern.
Use the mirror image for the second half.

center line

Bridal Garland

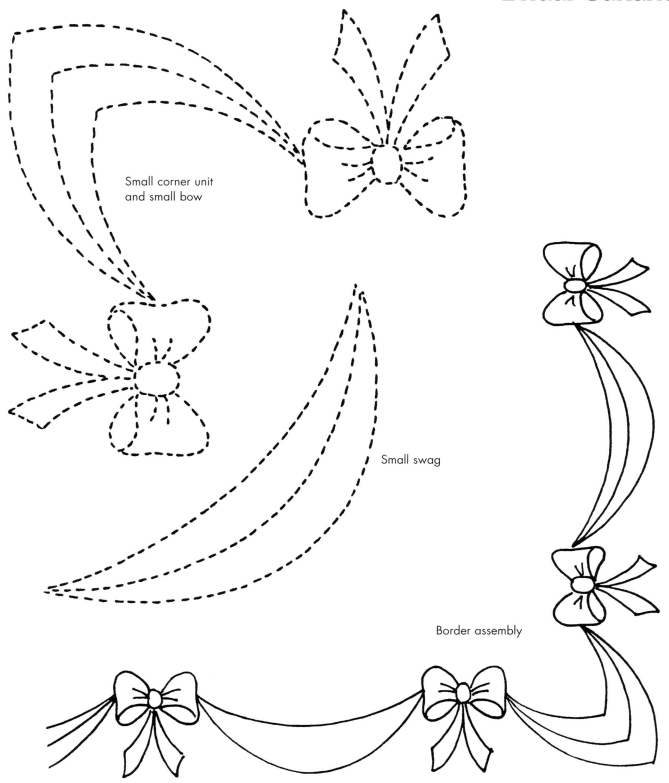

Small corner unit
and small bow

Small swag

Border assembly

Bridal Garland, continued

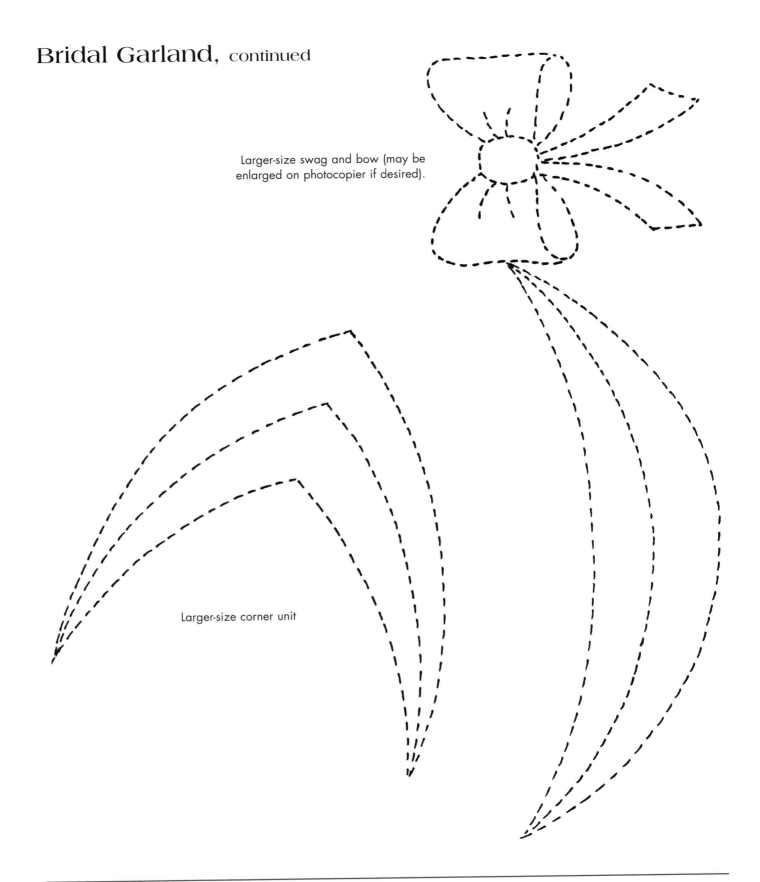

Larger-size swag and bow (may be enlarged on photocopier if desired).

Larger-size corner unit

Bridal Garland, continued

Half of a block pattern. Use mirror image for second half.

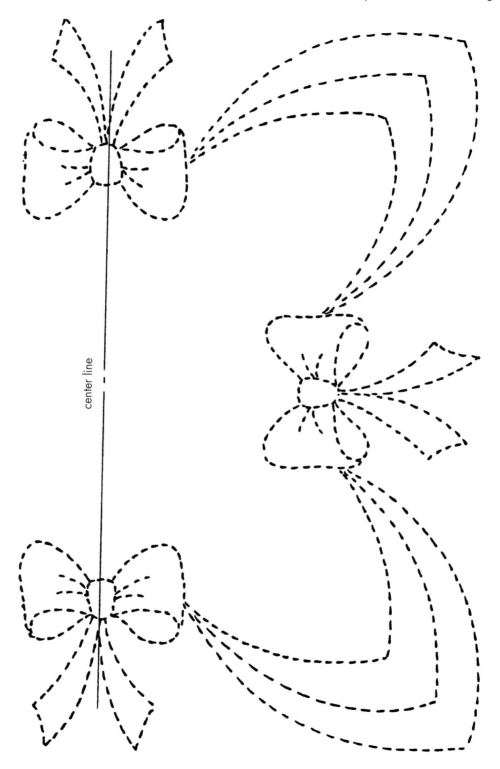

center line

Folk Art Flowers

Large flower pattern

Border assembly

Folk Art Flowers, continued

Block pattern

Diagram of a border repeat

Folk Art Flowers, continued

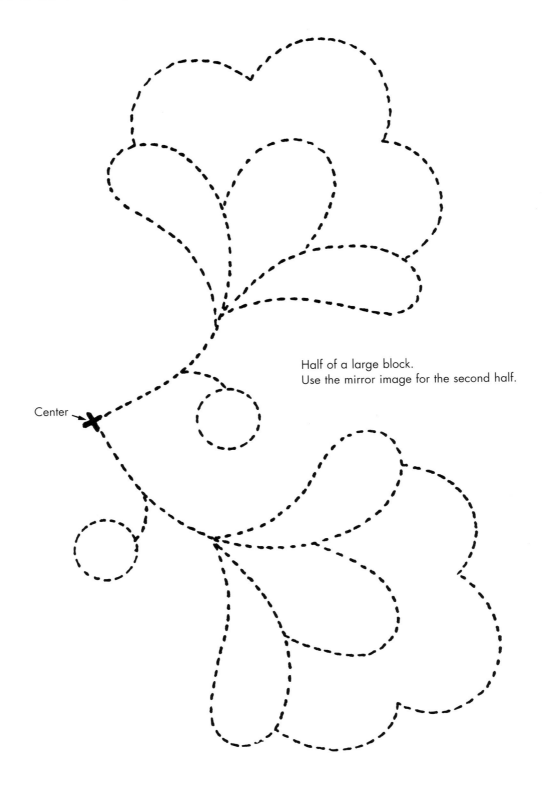

Half of a large block.
Use the mirror image for the second half.

Center

Medium-size flower pattern

Small border repeat

Folk Art Flowers, continued

Small block pattern

Small flower pattern

Large border buds

Swirling Hearts

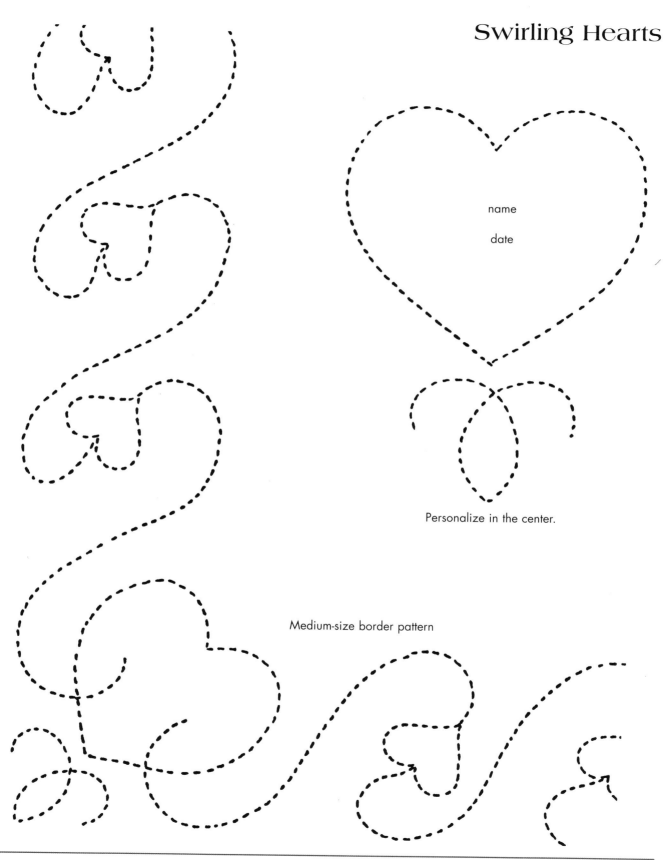

name

date

Personalize in the center.

Medium-size border pattern

Swirling Hearts,
continued

Block pattern

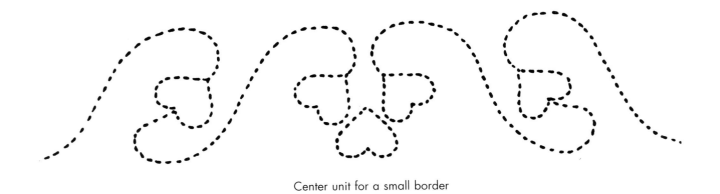

Center unit for a small border

Swirling Hearts, continued

Center unit for a large border

Stacked heart motifs as a border

Swirling Hearts, continued

Center unit for a medium-size border

Small border with corner

Block pattern

Swirling Hearts, continued

Layer the hearts for a border

Block pattern

Border arrangement using single heart units

Northern Lights

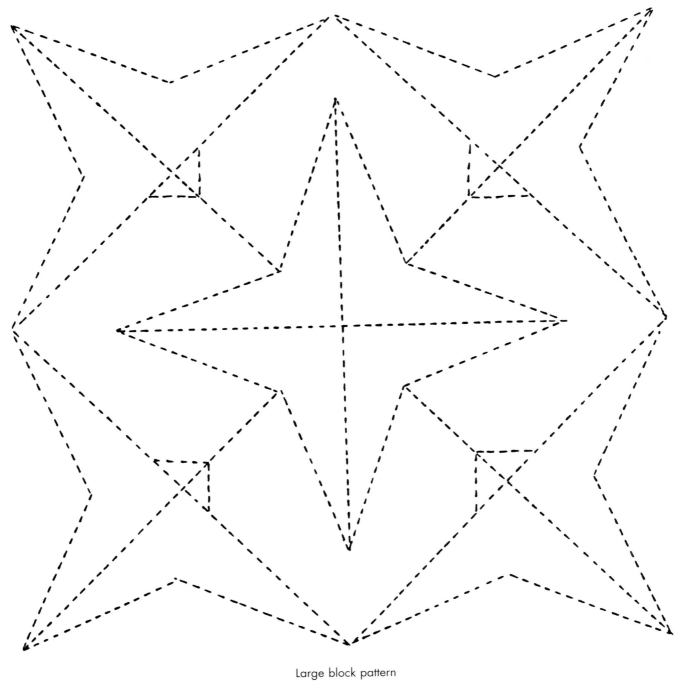

Large block pattern

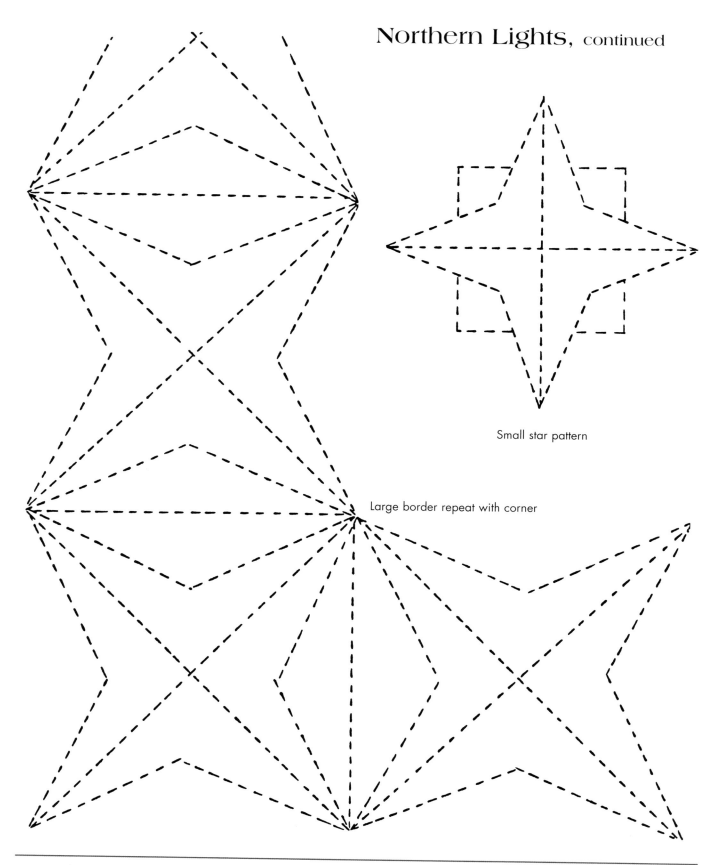

Small star pattern

Large border repeat with corner

Northern Lights, continued

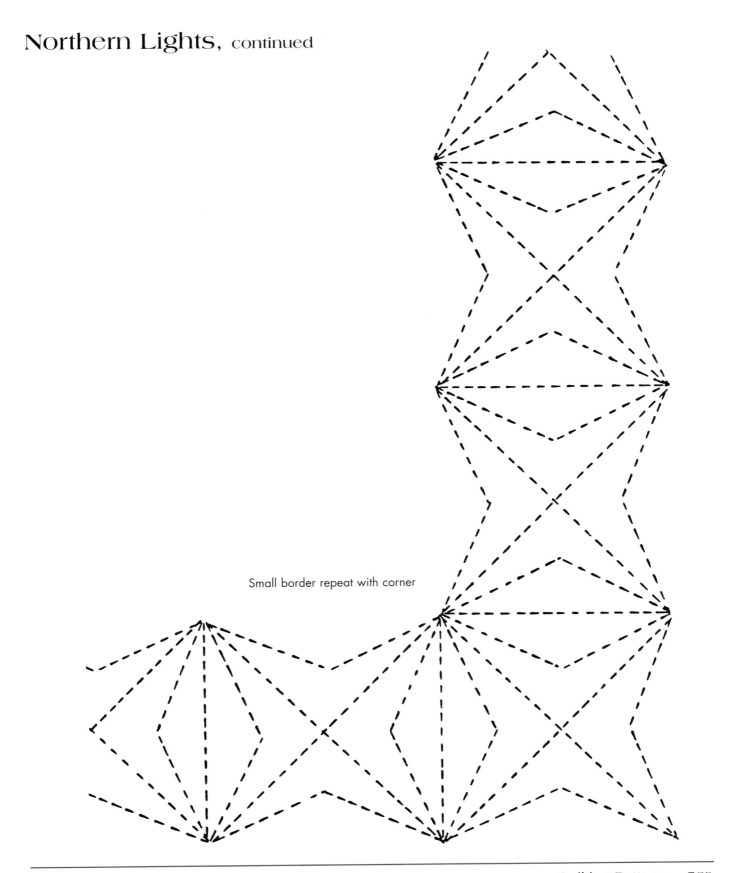

Small border repeat with corner

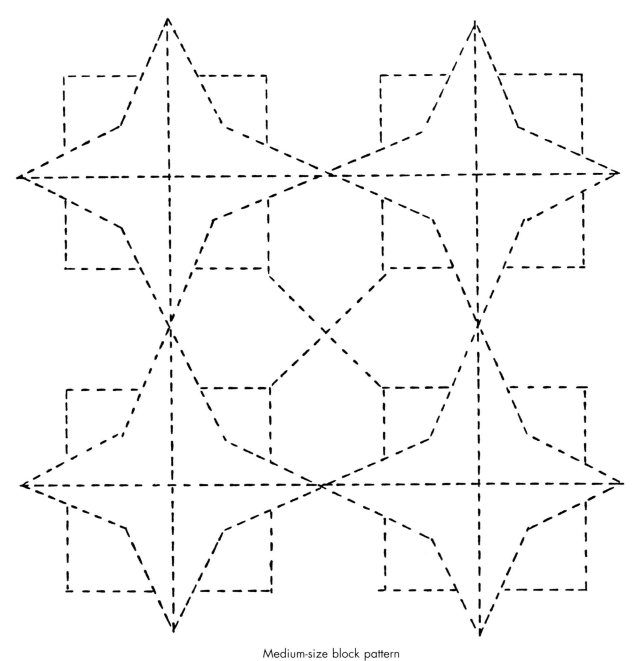

Medium-size block pattern

Shortcut Quilting Patterns

All of the quilting patterns that follow can be machine-stitched (see chapter 8—How To Quilt, page 440).

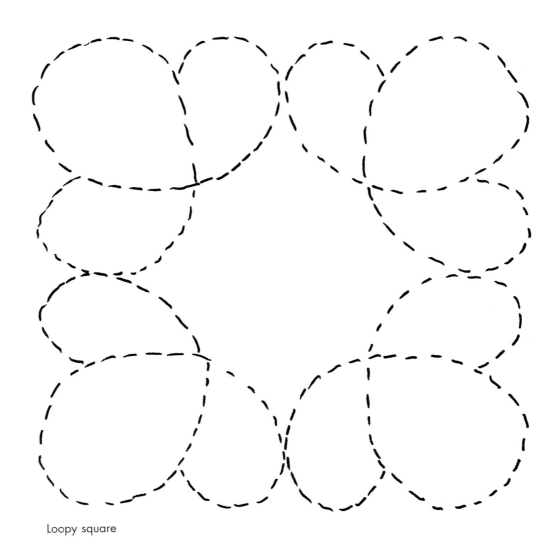

Loopy square

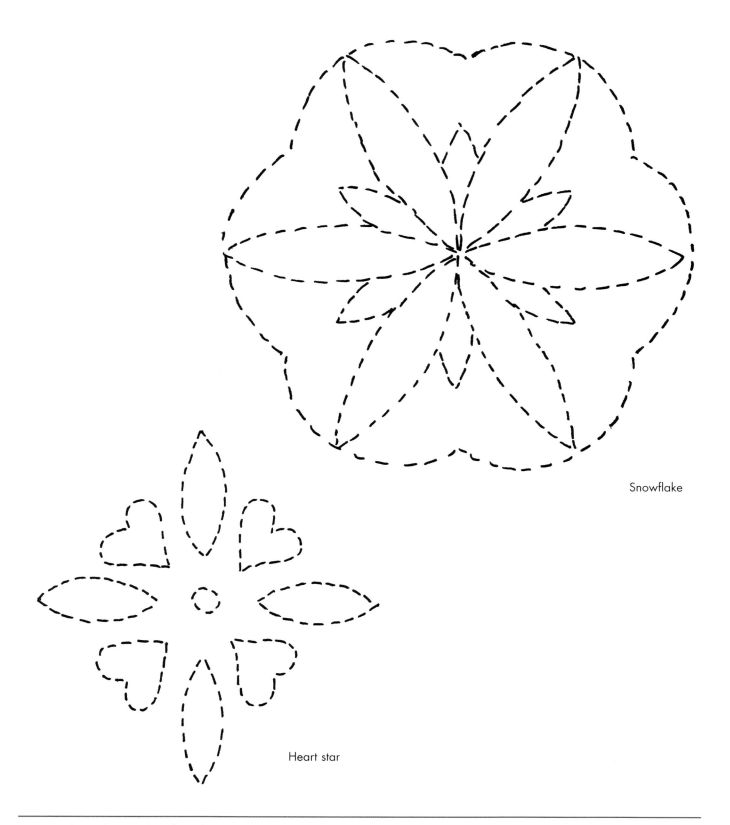

Snowflake

Heart star

Diamond Star

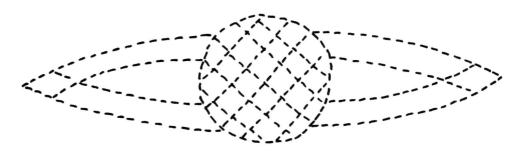

Diamond ring motif

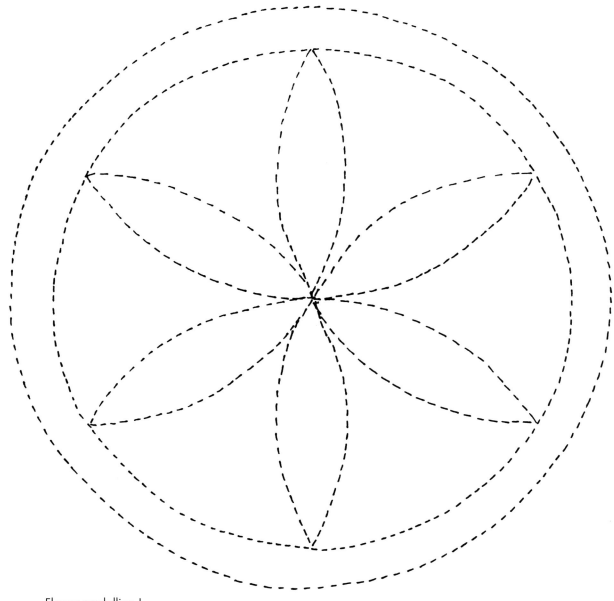

Flower medallion I

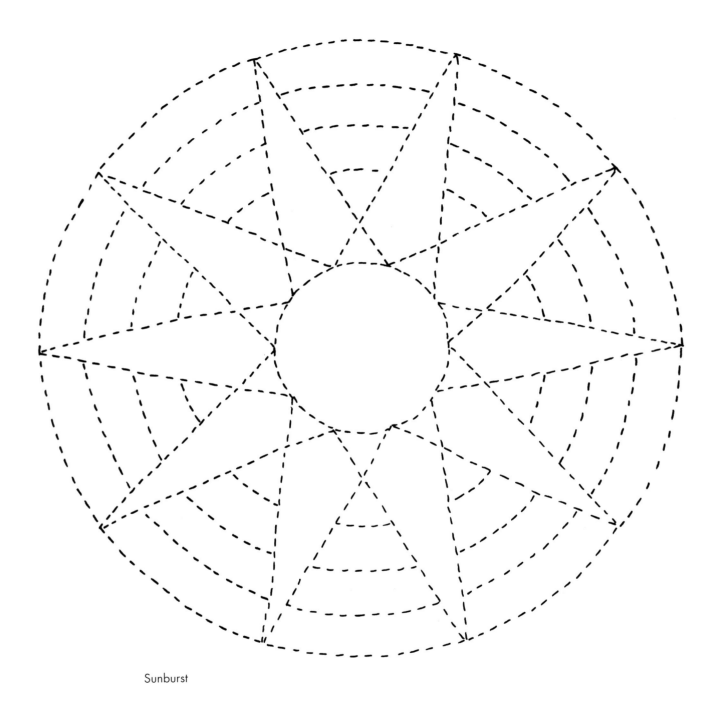

Sunburst

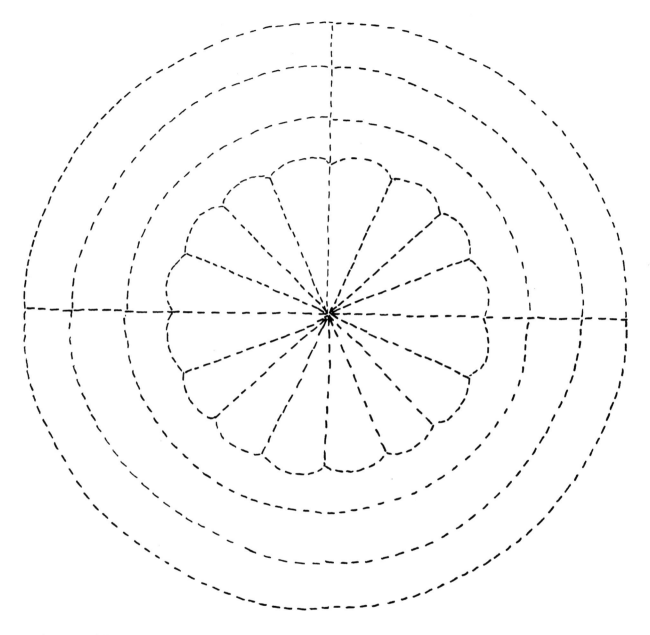

Flower medallion II

The three lines going out to the edge illustrate
various ways in which parts of the design can be used.

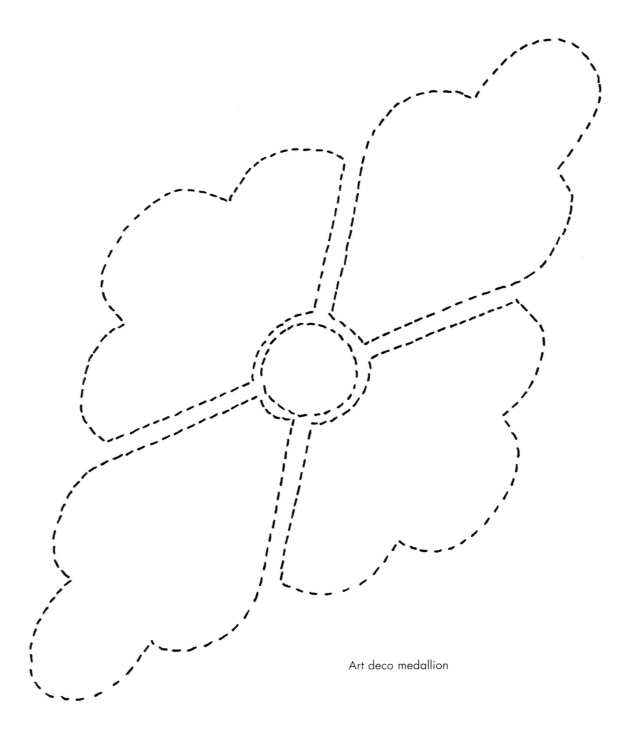

Art deco medallion

Damask rose

Dahlia

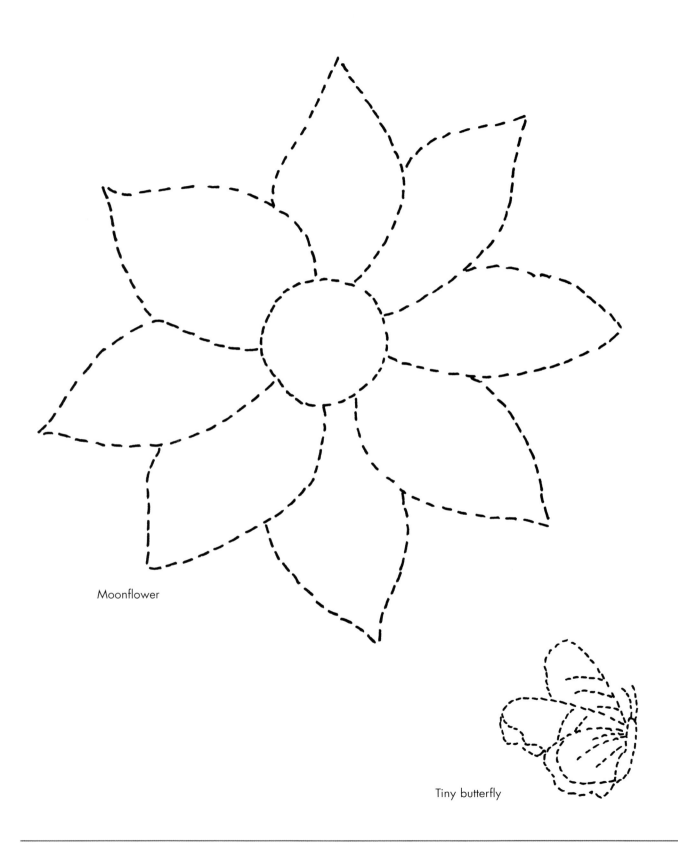

Moonflower

Tiny butterfly

Butterfly

Climbing vine

Singing bird

Tulip border A

Tulip border B

Tulip border C

Useful Charts

Metric Equivalents: Inches to Millimeters (mm) and Centimeters (cm)							
INCHES	**mm**	**cm**	**INCHES**	**cm**	**INCHES**	**cm**
1/8"	3	0.3	9"	22.9	30"	76.2
1/4"	6	0.6	10"	25.4	31"	78.7
3/8"	10	1.0	11"	27.9	32"	81.3
1/2"	13	1.3	12"	30.5	33"	83.8
5/8"	16	1.6	13"	33.0	34"	86.4
3/4"	19	1.9	14"	35.6	35"	88.9
7/8"	22	2.2	15"	38.1	36"	91.4
1"	25	2.5	16"	40.6	37"	94.0
1 1/4"	32	3.2	17"	43.2	38"	96.5
1 1/2"	38	3.8	18"	45.7	39"	99.1
1 3/4"	44	4.4	19"	48.3	40"	101.6
2"	51	5.1	20"	50.8	41"	104.1
2 1/2"	64	6.4	21"	53.3	42"	106.7
3"	76	7.6	22"	55.9	43"	109.2
3 1/2"	89	8.9	23"	58.4	44"	111.8
4"	102	10.2	24"	61.0	45"	114.3
4 1/2"	114	11.4	25"	63.5	46"	116.8
5"	127	12.7	26"	66.0	47"	119.4
6"	152	15.2	27"	68.6	48"	121.9
7"	178	17.8	28"	71.1	49"	124.5
8"	203	20.3	29"	73.7	50"	127.0

Yards to Meters

Yards	Meters	Yards	Meters	Yards	Meters	Yards	Meters	Yards	Meters
$\frac{1}{8}$	0.11	$2\frac{1}{8}$	1.94	$4\frac{1}{8}$	3.77	$6\frac{1}{8}$	5.60	$8\frac{1}{8}$	7.43
$\frac{1}{4}$	0.23	$2\frac{1}{4}$	2.06	$4\frac{1}{4}$	3.89	$6\frac{1}{4}$	5.72	$8\frac{1}{4}$	7.54
$\frac{3}{8}$	0.34	$2\frac{3}{8}$	2.17	$4\frac{3}{8}$	4.00	$6\frac{3}{8}$	5.83	$8\frac{3}{8}$	7.66
$\frac{1}{2}$	0.46	$2\frac{1}{2}$	2.29	$4\frac{1}{2}$	4.11	$6\frac{1}{2}$	5.94	$8\frac{1}{2}$	7.77
$\frac{5}{8}$	0.57	$2\frac{5}{8}$	2.40	$4\frac{5}{8}$	4.23	$6\frac{5}{8}$	6.06	$8\frac{5}{8}$	7.89
$\frac{3}{4}$	0.69	$2\frac{3}{4}$	2.51	$4\frac{3}{4}$	4.34	$6\frac{3}{4}$	6.17	$8\frac{3}{4}$	8.00
$\frac{7}{8}$	0.80	$2\frac{7}{8}$	2.63	$4\frac{7}{8}$	4.46	$6\frac{7}{8}$	6.29	$8\frac{7}{8}$	8.12
1	0.91	3	2.74	5	4.57	7	6.40	9	8.23
$1\frac{1}{8}$	1.03	$3\frac{1}{8}$	2.86	$5\frac{1}{8}$	4.69	$7\frac{1}{8}$	6.52	$9\frac{1}{8}$	8.34
$1\frac{1}{4}$	1.14	$3\frac{1}{4}$	2.97	$5\frac{1}{4}$	4.80	$7\frac{1}{4}$	6.63	$9\frac{1}{4}$	8.46
$1\frac{3}{8}$	1.26	$3\frac{3}{8}$	3.09	$5\frac{3}{8}$	4.91	$7\frac{3}{8}$	6.74	$9\frac{3}{8}$	8.57
$1\frac{1}{2}$	1.37	$3\frac{1}{2}$	3.20	$5\frac{1}{2}$	5.03	$7\frac{1}{2}$	6.86	$9\frac{1}{2}$	8.69
$1\frac{5}{8}$	1.49	$3\frac{5}{8}$	3.31	$5\frac{5}{8}$	5.14	$7\frac{5}{8}$	6.97	$9\frac{5}{8}$	8.80
$1\frac{3}{4}$	1.60	$3\frac{3}{4}$	3.43	$5\frac{3}{4}$	5.26	$7\frac{3}{4}$	7.09	$9\frac{3}{4}$	8.92
$\frac{7}{8}$	1.71	$3\frac{7}{8}$	3.54	$5\frac{7}{8}$	5.37	$7\frac{7}{8}$	7.20	$9\frac{7}{8}$	9.03
2	1.83	4	3.66	6	5.49	8	7.32	10	9.14

Yards to Inches

Yards	Inches	Yards	Inches
$\frac{1}{8}$	$4\frac{1}{2}$"	$1\frac{1}{8}$	$40\frac{1}{2}$"
$\frac{1}{4}$	9"	$1\frac{1}{4}$	45"
$\frac{3}{8}$	$13\frac{1}{2}$"	$1\frac{3}{8}$	$49\frac{1}{2}$"
$\frac{1}{2}$	18"	$1\frac{1}{2}$	54"
$\frac{5}{8}$	$22\frac{1}{2}$"	$1\frac{5}{8}$	$58\frac{1}{2}$"
$\frac{3}{4}$	27"	$1\frac{3}{4}$	63"
$\frac{7}{8}$	$31\frac{1}{2}$"	$1\frac{7}{8}$	$67\frac{1}{2}$"
1	36"	2	72"

Glossary

Because quilting has some unique terminology, it will be helpful to check over this glossary before you read further into the introductory material and choose a project.

Appliqué. The attaching of a small piece of fabric to a larger piece of background fabric by hand or machine stitching.

Backstitch. In hand sewing, to loop back over the stitch you've just taken to provide additional strength. On the sewing machine, to reverse three or four stitches at the beginning and end of a seam to lock the stitches.

Baste. To join together the layers of a quilted piece with long hand stitches. Basting threads are removed after quilting. (Some quilters use safety pins instead of hand-basting.)

Batting. The fluffy filler that is the middle layer of the quilt. Provides warmth and allows the quilting on the top layer to be more noticeable. Made of either cotton, cotton/polyester blend, polyester, wool, or silk.

Bias. The diagonal intersection of the lengthwise and crosswise threads of a piece of fabric, where the fabric has the most stretch. True bias is at a 45-degree angle to the straight grain.

Bias tape or binding. Strips of fabric, cut on the bias, used for binding edges. Purchase ready-made or make your own.

Blindstitch. An almost invisible hand stitch used for sewing hems, hanging sleeves, appliqués, and bias binding.

Block. Pieces of fabric sewn together to create a single unit; a traditional pieced quilt is made up of many blocks.

Ease in/ease to fit. To make two unequal lengths of fabric meet by gathering or pulling, in order to sew them together.

Echo quilting. To follow the pattern of quilting in a repetitive series of equally spaced rows of stitching.

Finger press. To use the fingertips instead of an iron to crease fabric or to press a seam.

Foundation-piecing. Creating a quilting block using a muslin base; the fabric pieces are sewn to the base as they are sewn to each other.

Hanging sleeve. A strip of fabric sewn to the back of a quilt. A rod or dowel is inserted through the sleeve to facilitate hanging for display.

In-the-ditch quilting. Quilting done as closely as possible to a seam line or appliqué edge.

Machine hem. To hem using the sewing machine. Press the raw edge under ¼"; fold the pressed edge to the desired depth of the hem, and stitch along the edge.

Mitered corner. A diagonal seam formed by two strips of fabric meeting at a 45-degree angle.

Outline quilting. Quilting that is done ¼" away from seams or appliqué pieces.

Patchwork. See Piece.

Piece. To sew together individual pieces of fabric to form a predetermined pattern; the fabric pieces are usually in geometric shapes.

Press. To use an iron in an up-and-down motion, rather than a back-and-forth ironing motion.

Quilt backing. The bottom layer of the traditional three-layer "sandwich" that a quilt comprises (top, batting, backing).

Quilting. Small, even, running stitches through all the layers of a quilt; it holds the layers together and forms a decorative pattern.

Quilting pattern. The design of the quilting stitches on the finished project.

Quilt top. The top layer of the quilt "sandwich," on which the quilting is executed.

Running stitch. The basic hand sewing stitch; the needle weaves in and out of the layers of fabric several times before it is pulled through.

Sandwich. The assemble the layers of a quilted project in preparation for basting and quilting.

Seam allowance. The tiny, usually ¼" area of fabric beyond the seam line, between the sewn seam and the raw edge of the fabric.

Scant. As in "a scant ¼"," this means "absolutely no more than, possibly slightly less" when you are sewing.

Shadow quilting. Quilting that is done along the outline of a piece of batting that is placed between two layers of fabric, one or both of which is transparent; the top piece must be transparent to achieve the desired effect.

Staystitch. To stabilize a fabric piece by stitching ⅛" from all raw edges; it prevents raveling. It also stabilizes foundation-pieced quilting projects.

Stencil. A pattern for a fancy quilting motif.

Strip piecing. Creating a quilting block using strips of fabric sewn to a muslin base.

Tack. To take small hidden stitch in order to hold a piece of fabric in place.

Template. A pattern, usually made from plastic (for repeated use) or thin cardboard (for one-time use) that is used for tracing shapes into fabric, which will then be cut out.

Topstitch. Machine stitching (sometimes hand stitching) done on the top or right side of fabric. A finishing stitch that is meant to be seen, topstitching can be sewn with matching or contrasting color thread.

Whipstitch. An overcasting hand stitch used to join edges.

Index